the festivals
in halachah

the festivals

by
Rabbi Shlomo Yosef Zevin

Translation / Shlomo Fox-Ashrei
Editor / Uri Kaploun
Contributing Editor / Meir Holder

המועדים בהלכה

VOLUME III

ın halachah

AN ANALYSIS OF THE DEVELOPMENT OF THE FESTIVAL LAWS

Published by

Mesorah Publications, ltd / New York

in conjunction with

HILLEL PRESS / Jerusalem

FIRST EDITION
First Impression ... March, 1982
Second Impression ... June, 1983

Published and Distributed by
MESORAH PUBLICATIONS, Ltd.
1969 Coney Island Avenue
Brooklyn, New York 11223
In conjunction with
HILLEL PRESS, Jerusalem

Distributed in Israel by
MESORAH MAFITZIM / J. GROSSMAN
Rechov Bayit Vegan 90/5
Jerusalem, Israel

Distributed in Europe by
J. LEHMANN HEBREW BOOKSELLERS
20 Cambridge Terrace
Gateshead
Tyne and Wear
England NE 8 1RP

ISBN
0-89906-910-X (hard cover)
0-89906-911-8 (paper back)

סֵפֶר בְּמִסְרָה
חֶבְרַת אַרְטְסְקְרוֹל בע״מ

Typography by Compuscribe at ArtScroll Studios, Ltd.
1969 Coney Island Avenue / Brooklyn, N.Y. 11223 / (212) 339-1700

Printed in the United States of America by Moriah Offset

Table of Contents

Table of Contents

PESACH

OMER

SHAVUOS

❧ Pesach

פֶּסַח בְּתוֹרַת שֵׁם הֶחָג

Pesach as the Name of the Festival

In 1939, when the evil legions of Amalek (May their memory be blotted out!) set out to destroy Jewry, their first target was Poland with its extensive Jewish population. Noteworthy yeshivos and influential chassidic dynasties were flourishing in that country — but none could equal in importance and sheer numbers Malchus Ger, "the kingdom of Ger." Although our People (הי״ד) underwent a martyrdom unequaled in human history, the enemy did not succeed. The dynasty of Ger is symbolic — it suffered so grievously that most predicted its demise, yet it not only survived but rebounded with almost unprecedented vitality. This is evident in the vigorous yeshivos, batei midrash and chassidic brotherhoods that have reestablished themselves in the last three decades (כן ירבו, אמן). And as if shaking off an evil dream the yeshivos and chassidic dynasties, each with their time-honored names and distinctive contributions to the rebuilding of the study and practice of Judaism, have with help of HaShem survived the long and bitter night, and are as strong in their love of HaShem and of the Torah as ever before.

It is fitting, therefore, that an early leader of Ger found this Jewish rebirth sybolized in the Torah passage dealing with the first festival which we were commanded to observe — the festival celebrating our emergence from the night of slavery in Egypt. Concerning the newborn moon which heralds the month of Nissan, and on which our calendar is based, the Torah says: "This month shall be for you the beginning of months; it shall be for you the first of the months of the year" (Exodus 12:2).

The famed Reb Aryeh Leib, the second Gerrer Rebbe, who is known by the title of his major work as the "Sfas Emes," explains: "We Jews fix our years by the moon, other nations by the sun. Those who depend on the sun are strong, and fight for their survival and existence as long as fortune shines on them — but as soon as their sun sets they vanish from the pages of history. Not so Am Yisrael, who live on and shine during the darkest stretches of the night — just like the moon, that sends forth its light in night's darkest hours."

Which Day is "Pesach"? To which day does the Torah actually refer in using the word "Pesach" as the name of festival — to the fourteenth of Nissan, the day on which the Pesach sacrifice is slaughtered, or to the fifteenth, the day on which the sacrifice is eaten?

No definitive answer is provided by the verse in *Numbers, And in the first month, on the fourteenth of the month [is] Pesach for HASHEM* (וּבַחֹדֶשׁ הָרִאשׁוֹן בְּאַרְבָּעָה עָשָׂר יוֹם לַחֹדֶשׁ פֶּסַח לה'),[1] for the word "Pesach" here is not used as the name of the day, but refers rather to the obligation of slaughtering and offering up the Pesach sacrifice. A similar use of the word is found in *Leviticus: In the first month, on the fourteenth of the month, towards evening, [is] the Pesach for HASHEM* (בַּחֹדֶשׁ הָרִאשׁוֹן בְּאַרְבָּעָה עָשָׂר לַחֹדֶשׁ בֵּין הָעַרְבָּיִם פֶּסַח לַה');[2] *Rashi* there explains, "*Pesach for HASHEM*: the offering up of the sacrifice called 'Pesach.' " To be interpreted in the same way is the verse in *Ezekiel,*[3] *In the first [month], on the fourteenth day of the month, shall be the Pesach for you* (בָּרִאשׁוֹן בְּאַרְבָּעָה עָשָׂר יוֹם לַחֹדֶשׁ יִהְיֶה לָכֶם הַפָּסַח). In all other places where the Torah uses the word "Pesach," it is clear that the reference is to the offering — with one exception, an exception which seems to provide explicit proof that "Pesach" as the name of a day means the fourteenth of Nissan. In *Numbers, parashas Masei,* we read, *On the morrow of the Pesach, the Children of Israel went out with a high hand before the eyes of all Egypt* (מִמָּחֳרַת הַפֶּסַח יָצְאוּ בְנֵי יִשְׂרָאֵל בְּיָד רָמָה לְעֵינֵי כָּל מִצְרַיִם).[4]

The question, however, is not yet resolved, for in contrast to this verse is another in *Joshua: And they ate from the grain of the Land, on the morrow of the Pesach, matzos and roasted grain, on that very day* (וַיֹּאכְלוּ מֵעֲבוּר הָאָרֶץ מִמָּחֳרַת הַפֶּסַח מַצּוֹת וְקָלוּי בְּעֶצֶם הַיּוֹם הַזֶּה).[5] According to a straightforward interpretation of this verse, it refers to the law that *chadash*, the new crop of grain, is not permitted for eating until after the sacrifice of the *omer*, the measure of crushed barley offered up on the sixteenth of Nissan. The verse tells us, then, that after Israel sacrificed the *omer* they ate from the new crop. Hence "Pesach" must mean the fifteenth of Nissan, not the fourteenth.

The Debate Over Joshua The problem presented by these two verses — in *parashas Masei* and in *Joshua* — in terms of determining which day is meant by *the morrow of the Pesach,* has stirred a wide-ranging debate. In the Jerusalem Talmud, *Amoraim* argue the question. In reply to an opinion that *chadash* was not forbidden to Israel at the time referred to by the verse in *Joshua*, i.e., immediately upon their entrance into the Land, but the prohibition only came into effect after the first fourteen years (seven of conquest and seven of apportionment), "Rabbi Bun bar Kahana answered, 'It is written, *And they ate from the grain of the Land on the morrow of the Pesach* — is this not the sixteenth?' " That is, since they did not eat this grain until the sixteenth, it must be that they were under the law of *chadash* even in that first year. "Rabbi Elazar bar Yosei answered him in the presence of Rabbi Yosei, 'But it is written, *On the morrow of the Pesach the children of Israel went out* — is this not the fifteenth?' "[6] That is, the term means the same in *Joshua* as it does in *Numbers; chadash* was not in effect, for they ate the new grain on the fifteenth of Nissan.

In the Babylonian Talmud we find, "they did not eat until the *morrow of the Pesach* after they sacrificed the *omer,*"[7] meaning that the *morrow of the Pesach* is the sixteenth of Nissan. This is in agreement with the opinion, cited above, of Rabbi Bun bar Kahana in the Jerusalem Talmud. *Rashi*, too, explains the verse in *Joshua* in accordance with this side of the debate. And *Rambam* held the same interpretation, as is evident from his use of the verse to disprove the opinion of the *Tzedokim* (Sadducees) concerning the correct date for sacrificing the *omer*.

The Torah, in *Leviticus* 23:11, gives the day of the *omer* sacrifice as *the morrow of the Shabbos*. The *Tzedokim* interpreted this in its more usual meaning, i.e., Sunday. The *Halachah*, however, states that in this case "*Shabbos*" means the first day of Pesach (for *Yom-Tov* is also a '*shabbos*,' a day of rest).° To demonstrate the truth of the *Halachah*, *Rambam* writes, "It is said, *And they ate from the grain of the Land on*

°[Throughout most of the Second Temple period, Jewry may be said to have been divided into two camps. On the one side were the Sages, known as the *Perushim* (Pharisees), who were followed by the overwhelming majority of the population, and on the other side an elitist group known as the *Tzedokim* (Sadducees).

The basic differences between these two groups may be summarized briefly as follows. The Sages taught that the Torah cannot be taken superficially, but must constantly be studied for its deeper implications, as we see in *Nechemiah*, when the Levites under the guidance of Ezra at a public gathering read *in the book, in the Torah of God, distinctly, and they gave the sense, and caused them to understand the reading* (בְּסֵפֶר בְּתוֹרַת הָאֱלֹקִים מְפֹרָשׁ וְשׂוֹם שֵׂכֶל וַיָּבִינוּ בַּמִּקְרָא; *Nechemiah* 8:8). To the *Tzedokim*, on the other hand, the Torah was a cult rather than a way of life, and not given to interpretation; in other words, they rejected *Torah She-be'al peh*, the Oral Law.

One of the great controversies between the *Perushim* and the *Tzedokim* concerned the date of the *omer* offering. The Torah states, *And he shall wave the omer to be accepted for you before HASHEM on the morrow after the day of rest* (וְהֵנִיף אֶת הָעֹמֶר לִפְנֵי ה' לִרְצֹנְכֶם מִמָּחֳרַת הַשַּׁבָּת; *Leviticus* 23:11). Since the Torah uses the expression, *Shabbos* ("day of rest"), the

the morrow of the Pesach, matzos and roasted grain; and if you argue that (the reason the day is called Pesach is because) that particular Pesach occurred on a *Shabbos*, as these fools have imagined — why would Scripture connect the permission to eat *chadash* to something which is neither its essence nor its cause, but purely a matter of chance? But in fact, since Scripture relates the matter to the morrow of the Pesach, it is clear that the morrow of the Pesach is the determining factor which makes the *chadash* permissible."[8] Thus, *Rambam* assumes that the *morrow of the Pesach* mentioned in *Joshua* means the sixteenth, the day of the *omer* sacrifice.

This interpretation, as found in the Babylonian Talmud, of the verse from *Joshua* stimulated a debate between Rav Avraham Ibn Ezra and Rabbeinu Tam. Ibn Ezra asks Rabbeinu Tam, "Must it not be true that *the morrow of the Pesach* is the fifteenth of Nissan, that is, the morrow of the slaughtering of the Pesach sacrifice, which is carried out on the fourteenth, as it is written in *parashas Masei: On the morrow of the Pesach the Children of Israel went out;* and that was on the fifteenth?"

Rabbeinu Tam's Solution

Rabbeinu Tam replied that the Babylonian Talmud did indeed make this very assumption — and nevertheless uses the verse in *Joshua* to prove that *chadash* was forbidden even in that first year of entrance into the Land. What is the proof? The verse must be read as consisting of two sentences. The first sentence reads, *And they ate from the grain of the Land on the morrow of the Pesach, matzos.* Here *the morrow of the Pesach* does indeed mean the fifteenth of Nissan; but *the grain of the Land* does not refer to *chadash*, the new crop, but rather to the previous year's crop; it was from this that they made *matzos.* The second sentence reads, *And [they ate] roasted grain on that very day.* Here, *roasted grain* means *chadash*, the new crop, while *that very day* means the sixteenth of Nissan, the day of the *omer*. (Thus, this second sentence is an echo of *Leviticus* 23:14, where *that very day* is also used to mean the day of the *omer* — *And you shall not eat bread, nor roasted grain, nor raw grain, until that very day* — וְלֶחֶם וְקָלִי וְכַרְמֶל לֹא תֹאכְלוּ עַד עֶצֶם הַיּוֹם הַזֶּה.)

Tzedokim, who refused any but the literal meaning of Scripture, argued that this verse must mean the morrow of the weekly Sabbath — an interpretation which of course would have distorted the whole calendar. In order to cause the *omer* to be offered on their preferred day, the *Tzedokim* were prepared to go to any lengths — the hiring of false witnesses to give evidence of an alleged sighting of the new moon is but one example.

In the Talmud, Rabbi Yochanan ben Zakkai refers to the *Tzedokim* as *shotim*, abnormal. *Rambam*, in the passage quoted here, describes them as "fools." — *Ed.*]

This interpretation by Rabbeinu Tam has the agreement of *Each* *in its* *Own* *Way* *Radak* in his commentary on *Joshua* (and *Meiri*, in his commentary on Tractate *Rosh HaShanah*, also cites this interpretation, attributing it to "some of the greatest sages who have interpreted Scripture"). Rabbeinu Tam's explanation fits in with the above passage from the Babylonian Talmud in terms of the subject matter, but does not fit well with the Talmud's wording, "They did not eat until ..." This discrepancy was noted by *Tosafos*;[9] thus an alternative explanation is offered in the name of *Ri*: °We must understand "the wording of the Torah in its way, the wording of the Prophets in its way, and the wording of the Sages in its way."[10] The Prophets (i.e., in *Joshua)* use "Pesach" to mean the fifteenth of Nissan, but in the Torah it is the fourteenth that is called "Pesach," and its *morrow* is the fifteenth. (For the meaning of "Pesach" as used by the Sages, see below.)

Ri was preceded in this interpretation by Rav Saadia *Gaon*, who is cited by *Ibn Ezra* in the latter's commentary on the Torah. "The *Gaon* says that there are two "Pesachim," the Pesach of HaShem and the Pesach of Israel. The Pesach of HaShem is the night of the fifteenth (on which the Pesach sacrifice must be eaten before midnight), and thus the *morrow of the Pesach* in *Joshua* is the sixteenth; while in the Torah (Pentateuch) *the morrow of the Pesach* means (the fifteenth, that is) the morrow of the slaughtering of the Pesach sacrifice"[11] (and thus the "Pesach of Israel" is the afternoon of the fourteenth, when the sacrifice is slaughtered). But *Ibn Ezra* himself challenges this interpretation of Rav Saadia *Gaon* with typically sharp-edged language: "This says nothing," and offers a different interpretation of his own. According to him, "Pesach" means the same thing in both places in Scripture, for even in *parashas Masei* it refers to the °°night of the fifteenth, "for the whole reason why the festival is called Pesach is that HaShem 'passed over' *(pasach)* the houses." How is it, then, that the Children of Israel went out *on the morrow of the Pesach?* The answer is that even though

°[This is a general principle often referred to in the Talmud which could be paraphrased thus: "The Torah has its own method of expression, so have the Prophets, and so have the Sages." Thus the same word used in the Torah to mean the fourteenth of Nissan could be used in the Prophets to mean the fifteenth of Nissan and by the Sages to mean the seven days of the Festival of Pesach starting on the fifteenth of Nissan. — Ed.]

°°[The Jewish day begins, of course, in the evening. *Ibn Ezra*, towards the end of his long and remarkable life, wrote the book, *Igeres HaShabbos*, in order to prove conclusively this very point. He takes strong exception to anyone who attempts to assert the opposite; one such opponent incurred Ibn Ezra's curse: "May his right arm wither and the sight of his right eye fade." — Ed.]

the date of the night and its following day are the same (e.g.,
the fifteenth of Nissan consists of the night and its following
day), nevertheless, in relation to the previous night the
morning is called "the morrow." Thus, in *parashas Masei*
"Pesach" means the night of the fifteenth, and its *morrow* is
the morning of the fifteenth; and similarly it is written, ... *that
whole day and the whole night and the whole morrow* (כָּל
הַיּוֹם הַהוּא וְכָל הַלַּיְלָה וְכֹל יוֹם הַמָּחֳרָת; *Numbers* 11:32).

Ritva[12] cites this interpretation, adding another piece of
evidence from *I Samuel: If you do not save your life tonight,
tomorrow you will be slain* (אִם אֵינְךָ מְמַלֵּט אֶת נַפְשְׁךָ הַלַּיְלָה
מָחָר אַתָּה מוּמָת).[13] But *Ritva* notes that in the majority of
cases, "tomorrow" and "the morrow" do mean the
subsequent date; and it is only in a few places that "Scripture
did not choose the more precise meaning of the term (לֹא דַּיֵּיק
קְרָא) and used it to mean the morning." And this last remark is
necessary in the context at hand; for we now wish to interpret
the verse in *Joshua* as meaning that the Children of Israel ate
chadash (not the previous year's crop) *on the morrow of the
Pesach*, and thus the meaning of *on the morrow* here must be
the sixteenth of Nissan.

*The Night
Comes
After
the Day*

A surprising alternative way of reconciling our two verses is
offered by the author of *Hamiknah*. He demonstrates through
several proofs that the rule, "the day comes after the night"
(הַיּוֹם הוֹלֵךְ אַחַר הַלַּיְלָה) — i.e., any given date consists of the
night and its following day — was an innovation instituted
when the Torah was given. Before the giving of the Torah,
"the night comes after the day," i.e., a given date consists of
the day and its following night (as reflected in the verse, *Day
and night shall not cease* — וְיוֹם וָלַיְלָה לֹא יִשְׁבֹּתוּ; *Genesis* 8:22).
In this light, there is no contradiction between the wording
used in *Masei* and that in *Joshua*. In both places, "Pesach"
means the time when the Korban Pesach is eaten, namely the
night of the fifteenth of Nissan. But this same night is
assigned two different dates, depending on the context. In
parshas Masei, which speaks of the time of the Exodus, before
the Torah was given, the night preceding the fifteenth of
Nissan is dated the fourteenth; therefore the day of the
fifteenth is called the *morrow of the Pesach*. But in *Joshua*,
events that occurred after the Torah was given are related,
therefore, the night preceding the fifteenth of Nissan is dated
the fifteenth, and therefore *the morrow of the Pesach* means
the sixteenth.[14]

All the above interpretations follow the opinion that the law *When* which prohibits *chadash* until after the sacrifice of the *omer* *the* was in effect immediately upon entrance into the Land. But *Manna* what about those who hold that the prohibition of *chadash* *Ceased* did not come into effect until after the fourteen years of יְרוּשָׁה וִישִׁיבָה (lit., inheritance and settling), the seven years during which the Land was conquered and the seven during which it was divided among the tribes and families? This question is considered by the Babylonian Talmud;[15] the explanation given from this point of view is that the Children of Israel waited until the sixteenth to eat the grain of the Land, not because it was prohibited to them before then, but because they did not need to eat it before then; for until then they were supplied with food by the manna that remained in their vessels. This fact is stated explicitly in the next verse in *Joshua. And the manna ceased on the morrow, ... and the children of Israel no longer had manna* (וַיִּשְׁבֹּת הַמָּן מִמָּחֳרָת ...; וְלֹא הָיָה עוֹד לִבְנֵי יִשְׂרָאֵל מָן *Joshua* 5:12). But in addition, the Talmud proves the same fact from verses in the *Chumash*.[18] According to this viewpoint, too, "Pesach" here means the fifteenth, for the *morrow* is interpreted as the sixteenth of Nissan.

"Pesach" in the Talmud

So far we have learned that in the Torah and the Prophetic *All* writings the term "Pesach," in so far as it refers to a day rather *Seven* than to the slaughter and sacrifice of the Korban Pesach, *Days* means either the fifteenth or the fourteenth of Nissan (depending upon which interpretation we accept). Neither of these, however, is the meaning of "Pesach" as used by the Sages of the Talmud. There, "Pesach" means the seven days of the festival, those seven days which in the Torah are termed "the festival of *matzos*." In passages beyond number, the *Tannaim* and *Amoraim* use the term "Pesach" to mean the festival of *matzos*. In the same sense, they use the terms *erev Pesach* (or *arvei Pesachim*) as meaning the day before the festival begins; and likewise, "the first *Yom-Tov* of Pesach," "the seventh day of Pesach," and "after the Pesach."

We find, as an exception to the rule, one place where "Pesach" *The* is used to mean the fourteenth of Nissan. A *mishnah* in *Fourteenth* *Pesachim* tells us, "Rabbi Meir said, 'We have learned from the Sages that one may burn undefiled *trumah* (תְּרוּמָה טְהוֹרָה) along with defiled *trumah* (תְּרוּמָה טְמֵאָה) on Pesach.' "

Normally, defiled and undefiled *trumah* must be kept apart, for it is forbidden to cause *trumah*, the portion of the crop given to the *kohen*, to be defiled; and contact with defiled grain would defile the pure *trumah*. However, the *mishnah* informs us, when *trumah* has fermented and become *chametz*, and must therefore be destroyed before Pesach, we are no longer obligated to guard it against defilement, since in any case it is עוֹמֶדֶת לִשְׂרֵיפָה, slated for burning. In this *mishnah* the term "Pesach" means specifically the day before Pesach, *erev Pesach* — this must be so, not because *erev Pesach* is the time when *chametz* is eliminated, for after all, grain which ferments during the seven-day festival is equally subject to the mitzvah, *You shall remove leaven from your houses* (תַּשְׁבִּיתוּ שְׂאֹר מִבָּתֵּיכֶם; *Exodus* 12:15), and must be destroyed even if it ferments after *erev Pesach*. But we know that "Pesach" here refers only to *erev Pesach* because the Talmud explains that the whole point of Rabbi Meir's statement is that even during the hour before noon on *erev Pesach*, when the prohibition of *chametz* is Rabbinic and not Scriptural, nevertheless we are permitted to burn undefiled and defiled *trumah* together.

The Jerusalem Talmud takes note of the exceptional use of the term here, and emphasizes it: "What is meant by 'Pesach'? — the fourteenth."[18] But the Jerusalem and Babylonian Talmuds understand this *mishnah* in different ways. According to the Babylonian Talmud, Rabbi Meir was speaking only of the pre-noon hour (שָׁעָה שִׁשִּׁית), for after that hour *chametz* is Scripturally prohibited — and Rabbi Meir's rule should be admitted even by those who disagree with Rabbi Meir about mixing undefiled and defiled *trumah* during the pre-noon hour. But according to the Jerusalem Talmud, Rabbi Meir was speaking of the whole afternoon of the fourteenth, for according to the *Yerushalmi*, Rabbi Meir holds that the prohibition of .*chametz* on *erev Pesach* is purely Rabbinic until sundown.[19]

The First Night In a number of places in the Mishnah we find the term "Pesach" not in reference to all seven days of the festival, but to the first night of Pesach alone. Two examples are found in Tractate *Pesachim*. "These are the [grains] with which one may fulfill his obligation on Pesach: wheat, barley ..."[20] *Rashi* explains, " 'fulfill his obligation' — the obligation of *matzah* on the first night, for one is obligated to eat *matzah*, as it is written, *In the evening you shall eat matzos* (בָּעֶרֶב תֹּאכְלוּ מַצֹּת; *Exodus* 12:18).[21] And similarly, "These are the vegetables with which one may fulfill his obligation on Pesach: *chazeres* ...''[22] Here, too, the reference is to the first night, during which there is an obligation to eat *maror*, bitter herbs.[23] Of course, this use of the term "Pesach" does not contradict its more usual meaning, i.e., the whole festival, for the first night is included in the festival as a whole and thus may also be called "Pesach." One commentary on the Mishnah, however — *Meleches Shlomo* — takes the word "Pesach" here in a different sense: not the point in time, but the sacrifice. The commandment of the Pesach sacrifice is that it should be eaten with *matzah* and *maror* — *With matzos and merorim they shall eat it* (עַל מַצּוֹת וּמְרֹרִים יֹאכְלֻהוּ; *Numbers* 9:11) — and it is to this that these two *mishnayos* refer. One fulfills his obligation when he eats them "on Pesach," that is, with the Pesach sacrifice. The interpretation may be described as ingenious; however, it departs from the plain meaning of the *mishnah*.

A completely different meaning of the word "Pesach" is *The* found in only one place: the first *mishnah* of Tractate *Chalah*, *Sixteenth* where the word is used for the sixteenth of Nissan. This *mishnah* states that to eat the five types of grain specified by the Torah is "forbidden, from the new crop *(chadash)* before the Pesach; and reaping [it is forbidden] before the *omer*."[24] What could be the meaning of the words, *"chadash* is forbidden before the Pesach"? The fact is that even when Pesach, the fifteenth of Nissan, passes, *chadash* is still forbidden. We are forced, then, to interpret the *mishnah* as does *Tosefos Yom-Tov*. "Before the Pesach" here means "before that day during Pesach on which the *chadash* is brought" (as the *omer* offering in the *Beis HaMikdash*). The reason for this peculiar wording is explained in terms of a dispute about what it is that makes the *chadash* permissible on the sixteenth of Nissan; is it simply the dawning of the day, or is it the offering of the sacrifice? If the *mishnah* had stated that eating *chadash* is forbidden 'before the *omer*,' this would have meant 'before the offering of the *omer* in the *Beis HaMikdash*.' But the author of the *mishnah* held the other opinion, and therefore used a term implying that the decisive factor is "the *day* during Pesach on which the *chadash* is brought."[25]

The difficulty remains evident — this does not seem to be the plain meaning of the phrase, "before the Pesach." There is, however, another version of this *mishnah*. The version just cited is indeed that printed in our current editions of the

Mishnah, and is accepted by *Rambam*[26] and *Ri ben Malkitzedek*.[27] But a second more exact version reverses the times stated and thus presents no difficulties of wording. It reads, "... forbidden, from the *chadash*, before the *omer*, and reaping [it is forbidden] before the Pesach." The meaning is simple. Eating *chadash* is forbidden before the sixteenth of Nissan, but reaping is forbidden before Pesach, for on the fifteenth of Nissan reaping is in any case forbidden because the day is *Yom-Tov*. [Thus, if the *mishnah* had stated that reaping is forbidden 'before the *omer*' this would have implied that it is only the law of *chadash* which makes reaping forbidden on the fifteenth. — *Ed.*] This second version is the one accepted by Rabbeinu Gershom *Meor Hagolah*, *Rashi* and *Tosafos*,[29] *Rash*,[30] *Or Zarua*,[31] *Gra*,[32] and others.[33]

The roots of these two versions of our *mishnah* reach back to the Jerusalem Talmud. "There are those who teach, 'before the Pesach,' and those who teach, 'before the *omer*.' "[34] The *Yerushalmi* also explains the halachic difference between the proponents of the two versions. "He who holds 'before the *omer*' supports Chizkiah."[35] This refers to a dispute between Rabbi Yochanan and Chizkiah over the issue already mentioned above. Rabbi Yochanan holds that even when the *Mikdash* is standing it is the dawning of the day that makes *chadash* permissible; therefore he reads, "before the Pesach," i.e., the *day* during Pesach on which the *omer* is brought. Chizkiah holds that when the *Mikdash* is standing it is only the offering of the sacrifice which makes *chadash* permissible; therefore he reads, "before the *omer*," that is, the offering of the *omer*.[36]

A Different Interpretation A completely different interpretation of the passage in the Jerusalem Talmud is given in the book *Nir*. According to this interpretation, the disagreement about "before the Pesach" vs. "before the *omer*" has nothing to do with the *mishnah's* first statement, about eating *chadash*. Without doubt, this author asserts, both sides agree that the correct wording is "before the *omer*." ("It is very far-fetched to interpret the term 'Pesach' as meaning 'the day during the Pesach festival that is the day of offering the *omer*.' ") What, then, is the disagreement? It is about the second part of the *mishnah*, "and reaping [is forbidden] before ..." The meaning of the disagreement is as follows. Rabbi Yochanan, who, as we know, holds that the *time* of offering the *omer*, rather than the act itself, is the determining factor permitting one to eat *chadash*, will hold the same opinion with regard to the permission to reap the *chadash*. The *time* of reaping is what makes the reaping permissible; therefore, immediately at the end of the first *Yom-Tov* day of Pesach, reaping is permissible. And since reaping is in any case a type of labor which is forbidden on *Yom-Tov*, it is proper to say that reaping is forbidden "before the Pesach." Chizkiah, on the other hand, who holds that only the actual sacrifice of the *omer* makes *chadash* permissible for eating, will hold the same concerning reaping: only the actual reaping of the *omer* sheaves makes the rest of the new crop permissible for reaping. Therefore, for Chizkiah it is impossible to say that reaping is forbidden "before the Pesach," for even when the first *Yom-Tov* day of Pesach has ended, as long as the sheaves of barley have not been cut for the *omer*, reaping *chadash* remains prohibited. Thus, the proper wording is "reaping [is forbidden] before the *omer*," meaning before the reaping of the *omer*.

(This idea, that the disagreement recorded in the Jerusalem Talmud has to do with the reaping of the *chadash*, rather than the eating, is also the opinion of *Gra* in his commentary on the *Yerushalmi*; however, *Gra* interprets the whole *mishnah* as speaking about the situation after the destruction of the Temple, and accordingly suggests an alternate reading of the entire passage in the Jerusalem Talmud.)[37]

And if in this *mishnah* from Tractate *Challah* the authorities argue, debate, and strain to determine the correct reading, in another place in the Talmud we find the term "Pesach" used in this same sense — as meaning the sixteenth of Nissan — without a murmur from anyone. In Tractate *Semachos*[38] there is a *baraisa* which lists all the laws that involve a time limit of three days. Among these laws is, "Seeds from the five kinds of grain [sown] three days before the Pesach are permitted." As usually understood, this *mishnah* informs us about the prohibition of *chadash*, and defines the boundary between the 'old crop' and the 'new crop.' If seeds were sown at least three days before the "Pesach," i.e., the sixteenth of Nissan, last year, then they are considered as the 'old crop,' and not prohibited as *chadash* the following Pesach. *Gra* amends the wording of the *mishnah* by adding, "less than this, prohibited;" that is, seeds planted less than three days before the "Pesach" are considered part of the new crop, since it is assumed that the plants will not have taken root in less than three days, and thus their time of taking root will have occurred after the "Pesach."

Here we have an amazing thing: *Gra* himself, in the *mishnah* from *Challah* discussed above, as well as in the passage from the Jerusalem Talmud, rejects the use of the word "Pesach" as meaning the sixteenth of Nissan, adopting the alternative reading of "before the *omer*" rather than "before the Pesach;" and here, where "Pesach" is again used to mean the sixteenth of Nissan, *Gra* lets it pass without comment, even though he was involved in amending the wording pertinent to this *halachah!* The present author, in his youth, offered an alternative explanation of our *baraisa* in *Semachos*, which renders *Gra's* comment — or lack of comment — understandable. The *mishnah* can be interpreted as dealing with a completely different topic; it does not deal with *chadash* at all, but rather with the prohibition of *chametz* on Pesach. Seeds sown in one's field shortly before Pesach are of course part of one's property; if the moisture of the ground should cause them to ferment and become *chametz*, then one would be obligated to eliminate them from one's possession along with all other *chametz*, before Pesach. Our *mishnah* comes to inform us that if the seeds were sown at least three days before Pesach they may be considered to have rotted and hence they are not prohibited as *chametz*. This is similar to the case, discussed in Tractate *Pesachim*, where *chametz* which is thoroughly charred by fire before Pesach, so that, as *Rashi* explains, it loses the taste and appearance of *chametz*, is permitted for use (e.g., fuel) after Pesach even though one had not eliminated it from his possession during the festival.[40] However, the *mishnah* says, seeds sown less than three days before Pesach must be assumed not to have rotted, but to have fermented, and therefore are forbidden for Jewish ownership on Pesach, like other *chametz*.

And how do we know that the time limit for this law is three days? This may be deduced from the Mishnah itself. A *mishnah* in Tractate *Kilayim* is concerned with the prohibition of sowing different types of seeds, such as wheat and barley, together — the prohibited mixture is called *kilayim*. The *mishnah* there tells us, "If one's field has already been sown with wheat, and one changes one's mind and wishes to sow it with barley, one should wait עַד שֶׁתַּתְלִיעַ. The Jerusalem Talmud states "until it is in the ground three days." *Rambam*, in his commentary on the Mishnah, explains the term as meaning that the seeds have become destroyed through mold and rot.[42] We see, then, that three days is the time during which seeds in the ground decay. (The time required for seeds to take root is subject to disagreement, but here we are concerned not with the time for taking root, but for rotting.)

There is record of a halachic inquiry directed to Rabbi Shmuel Landau (the son of the author of *Noda BiYehudah*), concerning one who had sown grain three days before Pesach, and wished to know whether the seeds were prohibited as *chametz* on Pesach. The reply was that "intuition suggests and reason dictates" that after three days the seed has rotted and been destroyed and is no longer fit for eating[43] (and therefore not prohibited as *chametz*). If our interpretation is correct, this inquiry and reply constitute an interpretation of the *halachah* given by our *mishnah* in *Semachos*.

This, then, is the term "Pesach" as used by the Torah, by the Prophets, and by the Sages. What remains is the meaning of the term as used by the man in the street (לְשׁוֹן בְּנֵי אָדָם). Common usage, *leshon bnei adam*, has determining force in *Halachah* mainly in connection with vows. There is a rule, בִּנְדָרִים הַלֵּךְ אַחַר לְשׁוֹן בְּנֵי אָדָם, "In connection with vows, follow common usage."[44] Thus, if one vows not to derive any benefit from a certain thing until Pesach, until precisely what day does the prohibition remain in force? The Talmud discusses three forms of such a vow: עַד הַפֶּסַח, until Pesach; עַד שֶׁיְּהֵא הַפֶּסַח, until Pesach will be; עַד פְּנֵי הַפֶּסַח, which can be interpreted either as 'until the front of Pesach,' or 'until the turning of Pesach.' Some accept an alternate reading of this third term, עַד לִפְנֵי הַפֶּסַח, which again can be understood either as 'until before the Pesach' or 'until the turning of the Pesach.' The Talmud explains each of these phrases in turn. If one's vow is phrased, עַד הַפֶּסַח, then the prohibition is effective until Pesach arrives. This means until the night of the fifteenth of Nissan, for, as *Ran* explains, in common usage the term "until" means up to but not including.

The second phrase, עַד שֶׁיְּהֵא הַפֶּסַח, results in a prohibition which lasts until the end of Pesach ("for in common usage this term means 'until it will have been entirely' ").

Concerning the third phrase, עַד פְּנֵי הַפֶּסַח, there is disagreement. Rabbi Meir says the prohibition lasts until Pesach arrives, while Rabbi Yosei says, until the festival ends.[45] Here there is no disagreement about the meaning of the term "Pesach." Both sides take it to mean the whole seven-day festival. The disagreement arises over the word פְּנֵי, i.e., whether it means "front" — "before the Pesach," or "turning" — "until Pesach shall have turned and passed."[46]

A second, similar *mishnah* presents a challenge of interpretation in connection with that just quoted. "Rabbi

The Man in the Street

Yehudah says, if one vows that 'he will not taste wine עַד שֶׁיְהֵא הַפֶּסַח (until the Pesach will be)' his intention is only until the night of Pesach, until the hour when the custom is to drink wine."[47] Does this mean that Rabbi Yehudah disagrees with the statement in our previous *mishnah*, "עַד שֶׁיְהֵא [means] the thing is forbidden until [the festival] ends"? The question whether or not Rabbi Yehudah disagrees with the other *mishnah* is itself the subject of disagreement among the *Rishonim*. Some hold that there is no contradiction between the two *mishnayos*. The previous *mishnah* deals with one who has vowed to refrain from other things, while Rabbi Yehudah was speaking of one who vowed specifically about wine. A vow about wine is different, for it is reasonable to make the assumption (אוּמְדָן הַדַּעַת) that the person intended to restrict himself only up to — but not including — Pesach night [when of course one is obligated to drink the Four Cups of wine during the *Seder*]. Other *Rishonim*, however, who believe that both *mishnayos* have to do with wine specifically, hold that Rabbi Yehudah disagrees with the previous *mishnah*.[48]

God and Israel Praise Each Other Why is it that in the Torah the festival as a whole is called "the festival of *matzos*," while we refer to it as "Pesach"? Rabbi Levi Yitzchak of Berdichev finds in this fact a parallel to the difference between the *tefillin* which we wear and those which the Holy One, Blessed Be He, wears, as it were. The Talmud tells us in Tractate *Berachos* that God and Israel praise each other; for in our *tefillin* are found the words "Hear, O Israel, HASHEM our God, HASHEM is one," while the *tefillin* of the Master of the Universe it is written, "And who is like Your people Israel, one nation, on the earth?"[49] It is the same with the name for Pesach. The Holy One, Blessed Be He, in His Torah calls it "the festival of *matzos*" in praise of Israel, who were so eager in carrying out the command of God "that there was not even time for the dough of our forefathers to ferment."[50] Israel, for their part, refer to the festival by a name which implies praise of the Holy One, Blessed Be He, for He passed over *(pasach)* the houses of the Children of Israel in Egypt" — thus the name "Pesach."[51]

***

The Word Itself What meaning is implied by the word "Pesach"? *Tannaim* disagree about the answer to this question, as we find in *Mechilta*. "וּפָסַחְתִּי עֲלֵכֶם (*Exodus* 12:13) — Rabbi Yoshiyah (יֹאשִׁיָה) says, In place of וּפָסַחְתִּי read וּפָסַעְתִּי, shall step, for the Holy One, Blessed Be He, skipped over the houses of the

Children of Israel in Egypt, as it is said, *The voice of my Beloved — behold He comes, skipping over the mountains* (קוֹל דּוֹדִי הִנֵּה זֶה בָּא מְדַלֵּג עַל הֶהָרִים; *Song of Songs* 2:8). Rabbi Yonasan says, וּפָסַחְתִּי עֲלֵכֶם, *On you I shall have pity*, but I shall not have pity on the Egyptians. If an Egyptian was in the house of one of Israel, we might think (since *HaShem* skipped over the houses of Israel) that the Egyptian would be saved. But the verse says, וּפָסַחְתִּי עֲלֵכֶם — *On you I shall have pity*, but not on the Egyptians.''

Rabbi Yonasan finds agreement from Rabbi Yishmael, further on in *Mechilta*.[53] And *HaShem* פָּסַח over the door — פְּסִיחָה means none other than mercy, as it is said, *As flying birds, so will the Lord of Hosts defend Jerusalem, He will defend and deliver it. He will have mercy* (פָּסוֹחַ) *and rescue it* כְּצִפֳּרִים עָפוֹת כֵּן יָגֵן ה' צְבָאוֹת עַל יְרוּשָׁלַיִם גָּנוֹן וְהִצִּיל פָּסוֹחַ וְהִמְלִיט; *Isaiah* 31:5).

The disagreement continues through later generations. *Onkelos* translates וּפָסַחְתִּי עֲלֵכֶם as ''And I shall have mercy on you,'' and likewise renders וּפָסַח ה' as ''And *HaShem* will have mercy.'' But *Rashi*, after citing an interpretation of the word וּפָסַחְתִּי as meaning ''I shall have compassion (וְחָמַלְתִּי)'' writes, ''I say that the term פְּסִיחָה always means skipping or jumping; He skipped over the houses of Israel to the houses of Egypt, for the houses were all intermingled. And similarly (we find that פְּסִיחָה means 'skipping') in the phrase, *How long will you skip between two opinions* (עַד מָתַי אַתֶּם פֹּסְחִים עַל שְׁתֵּי הַסְּעִפִּים; *I Kings* 18:21); and likewise, the word פִּסְחִים means the lame, because those who are lame walk as if jumping; likewise, *He will pass over* (פָּסוֹחַ) *and rescue it* (*Isaiah* 31:5 — the same verse used above by Rabbi Yishmael to prove the opposite of *Rashi's* opinion).

Defense and Salvation

Ibn Ezra cites both interpretations of the etymology of ''Pesach'' without indicating a preference. But Rav Mecklenburg in *HaKsav VehaKabbalah* writes,[55] ''It is more correct to interpret the word as meaning defense and salvation ... as it is said, *And our houses He saved* (וְאֶת בָּתֵּינוּ הִצִּיל; *Exodus* 12:27), rather than skipping or jumping — for how are we justified in needlessly concretizing the Creator, Blessed Be He, to such an extent? And likewise the sacrifice which is offered on the festival is called ''Pesach'' (in this same sense), as in the phrase, *And slaughter the Pesach* (וְשַׁחֲטוּ הַפָּסַח; *Exodus* 12:21); and likewise, *the sacrifice of the festival of Pesach* (זֶבַח חַג הַפָּסַח; *Exodus* 34:25); and similarly, all other occurrences of the word in the Torah — all of them derive from the meaning: compassion, defense, and salvation."

Considering Israel's situation among the nations, we, too, must say, "It is more correct to interpret it as a term of defense and salvation."

NOTES

[1] *Numbers* 28:16.

[2] *Leviticus* 23:5.

[3] 45:21.

[4] *Numbers* 33:3.

[5] *Joshua* 5:11.

[6] *Challah* 2:1.

[7] *Rosh HaShanah* 13a.

[8] *Temidin UMusafin* 7:11.

[9] See *s.v.* דאקריבו, *Rosh HaShanah, loc. cit.*

[10] See *Tosafos, Kiddushin* 37b.

[11] *Leviticus* 23:11.

[12] In his *Chiddushim* on *Rosh Hashanah*.

[13] *I Samuel* 19:11.

[14] See *Sefer HaMiknah* on *Kiddushin* 37b, and the same author's work, *Panim Yafos al HaTorah, Genesis* 9:22, *Exodus* 11:2, *et al.* And see responsa *Binyan Tzion*, by Rav Y. Etlinger, sec. 126.

[15] *Kiddushin* 38a.

[16] And see *Tosafos, loc. cit., s.v.* ובני ישראל.

[17] Mishnah *Pesachim* 1:7.

[18] *Pesachim* 1:8.

[19] See *Meleches Shlomo* on Mishnah *Pesachim, loc. cit.,* in the name of Rav Elazar Azkari, and *Mareh HaPanim* on the *Yerushalmi, loc. cit., s.v.* ר' יוסי.

[20] *Pesachim* 2:5.

[21] 35a

[22] *Pesachim* 2:6.

[23] And see also *Challah* 1:2,8, *et. al.*

[24] *Challah* 1:1.

[25] And see *Tosefos Yom-Tov, loc. cit.*

[26] In his commentary on Mishnah *Challah*.

[27] *Ibid.*

[28] In his commentary on *Menachos*.

[29] *Menachos, loc. cit.*

[30] In his commentary on *challah*.

[31] Part 1, sec. 328.

[32] In *Shenos Eliahu* on *Challah*.

[33] And see "Mishnah *Zera'im*," pub. by Machon HaTalmud HaYisraeli HaShalem, part 2, p.314, in the variant readings and in note 2.

[34] *Challah* 1:1.

[35] *Ibid.*

[36] See the *Yerushalmi, loc. cit.*, and its commentaries.

[37] *See loc. cit.*

[38] *Ch.6.*

[39] In *Kovetz HaMe'asef*, by Rav B.Z. Koinkeh (Jerusalem, 1912), sec.33.

[40] *Pesachim* 21b.

[41] *Kila'im* 2:3.

[42] And see *Rambam, Kila'im* 2:13.

[43] See responsa *Shivas Tzion*, sec. 9; this author does not mention the *mishnah* in *Kila'im.*

[44] *Nedarim* 30b, and several other places in this Tractate.

[45] Mishnah *Nedarim* 8:2.

[46] *Kiddushin* 65a. In *Nedarim* 61b this disagreement in the *mishnah* is interpreted differently.

[47] *Nedarim* 8:5.

[48] See *Ramban*, in his *Halachos*, and *Ritva, loc. cit*; *Ran, Meiri*, and *Shitah Mekubetzes, Nedarim* 63b. And see *Tur, Yoreh De'ah* 220 and its commentaries, and *Shach, loc. cit.*, sec. 18.

[49] See *Berachos* 6a.

[50] And see *Rashi* on *Jeremiah* 2:2: *"I have remembered for you the zeal of your youth — and what is the zeal of your youth? — Your going after me in the wilderness, and there were no provisions for the way."*

[51] *Tosafos Chadashim* on the *Mishnayos*, at the beginning of *Pesachim*, in the name of the *Tzaddik.*

[52] *Exodus* 12:13.

[53] *Loc. cit.*, v. 23.

[54] *Loc. cit.*, v. 27.

[55] *Loc. cit.*, v. 13.

עֲשִׂין וְלָאוִין בְּקָרְבַּן פֶּסַח ⧫

The Pesach Sacrifice: Its Positive and Negative Commandments

Every sacrifice that was offered in the Beis HaMikdash had its specific purpose and its distinctive halachos. However, as the author points out, Rambam enumerated no fewer that eleven Scriptural commandments governing the korban Pesach, the Passover sacrifice — a number not reached by any other korban.

One of these commandments is indicated by an interesting translation in Onkelos' Aramaic rendition of the Torah known as the Targum. The Torah says: כָּל בֶּן נֵכָר לֹא יֹאכַל בּוֹ — which is usually translated, "No alien shall eat thereof" (Exodus 12:43). Not so the Targum, which translates: "Any Jew who becomes an apostate (meshumad) shall not eat thereof." The author of Meshech Chochmah explains that the very wording of the commandment indicated this meaning. To whom, he asks, is the Torah speaking? to a Jew? — Then it should say, "You shall not feed the korban Pesach to any alien." To a non-Jew? He is not obligated to observe most of the Torah. We must therefore say that this verse forbids an apostate Jew to partake of the korban Pesach.

An original point is made in this connection by the author of Pardess Yosef. Why is it that on Yom Kippur eve we open the Kol Nidrei service with a solemn declaration allowing transgressors of this sort to join us in our fasting and prayers, yet on Pesach night we strictly insist that they keep away? And he answers his own question. When a Jew, however far away he has wandered, wishes to join us in our prayers and fasts, we may reasonably assume that we discern a spark of serious goodwill which we are anxious to encourage. If, however, that spark awakens when the aroma of the festive roast reaches his nostrils, and all he wants is to join us in our feasts and joys, we say, "Such partners we can do without ... "

A
Unique
Mitzvah

The *Pesach* sacrifice has a feature which makes it almost unique among all the commandments of the Torah — it is one of the two positive mitzvos (the other being מִילָה, circumcision) for which the punishment for failing to perform the *mitzvah* is *kares*, divine excision of the soul.[1] Even in our time, though the *mitzvah* can no longer be performed, its special importance has left its traces: for this is the only one of the sacrifices whose memory is kept alive not only by words — through prayer and Torah reading — but also by deeds: the eating of the *afikoman* at the end of the Pesach feast, and the setting out of the *zroa*, the bone of cooked meat, on the symbolic Pesach plate.[2] Further, when, during the days of Rav Zvi Kalisher, the possibility of performing the sacrifices in our own time was raised, the main focus of the debate was the question of offering the *Pesach* sacrifice. (See vol. II, p. 279.)

The special importance of the *korban Pesach* is also reflected by the place it occupies in the listing of the six hundred and thirteen mitzvos. The sheer number of positive and negative commandments concerned with this *korban* is noteworthy. *Rambam*, in *Hilchos Korban Pesach*, lists sixteen such *mitzvos*, four positive and twelve negative. It is true that one of these has to do with the *korban chagigah*, a separate sacrifice offered in conjunction with the *Pesach* sacrifice; and four others have to do with *Pesach Sheni*, the "second Pesach" observed by those who were prevented, by ritual impurity *(tumah)* or by inability to reach the *Beis Hamikdash*, from observing the festival at its proper time. But even after subtracting these five mitzvos, there remain eleven belonging to the main *Pesach* sacrifice. No other *korban* is honored with so many commandments.

Eleven
Command-
ments

Those eleven mitzvos are: (1) to slaughter the *Pesach* sacrifice at the proper time; (2) not to slaughter it while any *chametz*, leavening, remains in one's possession; (3) not to allow the night to pass without offering up those parts (אֵמוּרִים) of the sacrificial animal which are to be consumed on the altar; (4) to eat the meat of the sacrifice, with *matzah* and *maror* — unleavened bread and bitter herbs — on the eve of the fifteenth of Nissan; (5) not to eat the sacrifice partially roasted, nor cooked in liquid — that is, it must be completely roasted over a fire; (6) not to remove the meat of the sacrifice from the *chavurah* (the group of people who have joined together to eat that particular sacrificial animal); (7) that the sacrifice should not be eaten by a *mumar*, one who serves idols; (8) that it should not be eaten by a non-Jew (תּוֹשָׁב וְשָׂכִיר); (9) that it should not be eaten by one who is uncircumcised; (10) not to break the bones of the sacrifice; (11) not to leave over the remnants of the sacrifice until the morning.

Of these eleven commandments, nine are negative and two — the slaughtering and the eating of the *korban* — are positive mitzvos. Why is it that these two are counted as separate and distinct commandments? — After all, it is impossible to eat the sacrifice without slaughtering it. Furthermore, we see that concerning the *korban chatas*, sin offering, the slaughtering and the eating are commanded in separate verses: *The chatas shall be slaughtered* (תִּשָּׁחֵט הַחַטָּאת; *Leviticus* 6:18); and, *The kohen who sacrifices it as a sin-offering shall eat it* (הַכֹּהֵן הַמְחַטֵּא אֹתָהּ יֹאכְלֶנָּה; *ibid.* v. 19). The same is true of the *asham*, guilt offering, and the *shlamim*, peace offering. Nevertheless, the slaughtering and the eating of these sacrifices are not counted as two separate mitzvos. Why is the *Pesach* sacrifice different?

The question is discussed in *Ma'ayan Chachmah* (by the author of *Atzei Arazim*), and at the end of the discussion the author remarks, "I have not seen this point raised by any of those who enumerated the six hundred and thirteen mitzvos."[3] But if none of these authorities dealt with this question explicitly, there is one of the earliest of them who took the matter into account implicitly. *Yere'im HaShalem*[4] writes, "The Holy One, Blessed Be He, commanded Israel to offer the *Pesach* [sacrifice] ... and by offering the *Pesach* [sacrifice] is meant the slaughtering, the sprinkling of the blood, and the burning of the appropriate parts (אֵמוּרִים) on the altar — but not the eating, for it is written, *On the fourteenth of the month, towards evening, they shall sacrifice it at its appointed time* (בְּאַרְבָּעָה עָשָׂר יוֹם בַּחֹדֶשׁ הַזֶּה בֵּין הָעַרְבַּיִם תַּעֲשׂוּ אֹתוֹ בְּמֹעֲדוֹ; *Numbers* 9:3), and the eating was not on the fourteenth, but on the night of the fifteenth." That is, the two commandments have separate times. The slaughtering is commanded for the fourteenth (and may not be performed on the fifteenth), and the eating, for the fifteenth (and not the fourteenth). This is different from the case of the other sacrifices, for they are eaten on the same day that they are slaughtered.[5]

Chovas Another author who discusses this question is *Beis HaLevi*,[5*]
Gavra who makes a convincing distinction. With the other sacrifices, the eating is not a commandment relating specifically to the man who eats — that is, it is not a *chovas gavra*, an obligation upon the man himself — rather, the commandment is simply that the sacrifice should be eaten. Therefore the eating is only one of the details of the act of offering the sacrifice, such as slaughtering, burning on the altar, and so on. This is not the case with the *Pesach* sacrifice, for the command to eat this sacrifice is an obligation upon the person himself, "and is not included at all within the [act of] offering the *korban*." This is the reason why it is counted as a separate positive mitzvah.

An author of our time discusses another aspect of this topic: the relationship between the two mitzvos. "It is certain that the two mitzvos have a cause and effect relationship; hence the question arises, which is the cause and which the effect?" He concludes, "The essential mitzvah is the eating on the night [of the fifteenth], while the offering on the [previous] day is in the category of an 'enabling act' for the eating." [6] It is possible to discuss and debate the author's assertion that the slaughtering is merely an enabling act for the eating;'[7] but the fact that in general the eating is the essence of the mitzvah of the *Pesach* sacrifice cannot be disputed. The Talmud tells us, "A *Pesach* [sacrifice] which comes (to the Altar) in a state of *tumah* may [also] be eaten in a state of *tumah*,° for from the beginning it comes only for the eating."[8] *Rashi* explains, "When the *Pesach* [sacrifice] was commanded, it was essentially commanded for eating."[9]

Wrong This relationship between the eating and the slaughtering of
Intentions the *korban Pesach* is used by several authors as the basis for explaining a *halachah* which was first made explicit by *Rambam*. The *halachah* has to do with the thoughts and intentions of the person slaughtering an animal which is being offered as a sacrifice. For example, the animal may have been set aside by its owner as an *olah*, burnt offering, and the one slaughtering it intends while doing the sacrifice that it should be a *shlamim*, peace offering. For most types of sacrifice, such a thought does not disqualify the animal.°° There are two types

°[Although the general rule is that טוּמְאָה הוּתְּרָה בְּצִיבּוּר, that is, the prohibition of *tumah* does not apply to communal sacrifices (see vol. II, p. 52), this rule only goes so far as to allow a defiled sacrifice to be offered on the Altar; it could not be eaten as could an undefiled sacrifice, but instead had to be burned (see *Pesachim* 76b). However, the *korban Pesach*, even if defiled, could be eaten; for, as *Rashi* says, "it was essentially commanded for eating." — *Ed.*]

°°[Nevertheless, the sacrifice has not freed the owner from bringing a fresh *olah* and a fresh of sacrifice, however, where a thought of this type renders the animal altogether invalid for the Altar. The two are the *chatas* and the *Pesach*.

If an animal has been designated by its owner as a *chatas* or *Pesach* sacrifice, and the one slaughtering it intends that it should be offered as some sacrifice other than that designated by the owner, the animal is disqualified. In this respect, the *chatas* and *Pesach* sacrifices are distinguished from all others. The innovation of *Rambam*[10] consists in making a distinction even between the *chatas* and the *Pesach*. The *chatas* is invalidated only by an intention to switch it for some other sacrifice, but not by an intention to slaughter it for ordinary eating *(chullin)*. As the Talmud states, "Its own kind eradicates it; a different kind does not eradicate it"[11] — that is, the intention to switch it for a different sacrifice invalidates it, since even a different sacrifice is still "its own kind," still a sacrifice. However, the intention to switch it for something which is altogether not "its own kind," that is, not a sacrifice at all, does not invalidate it. With the *Pesach*, *Rambam* reveals, even the intention to slaughter it for ordinary eating invalidates it (as is written, *And you shall say, "It is the Pesach sacrifice for HASHEM" — Exodus 12:27*). The authorities have endeavored to understand how *Rambam* arrived at this conclusion, and have offered various explanations — but nearly all of them are based on this foundation, that the eating is the essence of the mitzvah of the *Pesach* sacrifice.

For example, *Or Same'ach* explains that with respect to the *chatas* offering, the slaughtering is for the Altar (לְצוֹרֶךְ גָּבוֹהַּ), while with respect to *chullin*, ordinary meat, the slaughtering is purely for the purpose of the eating; hence *chullin* is "a different kind" from the *chatas*. But with respect to the *Pesach* sacrifice, where the slaughtering is for the purpose of eating, we cannot say that *chullin* is an entirely different kind; it may be said that the *Pesach* offering is, if not "its own kind" (מִינָה), at least a closely related kind (בַּת מִינָה).[12]

A different explanation points out that the animal intended as a *Pesach* sacrifice is invalid if slaughtered שֶׁלֹּא לְאוֹכְלָיו, that is, if slaughtered for people who cannot perform the mitzvah of eating it (e.g., for sick people).[13] Since with *chullin* there is no mitzvah to eat it, when one slaughters an animal for the purpose of *chullin* it is as if he slaughtered it for those who cannot eat it.[14]

---

shlamim. In other words, it is not counted as a sacrifice as far as the owner's obligations are concerned. — *Ed.*]

Laws of the Slaughtering Connected to this mitzvah of slaughtering the *korban Pesach* are many particular laws. The Torah specifies the time when the slaughtering must be performed (after noon on the fourteenth of Nissan); the kind of animal *(of the sheep or of the goats, a year-old male —* מִן הַכְּבָשִׂים וּמִן הָעִזִּים; *Exodus* 12:5); the persons who are to participate in the sacrifice (both men and women participate, though there is disagreement among the *Tannaim* about whether the woman's participation is obligatory or optional);[15] and the place of the slaughtering. The place must be the courtyard (עֲזָרָה) of the Tabernacle or Temple; this excludes a 'private altar' *(bamas yachid),* even during those times when other types of sacrifices were permitted on a *bamas yachid* — i.e., during the period when Israel had entered the Land but had not yet established a permanent altar.° The exclusion is derived from the verse, *You may not slaughter the Pesach in one of your cities* (לֹא תוּכַל לִזְבֹּחַ אֶת הַפֶּסַח בְּאַחַד שְׁעָרֶיךָ; *Deuteronomy* 16:5). The Torah further specifies how those wishing to partake of the *Pesach* must be specified before the animal is slaughtered (as derived from the verse, *You shall designate the participants in the sheep —* תָּכֹסוּ עַל הַשֶּׂה; *Exodus* 12:4); and indicates that certain intentions on the part of the person who actually performs the slaughtering invalidate the sacrifice (e.g., if he has in mind to slaughter it for people who cannot eat it, for people other than those designated as participating in that animal, for people who are uncircumcised or in a state of *tumah,* and so on). The numerous general principles and specific details of these and similar laws are explained by *Rambam* in *Hilchos Korban Pesach,* based on the statements of the Sages as recorded in *Mechilta, Tosefta,* and the Jerusalem and Babylonian Talmuds.

In the Beis HaMikdash How is the *Pesach* sacrifice performed in the *Beis HaMikdash?* *Rambam* gives a description of the process, based on the Mishnah. "The *Pesach* [sacrifice] is slaughtered in three shifts (כִּתּוֹת), as it is written, *And the whole assemblage of the congregation of Israel shall slaughter it* (וְשָׁחֲטוּ אֹתוֹ כֹּל קְהַל עֲדַת יִשְׂרָאֵל; *ibid.,* v. 6) — *assemblage* and *congregation* and

---

°[The Talmud in *Zevachim* 112a explains that *'bamas yachid'* was only allowed for the first 14 years after the entry to *Eretz Yisrael* and during the interregnum between the *mishkan* of Shiloh which stood for 369 years and the building of the *Beis HaMikdash* in Jerusalem 57 years later. However, even during the first 14 years there was a central altar in Gilgal whilst during the 57 years between Shiloh and Jerusalem the central altar was first in Nov and then in Givon. During these two periods of 14 and 57 years one was allowed to bring certain sacrifices on a private altar but the *korban Pesach* had to be brought to the central altar. — Ed.]

Israel (imply three shifts). There must be at least thirty people in each shift ... The first shift enters until the courtyard is full; the doors of the courtyard are locked, and they begin to slaughter their [*Pesach* sacrifices]. And the whole time the people are slaughtering and offering [their sacrifices], the Levites recite the *Hallel (Psalms* 114-118). If they finish the *Hallel* before the first shift have finished their offerings, they repeat the *Hallel*. And if they have repeated it and the shift has not finished, they recite it a third time (and the Mishnah records, "Rabbi Yehudah says, in the whole history of the third shift [the Levites] never reached the words *'I love it that HASHEM hears ...'* [i.e., the middle of the *Hallel*]. For each recital [of the *Hallel*] three blasts are blown on the חֲצוֹצְרוֹת, the silver trumpets: a long steady blast (תְּקִיעָה), then a blast consisting of several short ones (תְּרוּעָה), then another long blast. Since there are no wine libations [with the *Pesach* offering] and hence the trumpets cannot be blown at the time of the pouring of the libations, they are blown at the time of slaughtering. The *kohanim* stand line after line, and in their hands are vessels of silver and vessels of gold (for the blood of the sacrifices). Each line is either all silver or all gold; and they do not intermingle (the gold with the silver) so as to enhance their beauty. The vessels do not have bases, so that they should not be set down lest the blood congeal. When a person has slaughtered, and the *kohen* has received the blood, he passes it to his fellow *kohen*, and that one to the next, so that many men should be involved in the mitzvah, until the blood reaches the *kohen* closest to the altar. He pours it out in one motion against the side of the altar over the base, receives a full vessel, and afterwards returns the empty one. They hang up and skin the entire animal, slit it open, and the *kohen* cleans out the innards, removing the excrement. He takes out the parts intended for the altar, puts them in a vessel, salts them, and burns them on the altar ... When [the first shift] have finished their offerings, the doors of the courtyard are opened, the first shift exit, and the second shift enter. When the second has exited, the third enter. The second and third shifts perform the sacrifice in the same way as the first. When the third shift have finished, they exit, and the courtyard is washed."[17]

The matter of the Levites reciting the *Hallel*, as described by *Rambam*, is not a settled fact. True, the procedure is thus set forth by *Tosefta*,[18] by *Rashi*,[19] and by *Tosafos*.[20] But the commentary of *Rashi* on other Talmud passages indicates that all the people in each shift recited the *Hallel*, rather than just the Levites on duty in the *Beis HaMikdash*. This is also implied by the wording of the *Gemara* in another place in Tractate *Pesachim*. The Talmud there discusses how we know that *Hallel* is to be recited on Pesach, and one of the reasons given is, "Can it be that Israel would slaughter their [*Pesach* sacrifices] or wave their *lulavim* and not recite *Hallel?*"[22] We see from this passage that the recital of *Hallel* is a law connected to the mitzvah of the *Pesach* offering — a mitzvah obligatory upon all Israel, just like the waving of the *lulav* on Sukkos — rather than one connected to the Temple services, whose mitzvos — the pouring of the blood, the recitation by the Levites and so on can be performed only by the *kohanim* and Levites.[23]

As for the 'pouring out' of the blood, mentioned by *Rambam*, this is not the wording of the Mishnah, [24] which says instead, "and [the *kohen*] sprinkles it with one toss (זְרִיקָה) onto the altar." Tossing is from a distance, while pouring out (שְׁפִיכָה) is a smoother motion, from nearby. The problem of the choice of terms goes back to a disagreement among the *Tannaim*.[25]

Slaughtering on Shabbos

When the fourteenth of Nissan, the time for slaughtering the *Pesach* sacrifice, falls on *Shabbos*, a *mishnah* in *Pesachim* tells us that "slaughtering [of the *Pesach* sacrifice], the tossing of its blood, the cleaning out of the intestines, and the burning of the fat (חֲלָבִים) on the Altar supersede (the prohibition against these kinds of work on) the *Shabbos;* but roasting [the meat] and the rinsing (הֲדָחָה) of the intestines do not supersede the *Shabbos*."[26] *Rashi* explains that this is because roasting the meat and rinsing the intestines are activities which it is possible to perform after dark, that is, when *Shabbos* is over. Concerning acts done in preparation for the sacrifice — for example, bringing things to the Temple on *Shabbos* from places outside the *techum*, the *Shabbos* boundary of the city — there is a dispute between Rabbi Eliezer and Rabbi Akiva as to whether such acts, normally forbidden on *Shabbos*, may be done when they are מַכְשִׁירִים, 'enabling acts' for the *Pesach* sacrifice. A stormy debate between these two *Tannaim* is recorded in this *mishnah* and in a *baraisa*.[27] The *halachah* is according to Rabbi Akiva, whose rule is: Every type of "work which it is possible to perform before *Shabbos* does not supersede the *Shabbos;* slaughtering, which (being commanded for the fourteenth) cannot be done before *Shabbos*, supersedes the *Shabbos*."[28]

The question of offering the *Pesach* sacrifice on *Shabbos* triggered a historic event which is recorded in a *baraisa:* "The Sages taught that this *halachah* escaped the memory of Bnei Besera." *Rashi* explains that Bnei Besera were at that time the *nesi'im,* the national leaders who headed the Sanhedrin, the supreme court in Jerusalem. "It once happened that the fourteenth fell on *Shabbos.* [Bnei Besera] forgot and did not know whether or not the mitzvah of the *Pesach* sacrifice superseded that of *Shabbos.* They asked, 'Is there a man who knows whether or not *Pesach* supersedes *Shabbos?'* They were told, 'There is one man who has come from Babylonia; Hillel the Babylonian is his name; he served the two greatest men of the generation, Shmayah and Avtalion, and he knows whether or not *Pesach* supersedes the *Shabbos.'* They sent for him and asked, 'Do you know whether or not *Pesach* supersedes the *Shabbos?'* He answered, 'Do we have only one *Pesach* each year which supersedes the *Shabbos?* Indeed, we have far more than two hundred *Pesachim* a year that supersede the *Shabbos* (meaning: the daily offerings and additional offerings — תְּמִידִים and מוּסָפִים — that are slaughtered every *Shabbos)!'* They asked, 'Whence do you derive this?' He answered, 'The Torah uses the expression *at its appointed time* concerning the Pesach sacrifice *(Numbers* 9:2), and also concerning the daily offering *(ibid.,* 28:2). Just as *its appointed time,* written concerning the daily offering, supersedes the *Shabbos,* so also *its appointed time,* written concerning the *Pesach* sacrifice, supersedes the *Shabbos.* Furthermore, this may be proved through קַל וָחוֹמֶר, *a fortiori.* If it is true that the daily offering, whose neglect is not punishable by *kares,* supersedes the *Shabbos,* then all the more must it be so that the *Pesach* sacrifice, whose neglect is punishable by *kares,* supersedes the *Shabbos.'* Immediately they set him at the head and appointed him *nasi* over them. And he lectured that entire day on the laws of Pesach. He began by remonstrating with them, saying, 'Who brought this upon you, that I should come up from Babylonia and become *nasi* over you? It was your own slothfulness, in that you did not serve the two great men of the generation, Shmayah and Avtalion.' They said to him 'Rabbi, what is the law concerning one who forgets to bring the slaughtering knife to the *Beis HaMikdash* before *Shabbos?'* He answered, 'This law I have heard but forgotten. But leave it to the people of Israel; if they are not prophets, they are the sons of prophets.' The next day *(Shabbos,* the fourteenth), those who were bringing a lamb for the sacrifice inserted the knife in its wool and those who were bringing a kid inserted the knife between its horns.

Hillel, on seeing the deed, remembered the *halachah*. He said,
'This is the tradition I received from Shmayah and
Avtalion.' "[29]

The One of the main stipulations of the mitzvah of eating the
Roasting *korban Pesach* is that it should be eaten roasted. *And they
shall eat the meat on that night, roasted by fire* (וְאָכְלוּ אֶת
הַבָּשָׂר בַּלַּיְלָה הַזֶּה צְלִי אֵשׁ; *Exodus* 12:8). If the sacrifice is not
roasted by fire, then one is forbidden to eat it at all; and if one
does eat it, this does not fulfill the mitzvah of eating the
korban Pesach.[30] How is this sacrifice roasted? One uses a
spit of pomegranate wood, inserting it through the animal's
mouth so that it reaches to the buttocks; the animal on the spit
is hung inside an oven, above the fire. Pomegranate wood is
used for the spit because this type of wood does not give off
liquid when heated — for any liquid might cause part of the
sacrifice to be cooked rather than roasted.[31] And why is it
that one may not use a metal spit? The reason is that metal is
an efficient conductor of heat; when any part of it is heated, it
becomes hot throughout; this would cause the *Pesach* sacrifice
to be roasted in part by the heated metal within it, and the
Torah says *roasted by fire* — and not roasted by something
else.[32] The *korban* must be roasted whole, not roasted in
pieces.[33] There is a disagreement among the *Tannaim* about
where the legs and innards are to be placed. Rabbi Yosei
HaGalili says they are to be put inside the animal; Rabbi
Akiva says they are to be hung on a spit outside the animal,
above its mouth, for if they were put within the animal, this
would be like a type of cooking.[34] The *Halachah* follows
Rabbi Akiva.[35]

With The mitzvah of eating the *korban Pesach* is related to another
Matzos mitzvah — that of *matzah* and *maror*. *And they shall eat ...
and* *roasted by fire, and matzos with maror, they shall eat it*
Maror (וְאָכְלוּ ... צְלִי אֵשׁ וּמַצּוֹת עַל מְרֹרִים יֹאכְלֻהוּ; *ibid.*). *Mechilta*,
noting the apparent redundancy of the second *they shall eat it*,
derives from this phrase a new law. "Whence may you know
that if they do not have *matzah* and *maror* they may
(nevertheless) fulfill their obligation with the *Pesach*
[sacrifice]? Because the Torah says *they shall eat it*.[36]
Concerning the proper way of eating the meat of the
korban Pesach with *matzah* and *maror*, there is a dispute
among the *Tannaim*, namely, between Hillel and the
Chachamim. According to Hillel, the foods are to be joined
together and eaten, while according to the *Chachamim*, each

of the items is to be eaten separately.[37] However, variant readings of the Talmud yield versions of Hillel's opinion which differ as to whether he joined together only the *matzah* and *maror*,[38] or whether he also joined with them the meat of the *korban*.[39] Further, the *Rishonim* disagree as to the extent of this dispute between Hillel and *Chachamim*. Were their *halachos* intended only to indicate the best way of performing the mitzvah (לְכַתְּחִילָה), or did they mean that if the eating was not performed in their prescribed way the mitzvah was altogether invalid (בְּדִיעֲבַד)?[40]

This disagreement between Hillel and the other Sages has been a focus of interest about which many authors have written, for the topic extends beyond the boundaries of the *Pesach*, to involve more general issues relating to the question of whether forbidden foods neutralize each other. The bridge between these general issues and the specific dispute about *matzah* and *maror* is the question whether or not "mitzvos neutralize each other" (מִצְוֹת מְבַטְלוֹת זוֹ אֶת זוֹ). The reason why the Sages held that each of the three foods should be eaten separately is that they believed "mitzvos neutralize each other" — that is, since the taste of the bitter herb is stronger than that of the *matzah*, then when they are eaten together the *matzah* is neutralized and does not count as a mitzvah. Since Hillel disagreed on this point, holding that "mitzvos do not neutralize each other," he was able to advocate eating the *matzah* and *maror* together.[41]

The Shiur of Maror

A number of *Acharonim* see in this disagreement between Hillel and the Sages yet another implication — it affects the problem of establishing the minimum amount (*shiur*) of *maror* which must be eaten to fulfill the mitzvah. We have a rule that סְתָם אֲכִילָה בִּכְזַיִת, that is, whenever the Torah speaks of "eating," and does not specify the minimum amount required, we are to assume that the minimum is a *kazayis*, the volume equivalent of an olive. In the verse from *Exodus* cited above, the Torah says *they shall eat it*. The question is whether this phrase refers only to the *korban Pesach*,[42] or whether it refers to the *matzah* and *maror*. The answer to this question does not affect the *shiur* of *matzah*, since for *matzah* there is a different verse, *In the evening you shall eat matzos* (בָּעֶרֶב תֹּאכְלוּ מַצֹּת; ibid. v. 18). But it does affect the *shiur* of *maror*. If the phrase *they shall eat it* refers to the *matzos* and *maror*, this means that the *maror*, too, has a *shiur* of *kazayis*;[43] whereas if the phrase refers only to the Pesach sacrifice, then no minimum *shiur* is established for *maror*.

Acharonim point out that according to the Talmud passage about the dispute between Hillel and the Sages, the answer to our question about the verse in *Exodus* depends upon that dispute. How so? According to Hillel, *they shall eat it* refers only to the *Pesach* sacrifice, and that is why the other two foods must be joined together with it; while according to the other Sages, *they shall eat it* refers to each one of the three items; therefore they can be eaten separately.[45] The Talmud establishes the *Halachah* according to neither Hillel nor the Sages, but rather a combination of their practices.[46]

The The time when the *korban Pesach* must be eaten is the subject
Time of a disagreement among the *Tannaim*. One opinion is that it
of must be eaten before midnight. The proof is: in one place the
Eating Torah says, *And they shall eat the meat on that night* (וְאָכְלוּ אֶת הַבָּשָׂר בַּלַּיְלָה הַזֶּה; *Exodus* 12:18), and farther it says, *And I shall pass through the land of Egypt on that night* (וְעָבַרְתִּי בְאֶרֶץ מִצְרַיִם בַּלַּיְלָה הַזֶּה; *ibid.* v. 12). Just as the latter verse means "before midnight," so also the former means "before midnight." The other opinion of *Tannaim* is that the *korban* may be eaten until dawn (עַמּוּד הַשַּׁחַר).[47] However, both sides agree that on the Rabbinic level the mitzvah is to eat the sacrifice before midnight — "to keep a distance between man and sin."[48] This disagreement about the *mitzvah* (on the Scriptural level) has a direct bearing on the *Halachah* in our own time; for it is stated in Tractate *Pesachim*[49] that in respect to the time limit, the Torah made a linkage (הֶקֵּשׁ) between *matzah* and the *korban Pesach;* hence those who hold that the *korban* must be eaten before midnight will hold the same about *matzah*.

Rosh adds:[50] Even those who hold that on the Scriptural level the time for eating *matzah* is the whole night until dawn, admit in any case that here, too, the Sages made a "fence" to keep a distance between man and sin, and stipulated as a Rabbinic mitzvah that *matzah* must be eaten before midnight.[51]

Widely disseminated in *yeshivah* circles is an opinion attributed to Rav Chaim Soloveitchik: Even according to those who hold that (on the Scriptural level) the *korban Pesach* must be eaten before midnight, in any case this is not a law applying to the object itself, viz., the *korban*, but rather to its owner; it is a law about the eating to be performed by the owner. Just as there are other laws specifically concerned with the eating of the *korban Pesach* — that it should be eaten roasted, etc. — so also there is this additional law about the time of the eating. However, this law only specifies when the man must eat, not when the *korban* must be eaten. This distinction has consequences in practice — it means that the uneaten remnants of the *korban Pesach* are not to be burned (i.e., do not become *nosar*) until dawn.

An even more far-reaching idea is suggested by *Or Same'ach*.[53] Not only do the remnants not become *nosar* until dawn, but on the Scriptural level it is even permissible to eat the *korban* until dawn. As *korban Pesach* it may only be eaten until midnight, but after that point it comes under the law of ordinary sacrificial meat (סְתָם קָדָשִׁים), which the Torah permits for eating until dawn. It is simply that after midnight, eating this meat no longer fulfills the mitzvah of eating the *korban Pesach*.[54]

All the sacrifices have a set time beyond which they can no longer be eaten, but the *korban Pesach* is unique in having as well a fixed time for the start of the eating — the beginning of the night of the fifteenth. One who eats the *korban Pesach* before this night has violated a positive commandment. From the positive mitzvah, *And they shall eat the meat on that night* (וְאָכְלוּ אֶת הַבָּשָׂר בַּלַּיְלָה הַזֶּה; *ibid.*, v. 8), the Talmud derives a negative mitzvah: "In the night, and not in the day." And when a negative is derived from a positive commandment, a person violating that negative commandment is considered as if he had violated a positive one.[55] In fact *Rambam* in his *Sefer HaMitzvos* counts this as one of the 248 positive commandments.[56]

The Start of the Eating

The Torah sets two requirements with regard to the place where the *korban Pesach* must be eaten — one general, and one individual. The general place is the city of Jerusalem in its entirety; that is, the *Pesach* sacrifice, like other קָדָשִׁים קַלִּים, offerings of 'lesser' sanctity, may not be eaten outside the limits of Jerusalem.[57] This *halachah* serves a number of authors as the basis for a question about a different law. It is forbidden to cook on *Shabbos*, and it is also forbidden to cook (as opposed to roasting) the *korban Pesach*. However, one who cooks on *Shabbos* by means of *chamei Tveryah*, the hot springs of Tiberias, is exempt (on the Scriptural level) from punishment, since such cooking is not by means of fire. The Talmud says that the same principle is applicable to the *korban Pesach*. Since this means of cooking does not involve a fire, it does not fall within the prohibition against eating the sacrifice "cooked." But with regard to the *Pesach* sacrifice,

The Place

there is a separate prohibition which forbids eating it in any way except roasted — for the whole verse reads, *Do not eat of it partially roasted or cooked, but rather roasted by fire* (אַל תֹּאכְלוּ מִמֶּנּוּ נָא וּבָשֵׁל מְבֻשָּׁל בַּמָּיִם כִּי אִם צְלִי אֵשׁ; *ibid.*, v. 9). The words beginning *but rather* are taken as a separate prohibition. Therefore, we read in Tractate *Pesachim*, "[One who eats] a *Pesach* [sacrifice] which was cooked in *chamei Tveryah* is punishable, for he has violated the verse [*but rather] roasted by fire*."[58]

Some authors are puzzled by the problem of how it could come about that the *korban Pesach* was cooked in the hot springs of Tiberias. The moment the sacrifice is removed from Jerusalem it becomes disqualified, just like any other type of *kodashim kalim* taken past the city walls. Some solve the difficulty by suggesting that the case could occur during the time when Israel had entered the Land but the Altar at Jerusalem had not yet been established and sacrifices were permitted on 'local' altars *(bamos)*. It is true that even in such times the offering up of the *korban Pesach* could only be done at the *bamah gedolah*, the central national altar at Nov or (later) Givon; but once the offering had been sacrificed at the *bamah gedolah*, it could be eaten in any of the cities of Israel.

Others suggest that *chamei Tveryah* is only a general term meaning hot springs like those at Tiberias. Another suggested solution is that the boiling hot waters might be brought from Tiberias to Jerusalem in some sort of vessel paralleling the modern Thermos bottle. Still others approach the problem in different ways.[59]

In One Besides this general location — the whole city of Jerusalem —
"House" the Torah also requires a specific location: *It shall be eaten in one house* (בְּבַיִת אֶחָד יֵאָכֵל; *ibid.* v. 46). The *Tannaim* disagree whether this means that the sacrifice must be eaten within one *chavurah*, or within one place.[60] The *Gemara* discusses this law with regard to various situations; for example, that of a *chavurah* who, in the midst of their eating, are divided into separate groups by the setting up of a partition;[60] and the opposite case, that of two separate *chavuros* whose partition is removed while they are eating.[61] The *Gemara* also discusses the precautionary steps necessary to prevent violation of this law of *one house* in the situation where a servant must serve both his own and another *chavurah*,[62] while he himself is eating the *korban*.

Two *shiurim*, required quantities, apply to the mitzvah of **Two** eating the *korban Pesach*. To perform the mitzvah in the best **Shiurim** way, one should eat the meat of the sacrifice until one's appetite is satisfied (כְּדֵי לִשְׂבּוֹעַ מִמֶּנּוּ): but eating only one *kazayis* meets the minimum requirement for fulfillment of the mitzvah.[63]

Shaagas Aryeh[64] makes an interesting assertion, stating it as a matter of plain fact: that the mitzvah of eating applies to the entire sacrificial animal. All the authorities agree that the sacrifice should be eaten in its entirety. But the usual reason given for this is the Torah commandment that any of the meat which is not eaten before morning must be burned; if any meat remains uneaten, there is the danger of inadvertently violating this commandment. But to this reason *Shaagas Aryeh* adds a more direct one — the positive commandment to eat the *korban Pesach* means to eat it in its entirety.[65]

The Talmud sets forth various stipulations about the eating of **The** the *korban Pesach*. It should be eaten on a full stomach **Manner** (עַל הַשּׂוֹבַע), and should be the last course of the meal. As a **of** *mishnah (Pesachim* 119b) states, "No dessert *(afikoman)* **Eating** should be brought after the [*korban*] *Pesach.*" The reason given by *Rashi* is, "so that they should enjoy the eating [of the sacrifice] and it should be precious to them." *Rashbam*[67] gives a different reason: "So that one should not lose the taste of the [*korban*] *Pesach.*" Furthermore, the eating of the sacrifice should not be *achilah gassah* — literally, "coarse eating." The source for the latter prohibition about "coarse eating" is a passage in Tractate *Nazir.*[68] "*For the ways of Hashem are straight; the righteous shall walk in them, and the wicked shall stumble in them* (כִּי יְשָׁרִים דַּרְכֵי ה' וְצַדִּקִים יֵלְכוּ בָם וּפֹשְׁעִים יִכָּשְׁלוּ בָם; *Hosea* 14:10) — this may be exemplified by two who roasted their Pesach sacrifices. One man ate his for the sake of the mitzvah; the other, for the sake of *achilah gassah.* Concerning the one who ate for the sake of the mitzvah, it is said, *The righteous shall walk in them.* Concerning the one who ate for the sake of *achilah gassah* it is said, *And the wicked shall stumble in them.*"

Another rule about the eating is that only those people who have been 'designated' (נִמְנוּ) for a given *Pesach* animal may eat of it; i.e., that group of people must designate themselves as the eaters of that specific animal by contributing towards the money used to purchase it.[69]

Rabbeinu Shimshon of Shans[70] makes an assertion of great import about this law. He states that the eating of a particular *korban Pesach* by those not designated for it is not forbidden, but simply fails to fulfill the mitzvah of eating the *korban*.

The eating of the sacrifice must be accompanied by the recital of *Hallel*. The Talmud derives this from *Isaiah* 30:29. *"You shall have song as on the night of the sanctification of a festival* (הַשִּׁיר יִהְיֶה לָכֶם כְּלֵיל הִתְקַדֶּשׁ חָג) — a night sanctified for a festival requires the recitation of *Hallel."*[71] This recital of *Hallel* during the eating of the *korban Pesach* was done with such great festive spirit that it resulted in a saying: "A *kazayis* of the *Pesach*, and the *Hallel* shatters the roof."[72] *Rashi:* "They used to designate large *chavuros*, to the point that when the sacrificial animal was portioned out each person received only a *kazayis*," and because of "the tumultuous sound of the multitudes singing the *Hallel*, it seemed as if the roofs were splitting."

Rav Meir Simchah of Dvinsk finds a source in Scripture for the prohibition against *achilah gassah*. He cites the verse, *And if the house is insufficient for a sheep ... each man according to his eating* (וְאִם יִמְעַט הַבַּיִת מִהְיוֹת מִשֶּׂה ... אִישׁ לְפִי אָכְלוֹ; *Exodus* 12:4), and interprets it as meaning that even if there are only a small number of people in the house, they should guard against eating *achilah gassah*, but rather, each person should take only as much as he normally eats *(each man according to his eating)*; therefore, *He and his neighbor shall take* [a sheep] (וְלָקַח הוּא וּשְׁכֵנוֹ; *ibid.).*[73]

The Negative Commandments

Not With Chametz The first negative commandment in the list given by *Rambam* is that stated in the verse, *Do not slaughter the blood of My sacrifice [while possessing] chametz* (לֹא תִזְבַּח עַל חָמֵץ דַּם זִבְחִי; *Exodus* 23:18). A *mishnah* tells us, "One who slaughters the *Pesach* sacrifice [while possessing] *chametz* violates a negative commandment."[74] *Rambam* details the *halachah* as follows. "The law applies equally to the one who slaughters the animal, the one who sprinkles the blood against the altar, and the one who offers up the appropriate parts of the animal on the altar by burning: if any of these men, or any of the members of the *chavurah* who are to eat this sacrifice, have in their possession a *kazayis* of *chametz* at the time when the sacrifice is offered, that person incurs lashing."[75]

Shaagas Aryeh[76] discusses the problem of how such a penalty of lashing could ever actually be incurred. In order to impose the penalty, the court must know for certain that the person received a clear warning at the time that he committed the offense. Furthermore, the law concerning *chametz* is that one may validly remove it from one's possession simply by resolving in one's heart to regard the *chametz* as of no importance (בָּטֵל), "like the dust of the earth." In this case, then, the defendant can always claim that he made such a resolution in his heart before the deadline for the removal of *chametz*, and thus avoid punishment. In addressing himself to this problem the author proves at length that there is a way in which one can "possess" *chametz* on which such a resolution of the heart will have no effect — namely, in the case of one who accepts financial responsibility for keeping charge of *chametz* which belongs to someone else.° This discussion of *Shaagas Aryeh* is the subject of intricate debate among the *Acharonim*.[77]

The violation of this commandment, *Do not slaughter ...* [while possessing] *chametz* does not, however, result in the invalidation of the *korban* itself; the animal remains fit for eating in fulfillment of the mitzvah. This law is derived, in the *Talmud Yerushalmi*, from the word זִבְחִי, *My sacrifice*, in the verse cited above. "The Torah calls it *My sacrifice*," that is, a valid sacrifice, even though a commandment has been violated.[78] This law gives rise to discussion among the *Acharonim* because it seems to contradict a rule that "Whenever one does a thing which the Torah has told us not to do, one's doing has no effect" (כָּל מִילְתָא דְּאָמַר רַחֲמָנָא לֹא תַעֲבִיד, אִי עָבִיד לֹא מְהַנֵּי). Why, then, should violation of this negative commandment about the slaughtering of the *korban Pesach* [while possessing] *chametz* result in a sacrifice which is still valid?[79]

A different law, first pointed out by *Mishneh LeMelech*, has also stimulated discussion. *Mishneh LeMelech*[80] states that if the *korban* is rendered invalid through improper slaughtering, and those who subsequently sprinkle the blood and offer up the אֵמוּרִים on the altar have *chametz* in their possession, they do not thereby violate our commandment, *Do not slaughter ...* [while possessing] *chametz*; for the Torah in this verse is warning us about a valid (כָּשֵׁר) *korban*, not about one that is invalid (פָּסוּל). In a *mishnah* there is disagreement about a related matter: whether the one himself who performs the improper slaughtering violates the commandment in question if he has *chametz* in his possesion. Rabbi Shimon says there is no violation, since slaughtering

° [In this case the *chametz* is his responsibility and yet is not his property that he can abandon at will. — *Ed.*]

performed improperly "is not considered slaughtering." But the majority of the Sages say there is a violation, since "Improper slaughtering is still considered slaughtering."[81] According to this latter opinion, how can we explain the law stated by *Mishneh LeMelech?* If the improper slaughtering is considered nevertheless to fit the definition of slaughtering, and the one who performs it with *chametz* in his possession is thereby guilty, why are not those who toss the blood and offer up the parts on the Altar likewise guilty?

This question was addressed to the author of *Shaar HaMelech*, who replied by pointing out a distinction between the one who slaughters and those who perform the subsequent sacrificial acts. It is true that the one who, with *chametz* in his possession, performed the slaughtering, was only involved with an invalid sacrifice, not a valid one; but that fact is the result of his own action, i.e., the improper slaughtering. (It should be noted that in the case under discussion, what rendered the slaughtering invalid was that the one performing it did not have the correct intentions that are necessary when slaughtering a *korban Pesach.*) Therefore, since he himself is responsible for the fact that the slaughtering is improper and the sacrifice invalid, he remains guilty of violating the commandment. On the other hand those who perform the subsequent sacrificial acts on the invalid *korban* are not guilty, even though they possessed *chametz*, because the disqualification of the sacrifice was not their own doing.

A More Basic Distinction If you like, however, this problem can be solved without need for the above distinction. For there is a difference between improper slaughtering and improper tossing of the blood (or offering up of the אֵמוּרִים). This improper act of slaughtering invalidated the *korban* because of an incorrect intention; even though the sacrifice cannot be eaten, nevertheless the slaughtering was effective in that it removes the animal from the category of *nevelah*, one that died without being slaughtered according to the law. For this reason, the act still comes within the definition of slaughtering, and since the one who performed it possessed *chametz*, he is guilty. On the other hand, the sprinkling of the blood, if it does not bring about the validation of the *korban*, has no effect whatsoever, and hence does not even come within the category of "sprinkling of the blood." As the Talmud states in a related connection, "It is as if he had sprinkled ordinary water."[83] Therefore, though he possessed *chametz*, he is not guilty.

The negative commandment about *emurim*, the parts of the animal that must be burned on the altar, prohibits *halanah*, leaving them overnight; they must be offered up before the morning. Even though *Rambam* counts this as one of the negative commandments of the *korban Pesach*, it is not restricted to the *Pesach* sacrifice alone. As *Rambam* himself states elsewhere, "The Torah has warned us not to leave the *emurim* of the *Pesach* without sacrificing them lest they become invalidated through being left overnight. This is the meaning of the verse, *And the fat of My festival offering shall not remain overnight until the morning* (וְלֹא יָלִין חֵלֶב חַגִּי עַד בֹּקֶר; *Exodus* 23:18); and the same law applies to the *emurim* of all the other sacrifices."[84]

Not Partly Roasted nor Cooked

The verse, *Do not eat of it partly roasted, nor cooked* (אַל תֹּאכְלוּ מִמֶּנּוּ נָא וּבָשֵׁל מְבֻשָּׁל; *ibid.* 12:19), constitutes, according to *Rambam*, one negative mitzvah;[85] while other *Rishonim* consider it to be two negative mitzvos, one for *partly roasted* and one for *cooked*.[86] This disagreement has a practical consequence, namely, in the case of one who eats simultaneously both half-roasted and cooked meat from the *korban Pesach*. According to *Rambam*, this would incur one penalty of lashing; according to the other opinion, two such penalties.[87] *Minchas Chinuch* discovers another practical consequence of this disagreement, based on the fact that, to incur the penalty, one must eat at least a *kazayis* of improperly prepared meat. If one were to eat half a *kazayis* of partly roasted, and half a *kazayis* of cooked meat together, he points out, according to *Rambam*, the two halves would be added together and the penalty incurred; according to the other opinion, the two halves would not be added together, and no penalty at all would be incurred.

There is also a disagreement between *Amoraim* (Abbaye and Rava) over the interpretation of this verse just cited, *Do not eat of it partly roasted, nor cooked, but rather, roasted by fire*. The disagreement is whether one who eats, for example, partly roasted meat from the *korban*, receives only one penalty or two, one for *partly roasted* and one for *but rather, roasted by fire* — that is, the dispute is whether the words *Do not eat* apply separately to both phrases, or whether the phrase, *but rather, roasted by fire* is to be considered a לָאו שֶׁבִּכְלָלוּת, that is, a negative commandment included in an overall statement, and therefore not bearing a penalty [of lashing]. The term *lav shebichlalus* refers to the situation when the Torah gives a negative commandment, such as one beginning "Do not ... ", which includes a number of items rather than just one.

The word נָא, *partly roasted*, is defined by *Rambam* as "meat on which the fire has begun to act, and which is somewhat roasted, but which is not yet fit for human eating."[90] *Tzafnas Paane'ach* discovers a general principle: "There are certain things whose existence is only in law, and except for the law they have no existence whatsoever." An example is the meat described by our word, *na*. "With the exception of the law, this term refers to nothing at all. Meat fitting the term *na* exists only in an infinitesimally thin layer; for part of the animal is completely roasted, and part of it is completely raw — which is נָא. Consider the words of our Teacher in *Moreh Nevuchim*, part 2, seventh Proposition: 'Everything that is changeable is divisible' — if so, there is no meat to which this negative commandment applies, for the roasted part is fit for the mitzvah, while the raw part is forbidden only by a positive commandment" (but not by this negative one). The author provides, at length, several other examples to illustrate his principle.

If the *Pesach* sacrifice is in fact cooked, it becomes forbidden not only for eating, but for any benefit whatsoever.[92]

The *Acharonim* analyze another question: whether, in violating the prohibition against eating the *korban Pesach* cooked, one also violates a second negative mitzvah, viz., that referred to by the Talmud's dictum, "The Torah has given a negative commandment against eating any sanctified food which has become *pasul* (invalidated)."[93]

In connection with this negative commandment against eating the *korban Pesach* cooked or partly roasted, the Talmud discusses various subordinate questions; for example, the law when the *korban* is cooked, but in liquids other than water; when it is first roasted, then afterwards cooked, or vice-versa; when it is cooked in *chamei Tveryah;* and other problems.[94]

One who eats the *korban Pesach* raw has violated the positive commandment implied in the words *roasted by fire,* but has not violated a negative commandment.[95] However, according to *Rashi* such an act violates a negative mitzvah implied in the words, *Do not eat ... but rather, roasted by fire.*[96]

The negative commandment against taking the meat of the *Removing* Pesach sacrifice away from where it is being eaten — לֹא תוֹצִיא *It* — includes two prohibitions: not to remove it from the house, *From* and not from the *chavurah*.° The Talmud derives the second *the* of these from a seeming redundancy in the verse, *"Do not* *"House"* *remove any of the meat from the house to the outside* (לֹא תוֹצִיא מִן הַבַּיִת מִן הַבָּשָׂר חוּצָה; *ibid.*, v. 46). — This teaches me only [the prohibition against removing the meat] from house to house; whence do I learn that against removing it from *chavurah* to *chavurah*? From the [seemingly extraneous] words, חוּצָה, *to the outside*. It means: 'outside the *chavurah* where it is eaten.' "

The definition of 'removal,' הוֹצָאָה, with regard to this negative *mitzvah* is the same as for the prohibition against removing things from the private to the public domain on *Shabbos*. That is, one has not committed the act of 'removal' until one has both picked up the object from its place and set it down in the new place.[98] The minimum punishable amount of food, however, is different for this mitzvah than for that of *Shabbos*; on *Shabbos* the amount is *kigrogeres*, the equivalent of a dried fig; for the *korban Pesach*, the *shiur* for removal is *kazayis*.[99]

Minchas Chinuch raises questions and gives new rulings concerning the various aspects of this prohibition against *ho-tzaah*. For example, he discusses the case of two people who perform the act, one picking up the meat, and the other setting it down; the case of one who, rather than taking the meat outside, puts or throws it outside; and the case when the *hotzaah* is performed after the sacrifice has already become *pasul*.

The *son of a stranger*, בֶּן נֵכָר, of whom the Torah (*ibid.*, v. 43) *The Son* says he *shall not eat* from the Pesach sacrifice refers not only *of a* to a non-Jew, but also to a Jew who rejects the Torah, i.e., a *Stranger* *mumar*. The inclusion of the latter is derived by *Mechilta*, which states that *No son of a stranger ...* means both "him of uncircumcised heart and him of uncircumcised flesh."[100] For "stranger," נֵכָר, can be interpreted as *mumar*, in the sense of "one whose deeds have become estranged from his Father in heaven."[101]

This negative commandment presents a basic problem. To whom is the Torah's warning directed? Is it addressed to the

° [That is, if several *chavuros* are in the same house each one is legally separate, and if one removes part of the *korban* from one *chavurah* to the next, though they are in the same room, he has transgressed against לֹא תוֹצִיא. — *Ed.*]

son of a stranger himself, commanding him not to eat; or is it
addressed to the observant Jew, telling him not to feed the
korban Pesach to a ben nechar? Rambam and Sefer
HaChinuch write that the prohibition is against feeding the
sacrifice to a ben nechar; as Kesef Mishneh explains, "Since
the ben nechar would not take heed of the verse's warning, it
must be that it is addressed to the Jew, warning him not to
feed [this sacrifice] to a ben nechar." However, Semag rules
that the prohibition is not against feeding, but against
eating;[102] that is, it is addressed to the ben nechar himself.
The same problem and the same disagreement among the
authorities are found in regard to the related prohibition,
which says, תּוֹשָׁב וְשָׂכִיר לֹא יֹאכַל בּוֹ; literally, No resident nor
hired person shall eat it (ibid., v. 45). The term toshav vesachir
is, however, not to be taken literally. Chinuch, based on the
Talmud, defines them as follows. "Toshav means a non-Jew
who undertakes not to worship idols, but may still (for
example) eat meat which has not been slaughtered according
to the Law. Sachir means a non-Jew who has been circumcised
but has not yet immersed himself in the mikveh, ritual bath
(for the sake of conversion)."[103]

Rambam was the first to point out that these two
prohibitions do not involve the penalty of lashing. Chinuch
adds an explanation. He says that these two mitzvos are in the
category of לָאו שֶׁאֵין בּוֹ מַעֲשֶׂה, a negative commandment
which can be violated without performing an act. Minchas
Chinuch, the commentary on Chinuch, questions this
explanation, pointing out that Rambam defines the mitzvah as
prohibiting one from feeding the sacrifice to a ben nechar or to
someone in the category of toshav vesachir — and is not
feeding an act? (And see Kesef Mishneh, where there is a
different explanation for the absence of the penalty.)

Ravad, in his critical commentary (Hasagos) on Rambam,
finds an additional prohibition in the negative commandment
of toshav vesachir. He says it also implies a negative mitzvah
prohibiting the eating of any particular korban Pesach by one
who is not part of the chavurah designated for that
korban.[104]

The **Who** is the עָרֵל, uncircumcised one, whom the Torah
Uncircum- prohibits from eating the Pesach? The Rishonim are in
cised disagreement over this question. Some say the law refers to
one of whom the Torah does not require circumcision, e.g.,
one whose brothers died as a result of circumcision.[105]
Others say that since the lack of circumcision in such a person

is due to circumstances beyond his control (אָנוּס), he is allowed to eat the *korban*. According to this opinion, the prohibition against eating applies to one who is uncircumcised simply because of fear of the pain involved.[106]

Just as one who is uncircumcised may not perform the mitzvah of the *korban Pesach*, so also one whose "males," i.e., sons or slaves, remain uncircumcised may not perform the mitzvah — neither the offering nor the eating.[107] And even "males" who were under no obligation to be circumcised at the time when the sacrifice was offered, but became obligated for circumcision by the time of eating the *korban*, prevent their father or owner from eating it.[108] As for one who was circumcised and subsequently his foreskin drew forward so that it conceals the circumcision, this does not prevent him from eating the *Pesach*, since the mitzvah of *bris milah* was fulfilled for at least some time.[109] This last *halachah* is used by *Netziv* in his book, *Ha'amek Davar*, to interpret the verse, *And every slave, a man bought for money, if you have circumcised him, then he shall eat [the korban]* — (וְכָל עֶבֶד אִישׁ מִקְנַת כָּסֶף וּמַלְתָּה אֹתוֹ אָז יֹאכַל בּוֹ; *ibid.*, v. 44). The word, *then,* says *Netziv*, refers not to the subsequent clause, but to the preceding. If you circumcised him *then,* when you bought him, even if afterwards his circumcision is concealed, he may eat the *korban*.

Maharsha,[110] based on a careful reading of *Rashi*, arrives at a new halachic conclusion of great significance: In spite of the fact that the Torah does not obligate a woman to circumcise her son (the obligation resting on the father alone), a woman is nevertheless disqualified from eating the *Pesach* sacrifice if her son remains uncircumcised.[111]

The *shiur* applicable to the negative commandment against *Breaking* breaking the bones of the *korban Pesach* is the same as that *the Bones* for a defect in the surface of the Altar; the Altar is rendered defective, or the bone considered broken, by a dent large enough to catch one's fingernail as it slides over the surface (בַּחֲגִירַת צִפּוֹרֶן).[112] One is not liable for punishment for violating this commandment unless the bone broken has on it a *kazayis* of meat, or has marrow in it.[113] This last fact is used elsewhere in the Talmud to prove a fundamental principle, i.e., in the *Beis HaMikdash*, a positive commandment does not supersede a negative one. If this were not true, then there could be no prohibition against breaking a bone of the *korban Pesach* which has marrow in it; for the positive commandment of eating the marrow would supersede the negative commandment against breaking the bone.[114]

One who breaks a bone of the *Pesach* after it has already been broken by someone else, receives the penalty of lashing[115] for violating the commandment. As the *Talmud Yerushalmi* says, "One can break (i.e., receive the penalty for breaking) a bone that has already been broken, but one cannot remove a piece of the sacrifice that has already been removed,"[116] that is, if the piece was removed and then brought back into the *chavurah*, removing it a second time does not constitute a violation. The reason for this rule is that breaking a bone does not invalidate that part of the *korban*, whereas removing a piece of meat from the house or *chavurah* invalidates the meat.

A fine hint of this last law in a verse is discovered by Rav Zalman of Vilna, as cited by *Toldos Adam*.[117] The verse says, *Do not remove it from the house to the outside, and do not break a bone in it* (לֹא תוֹצִיא מִן הַבַּיִת מִן הַבָּשָׂר חוּצָה וְעֶצֶם לֹא תִשְׁבְּרוּ בוֹ; *ibid.*, v. 46). The unusual wording is evident in the Hebrew. The word for *remove* is written in the singular, and the word for *break*, in the plural. But Rav Zalman perceives the *halachah*, as stated in the *Yerushalmi*, "ensconced in this verse:" for "removal" only one person can become punishable; that is, the first person to remove the meat; while for "breaking" a single bone, many people could become punishable, i.e., each one who breaks it. As for the tendons, breaking them is not a violation of the mitzvah. On the other hand, even though they may be edible, one cannot be "designated" (נִמְנָה) for the *korban* on the basis of eating the tendons.

How It Is Eaten This is the procedure for eating the *korban Pesach* as set forth by *Rambam*: "When a person eats the *Pesach*, he cuts the meat and eats, and cuts the bones from the joint and disjoints them if he wishes. When he arrives at the *gid hanasheh*, the sciatical tendon (which is forbidden for eating), he removes it and sets it aside with the rest of the tendons, bones, and membranes; for the *korban Pesach* is not cleaned out previous to eating as is other meat, and is not cut in pieces before cooking, but is roasted whole."[118] The language of *Ravad* here in criticizing *Rambam* is characteristic of the former's style throughout the *Hasagos*. "By the life of my head, there is no greater prohibition than this, that one should roast the *Pesach* with the *gid hanasheh* and with its fat ... and if I should have the merit to eat the *Pesach*, and he were to bring before me a sacrifice roasted in this manner, I would dash it to the ground in front of him."[119]

The final negative commandment in the list of *Rambam* —
And do not leave over from it until morning (וְלֹא תוֹתִירוּ
מִמֶּנּוּ עַד בֹּקֶר; *ibid.* v. 10) — has a double application: to the
Pesach, and to *kodashim*, other sacrificial meat. For each of
these there is a specific negative mitzvah. *Minchas Chinuch*
was the first to point out the *chiddush*, halachic discovery,
that in leaving over the meat of the *Pesach* until morning one
violates both of these negative mitzvos — for the *Pesach*
sacrifice, too, is included in the general category of
kodashim.[120] Long discussions are presented in *Minchas
Chinuch* on such questions as that of the *shiur* for this
prohibition, whether the minimum amount punishable is a
kazayis, or whether it is *kolshehu* — the latter meaning any
amount, no matter how small;[121] the author also discusses
whether this prohibition applies to a *korban Pesach* which has
become invalid *(pasul)*; whether the prohibition applies to the
tendons and bones; and other questions.

No punishment of lashes is attached to this negative
commandment, because it is in the category of לָאו הַנִּיתָּק
לַעֲשֵׂה, a negative commandment, the violation of which may
be corrected by performing a positive commandment. In this
case, the relevant positive commandment is, *And that which is
left over from [the korban] you shall burn by fire* (וְהַנֹּתָר
מִמֶּנּוּ עַד בֹּקֶר בָּאֵשׁ תִּשְׂרֹפוּ; *ibid.*).[122] In the *Gemara* two other
reasons for the lack of penalty are given. First, that this is a *lav
she-ein bo ma'aseh*, since the violation is one of omission
rather than commission; second, that it is impossible to
receive an unequivocal warning before violating the
commandment [since up until the last moment there is always
the possibility that the meat may be eaten and not left
over].[123]

*Leaving
It
Overnight*

NOTES

[1] Mishnah, beginning of *Krisos*.

[2] See below, *The Seder*.

[3] First *aleph-beis*, sec. 21.

[4] Sec. 415.

[5] And see *Tosafos R'em.*, *loc. cit.* In the
commentary of Rav Y. Perla on *Sefer
HaMitzvos* by Rav Saadiah Gaon, positive
commandment 47, Rav Perla interprets
Rasag as counting the slaughtering and the
eating as one mitzvah. All the other works
enumerating the 613 mitzvos count these as
two mitzvos, as does *Rambam*.

[5*] Part 1, sec. 2. This author does not cite
Yere'im.

[6] *Nezer HaKodesh*, *Zevachim* 86.

[7] And see *Pesachim* 78b.

[8] *Mishnah*, *Pesachim* 76b.

[9] *Rashi*, *loc. cit.*

[10] *Rambam*, *Pesulei HaMukdashim* 15:11.

[11] *Zevachim* 3a.

[12] *Or Same'ach*, *Pesulei HaMukdashim*,
loc. cit.

[13] *Mishnah*, *Pesachim* 61a.

[14] *Marcheshes*, part 1, sec. 7. And see *Meshech Chachmah, parashas Bo; Levush Mordechai, Kadashim*, sec. 1; *Derech HaKodesh*, by Rav Moshe Avigdor Amiel, 13:8; *Chemdas Daniel*, by Rav D. Zaks, *Zevachim* 2; *et al.* Incidentally: My friend Rav B.Z.Y. Rabinowitz-Teomim, *zal*, has drawn my attention to a source in the *Gemara* which would be consistent with the ruling of *Rambam*. "It is said, concerning the Pesach sacrifice, הוא (*And you shall say, It is a Pesach sacrifice* — וַאֲמַרְתֶּם זֶבַח פֶּסַח הוּא). [This is said] concerning the slaughtering, and is an essential requirement." — *Zevachim* 7, end of side b; and see the commentary of *Rashi*, who is hard pressed for an interpretation.

[15] *Pesachim* 21b et. al.

[16] *Zevachim* 114b. According to *Ramban*, this is to be counted separately as one of the 365 negative mitzvos.

[17] *Rambam, Korban Pesach* 1:9-15, based on *Pesachim* 64.

[18] *Pesachim*, ch. 4.

[19] *Arachin* 10a, *s.v.* וְלֹא הָיָה.

[20] *Pesachim* 64a.

[21] *Pesachim, loc. cit., s.v.* קָרְאוּ, and *Sukkah* 55b, *s.v.* עֶרֶב הַפֶּסַח.

[22] *Pesachim* 95b.

[23] And see *Chukas HaPesach*, by Rav Y. Gershoni, pp. 84-7, in the name of Rav Y.Z. Soloveitchik of Brisk, where the author argues at length that there are two distinct laws of *Hallel* over the slaughtering of the Pesach sacrifice — one relating to the sacrifice [as an offering made on the Altar, like all the other offerings performed in the *Beis HaMikdash*], and one relating to the Pesach [i.e., the specific mitzvah of bringing the Pesach offering].

[24] *Pesachim* 64a.

[25] *Ibid.* 64b, and 121a.

[26] *Mishnah, ibid.* 65b.

[27] *Ibid.* 69a.

[28] *Ibid.* 69b; *Rambam*, 1:18.

[29] *Baraisa, Pesachim* 66a.

[30] *Minchas Chinuch*, mitzvah 7.

[31] *Mishnah, Pesachim* 74a.

[32] *Gemara, loc. cit.*

[33] *Tosefta, Pesachim*, ch. 5; *Rambam*, 10:11.

[34] *Mishnah, loc. cit.*, and *Rashi*.

[35] *Rambam*, 8:10.

[36] *Mechilta, Exodus* 12:8; *Rambam*, 8:2; and see *Sefer HaMitzvos*, positive commandment 56.

[37] *Pesachim* 115a and *Zevachim* 79a.

[38] As in the version printed in the current editions of the Talmud, *Pesachim* and *Zevachim, loc. cit.* And see *Rambam* 8:6,7, and *Lechem Mishneh* there.

[39] *Yerushalmi, Challah* 1:1, and this is the version accepted by *Rashi* in *Zevachim*, and by *Rashi, Rambam*, and *Meiri* in *Pesachim, loc. cit.*

[40] See *Rashbam, Tosafos, HaMaor, Ramban* in *Milchamos*, and *Meiri* on *Pesachim, loc. cit.*

[41] See (in addition to the commentaries on *Pesachim* and *Zevachim*): *Baruch Taam, shaar* 1; *Yeshuos Yaakov*, sec. 475; responsa *Toras Chesed*, sec. 49; responsa *Kesav Sofer, Orach Chaim*, sec. 86; *Levush Mordechai, Kadashim*, sec. 15; responsa *Divrei Yissachar*, sec. 40; *et. al.*

[42] And this is in fact the opinion of *Trumas HaDeshen*, sec. 245, based on *Rosh*. And see *Shaagas Aryeh*, sec. 100.

[43] See below, *The Seder*: "Maror".

[44] 115a.

[45] See responsa *Toras Chesed*, 49; *Kesav Sofer*, sec. 86; *et. al.*

[46] *Pesachim, loc. cit.* And see below, *The Seder*.

[47] *Berachos* 9a.

[48] *Zevachim* 57b. And see *Rashba, Berachos, loc. cit.*, where this *Rishon* states that according to those who hold that the time limit is dawn, there is no preventive limit of midnight even on the Rabbinic level.

[49] 120b.

[50] End of *Pesachim*.

[51] And see *Beis HaLevi*, part 1, sec. 34.

[52] And see the wording of *Rashi, Berachos* 9a, *s.v.* שָׁם תִּזְבַּח.

[53] *Chametz UMatzah* 6:1.

[54] And see *loc. cit.* for a lengthy explanation of the *sugios* which would seem to contradict this conclusion; and see also *Chazon Yechezkel* on *Tosefta, Pesachim*, ch. 5; responsa *Degel Reuven*, part 2, sec. 10; *HaPardes* (Rabbinic journal pub. in Chicago, Sivan 5703 — 1943), sec. 17.

[55] *Pesachim* 41b.

[56] And see *Megillas Esther, loc. cit.*, and *Mishneh LaMelech, Korban Pesach* 8:5.

[57] *Mishnah, Zevachim* 56b.

[58] *Pesachim* 41a.

[59] See responsa *Pri Yitzchak*, part 1, sec. 20; *Karnei Re'em* on *Pesachim* [by Rav Eliezer Mordechai Kovner] (Vilna, 5624 — 1864), *loc. cit.*; *Cheshek Shlomo* (in the *Shas Vilna*), *Pesachim*, *loc. cit.*; responsa *Shem Aryeh*, *Yoreh De'ah*, sec. 32; responsa *Zecher Yehosef*, sec. 193; responsa *Machazeh Avraham*, sec. 117; *Omer UDevarim*, by Rav Braunrot, *Exodus* 13; et. al.

[60] *Pesachim* 86.

[61] *Ibid.*

[62] *Mishnah, loc. cit.*

[63] *Rambam*, 8:3.

[64] *Sec. 96.*

[65] And see *Chasam Sofer*, *Orach Chaim*, sec. 49; *Minchas Chinuch*, mitzvah 102.

[66] *Rashi*, *Pesachim* 70a.

[67] *Rashbam*, 119b. In the *Yerushalmi*, 6:4, a different reason is given: so as to reduce the likelihood of one's breaking a bone of the sacrifice. [Breaking any of the bones is prohibited.]

[68] *Nazir* 23a.

[69] *Rashi*, *Zevachim* 56b.

[70] In his commentary on *Toras Kohanim*, *Tzav*, ch. 13. And see commentary of Rav Y. Perla on Rav Saadiah Gaon's *Sefer HaMitzvos*, 175, and responsa *Beis Zevul* by Rav Y.M. Charlap, sec. 23.

[71] *Pesachim* 95b.

[72] *Ibid.* 85b.

[73] *Meshech Chachmah*, *Bo*.

[74] *Mishnah*, *Pesachim* 63a.

[75] *Rambam*, 1:5, based on the *sugya* in *Pesachim*, *loc. cit.*

[76] *Sec. 77.*

[77] See responsa *Oneg Yom-Tov*, sec. 24; *Mekor Chaim*, sec. 448; *Imrei Binah*, sec. 2; et. al.

[78] *Yerushalmi* 5:4. And see *Tosafos*, *Pesachim* 63a, and *Temurah* 4b.

[79] See *Shaar HaMelech*, *Korban Pesach* 1:5; *Shoel UMeshiv*, first ed., part 2, sec. 42; *Tiferes Yisrael* on the *Mishnah*, *Pesachim* 5:4; *Chazon Yechezkel*, *Tosefta*, *Pesachim*, ch. 4; et. al.

[80] *Korban Pesach* 1:5.

[81] *Pesachim* 63a, and *Rashi*.

[82] See *Chullin* 85a.

[83] *Zevachim* 42b. And see *Tosafos*, *loc. cit.*, concerning an invalid act of burning a minchah offering on the Altar, where *Tosafos* uses the phrase, "It is merely dust that he burns." And there is a halachic consequence involved here: If, while in possession of *chametz*, one threw the blood of the Pesach sacrifice with the intent that it should be a different type of sacrifice (שֶׁלֹּא לִשְׁמוֹ), according to the position of *Shaar HaMelech* one would nonetheless be guilty of having performed the Pesach sacrifice while in possession of *chametz* [since in fact the throwing was performed, though invalidly]; while according to what we have stated, it is possible to say that one would not be guilty of this offense [since no throwing took place at all, halachically speaking].

[84] *Sefer HaMitzvos*, negative commandment 116. And see *Chinuch*, mitzvah 90; *Mishneh LaMelech*, *Korban Pesach* 1:7.

[85] *Sefer HaMitzvos*, negative commandment 155.

[86] *Ramban*, in *Sefer HaMitzvos*, *shoresh* 9; *Semag*, negative commandments 350 and 351.

[87] And see *Rambam* and *Ravad*, *Sanhedrin* 18:3.

[88] Mitzvah 7.

[89] *Pesachim* 41.

[90] *Rambam* 8:6.

[91] *Kuntres Hashlamah*, p. 6.

[92] *Rashi*, *Chullin* 115b.

[93] See *Bris Avraham*, sec. 31; *Tzafnas Paane'ach*, *Kila'im* 10:27; *Zera Avraham*, by Rav M. Zemba, הי"ד (murdered by the Nazis during Pesach, 5703 — 1943), secs. 10,11.

[94] See *Pesachim*, end of ch. 2, and *Rambam*, ch. 8.

[95] *Rambam*, 8:6, based on *Pesachim* 41a; *Tosafos*, *ibid.* 41b; *s.v.* אִיבָּא, in the name of Rabbeinu Tam.

[96] *Rashi*, *ibid.* 41a; *s.v.* יָכוֹל; and see *Rashi* on *Exodus* 12:9, and *Meiri*, *Pesachim*, *loc. cit.*

[97] *Pesachim* 85b.

[98] *Ibid.*

[99] *Rambam* 9:1. *Minchas Chinuch*, mitzvah 15, attempted to find a source for the *shiur* of *kazayis* here, and did not find the source, concluding: "It is certain, however, that *Rambam* found this somewhere." And in fact there are two explicit sources on this: in *Tosefta*, *Makos*, beginning of ch. 4, and in the *Yerushalmi*, *Pesachim* 7:13.

[100] *Mechilta*, *Bo*.

[101] *Rashi*, *Pesachim* 28b.

[102] Negative commandment 353. And see
Tzelach, Pesachim, 73a, where it is stated that
even according to *Rambam,* the person
feeding the meat of the sacrifice to the *nachri*
violates only the prohibition against "putting
a stumbling block in the way of the blind" —
לִפְנֵי עִוֵּר לֹא תִתֵּן מִכְשׁוֹל — but a careful reading
of *Sefer HaMitzvos,* negative command-
ments 126 and 127, will show that this
interpretation of *Rambam* is untenable. And
see *Minchas Chinuch,* mitzvah 13.

[103] *Chinuch,* mitzvah 14 based on the
sugya in *Yevamos* 71a.

[104] And see the explanation of this
conclusion in *Maharsha, Yevamos* 70b, and
in the commentary of Rav Y. Perla on *Sefer
HaMitzvos* of *Rasag,* negative commandment 175.

[105] *Rashi, Pesachim* 28b, and in his
commentary on the Torah, *parashas Bo;
Tosafos, Pesachim* 120a; *Chinuch,* mitzvah
17.

[106] Rabbeinu Tam in *Tosafos, Chagigah*
4b, and *Zevachim* 22b. And see *Haamek
She'elah* by *Netziv, She'ilta* 10.

[107] *Yevamos* 70b.

[108] *Ibid.* 71a. And see *loc. cit.* for a
number of possible ways this could occur in
reality — for obviously if a son were born
between the time of the slaughtering and the
eating, he would not invalidate the mitzvah
since he would not yet be eight days old.

[109] *Mechilta, Bo.*

[110] *Yevamos* 71b.

[111] And see *Shaagas Aryeh,* sec. 53;
responsa *Degel Reuven,* part 2, sec. 21. And
none of these authors took into account the
statement of *Or Zarua,* part 2, *Hilchos Milah,*
sec. 96, which indeed, in the time of
Maharsha and *Shaagas Aryeh,* had not yet
appeared in print.

[112] *Chullin* 17b.

[113] *Pesachim* 85a.

[114] *Zevachim* 97b.

[115] *Rambam* 10:4.

[116] *Yerushalmi,* end of ch. 7.

[117] *Toldos Adam,* by Rav Zalman of
Vilna, the brother of Rav Chaim of Volozhin,
ch. 4.

[118] *Rambam* 10:11.

[119] And for an explanation of *Rambam's*
reasoning, see *Chikrei Halachos,* by Rav
M.N. Maskil L'Eisan, sec. 25.

[120] Mitzvah 8.

[121] And see *Tzafnas Paane'ach,
Maachalos Asuros* 14:4, where the author
argues at length that although the minimum
shiur for the offense of leaving uneaten
remnants of a sacrifice is a *kazayis* as regards
all other sacrifices, for the Pesach sacrifice
even the tiniest amount (כָּל שֶׁהוּא) constitutes
a violation.

[122] *Rambam, loc. cit.*

[123] *Makos* 16a. And see *Kesef Mishneh,
Pesulei HaMukdashim* 18:9.

חָמֵץ וּמַצָּה ـ

Chametz and Matzah

In those happy days, may they soon return, when the Beis HaMikdash stood in all its splendor, when the "kohanim were at their service and the Levites at their song," the Pesach sacrifice was one of the twin pillars on which this great Yom-Tov rested. In our days, however, the one remaining pillar — the prohibition of chametz and the commandment to eat matzah — towers alone. And if our author counts, with Rambam, no fewer that sixteen Scriptural commandments connected with the Pesach sacrifice, in this chapter on chametz and matzah he elucidates (perhaps not by accident?) sixteen main topics.

Here as always, our Teachers and Rabbis of all the generations have found lessons to be learned and insights to be discovered in each detail of the halachos involved. A characteristic and — for our generation — especially apt teaching is given in a work entitled Noam Megadim, first published early last century. The Halachah stipulates that only those grains that can become chametz, may be used for the matzah we are commanded to eat. On the face of it since a reasonable sort of matzah could be produced from grains that cannot become chametz, ought we not to prefer them for this great mitzvah? Not so, writes the author of Noam Megadim. "The Torah is teaching us here how to serve HaShem. No man should seclude himself from the world and live in a wilderness in solitude, in order to ensure that he has no opportunity to transgress against the Torah — for under such circumstances his observance is not subject to his choice. Rather it is when one lives together with other people, works with them, does business with them, and yet overcomes all evil inclinations, that is the true way of serving HaShem: to be in a situation where one could become chametz, and yet succeeds in not doing so" — just like the matzah. For it is only when matzah is made of a substance that could become chametz, but is zealously guarded against this risk, that one can us it for the fulfillment of its mitzvah.

Numerous indeed are the subjects covered by the halachic literature on Pesach. Without going into the details of the laws, their explanations, and the new inferences to be drawn from them — for the multiplicity of these is beyond number — even when we merely list the general topics, we shall find the list a full one. It includes searching for *chametz* (בְּדִיקַת חָמֵץ); annulling it (בִּיטוּלוֹ): eliminating it from one's possession (בִּיעוּרוֹ); selling it (מְכִירָתוֹ); deriving benefit from it (הֲנָאָתוֹ); mixtures containing it (תַּעֲרָבְתּוֹ); seeing it (רְאִיָּתוֹ); and its presence in one's possession (מְצִיאוּתוֹ). *Matzah:* guarding it (שִׁימוּרָהּ); kneading it (לִישָׁתָהּ); and baking it (אֲפִיָּתָהּ); the *Haggadah;* the Four Cups; and all the details of the *Seder.*

One would expect that the discussions and investigations of these topics would deal primarily not with underlying definitions, but with clarification of the laws in practical terms and with rendering decisions on disputed issues. But this is not the case. A considerable portion of the literature on Pesach, not only that of the *Rishonim,* but even of the *Acharonim,* is devoted to the examination of the basic concepts themselves.

Bedikas Chametz

To begin at the beginning: The first *halachah* of Pesach concerns the search *(bedikas chametz)* for products of leavened grain in all their forms. And it is with this *halachah* that the first *mishnah* of Tractate *Pesachim* begins. This is a *mishnah* of ancient origin. Even though the whole concept of *bedikas chametz* in essence is purely Rabbinic, for on the Scriptural level, "simply annulling it in one's heart is sufficient"[1] — all the same, the requirement of *bedikas chametz* constitutes a *halachah* of great antiquity, concerning which there was already debate in the time of *Beis Shammai* and *Beis Hillel.* "And why," asks the *mishnah,* "did the Sages say [that the search for *chametz* must include] two rows [of wine barrels] in a cellar? — [because] it is a place where people bring *chametz. Beis Shammai* say: two rows along the whole front of the cellar. *Beis Hillel* say: the two outer rows, that is, the upper ones."[2] From this we see that *Beis Shammai* and *Beis Hillel* are debating the correct interpretation of an ancient *halachah* which they have received from tradition (i.e., the law of "two rows in a cellar").

What is the purpose of this search, and why is it needed at all? *The*
It serves, of course, as a preliminary to the subsequent *biur*, *Purpose*
the act of burning or otherwise eliminating all *chametz* from
one's possession. But why did the Sages not feel that mental
renunciation, *bitul*, was sufficient by itself, as is the case on
the Scriptural level? This is a question considered by the
earliest commentators: *Tosafos, Ran,* and others. Two reasons
for the Rabbinic amendment are given. (1) Since mental
renunciation, *bitul*, depends on a psychological state, the
Sages feared lest one's *bitul* might not be whole-hearted [and
hence might be halachically ineffective]. (2) Since people are
used to eating *chametz* all through the year, there is a danger
that one might forget momentarily and eat *chametz* found on
Pesach, even though one had renounced it. The first
explanation has reference to the prohibitions of *bal yera'eh*
and *bal yematzeh*, which stipulate that *chametz* which one
owns may neither be seen *(bal yera'eh)* nor be present in one's
possession *(bal yematzah)* during the seven days of Pesach.
The second explanation serves as a shield against the violation
of eating *chametz* during Pesach.

At the same time, it should be noted that there are *poskim*
who hold that in a case where one has not performed *bitul*
chametz, the obligation of *bedikas chametz* has Scriptural
force; for in that case it is not sufficient simply to have
destroyed that *chametz* which one is aware of. The debate
over this issue revolves around the question whether or not
chametz of which one is unaware violates the prohibitions of
bal yera'eh and *bal yematzeh*. This debate is the subject of
extended discussions in the works of the *Acharonim*.[3]

Even though the mitzvah of *bedikas chametz* is of Rabbinic *The*
origin, the *Talmud Yerushalmi* associates it with a verse in the *Source*
Torah, *And you shall guard the matzos ...* (וּשְׁמַרְתֶּם אֶת הַמַּצּוֹת;
Exodus 12:17). In the *Yerushalmi* it is first proven that this
verse is not needed to inform us of the date when we began to
eat only *matzah*, for that date can be deduced from nearby
verses. Hence, concludes the *Yerushalmi*, "If it does not refer
to the eating of *matzah*, we may understand it as relating to
biur chametz (אִם אֵינוֹ עִנְיָן לַאֲכִילַת מַצָּה, תְּנֵהוּ עִנְיָן לְבִיעוּר
חָמֵץ)."[4]Not only this, but even the precise time when the
bedikas chametz must take place — the evening which begins
the fourteenth of Nissan — is related by the *Yerushalmi* to this
same verse."*And you shall guard this day for your*
generations, an eternal statute" (וּשְׁמַרְתֶּם אֶת הַיּוֹם הַזֶּה לְדֹרֹתֵיכֶם
חֻקַּת עוֹלָם; *ibid.)* — [This implies that] we must ensure that

both the day and the night [i.e., *this day* in its entirety] are
'guarded' [— hence, the *bedikah* must take place at the
beginning of the evening so that the "guarding" effected
thereby will cover the entire night and following day].[5]

The Babylonian Talmud, in explaining the reason for the
prescribed time of *bedikas chametz*, states that it is "the time
when people are at home; and the light of a candle is well-
suited for *bedikah*."[6] This requirement itself — that the
search be conducted by the light of a candle — is associated
with scriptural verses. The Torah writes of *chametz*, *It shall
not be found ...* (לֹא יִמָּצֵא; *ibid.* v. 19); and "finding" comes
about through "searching" (חִיפּוּשׂ) as it is written, *And he
searched, beginning with the eldest and ending with the
youngest, and the cup was found ...* (וַיְחַפֵּשׂ בַּגָּדוֹל הֵחֵל וּבַקָּטֹן
כִּלָּה וַיִּמָּצֵא; *Genesis* 44:12). And "searching" is by means of a
candle, as it is written, *At that time I shall search Jerusalem
with candles* (בָּעֵת הַהִיא אֲחַפֵּשׂ אֶת יְרוּשָׁלַיִם בַּנֵּרוֹת; *Tzefaniah*
1:12).[7]

A number of details are given in the *Halachah* concerning
which places need and which do not need to be searched. The
basic rule is: Any place where *chametz* is never brought does
not require *bedikah*[8] — but one must check all the places
where there is any suspicion that *chametz* was brought, or
where people sometimes go carrying bread in their hand.[9]

The A disagreement in the *Gemara* concerns the wording of the
Blessing blessing which precedes *bedikas chametz*. Should one say,
"Blessed are You *HaShem* our God who has sanctified us with
His commandments and commanded us to *destroy chametz*"
(לְבַעֵר חָמֵץ) — or " ... and commanded us *concerning the
destruction of chametz*" (עַל בִּיעוּר חָמֵץ)? One authority holds
that [the term "concerning the destruction of"] indicates the
past. (*Rashi:* "[This wording would imply] 'concerning the
destruction which I have carried out,' but in fact one has not
yet searched, for the blessing precedes the search.") And the
other authority maintains that ["concerning the destruction
of"] refers to the future.[10] The decision rendered in the
Gemara favors the wording "concerning the destruction" —
but the *Rishonim* are divided as to whether this means that
this is the only acceptable wording, or whether it simply gives
us permission to use either term in the blessing.[11]

Our present custom, as determined by *Shulchan Aruch*, is
to say " ... and commanded us concerning the destruction of
chametz." And there is no blessing " ... concerning the search
for *chametz*," because the culmination of the mitzvah is not

the search, but the destruction of the *chametz* found.[12]

Nine sections[13] of *Shulchan Aruch* clarify numerous articles of the law of *bedikas chametz*.

Bitul Chametz

If *bedikas chametz* has given rise to disputes concerning the reason for the decree, *bitul chametz*, the mental renunciation of all leavening and its products, is the subject of disagreement about the very nature of the concept. What is the definition of this *bitul*? *Rashi* and *Tosafos*[14] would seem at first glance to disagree only about which Torah verse serves as the source of this mitzvah. But in essence this is not simply a difference of opinion about the source. The choice of source implies different definitions of the essential nature of *bitul chametz*.

According to *Rashi*, the mitzvah of *bitul* is the content of the Torah's commandment, *You shall cause leavening to cease from your houses* (תַּשְׁבִּיתוּ שְּׂאֹר מִבָּתֵּיכֶם; *Exodus* 12:15). *Tosafos*, on the other hand, holds that the mitzvah of *bitul* is derived by exegesis of the verse, *It shall not be seen with you* (וְלֹא יֵרָאֶה לְךָ: *ibid.* 13:7). The Sages interpret the expression *with you* (לְךָ) to mean, "You may not see *yours*; but you may see that which belongs to others or to heaven" (i.e., *chametz* belonging to the Temple). According to *Tosafos*, one carries out *bitul* in order to fulfill this commandment, for once one has renounced the *chametz*, and annulled one's ownership of it, it no longer can be called "yours." Thus the definition of *bitul* according to this opinion is clear and obvious — it consists of *hefker*, the renunciation of ownership. Indeed, the concept of *hefker* is itself subject to various interpretations; is it to be conceived of as the withdrawal of the ownership of the owners over the object, or the removal of the object from the ownership?° But in any case, these questions are not restricted to the topic of *chametz*. However we define *hefker* throughout the Torah, that same definition will apply here.

Definitions

° [The author alludes to an abstract inquiry posed by the Gaon of Rogachov into the essential nature of the concept of *hefker*. The state of *hefker* may be regarded as a new form of ownership resulting directly from the owner's action of repudiating his title to the object. In this view, the status of *hefker* is a *new* type of jurisdiction to which ownership of the object is transferred. If so, the act of making an object *hefker* is similar to a formal transfer of title (קִנְיָן) whereby ownership is actively conferred upon the recipient by the giver. Another view of *hefker* is that it is merely an owner's repudiation of his title, upon which the object involved automatically acquires the status of *hefker*, meaning simply that anyone may take it because it is ownerless (see *Encyclopedia Talmudis*, Hebrew edition, s.v. הפקר, p. 55). — Ed.]

Bitul, however, in the sense of "causing to cease" *(hashbasah)* as *Rashi* defines it, is not so easily understood. What is the nature of the *bitul* which "causes to cease"? *Ramban*, in his *Chiddushim* on Tractate *Pesachim*, clarifies this concept as follows. "[*Hashbasah* implies] *bitul* in the usual sense of the word; that in one's heart one nullifies the standing of this object as *chametz* and no longer has any desire for its existence — and this is the meaning of the term *hashbasah* wherever it appears, as in the verse, *You shall not cause the salt of the covenant of your God to cease* (וְלֹא תַשְׁבִּית מֶלַח בְּרִית אֱלֹקֶיךָ; *Leviticus* 2:13), meaning, 'You shall not nullify,' and likewise this is the meaning of [the noun from the same root as *hashbasah*,] *cessation* (שְׁבִיתָה); it means nullification *(bitul)* [of activity]. And thus the Aramaic translation by] Onkelos renders [for תַשְׁבִּיתוּ שְׂאוֹר "תְּבַטְּלוּן חֲמִירָא" [that is, the verb form of *hashbasah* — *tashbisu* — is rendered by the verb form of *bitul* — *tevatlun*]. *Ramban* goes on to explain that since the Torah forbids *chametz* for any use whatever [during Pesach], it no longer has the legal status of "property" *(mamon)*. Hence, in order to forestall the possibility of violating *bal yera'eh* and *bal yematzeh*, it is sufficient for a man that through his renunciation *(bitul)* "his intention agrees with that of the Torah" that the item in question shall have no significance as property [and it is not necessary to make it formally *hefker* in the usual manner]. In addition, *Ramban* argues at length to uphold the interpretation of *Rashi* in opposition to that of *Tosafos*. By contrast, *Shaagas Aryeh*, one of the greatest of the *Acharonim*,[15] writes at length to prove the correctness of *Tosafos'* opinion. (This author does not mention the comments of *Ramban* on the subject.)

The opinion of *Rambam* on this issue is in agreement with that of *Rashi*.[16] The existence of two different versions of *Rambam's* statement on this law has given rise to much involved argumentation. Our current editions of *Rambam* read, "And what is the *hashbasah* which the *Torah* commands? It means that one should nullify [the *chametz*] in one's heart and consider it as dust ... " In the commentary *Kesef Mishneh*, however, a different version is cited: "And what is this *hashbasah* commanded by the Torah? It means that one should remove from his possession the *chametz* that is known to him, and nullify in his heart that which is not known to him ... " In legal terms, the difference between the two versions concerns whether or not *bitul* is effective for *chametz* which is known to one. By citing the alternate version of *Rambam, Kesef Mishneh* is in effect introducing a new *halachah*, namely, that *bitul* is valid only for that *chametz* of which one is unaware. The many works dealing with *bedikah* and *bitul* do not "pass-over" this halachic innovation, and much space is devoted to discussing it.

Even though the Sages have obligated us to search for and eliminate our *chametz* from our possession, nevertheless it is still necessary to perform *bitul*. As the Talmud states, "He who searches must perform *bitul*."[17] The explanation is that this is necessary lest during Pesach one should find "a fine white roll" (גְּלוּסְקָא יָפָה) and be reluctant to burn it. If one were to hesitate even one moment before destroying it, one would already have violated the prohibitions of *bal yera'eh* and *bal yematzeh*.[18] And there is an opinion that if one does not perform *bitul* one is in violation of *bal yera'eh* and *bal yematzeh* even during the time one was unaware of the existence of the *chametz*; this would be comparable to one who eats forbidden fat (חֵלֶב) without being aware that this is what he is eating.[19] *Bitul* is only effective if perfomed before the time when *chametz* becomes forbidden; once the *chametz* is forbidden for all use, one no longer has ownership over it and hence cannot nullify it.[20]

Bitul must be performed twice. The first time is in the evening which begins the fourteenth of Nissan, immediately after the *bedikah*. At this time one nullifies only the *chametz* which is not known to one, i.e., that which was not found during the search; for one needs to leave over some *chametz* for eating the next day until the time when it becomes forbidden. Thus the wording of this first *bitul* speaks only of the *chametz* "which I have not seen and which I have not eliminated from my possession" (דְּלָא חֲמִיתֵיהּ וּדְלָא בִיעַרְתֵּיהּ). The second *bitul* is performed the next day, immediately after burning one's *chametz*, for in the course of the final *chametz* meal in the morning, some crumbs may have fallen into a crack or corner, and the *bitul* is necessary lest these lead to a violation during Pesach. This second *bitul* includes even the *chametz* which one has seen and is aware of. Hence the wording is, " ... which I have seen and which I have not seen, which I have eliminated from my possession and which I have not eliminated from my possession" (דַּחֲזִיתֵיהּ וּדְלָא חֲזִיתֵיהּ דִּבִיעַרְתֵּיהּ וּדְלָא בִיעַרְתֵּיהּ).[21] This *bitul* should be performed only after the burning of the *chametz*, so that the burning will have been performed with *chametz* which one still owns.[22]

The law is that one may say the formula of *bitul* in

Bitul is Performed Twice

whatever language one understands; but "those who do not understand [the words] at all, and believe that they are saying some sort of request (תְּחִינָה), undoubtedly do not fulfill the mitzvah."[23]

Biur Chametz

The nature of the elimination of chametz — biur — is a matter of disagreement among the Tannaim. According to Rabbi Yehudah, "Biur chametz is none other than burning." But Chachamim assert that biur is "also crumbling and scattering it to the wind, or putting it into the sea."[24] If you wish, you may see this difference of opinion as reflecting a disagreement about the basic definition of the mitzvah of biur. Is this mitzvah an end in itself, or is it purely a means to an end? In other words, does the very activity of destruction as performed on the chametz constitute the fulfillment of a mitzvah, or does the mitzvah consist entirely in the fact that one's possessions are free of all chametz, in which case the work of biur is only a means to the destruction and absence of chametz? It would seem that Rabbi Yehudah, who is particular about the exact method of biur, insisting on burning alone, believes that the mitzvah is in the biur itself; while Chachamim, who assert that the elimination of chametz may be done by any method, hold that the mitzvah does not reside in the eliminated chametz as an object, but rather in the result of that elimination, namely, the absence and eradication of chametz from one's possession.

This way of understanding the disagreement between Rabbi Yehudah and Chachamim is presented in the writings of Rav Chaim Soloveitchik.[25] On this basis, Rav Soloveitchik explains a law stated by Rambam, that "If one buys chametz on Pesach, or causes [grain] to become chametz, by performing a positive action," one is liable to the punishment of lashing.[26] This statement has given rise to much comment and discussion, for there is a general rule that the punishment of lashing does not apply to a "negative commandment which is connected to a positive one," (לָאו הַנִּיתָּק לַעֲשֵׂה), that is, a negative commandment which may be counteracted by the performance of a positive commandment. Here we would seem to have just such a case, for the negative commandments of bal yera'eh and bal yematzeh may be counteracted by the positive commandment of biur chametz. Why, then, should the punishment of lashing be applicable?

Rav Soloveitchik explains Rambam's reasoning as follows.

When the *Gemara*[27] characterizes *bal yera'eh* as a *lav hanitak le-aseh*, this is only intended in accordance with the opinion of Rabbi Yehudah, for whom the commandment, *You Shall cause leavening to cease* (תַּשְׁבִּיתוּ) is a mitzvah residing in the *chametz* itself as an object. But *Rambam* determines the Halachah as being in accordance with the opinion of *Chachamim;* who hold a different view of this commandment. According to them, *You shall cause to cease* is not really a positive commandment, but simply a positive statement of a negative commandment (אִיסוּר עָשֵׂה), that there should be no *chametz* in one's possession. Hence there is no question here of *lav hanitak le-aseh*. Rather, this is like any other prohibition which the Torah chooses to state in both negative and positive terms (בְּלֹא תַעֲשֶׂה וְעָשֵׂה).°

This basic conceptual question about the nature of the mitzvah of *biur* is discussed by the author of *Minchas Chinuch*.[28] This author does not relate the problem to the disagreement between Rabbi Yehudah and *Chachamim*, but he exerts himself at great length to prove that the issue underlies a disagreement among the *Rishonim*. *Minchas Chinuch* draws surprisingly far-reaching conclusions from this disagreement. In his opinion, those who hold that the activity of destroying the *chametz* is a mitzvah in itself would rule that if a person does not have any *chametz* before Pesach it is a mitzvah for him to acquire some in order to perform the commandment of *You shall cause to cease* — just as it is a mitzvah to wear a four-cornered garment in order to be obligated to add *tzitzis* to it.

From the halachic standpoint, the matter perhaps appears strange and unusual — buying *chametz* in order to destroy it?! Furthermore, *Minchas Chinuch* had not seen the comment of *Maharik*,[29] who takes the contrary as an obvious assumption: "Could one possible suppose that one who had no *chametz* at all, even if his supply had been exhausted more than thirty days before Pesach, should be required to purchase *chametz* in order to burn it and fulfill the mitzvah of *You shall cause to cease?*" But the fact is that a similar device is the accepted practice. For indeed it is the custom of all Israel to leave over pieces of *chametz* especially in order to burn them,

°[The classic example of *lav hanitak le-aseh* is the prohibition against taking a mother bird with her chicks (see *Deuteronomy* 22:6-7), which may be counteracted by performing the positive commandment of sending the mother bird away. An example of a prohibition stated in both negative and positive terms is *Shabbos*, concerning which the Torah tells us not only *You shall not do any work* (לֹא תַעֲשֶׂה כָל מְלָאכָה; *Exodus* 20:10), but also, *And on the seventh day you shall rest* (וּבַיּוֹם הַשְּׁבִיעִי תִּשְׁבֹּת; *Exodus* 23:12). — Ed.]

even though essentially there is no need to do so, since in our time we sell all our *chametz* to a non-Jew. The custom has support as well from the *Kabbalah*, which prescribes that before the *bedikah*, one should have ten pieces of *chametz* already prepared.[30]

The Time of Biur
The time to perform *biur chametz* is *erev* Pesach [i.e., the morning of the day before Pesach]. This is the meaning of our verse, *But on the first day you shall cause leavening to cease*. *Rambam* states, "We learn from tradition (מִפִּי הַשְׁמוּעָה) that this phrase, *the first day*, refers to *erev* Pesach."[31] The Talmud gives several ways of inferring this fact.[32] Two of these are cited by the *Rishonim*. (1) The verse, *For seven days leavening shall not be found in your houses* (שִׁבְעַת יָמִים שְׂאֹר לֹא יִמָּצֵא בְּבָתֵּיכֶם; *Exodus* 12:19), implies that during these seven days leavening should not be in one's house for even one moment; and if one were to wait until the first day of Pesach to destroy the *chametz*, this would mean that for a certain amount of time during the seven days leavening would be present in one's house.[33] (2) The Torah says, *You shall not slaughter the blood of My sacrifice with chametz* (לֹא תִשְׁחַט עַל חָמֵץ דַּם זִבְחִי; *Exodus* 34:25); that is, you shall not slaughter the Pesach sacrifice while *chametz* is still in existence [in your possession]; and the time for slaughtering the Pesach sacrifice is the fourteenth of Nissan.[34]

Even though, on the Scriptural level, one fulfills one's obligation by *bitul* alone [without *bedikah* and *biur*], nevertheless if one has not performed *bitul*, or if the time has arrived when *chametz* is forbidden, so that it is no longer within one's power to perform *bitul*, there is a Scriptural obligation to destroy the *chametz*.[35]

On the Scriptural level, the time for *biur chametz* begins with the seventh hour [from dawn or sunrise], that is, immediately after the noon hour on *erev* Pesach, which is the time for the slaughtering of the Pesach sacrifice. However, the Sages decreed that one should destroy the *chametz* at the beginning of the sixth hour [i.e., in the vicinity of 11:00 a.m.; the exact time varies for different geographical locations]; this is a precaution as people are liable to err about the exact time of day.[36] And the mitzvah of *biur* continues in force throughout the seven days, as long as one could be in violation of *bal yera'eh*.[37]

When *erev* Pesach falls on *Shabbos*, so that it is impossible to *Biur* burn the *chametz* that day, the *biur* is performed the previous *Before* day, and one leaves over enough *chametz* for two *Shabbos Shabbos* meals.[38] [This is the law as stated by the Talmud; but the practice now in some communities is that *se'udah shlishis*, the third *Shabbos* meal, is eaten even in this situation, with special arrangements to ensure that this does not conflict with the prohibition against eating *chametz* after the fifth hour of the morning. — Ed.] And even when *biur* is performed the day before such a *Shabbos*, i.e., on the thirteenth rather than the fourteenth, it is proper to perform it before the middle of the day *(chatzos)* so as to prevent people from making an error and thinking that in ordinary years also *biur* is permitted after *chatzos*.[39] [*Chatzos* here does *not* mean exactly 12:00; a Rabbinic authority or authoritative calendar must be consulted for the exact hour in each locality. Furthermore, *Rama* in *Shulchan Aruch* states that the requirement is to burn the *chametz* at the fifth hour approximately two hours before *chatzos*. — Ed.]

According to *Tzafnas Paane'ach*,[40] one may infer that this requirement to burn the *chametz* before *chatzos* even when *biur* is done on the thirteenth is not simply a stringency introduced by the *poskim*, but in fact a law stated explicitly in the Mishnah. This author gives a surprising and interesting interpretation of the relevant *mishnah*, which reads, "When the fourteenth falls on *Shabbos*, all [*chametz*, including both ordinary *chametz* and that which has been given special sanctity by being set aside as *trumah* for the *kohanim*] must be burned before *Shabbos*. This is the opinion of Rabbi Meir. But *Chachamim* say, 'at its time.' Rabbi Elazar bar Tzadek says, 'Trumah, before *Shabbos*, and ordinary [*chametz*] at its time.' " [41] The standard interpretation of this *mishnah* is that "at its time" means on the fourteenth as usual, that is, on *Shabbos*. Since burning cannot be done then, *biur* is accomplished by eating all the *chametz*. The distinction between *trumah* and ordinary *chametz* is that those qualified to eat *trumah* are few (*kohanim* only). Hence Rabbi Elazar bar Tzadok holds that it should be destroyed before *Shabbos*, lest no one be found to destroy it by eating on *Shabbos*; whereas for ordinary *chametz*, which anyone may eat, one may rely on the probability of finding people to eat it on *Shabbos*.

This interpretation has points of difficulty. For even Rabbi Meir, who says that the *chametz* should be destroyed before *Shabbos*, agrees that enough should be left over for two meals on *Shabbos*. If there is disagreement between him and

Chachamim, then, it must be that *Chachamim* assert that the amount to be destroyed on *Shabbos* may be even more than that required for two meals. How is it possible deliberately to rely on the chance of finding enough people to eat even more *chametz* than one will need for one's meals?

The Gaon of Rogachov, author of *Tzafnas Paane'ach*, thus proposes a different interpretation. According to him all sides of the dispute agree that the time for *biur* in such a case is on *erev Shabbos*, the thirteenth. Their disagreement concerns only that day itself. According to Rabbi Meir, there is no need to do *biur* before *chatzos*, since eating *chametz* is permissible all that day, and hence it is sufficient to destroy the *chametz* "before *Shabbos*," even just before dusk. When *Chachamim* say, "at its time," they mean at the time normally set for destroying *chametz* every year, that is, before *chatzos*. Rabbi Elazar distinguishes between *trumah* and ordinary food. *Trumah*, which because of its special sanctity should not be destroyed needlessly, should be left until the last possible time, i.e., "before *Shabbos*." How is it possible to destroy it before then, since it is still permissible for eating? But ordinary *chametz*, having no special sanctity, may be destroyed at the normal time, before *chatzos*.

Various details of the laws of *biur* are discussed by the *poskim*. These include the minimum amount *(shiur)* that necessitates *biur* (Some say the minimum is the volume equivalent of an olive — *kazayis* — [42] and others say that even less than a *kazayis*[43] requires *biur*, unless it can be assumed to be of no significance to the owner, such as *chametz* which is stuck to a wall and the like; but in the words of *Rosh*, as cited in *Shulchan Aruch HaRav*, "Israel are holy, and the custom is to be strict; they are careful to eliminate *chametz* that is present, even the tiniest amount, and even if it is stuck to a wall or a vessel.")[44] Also discussed are questions such as *taaroves chametz*, that is, mixtures containing *chametz*, — whether or not they are subject to *biur*[45]; the taste of *chametz* when it has merged imperceptibly into some cooked food [and there is no actual substance of *chametz* in the food] — whether or not this may be considered as if already destroyed, since it is not perceptible;[46] the proper procedure for dealing with *chametz* discovered on *Yom-Tov*, when burning it would be forbidden;[47] and other issues.

Here we arrive at a topic which occupies an important place, especially in the responsa literature — namely, the sale of *chametz* to a non-Jew. However, we have devoted the next chapter specifically to this subject.

The various stages of prohibition against eating or deriving benefit from *chametz* take effect at a number of different times. On *erev* Pesach, two hours before *chatzos*, *chametz* becomes Rabbinically forbidden for eating. One hour before *chatzos*, it becomes Rabbinically forbidden for any benefit whatsoever.[48] From *chatzos* on, the Scriptural prohibition against eating or deriving benefit from it takes effect; but at this stage the Scriptural prohibition is an *issur lav*, a negative commandment, and is not punishable by *kares*.[49] During the seven days of the festival, eating *chametz* is punishable by *kares*, while deriving benefit from it is an *issur lav*.[50] Outside *Eretz Yisrael*, where there is an eighth day of Pesach, eating *chametz* or deriving benefit from it on this last day are Rabbinically forbidden. Finally, even after Pesach, *chametz* which had been in the possession of a Jew during Pesach is forbidden for eating and for all other benefit. This last prohibition is a penalty (קְנָס) against those who have transgressed, so that there should be no legal benefit from the results of the transgression. It is "the penalty of Rabbi Shimon" (קְנָסָא דְרִ' שִׁמְעוֹן).[51]

The Prohibition against Eating Chametz

The eating of *chametz* on Pesach is actually the central point of all the prohibitions concerning *chametz* and all the related laws, and this fundamental point requires clarification. Does the prohibition apply to the *chametz* itself as an object, as is the case with forbidden foods such as non-kosher meat (נְבֵילָה וּטְרֵיפָה) and the like; or, since the entire prohibition is a temporary one, does that mean that the *chametz* itself as an object is not affected, but rather it is the man who is forbidden to eat it, as is the case, for example, with the prohibition against eating on Yom Kippur? To put the question in the terminology of the Talmud: Is the prohibition of *chametz* on Pesach an *issur cheftza*, "prohibition of the object," or an *issur gavra*," prohibition of the man?" The first authorities to devote extensive discussion to the definition of prohibitions in terms of *cheftza* and *gavra* did not deal exclusively with the prohibition of *chametz*. The first to devote attention to the difference between *chametz* and other prohibitions, in that the prohibition of *chametz* depends upon the time of year, was the author of *Taam HaMelech*; and this, not in his commentary on the laws of *chametz* and *matzah*, but rather as an incidental remark at the end of his essay on the problem of whether or not it is possible for two prohibitions to apply to the same thing at the same time (אִיסוּר חָל עַל אִיסוּר), an essay which appears in his commentary on the laws of forbidden relations. There the author remarks briefly that there is reason to compare the prohibition of *chametz* on Pesach to that of eating on Yom Kippur. However, he does not fully clarify the matter. The author of *Tzafnas Paane'ach*[52] also investigates the topic. In his words, the question is "whether *chametz* is a prohibition in itself, such that it is forbidden to eat it on Pesach, or whether it is simply that during Pesach it is forbidden to eat *chametz*." *Tzafnas Paane'ach* writes at length on the question, connecting it with the disagreement between Rabbi Yehudah and Rabbi Shimon as to whether *chametz* which had been in the possession of a Jew during Pesach is forbidden or permitted on the Scriptural level after Pesach. "He who says that it is forbidden believes that the prohibition is in the object and not in the time of year, while he who says that it is permitted believes that the prohibition is in the time of year."° [53]

If you wish, you may say that this conceptual problem underlies a disagreement among the *Rishonim* as to whether *chametz* which has been absorbed into the sides of a vessel before Pesach is categorized as "the absorption of a forbidden thing" or "the absorption of a permitted thing" (אִיסוּרָא בָּלַע or הֶתֵּירָא בָּלַע).[54] How can it be called "the absorption of a forbidden thing" when in fact before Pesach it was perfectly permissible? The answer is that the term "the absorption of a forbidden thing" means that when the time of prohibition arrives the prohibition applies to the taste of *chametz* inhering in the walls of the vessel, while "the absorption of a permitted thing" means that the new status of prohibition does not apply to it.[55] Thus, if one holds that the prohibition of *chametz* on Pesach depends on the man rather than the object, then it is not necessary at all for the new category of "prohibition" to apply to the object (i.e., the *chametz* inhering in the vessel). Just as it was in the category of *chametz* before Pesach, so it remains in that category during Pesach; it is simply that previously the man was permitted to eat things in this category and now he is prohibited from doing so. This is the intent of those who hold that *chametz* is a case of "absorption of a forbidden thing." In their words, "*Chametz* retains its name" [i.e., remains in the same category as

°[If we say that the prohibition is inherent in the object the end of Pesach does not affect the prohibition. If on the other hand it is the time that is the reason for the prohibition the end of the time, i.e. the end of Pesach, entails the end of the prohibition. — *Ed.*]

always]. But if, on the other hand, one holds that the prohibition of *chametz* on Pesach applies to the object itself, this means that each year when Pesach arrrives the quality of "prohibition" must take hold of and affect the *chametz*, and hence, if the "object" is only a taste, i.e., a thing which is light and weakened (קַל וְקָלוּשׁ), then it does not have sufficient substantiality to be affected by the new category of "prohibition.' Thus we say that before Pesach it was a case of "the absorption of a permitted thing."

Taaroves Chametz

Branching out from the prohibition against eating *chametz* is one of the most important topics within *hilchos* Pesach, and that is *taaroves chametz*, mixtures containing *chametz*.° In *Halachah* there are various *halachos* concerning mixtures of permitted and forbidden things, but *taaroves chametz* is amongst the most stringently regarded of all *taarovos*, for while others have some minimum percentage of forbidden substance below which its presence is considered nullified, there is no such minimum for *chametz*; even the tiniest amount, during Pesach, makes the whole mixture forbidden. The *Rishonim* are in disagreement as to the reason for this extra stringency. *Rambam* considers it to result from the rule that "those things which have some way of becoming permitted are not nullified even in a mixture of one to a thousand" (דָּבָר שֶׁיֵּשׁ לוֹ מַתִּירִין אֲפִילוּ בְּאֶלֶף לֹא בָּטֵל). [*Taaroves chametz* has a "way of becoming permitted" in that (on the Scriptural level) it may be eaten after Pesach. — *Ed.*] But according to the other *Rishonim*, the Sages were especially strict with regard to *chametz* because of the severity of the basic prohibition — first, that eating is punishable by *kares*; and second, that even the possibility of seeing it in one's house is forbidden *(bal yera'eh)*; and a further reason for extra stringency is the fact that people are in the habit of eating *chametz* throughout the rest of the year.[56]

The *Acharonim* have written at length to explain this

°[As a rule, when a forbidden substance becomes mixed with a permitted substance, if the forbidden is such a small proportion that in the words of *Rambam* "it is lost by virtue of its minuteness in comparison to the whole and is no longer of any significance," it becomes nullified *(batel)*. How small a proportion of the forbidden can become nullified is laid down by the Rabbis. In some instances we need a preponderance by the permitted of 60 to 1; in other cases, 100 to 1, or even 200 to 1. There are however exceptions, when we say that even 1000 to 1 will not nullify the forbidden, i.e., the mixture will always remain forbidden (the figure of 1000 to 1 being a hyperbolic term denoting that under no circumstances will the mixture become permitted). Of such substances we say that even if when compared to the whole the forbidden is an infinitesimally small quantity *(mashehu)* the prohibition remains and the whole mixture is forbidden. — *Ed.*]

disagreement among the *Rishonim* about the reason for the extra stringency of *taaroves chametz*. In responsa *Toras Chesed*,[57] the author enumerates in detail six differences of law which result from the difference between the reason given by *Rambam* and that given by the other *Rishonim*; and the author adds that these are only a few of the legal consequences of the disagreement. Here we shall indicate the first two: (1) The case of *chametz* which becomes part of a mixture on *erev* Pesach after *chatzos* — if the reason for the lack of a minimum amount is *davar sheyesh lo matirin*, i.e., the fact that *chametz* will later become permissible, then here too even the tiniest amount cannot be nullified by the mixture, for this reason applies equally on *erev* Pesach. But if the reason for the lack of a minimum is the severity of the punishment of *kares*, then the law does not apply here, for on *erev* Pesach the punishment is lashing rather than *kares*; hence the *chametz* would be subject to the same minimum as other forbidden substances mixed with permissible ones. (2) The case of inedible *chametz (chametz nukshe)* — eating this type of *chametz* does not incur *kares* (or, according to another opinion, is not even forbidden Scripturally, but only Rabbinically). If *chametz nukshe* is mixed with permissible food, what is the minimum amount of *chametz nukshe* which causes the whole mixture to be forbidden? If we hold that the reason for extra stringency is *davar she-yesh lo matirin*, then here too there would be no minimum. But according to the other explanation, which refers to the severity of punishment, there would be a minimum.[58]

The laws of *taaroves chametz* occupy much space in works of halachic responsa because of various kinds of practical situations which constantly arise. The saying is that "the individual case does not recur" (הַמִּקְרֶה לֹא יַתְמִיד). But individual instances involving *taaroves chametz*, in one form or another, do recur always. Again, of all the practical queries concerning Pesach that are put to Rabbis and halachic authorities, the majority concern *taaroves chametz*. However, most of these cases and queries have to do with mixtures which came about before Pesach, which means that there are fewer stringencies than for a mixture which occurs during Pesach. In *Shulchan Aruch* and its commentaries, the laws of *taaroves chametz* are mainly concentrated within three sections.[59]

One of the questions stemming from the prohibition of *Milk*
taaroves chametz, and arising as a practical problem each year *on*
— and this one does in fact concern a mixture produced during *Pesach*
Pesach — has stimulated numerous debates in the responsa
works. Is it permissible to drink the milk of a cow which
belongs to a non-Jew and is fed *chametz* during Pesach? This
is the question — and a decisive, unanimous ruling on it has
not yet been reached. There are those who forbid such milk,
and those who permit it. But in the course of the debate on this
question a number of basic concepts° have received
clarification. These include the concept of "twin causes" (זֶה
וְזֶה גּוֹרֵם — the question whether a product is forbidden if it
results from two causes, one of which is forbidden and the
other, permitted); the concept that it is sometimes permissible
to benefit from a forbidden item when this is done in a way
"other than the normal way of benefiting" (שֶׁלֹּא כְּדֶרֶךְ הֲנָאָתוֹ);

° [The text here discusses four concepts:
(1) זֶה וְזֶה גּוֹרֵם — "twin causes" — This is a usual ruling in *Halachah*, though the subject of
many qualifications and some disagreements, which states that whenever there are two causes,
one of which is permitted and the other forbidden, the end result is permitted.
In this instance the *chametz* consumed by the animal could not of itself turn into milk
without the animal. Therefore one cannot say that the *chametz* produced the milk of its own
accord; rather it is the animal which produced the milk out of the *chametz*. Hence we say the
milk has twin causes and is permitted.
(2) שֶׁלֹּא כְּדֶרֶךְ הֲנָאָתוֹ — "other than the normal way of benefiting" — The Talmud (*Pesachim*
24b, according to one version) states, "Rabbi Abbahu said in the name of Rabbi Yochanan,
'All forbidden foods do not incur the penalty of lashes unless used in their normal manner.'"
In our instance, we would say that to have it pass through an animal's stomach is not the
normal way of using *chametz*.
(3) חָרְבּוּ קוֹדֶם זְמַנּוֹ — "he has burned (or otherwise ruined) the *chametz* before it became
forbidden." — The rule is that if one has spoiled the *chametz* before it becomes prohibited in
such a way that "even a dog will not eat it" one may benefit from it during Pesach. The process
of digestion in the cow's stomach spoils the *chametz* to the extent that "even a dog would not
eat it." Since the prohibition of *chametz* does not apply to the non-Jew even during Pesach, it
is as if it was being ruined before any prohibition could apply.
(4) הוֹאִיל וְאִשְׁתְּרֵי אִשְׁתְּרֵי — "since it has been especially permitted, it remains permitted" —
In Tractate *Bechoros* (6b) we learn that the eating of milk would come within the prohibition
.of *ever min hachai*, which forbids eating part of an animal which is taken while the animal is
still alive. Therefore a special verse is required to make milk permissible. Since this permission
is a *chiddush*, a halachic innovation, on the part of the Torah, it could be inferred that the
chiddush extends even to kinds of milk which would otherwise be forbidden — for example,
even the milk of non-kosher animals. That such an inference has validity is borne out by the
fact that yet another verse is required to prohibit the milk of non-kosher animals. Thus we see
that in the case of milk, "Since it has been permitted [when taken from a kosher animal], it
remains permitted [even when taken from a non-kosher animal]" — and a special verse is
required to cancel the permission regarding the non-kosher animal. Our question is whether or
not it is valid to conclude that "Since it has been permitted [when taken from a cow that ate
"kosher" — i.e., pre-Pesach — *chametz*], it remains permitted [when taken from a cow that ate
forbidden *chametz*]."
Although questions may be raised about each of the above four reasons individually,
nevertheless taken together they provide the answer to the question why milk should be
permitted on Pesach. There are, nevertheless, some especially meticulous people who restrict
themselves during Pesach to milk which has been milked before Pesach. — *Ed.*]

the concept of *chametz* which the owner "burns [or otherwise ruins] before the time [of prohibition]" (חֲרַבּוֹ קוֹדֶם זְמַנּוֹ); the rule that "since it has been permitted, it remains permitted" (הוֹאִיל וְאִשְׁתְּרֵי אִשְׁתָּרֵי) and others.[60]

Hagalas Kelim Under the heading of *taaroves chametz* are to be included as well the numerous laws of *hagalas kelim*, the process in which the taste of *chametz* is cleansed from the walls of vessels by boiling them in water. The reason for this precaution of *hagalah* is care to prevent the taste of *chametz* which has been absorbed into the vessel from becoming mixed with permitted food which may be cooked in that vessel, thus forming a *taaroves*.

The essential place for the laws of *hagalas kelim* in *Shulchan Aruch* is the division called *Yoreh De'ah*, where forbidden and permitted foods in general are discussed.[61] Nevertheless, all the details of this law are set forth with full clarification, not there, but in *Hilchos Pesach*.[62] Not only that, but the author of *Shulchan Aruch* himself, in *Yoreh De'ah*,[63] refers the reader to the other location, stating: "The laws of *hagalah* and of *libun* [cleansing certain utensils by heating them to glowing heat] are written in *Hilchos* Pesach." In the Talmud, too, the precedent had already been set, for a number of the laws of *hagalah* are introduced in Tractate *Pesachim*.[64] And the *Rishonim* also placed these laws within those of Pesach. Their reason is evident. In relation to forbidden and permitted foods in general, the device of *hagalah* comes into play only irregularly and infrequently, whereas in relation to *chametz* on Pesach the process is a fixed and recurring feature of the preparations for the festival every year.

The basic principle underlying the rules of *hagalah* is: כְּבוֹלְעוֹ כָּךְ פּוֹלְטוֹ — "As it was absorbed, so likewise is it dislodged." If the taste of *chametz* was absorbed into a vessel that has rested on the fire (such a vessel is a *kli rishon* or "first vessel"), then its *hagalah* must be carried out by placing it into a vessel which is resting on the fire, and in which the water is boiling. If the absorption took place by pouring from a *kli rishon* into a second vessel (*kli sheni*), then the *hagalah*, likewise, takes place by pouring boiling water into the vessel from a *kli rishon*. If *chametz* was put into a vessel which is a *kli sheni*, then its *hagalah*, too, may be by means of hot water in a *kli sheni*. If, however, the *chametz* was cooked in the vessel by means of direct fire, without the intervention of liquid — for example, in the case of a spit (שַׁפּוּד) or frying pan (Aramaic, אַסְכָּלָא; Hebrew, מַחֲבַת) — then the means of hagalah is subject to disagreement among the Rishonim. At first glance it would seem obvious that the cleansing of such a vessel should be through libun, that is, heating to red heat by direct fire. However, the Gemara[65] explains that this is the law only in the case of issura bala, "the absorption of a forbidden substance"; whereas in the case of heteira bala, "the absorption of a permitted substance," hagalah is sufficient. (An example of "absorption of a permitted substance" may be drawn from the laws of sacrifices. [The meat of sacrifices must be eaten within a certain time limit after the sacrifice is offered up on the Altar — the time limit varying for different types of sacrifice. Up to that time limit, the meat is permissible; afterwards, forbidden. If the meat were roasted on a spit before the time limit, then the taste remaining in the metal could be dislodged by hagalah alone, for the absorption of this taste was "the absorption of a permitted substance."]) The reason why hagalah is sufficient for heteira bala is that whatever taste may remain in the vessel after hagalah is too light and weakened (kal vekalush) to be affected by the new category of "prohibition" when the time arrives. The dispute among the Rishonim concerns whether or not chametz before Pesach is in the class of issura bala or heteira bala.[66] If the former, then libun is necessary; if the latter, hagalah is sufficient.

The laws of hagalah and their details are very numerous, and "therefore it is proper and desirable," states Shulchan Aruch HaRav, "that a scholar conversant with the laws of hagalas kelim should be the one to perform hagalah with the vessels, and not as is the present custom."[67]

Bal Yera'eh and Bal Yematzeh

The moment the evening of the fifteenth of Nissan begins, the first law of Pesach to take effect is bal yera'eh, the prohibition which stipulates that one's chametz "shall not be seen." Together with this prohibition is its twin, bal yematzeh, stipulating that no chametz shall exist in one's possession. [Thus, if chametz which one owns is present on Pesach, one violates two prohibitions; first, that it is in one's possession, and second, that it is "seen."] Most poskim[68] agree that these two prohibitions do not apply on erev Pesach, when there is only the commandment, You shall cause to *cease*, and the prohibition against eating or deriving benefit from *chametz*. These two prohibitions, *bal yera'eh* and *bal yematzeh* are always mentioned together. But is it true that it is impossible for one of them to be violated without the other? [Obviously, it is impossible to violate *bal yera'eh* without violating *bal yematzeh*, for if the *chametz* is not "present," it cannot be "seen." The question, is, then, whether *chametz* can be "present" without being "seen." — *Ed.*]

This question depends on another. What is the nature of the "seeing" implied by *bal yera'eh*? Does it mean actual seeing with the eyes, or simply the possibility of being seen? *Rosh*[69] writes, "One is in violation of *bal yera'eh* even if one does not see [the *chametz*], for the Torah did not write, *You shall not see*, but rather ... *shall not be seen*, implying 'You shall not have any *chametz* in a place which is capable of being seen.'" *Kesef Mishneh*, however, without citing *Rosh*, records the opposite conclusion. "It appears to me that the phrase ... *shall not be seen* implies [that the violation is committed] only when [the *chametz*] is actually seen by the eyes — but if the *chametz* is hidden away (טָמוּן), one transgresses only against the commandment, ... *shall not be present* [*bal yematzeh*]."[70] Here then, we have a fundamental disagreement among the *Rishonim* about the definition of the concept, *bal yera'eh*. The subsequent Talmudic literature has let this disagreement pass almost without comment.

A Scriptural "Seyag" There is a different point worth considering in connection with *bal yera'eh* and *bal yematzeh*. It is ordinarily supposed that supplementary restraints (סְיָגִים), precautionary enactments (גְּזֵירוֹת) and "fences" (גְּדָרִים) are the province of Rabbinic legislation alone. Scriptural laws stand on their own right; one Torah commandment does not serve as a supplementary restraint for another. This supposition, however, is not always correct. *Ran*[71] writes that the reason why the Torah was especially severe towards *chametz*, making even seeing it a transgression, is in order to prevent one from eating it, since this is the accustomed habit throughout the year. *Rashbatz*, in *Yavin Shemuah*, reaches the same conclusion.

If you wish, you may say that this line of thought is explicitly indicated by the Torah. *For seven days leavening shall not be present in your houses, for whoever eats leavened grain, that soul shall be cut off* ... (שִׁבְעַת יָמִים שְׂאֹר לֹא יִמָּצֵא בְּבָתֵּיכֶם כִּי כָּל אֹכֵל מַחְמֶצֶת וְנִכְרְתָה; *Exodus* 12:19). The word, *for*, in this verse indicates that a reason is being stated —

[the reason for *bal yematzeh* is that the prohibition against eating is punishable by *kares*]. And this is how Abarbanel interprets this verse in his commentary on the Torah. The author of *Chasam Sofer*[72] has suggested that the opinion of *Ran* — that *bal yera'eh* is a *siyag* for the prohibition against eating — depends on the outcome of a disagreement between Rabbi Shimon and *Chachamim* as to whether or not it is possible to derive laws from the reasons behind the Torah's commandments (דּוֹרְשִׁין טַעֲמָא דִּקְרָא). If one may draw conclusions about the reasons for Torah commandments, then the opinion of *Ran* is valid; and if not, not. But if we understand the verse in the way Abarbanel does, no such distinction is necessary; for the reason behind the commandment is explicitly given by the Torah, and in that case both Rabbi Shimon and *Chachamim* agree that it is possible to draw conclusions about the reason for a commandment.[73] The truth is that there are other places in the Torah, as well, where Scriptural commandments perform the function of *gezeiros*, precautionary enactments.[74]

The prohibitions of *bal yera'eh* and *bal yematzeh* are limited in a way that does not apply to the prohibitions against eating *chametz* or deriving benefit from it; and that is with respect to ownership. For as we have already seen, the word לְךָ, *with you*, is interpreted to imply that "You may not see *yours*, but you may see that which belongs to others or to heaven." This limitation has opened the way for lengthy discussions among the commentators and *poskim* on such topics as the depositor of *chametz* and he with whom it is deposited (מַפְקִיד וְנִפְקָד); the thief and he from whom it is stolen (גַּזְלָן וְנִגְזָל); the borrower who gives *chametz* as security and he who holds the *chametz* as security for the loan (מְמַשְׁכֵּן וּמְמוּשְׁכָּן). In all these instances the question is, which of the two has violated the prohibitions of *bal yera'eh* and *bal yematzeh* if the *chametz* is not destroyed, nullified, or sold to a non-Jew before Pesach?[75] One passage, especially, from *Mechilta*, *parashas Bo*, serves as a focal point of these discussions. This *midrash* is known as "the *Mechilta* of ... *in your houses*" (הַמְּכִילְתָּא דְּבָתֵּיכֶם). It reads: "Why does the Torah say, ... *in your houses*? [Since it has already prohibited *chametz* "in your vicinity" (בְּכָל גְּבֻלֶךְ; *Exodus* 13:7), the prohibition of *in your houses* would seem unnecessary, for "vicinity" includes "house." But the meaning is that] just as 'your house' is in your possession so also the law about "your vicinity" is restricted to that which is in your possession. This is to exclude [from the prohibition] the *chametz* of a non-Jew which is in the possession of a Jew; for it is in his house, but he cannot destroy it. It is also to exclude the *chametz* of a Jew which is in the possession of a non-Jew, for it is his [i.e., the Jew's], but it is not in his possession." Both *Rishonim*[76] and *Acharonim*[77] are much occupied with the correct interpretation of this *Mechilta*.

The
Shiur
As for the *shiur*, the minimum quantity which causes one to be punishable for *bal yera'eh*, according to *Beis Shammai*, is *kazayis*, the volume equivalent of an olive, for leavening;° and for *chametz* it is *kakoseves*, the volume equivalent of a date. According to *Beis Hillel*, the minimum quantity is *kazayis* for both *chametz* and leavening.[78] The reason for the *shiur* of *kazayis* is that the law of *biur* is derived from the law about eating. Just as the *shiur* for the prohibition against eating is *kazayis*, as with all prohibited eating, so too this is the *shiur* for the minimum amount of *chametz* which requires destruction on Pesach.[79]

All the same, there is a difference between the *shiur* for eating and that for seeing. With eating, even less than the *shiur* is Scripturally forbidden;[80] the *shiur* simply determines the minimum for which one may receive punishment; whereas with seeing, the *Acharonim* agree that an amount less than the *shiur* is not prohibited at all on the Scriptural level. Two explanations are offered for this difference between eating and seeing. (1) The reason why even an amount less than the *shiur* is Scripturally forbidden in most cases is that one performs a positive action (for example, one eats the *chametz*), and this positive action lends significance to the amount acted upon, so that even though such a small amount normally is considered insignificant, and hence not punishable, nevertheless, it remains forbidden. This is not the case with *bal yera'eh*, for simply to see something does not involve positively acting upon it. Thus by seeing the small amount it cannot be said that one has added significance to it, and it remains insignificant not only with respect to punishment but even with respect to prohibition.[81] (2) Normally, the prohibition of an amount less than the *shiur* involves the reason that such an amount, though not punishable by itself, is "fit to be added" (חֲזִי לְאִצְטָרוּפֵי);[82] For example, if one eats half the *shiur*, and then within a certain

---

°[In the time of the Talmud, "leavening" did not mean the yeast which is used nowadays to make bread. Rather, moist dough was set in a warm place to ferment naturally from the yeast in the air, and this fermenting dough was then used to speed the fermentation of the main mass of dough used for the bread. — Ed.]

time limit eats another half, the first half is added to the second and punishment is incurred. (The time limit is that amount of time required to eat half a loaf of bread — *kedei achilas pras.*)°[82*] Here again, seeing is an exception; one instance of seeing cannot be added to another. Even if, after one found a half-*shiur* of *chametz*, a second half was found, the transgression begins only from the moment the whole *shiur* was seen; the first half of the *shiur* does not retroactively become part of the transgression.[83] All the above, of course, refers to the Scriptural level. On the Rabbinic level (מִדְבְרֵי סוֹפְרִים), the *poskim* are divided as to whether or not an amount of *chametz* less than a *kazayis* must be destroyed.[84]

There is yet another difference between the prohibition *The* against eating *chametz* and that against seeing it. For eating, *Punishment* there is a punishment prescribed by the Torah — either *kares*, the "cutting off" of the soul carried out by the heavenly court, or *malkos*, the lashing administered by the earthly court (as is always the case with those liable to *kares* — if they receive a lashing, they become exempt from the *kares*).[85] But for seeing, there is no punishment on the Scriptural level; for, *Rambam* explains, "A negative commandment that does not involve a definite action does not incur lashing" — לָאו שֶׁאֵין בּוֹ מַעֲשֶׂה אֵין לוֹקִין עָלָיו.[86] However, on the Rabbinic level there is a punishment of lashing (מַכַּת מַרְדוּת).[87]°° Furthermore, *Rambam* adds, since the absence of a penalty of lashing on the Scriptural level is only due to the fact that no *maaseh*, definite action, is involved in the transgression, it follows that if there does happen to be such an action — for example, if one purchases *chametz* or does the work necessary to make grain ferment — then, even Scripturally, a lashing is incurred.[88] This is the explanation of *Rambam*. But in the *Gemara*, a different reason is given for the absence of a Scriptural penalty of lashing; namely, that this is a *lav hanitak le-aseh*, a negative commandment which may be counteracted by the performance of a positive one; the positive commandment being, in this case, *You shall cause to cease* (תַּשְׁבִּיתוּ).[89] Much scholarly debate is recorded in the works of

° [See the present work, vol. I, pg. 216. — Ed.].

°° [The main difference between a lashing on the Scriptural level and on the Rabbinic level is that the former is mandatory and of a fixed number, 39, while the latter is determined by the view that the *Beis Din* take of the gravity and the circumstances of the transgression, the *Beis Din* having the power to fix a lesser amount of lashes or alternatively order a larger number. — Ed.]

the *Acharonim* to explain why *Rambam* did not give the explanation provided by the *Gemara*.[90]

The scholars have not neglected yet another difficulty in this opinion of *Rambam*. How could it be that one could "purchase *chametz*" on *Pesach*? After all, it is forbidden for any benefit whatsoever, i.e., it is an *issur hana'ah*; and one cannot legally acquire an *issur hana'ah* — the legal mechanism of acquisition simply does not function in such an instance. Even concerning one's own *chametz* the Talmud states, "There are two things which do not belong to a person but which the Torah nevertheless treats as if they belonged to him; and these are an open pit in the public thoroughfare (בּוֹר בִּרְשׁוּת הָרַבִּים)° and *chametz* after the sixth hour [on *erev* Pesach]."[91] If this is true even of *chametz* which was one's own, how is it possible that on Pesach one could legally acquire *chametz* which had never been one's own?

An answer to this question appears indirectly in the commentary of *Ran* on Tractate *Avodah Zarah*.[92] *Ran* explains that even though an item used by a non-Jew for idol worship is an *issur hana'ah*, it is possible for a Jew to acquire such an item, because there is a way for the item to become permissible; namely, if the non-Jew, by disfiguring it, shows that he has renounced it as an object of worship. Since the item does have a way of becoming permissible, it can be acquired by a Jew even if it has not in fact become permissible. Similarly, a Jew could acquire the *chametz* of a non-Jew. The author of *Or Same'ach*[93] explains that since the *chametz*, too, has a way of becoming permissible [on the Scriptural level] — namely, when Pesach ends — therefore it falls within the category of "property" *(mamon)* and is capable of being acquired. It may be objected that as soon as a Jew acquires the *chametz* during Pesach it becomes forbidden for all benefit, and hence cannot be in the category of *mamon*. But the answer is that this prohibition comes about as a result of acquisition by a Jew, and "How could it be that a *result* could take precedence over a *cause*, canceling the validity thereof before it had yet been caused by it?"

Concerning the other punishable *maaseh* mentioned by *Rambam* — doing the necessary action to cause grain to

° בּוֹר בִּרְשׁוּת הָרַבִּים — "a pit in the public thoroughfare." If one digs a hole in a public place, whatever damage is caused by this action is the responsibility of the one who has opened the hole, even though he does not own the road; and it remains his responsibility until the hole is filled up again. Furthermore, even if he is prevented from filling the hole (for example, by a non-Jew of whose violence he is afraid), he remains responsible. We have thus a situation whereby the Torah makes him the 'owner' of a public hazard though he has in fact never owned, in the ordinary sense, the place where the hazard exists. — *Ed.*]

ferment and become *chametz* — *Tzafnas Paane'ach*[94] remarks that this does not necessarily mean only when one puts the leavening into the dough to make it ferment. This is the action necessary to become liable for a different transgression mentioned by the Talmud, viz., causing a meal offering (a *mincha*, which must consist of *matzah*) to become *chametz*.[95] But in our case, explains *Tzafnas Paane'ach*, even if one simply kneads dough and then leaves it unattended so long that it naturally begins to ferment, this too is considered a definite action, *maaseh*, and is punishable by lashing on the Scriptural level.

On the question whether the prohibition of *bal yera'eh* applies to *taaroves chametz*, just as the prohibition against eating applies to it on the Scriptural level, the *Rishonim* are in disagreement. The issue depends on the correct interpretation of the *mishnah* which lists various kinds of *taaroves chametz* and which begins with the words, וְאֵלּוּ עוֹבְרִין בְּפֶסַח.[96] The word עוֹבְרִין used here can have different meanings, "to transgress" and "to pass by." *Rashi* interprets the phrase to mean, "These are the things for which one transgresses on Pesach." In his words, " ... for these, one transgresses *bal yera'eh* and *bal yematzeh*." Rabbeinu Tam, as cited in *Tosafos*, interprets the phrase to mean, "These are the things which must pass by the table," that is, which are forbidden for eating; but according to him they are not subject to the prohibition of *bal yera'eh*. *Taaroves chametz* is included even in the prohibition against eating only by virtue of a special word in Scripture. In the verse, *You shall not eat any leavening* (כָּל מַחְמֶצֶת לֹא תֹאכֵלוּ; Exodus 12:20), the word *any* is apparently superfluous, and is thus interpreted to indicate the inclusion of *taaroves chametz* in the prohibition against eating. The majority of the *poskim* rule, like *Rashi*, that *bal yera'eh* and *bal yematzeh* do apply to *taaroves chametz*.[97]

* * *

Matzah

Time alone, it would seem, forms the connection between *chametz* and *matzah*. At that time of year when *matzah* is to be eaten, *chametz* becomes forbidden; other than this, the two concepts are not intrinsically bound up with each other. So it would seem; but the truth is otherwise. It is not for nothing that the Torah mentions these two *bedibur echad*, in one utterance [see *Exodus* 12:15; *Deut.* 16:3]. For *matzah* is defined in terms of *chametz*. What is *matzah*? One could reply that it is the product of dough which has not fermented and

Matzah Defined by Chametz

become *chametz*. This alone is not an adequate definition, however — for flour made from *kitnios* (rice, peanuts, sesame, and the like) also does not ferment and rise and yet one cannot use such flour to bake *matzah*. This does, nevertheless, lead us to a sufficient definition of *matzah*; it is that which is capable of fermenting and rising, but which has not done so — in other words, baked goods made from the unfermented dough of the five types of grain[98] [wheat, barley, oats, rye and spelt חִיטִין וּשְׂעוֹרִין וְכֻסְמִין, שִׁיבּוֹלֶת שׁוּעָל וְשִׁיפוֹן]. Those who enjoy metaphorical interpretation, by the way, find in this fact — that *matzah* can only be made from that which is capable of being *chametz* — another significance. It recalls the reason given by the Midrash for the fact that Torah was given to man and not to the ministering angels. In the *midrash*, Moshe Rabbeinu claims the Torah for Israel, arguing, "Is there any jealousy among you [angels]? Is there any Evil Inclination among you?"°

From the halachic standpoint, the author of *Oneg Yom-Tov*[99] draws far-reaching consequences from this relationship between *chametz* and *matzah*. He asserts that by eating *matzah* on the first night of Pesach, one accomplishes two things; one performs the positive commandment of eating *matzah*, and one obeys the prohibition against eating *chametz*. Through this very eating of *matzah*, one fulfills the commandment, *You shall not eat ... chametz* (... לֹא תֹאכַל חָמֵץ; *Deuteronomy* 16:3). By means of this innovative interpretation, the author resolves a number of problematic issues. But even if we do not go so far as to accept the *chiddush* proposed by *Oneg Yom-Tov*, in any case we have seen that the very definition of *matzah* stems from the concept of *chametz*.

Matzah is dependent upon the prohibition of *chametz* in another way — in terms of the question, Who is obligated by the mitzvah? Basically, women should be exempt from eating *matzah* on the first night of Pesach, for this is a *mitzvah she'hazman grama*, a mitzvah which must be performed at a specific time, and women are usually exempt from all such obligations. But the Talmud tells us that women are in fact included in this mitzvah, for "Whoever is included in the prohibition against eating *chametz* is included in the obligation to eat *matzah*."[100]

The concept of *chametz* qualifies the definition of *matzah* in yet another way. It was stated above that *matzah* must be

---

° [The rabbis equate the evil inclination to which man is subject to the fermentation that makes the dough rise. — *Ed.*]

made from that which is capable of being *chametz*, i.e., the five kinds of grain. But there are times when even *matzah* made from one of these five kinds does not fulfill the mitzvah. In a case where such dough, had it fermented, would not be subject to the prohibition of *chametz*, it also cannot be used to fulfill the mitzvah of *matzah*. What is such a case? It can occur, according to one opinion, if the prohibition against *chametz* is prevented from taking effect because it has been preceded by a prior prohibition; for example, the prohibition of *tevel*, grain which is forbidden because *trumah*, the portion due the *kohen*, has not been separated from it.

According to this opinion, the fact that the first prohibition prevents the second — i.e., there is no prohibition of *chametz* because the prohibition of *tevel* already preceded it — is derived from a verse. "One might suppose that a person could fulfill the obligation [of eating *matzah* on the first night of *Pesach*] with [*matzah* made from] *tevel*. But the Torah indicates otherwise, saying: *You shall not eat chametz with* [*the Pesach sacrifice*] (לֹא תֹאכַל עָלָיו חָמֵץ; *Deuteronomy* 6:3). This is to restrict the prohibition to those things whose prohibition derives from the command, *You shall not eat chametz with* [*the Pesach sacrifice*], thus excluding those things whose prohibition does not derive from the command not to eat *chametz*, but rather from the command not to eat *tevel*."[101] This law, however, applies only in accordance with the opinion of Rabbi Shimon, who holds that a second prohibition cannot take effect upon a given item if another prohibition has already preceded it — even if that second prohibition is more general than the first and includes it (אִיסוּר כּוֹלֵל). The *Halachah* rules otherwise. According to the *Halachah*, if the second prohibition is of a general nature, then both prohibitions can be in effect simultaneously. And in our case, *chametz* is a more general prohibition, including even grain which is not *tevel*, and therefore can take effect upon *tevel* as well.[102]

In the end it transpires that in any case *matzah* from *tevel* cannot be used to fulfill the commandment of eating *matzah*, but for a different reason — it is a case of *mitzvah habaah be-averah*, a mitzvah which is fulfilled by means of a transgression.[103]

There is a difference between the first night (outside *Eretz Yisrael*, the first two nights) and the remaining days of Pesach. On the first night(s), eating *matzah* is obligatory; on the remaining days, optional. This law is derived from a verse.

The Obligation to Eat Matzah

"You shall eat matzos for six days and on the seventh day, a gathering for HaShem your God (שֵׁשֶׁת יָמִים תֹּאכַל מַצּוֹת וּבַיּוֹם הַשְּׁבִיעִי עֲצֶרֶת לַה' אֱלֹקֶיךָ; Deuteronomy 16:8). Just as on the seventh day eating matzah is optional, so also on the six days it is optional."[104] The reasoning here is based on one of the thirteen exegetical principles by which Halachos are derived from Torah verses. The principle is, "A thing which was included in a general category and then was exempted from that category in order to teach something, was not exempted only in order to teach about itself, but rather to teach about the entire category." Here the "seventh day" had previously been included in the "general category" of You shall eat matzos for seven days (שִׁבְעַת יָמִים מַצּוֹת תֹּאכֵלוּ; Leviticus 23:6). In the verse in Deuteronomy it is exempted from this general category [since it is only the six days that are included in the command, You shall eat matzos]; the purpose is to teach that eating matzah is optional. Since our principle tells us that what is taught in such a case applies to "the entire category," it would be proper to conclude that even on the first night eating matzah is optional; however, the law regarding that night is derived separately from other verses. For times when the Temple is standing we have the verse, You shall eat [the Pesach sacrifice] with matzos and maror (וּמַצּוֹת עַל מְרֹרִים יֹאכְלֻהוּ; Exodus 12:8); for times when the Beis HaMikdash is not standing we have the commandment, In the evening you shall eat matzos (בָּעֶרֶב תֹּאכְלוּ מַצֹּת; ibid. v. 18).[105]

The author of the Torah commentary, Chizkuni, in parashos Bo, interprets the verses as meaning that even though there is no obligation to eat matzah all seven days, nevertheless throughout these days the eating of matzah constitutes the fulfillment of a mitzvah. The Gaon of Vilna, likewise, "had a great love for the mitzvah of eating matzah all seven days, and on the final Yom-Tov day he would eat a third meal (סְעוּדָה שְׁלִישִׁית)[106] even though he did not eat a third meal on the other festivals; [but he did so on the last day of Pesach] because of the preciousness of the mitzvah of eating matzah, whose time was now passing away."[107] In any case, all agree that the blessing, " ... Who has sanctified us with His commandments and commanded us concerning the eating of matzah" (עַל אֲכִילַת מַצָּה) may be recited only on the first night.[108]

Guarding the Matzos The grain from which matzah is made must of course be kept from contact with water so as to prevent any possibility of fermentation; and this requirement involves two aspects:

guarding, and knowledge (שִׁימוּר וִידִיעָה). The obligatory matzah of the first night of Pesach (מַצַּת חוֹבָה) requires actual guarding, as implied by the verse, And you shall guard the matzos (וּשְׁמַרְתֶּם אֶת הַמַּצּוֹת; Exodus 12:17). For the optional matzah of the seven days of Pesach (מַצַּת רְשׁוּת), the requirement is satisfied through investigation and knowledge that the grain and flour did not ferment. A disagreement among the Rishonim, with roots in the Talmud, concerns the nature of "guarding." There are three opinions as to the time when the guarding must begin. (1) from the time of the reaping; (2) from the time of grinding; (3) from the time of kneading. This is the origin of three basic terms encountered in the halachic literature: guarded flour (קֶמַח שְׁמוּרָה), "Pesach flour" (קִמְחָא דְפִּסְחָא) and "flour from the marketplace" (קֶמַח מִן הַשּׁוּק). In normal times, even the matzos for the seven days should be baked only from "Pesach flour" (guarded from the time of grinding), and the matzos used to fulfill the mitzvah of the first night are baked from shmurah, flour guarded from the time of reaping. Those who are especially meticulous bake with shmurah for the entire festival week. The author of Aruch HaShulchan[109] finds this practice of using shmurah during all of Pesach to be not only a matter of custom, but of actual law according to the opinion of certain Rishonim (at least according to that author's interpretation of those Rishonim).

In difficult times, when "Pesach flour" is unavailable, it is permissible to rely on the opinion that "guarding" is from the time of kneading, and thus the obligation may be fulfilled with matzah made from "flour from the marketplace."[110]

A halachic innovation by Ridbaz of Slutzk asserts that the definition of the "guarding" required for shmurah is similar to the definition given in the Talmud by Rabbi Yehudah for the guarding of an ox which has been certified as a gorer. Rabbi Yehudah states that a minimal guarding, such as a door strong enough to withstand an ordinary wind, is sufficient in the case of the goring ox.[111] Here, too, writes the author, a minimal guarding is sufficient; it is enough that the grain be guarded from ordinary rain,° and it need not be guarded against extraordinary rainfall.[112]

On the other hand, an original suggestion on the part of Rav Yosef Shaul Natansohn tends towards the other extreme. This author writes that since the Torah says, And you shall

° [In other words, the store room has to be of such a nature as not to permit an ordinary rain to penetrate but need not be able to withstand an extraordinary rainstorm; and unless we know otherwise, we assume that the wheat from such a store room has been guarded. — Ed.]

guard (וּשְׁמַרְתֶּם; *Exodus* 12:17), the requirement is for sure and certain guarding from fermentation, and hence one may not even rely upon high probabilities (רוב and סְפֵק־סְפֵיקָא). This opinion is based on a statement by *Ramban*[113] concerning *tumah*, ritual impurity. The usual rule is that an item concerning which there is doubt as to whether or not it has contracted *tumah* is considered *tahor*, pure, if the doubt arose in the public domain (רְשׁוּת הָרַבִּים).° But, says *Ramban*, this does not apply to *kadashim*, items sanctified for the Altar, for concerning these the Torah uses the term *mishmeres* — from the same root as "guarding" — and hence as long as there is any doubt the item may not be considered "guarded."[114]

Kneading... The kneading and baking of the *matzah* are themselves the subject of many laws. The Sages of the Mishnah were already occupied with the proper method of kneading. "Rabban Gamliel says that three women may knead simultaneously and bake in the same oven, one after the other *(Rashi: " ... and no fermentation takes place even though one woman waits until the other two have baked")*. But *Chachamim* say that three women should work on the dough together; one kneading, one shaping the dough, and one baking. (A *baraisa* explains this procedure: as soon as the first woman has finished kneading, she shapes the dough she has kneaded and the second woman begins to knead; when the first woman has finished shaping the dough, she begins to bake while the second one shapes her dough and the third begins to knead; when the first woman has finished baking she begins to knead again while the second woman bakes and the third shapes the dough; and so on.) [By this procedure, there is never any waiting period for the dough; it is always being either kneaded or shaped until the moment of baking.] Rabbi Akiva says, Not all women nor all firewood nor all ovens are the same."[115] Here, of course, the *mishnah* is speaking with reference to small ovens. The *Halachah* follows the opinion of *Chachamim*, i.e., that the dough may not be allowed to stand without being worked, once the kneading has begun, "She must not raise her hand from the oven until the entire baking is finished" *(Rashi: "that is, she must be occupied with the dough at every moment")*.[116] If she leaves the dough without handling it for the length of time required to walk the distance of a *mil* — it has fermented.[117] (Concerning the length of time it takes to walk a *mil* there are varying opinions; the shortest time is 18 minutes, the longest, 24.)

The *Halachah* further stipulates that the kneading may

only be done with *mayim she-lanu*, water which has stood overnight;[118] that one may not knead with hot water;[119] and that one may not knead a mass of dough larger than the minimum size which obligates one to set aside *challah*, the portion of dough given to a *kohen*.[120] The custom is to be lenient with regard to this last law (regarding the amount of dough) because the Sages were concerned about this only in their time, when one person would knead and shape the dough, and using a large amount would necessarily entail delay; but in our time, when *matzos* are baked with many helpers, and furthermore our ovens are extremely large and the kneading, shaping and baking is done with great speed and care, we should not be strict about this [limitation on the maximum amount of dough] even when a large amount is kneaded at one time.[121] A number of halachic details are set forth concerning these laws and other aspects of the kneading process.

A number of halachic details are likewise involved in the process of baking. They include the method of making the oven kosher for Pesach ("the coals must make contact with the entire surface [of the oven] and sparks must be given off from it");[122] the problem of *matzah* which becomes folded in the oven and is stuck together to the extent that the fire does not reach part of the *matzah*; the problem of *matzah* which swells in the middle; and others. (Concerning the latter two problems the practice is to rule on the side of strictness.[123]) ...*and Baking*

There is a disagreement in the *Gemara* and among the *poskim* concerning whether or not *mei peros* — wine, oil, honey, milk, eggs, and other liquids not deriving from water — cause fermentation. The ruling accepted as *Halachah* is that these liquids themselves, without admixture of water, do not cause fermentation; but *matzah* made with them cannot be used to fulfill the mitzvah on the first night of Pesach because this is *matzah ashirah*, "rich *matzah*," and the Torah writes of *lechem oni, the bread of poverty* (see *Deuteronomy* 16:3). If these liquids are mixed even with a little water, then dough made with them ferments even more rapidly than ordinary dough. The practice is not to knead the dough with *mei peros*, even without water, except in situations of special need, as for the aged or the sick.[124] *Rich Matzos*

Special laws apply to the kneading and baking of *matzas mitzvah* for the first night. These *matzos* may not be kneaded or baked by a non-Jew, nor by a Jew who is deaf-mute,

mentally incompetent, or a minor (חֵרֵשׁ שׁוֹטֶה וְקָטָן). The reason
is that these persons, being exempt from the mitzvos, are not
able to guard the matzos for the sake of the mitzvah (אֵינָם
בְּנֵי שִׁימוּר לִשְׁמָה).[125] As to whether such persons may knead or
bake if a qualified person supervises them, the poskim are
divided.[126]

Shulchan Aruch records that "Rosh would make special
efforts for the matzas mitzvah; he would supervise the
making of them, urge on the workers, and aid in shaping the
matzos; and this is the proper way for everyone to do."[127]
Others have written that the same special care should be taken
with all the matzos for the week,[128] while Shibolei HaLeket
states that "Torah sages and most of the rabbis clean the
wheat with their own hands; they themselves take it to the
mill to be ground, and supervise the sifting of the flour, as
well as the kneading and baking."[129]

A special custom with matzas mitzvah is to reserve the
kneading and baking of these matzos for erev Pesach after the
noon hour. This custom has been associated with a verse, And
you shall slaughter a Pesach sacrifice ... For seven days you
shall eat matzos with it (שְׁבְעַת יָמִים תֹּאכַל עָלָיו ... וְזָבַחְתָּ פֶּסַח
מַצּוֹת; Deuteronomy 16:2-3). Here we see that the Torah has
made a connection between the matzos and the Pesach
sacrifice; and the latter was offered after the noon hour on the
day before Pesach. Certain of the Rishonim were strict in this
matter, regarding it as not only custom, but law; the poskim,
however, are in agreement that this is not an essential
requirement from the standpoint of law.[130]

The
Challenge
of
Technology
With the invention of technical innovations in the processes
of grinding and baking, various halachic doubts and questions
arose, causing numerous debates among the great Torah
scholars. With regard to the modern milling machines, the
main problem was that because of the heat generated during
the grinding of the grain, the mills gave off moisture which
caused the flour to form lumps. A revealing passage about this
problem is found in responsa Divrei Yissachar, by the Rav of
Bendin.[131] "If my honored correspondent will be good
enough to refer to Korban Nesanel on Perek Kol Shaah, s.v.
בִּשְׁנַת תק"א לְאֶלֶף הַשִּׁשִּׁי פֹּה בִּפְרָאג, it will be seen that at that
time the problem was a new one, since these large mills had
just been invented; for until that time they were not in
common use. And when it was seen that with these mills there
was moisture on the internal walls within the casing, there
were some people who refrained from eating [matzos made

with flour from this type of grinding machine] ... and nowadays what have we to say for ourselves?; for throughout the whole Dispersion of Israel all the mills are now of this type, and within the casing there is always dough formed by the moisture, and no one any longer raises his voice to advise stringency on this matter, until afterwards, in our own day, the cylindrical mills with elevators (וַאלְצָאנוֹע עִם עֶלְעָוַואטוֹרִין) were invented and a fresh uproar was made. But the truth is that there is no difference between the one and the other; on the contrary, the cylindrical mills grind at a cool temperature ... " Concerning the "uproar" that arose over the cylindrical steam powered mills (waltzava), a lengthy discussion may be found in Sdei Chemed.[132] In responsa Gevul Yehudah by Rav Zirlson, הי"ד[133] the author sees valid reason to "remove all doubts" about these machines, not only from the legal standpoint, but also from the standpoint of scientific investigation, through understanding the essential nature of this type of milling process.

An even greater "uproar" was caused by the invention of machines for the baking of matzos. This matter aroused a great disagreement among the halachic authorities. In every country there were those who forbade matzos made by this method, and others who permitted them,. In Galicia Rav Shlomo Kluger of Brodi forbade them emphatically, while Rav Yosef Shaul Natansohn of L'vov found ample grounds to permit them. Special pamphlets were published by both sides of the controversy. One such publication, "An announcement to the House of Israel," (מוֹדָעָה לְבֵית יִשְׂרָאֵל) was greeted from the other camp with a work entitled "Cancellation of an Announcement" (בִּיטוּל מוֹדָעָה). The debate was carried on in the columns of the then current newspaper for the observant, HaLevanon.[134]

When, in America, matzah machines powered by electricity were invented, yet another debate arose among the rabbanim.[135] In the end, as we know, these machines have come into use everywhere. They have all but acquired "full citizenship." The "loyalists" of the hand-matzos would seem to be in the minority, although those who are extremely meticulous about the mitzvos (הַמְהַדְרִין מִן הַמְהַדְרִין) do not use machine matzos. It has been justly said that in this matter everything depends upon the quality of the machine and the quality of the supervision. If these two factors are not in order, there is room for all the doubts and reservations of those who forbid machine-made matzos; while if the machine and the vigilance of those who operate it are at the proper level, the halachic validity of such *matzos* is above all doubt; and according to some, perhaps even above the level achieved by the hand-*matzah* factories.

The boundaries of the halachic territory called Pesach are broad indeed. Here we have limited ourselves to a general outline of the principle concepts and topics in *Hilchos* Pesach.

NOTES

[1] *Pesachim* 4b.

[2] *Mishnah*, beginning of *Pesachim*.

[3] See *Pnei Yehoshua*, beginning of *Pesachim*; *Or Chadash*, in his introduction to *Pesachim*; *Mekor Chaim*, sec. 431; *Magen HaElef*, introduction to sec. 434; *Yeshuos Yaakov*, sec. 434; *et. al.*

[4] 1:1; and see the commentaries there.

[5] *Ibid.*; and see *Biur HaGra* 431, para. 8.

[6] *4a.*

[7] *7b.*

[8] *Mishnah*, beginning of *Pesachim*.

[9] *Shulchan Aruch* 433:3.

[10] *7b.*

[11] And see *Rashi, Tosafos, Rosh, Ran,* and *Meiri, loc. cit.* And see *Rambam, Hilchos Berachos* 11:15.

[12] *Beis Yosef* 432.

[13] *431-439.*

[14] *4b.*

[15] *Shaagas Aryeh*, sec. 77.

[16] *Hilchos Chametz UMatzah* 2:2.

[17] *6b.*

[18] *Ibid.*, and *Rashi* there.

[19] *Magen Avraham* 434, para. 5, based on *Tur*; and see *Tosafos*, 21a, s.v. ואי; *Yeshuos Yaakov* 434; *Kuntres Acharon* to *Shulchan Aruch HaRav*, 433; *et. al.* Nearly all disagree with this opinion, and rule that if one does *bedikah* but not *bitul*, there is no retroactive transgression for *chametz* found later.

[20] *7a.*

[21] *Shulchan Aruch* 434. And see *Taz* there, para. 5.

[22] *Rama*, end of 434.

[23] *Rama*, 434, and *Magen Avraham* there, para. 6.

[24] *Mishnah*, 21a.

[25] *Chiddushei Rabbeinu Chaim HaLevi, Hilchos Chametz UMatzah.*

[26] *Chametz UMatzah* 1:3.

[27] *Pesachim* 95a.

[28] *Mitzvah* 9.

[29] *Shoresh* 174.

[30] See *Rama*, end of 432, and *Chok Yaakov* and *Shulchan Aruch HaRav, loc. cit.*

[31] *Rambam, Chametz UMatzah* 2:1.

[32] 4b and 5a.

[33] *Abbaye* in the *Gemara, loc. cit.*, and *Rashi, s.v.* שבעה; *Rif, loc. cit.; Tur*, 431.

[34] *Rabbi Yishmael* in the *Baraisa* cited by the *Gemara, loc. cit.*, and *Rava; Rambam, loc. cit.*

[35] *Ran*, beginning of *Pesachim.*

[36] *Pesachim, loc. cit.; Mishnah* at 11b, and *Gemara* there.

[37] *Noda BiYehudah*, second ed., secs. 60 and 61; and see an extensive discussion of this law in responsa *Pri Yitzchak*, sec. 13.

[38] 13a.

[39] *Tur* and *Shulchan Aruch*, 444; and see *Mishnah Berurah*, para. 9.

[40] *Chametz UMatzah* 3:3.

[41] 49a.

[42] *Tur*, end of sec. 442. And see *Kuntres Acharon* to *Shulchan Aruch HaRav*, sec. 446, where it is shown that this is the opinion held by several *Rishonim.*

[43] *Magen Avraham* 442, para. 12, and 444, para. 14.

[44] *Shulchan Aruch HaRav*, 442.30, based on *Tur* and *Shulchan Aruch.*

[45] See *Magen Avraham* 442, para. 1; *Bach*, 442, in the name of *Semag* and others; *Shulchan Aruch HaRav, loc. cit.*

[46] See *Chok Yaakov*, and *Kuntres Acharon* to *Shulchan Aruch HaRav*, 442.

[47] See *Shulchan Aruch* and its commentaries, sec. 442.

[48] In accordance with the opinion of Rabbi Yehudah in the *mishnah* at 11b.

[49] In accordance with the opinion of Rabbi Yehudah in *Pesachim* 28b; the ruling of Rabbi Yehudah is followed by *Rambam*, 1:7, and by the other *Rishonim* cited by *Maggid Mishneh* there. *Ravad* in his *Hasagos* adopts the ruling of Rabbi Shimon, to the effect that between noon and nightfall there is no punishable prohibition (לָאו), but rather an implied, non-punishable one (אִיסוּר עֲשֵׂה), and that on the Scriptural level only eating is prohibited, but deriving benefit from the *chametz* is allowed.

[50] 21b; *Rambam*, 1:2.

[51] 29a and 30a.

[52] *Chametz UMatzah* 1:6.

[53] And see *Chelkas Yoav*, second ed., sec. 20.

[54] See *Ran, Pesachim*, ch. 2, in the name of *Ramban* and others.

[55] See *Shulchan Aruch HaRav*, 447:45, and *Hagah*, 451:13.

[56] See *Maachalos Asuros* 15:9; *Rama, Shach*, and *Taz, Yoreh De'ah* 102; *Magen Avraham* 547, para. 40; *et. al.*

[57] Sec. 20.

[58] And see responsa *Mishnas Rav Eliezer*, by Rav E. Barkohen, sec. 12, where the author gives two more halachic consequences of the difference between the two explanations.

[59] 442, 447, and 467.

[60] See *Yeshuos Yaakov* 448; responsa at the end of *Avnei Miluim*, secs. 6 and 7; *Nishmas Adam, she'elah* 9; responsa *Beis Ephraim, Orach Chaim*, sec. 35; responsa of *Ramatz, Orach Chaim*, sec. 28; responsa *Toras Chesed*, sec. 21; responsa *Mishnas Rav Eliezer*, sec. 9; responsa *Chelkas Yoav*, second ed., sec. 20; *et. al.*

[61] Secs. 121 and 122.

[62] Secs. 451 and 452.

[63] 121:3.

[64] Ch. 2.

[65] End of *Avodah Zarah*.

[66] See *Ran, Pesachim*, ch. 2.

[67] *Shulchan Aruch HaRav, Orach Chaim*, end of sec. 452, based on *Sefer Chassidim* and *Magen Avraham.*

[68] *Rashi, Pesachim* 63a in the *mishnah*; and see *Tosefos Yom-Tov* on that *mishnah*; *Ravad, Chametz UMatzah* 3:8; *Magid Mishneh, loc. cit.*, on the opinion of *Rambam*; responsa *Maharam ben Rav Baruch* (ed. Prague), sec. 162; *Magen*

Avraham 443, para. 1; *Shulchan Aruch HaRav, loc. cit; et. al.* The author of *Noda BiYehudah*, in the first edition, *Orach Chaim*, sec. 20, testifies that: "According to the known views of the *poskim*, not a single *posek* disagrees about this." However, the author of *Noda BiYehudah* himself writes at length there to prove that according to *Rambam* the prohibitions of *bal yera'eh* and *bal yematzeh* are in effect beginning at noon on *erev* Pesach, and this is the opinion of *Rashi, Bava Kamma* 29b, and *Migdal Oz, Chametz UMatzah, loc. cit.* In the *Yerushalmi, Pesachim* 1:4 it is explained that according to Rabbi Yehudah the possessor of *chametz* is in violation of a negative commandment (לא תעשה) on *erev* Pesach. And see the version of *Sefer HaMitzvos*, by *Rambam*, in the edition of Rav. Ch. Heller, positive commandment 156. According to this version, by the way, it would seem that *Noda BiYehudah* was correct concerning the opinion of *Rambam.*

[69] *Pesachim*, ch. 1, sec. 9.

[70] *Chametz UMatzah* 1:3.

[71] Beginning of *Pesachim.*

[72] *Orach Chaim*, sec. 108.

[73] And see *Or Same'ach, Chametz UMatzah* 4:3.

[74] See *Avos DeRabbi Nasan*, ch. 2: "Which is the 'fence' that the Torah made for its own words ... " And see *Rashi, Sanhedrin* 18a, s.v. כהן גדול; *Kuntres Acharon* on *Shulchan Aruch HaRav*, 445, para. 2; *Beis HaLevi*, part 1, sec. 1; *Lekach Tov* by Rav Y. Engel, *klal* 8.

[75] See *Tur, Shulchan Aruch* and their commentaries, secs. 440 and 441.

[76] See *Ramban* on the Torah, *parashas Bo; Rosh, Pesachim*, ch. 1; *Ran*, there; *et. al.*

[77] See *Shaagas Aryeh*, sec. 83; *Mekor Chaim*, sec. 440; *Oneg Yom-Tov*, sec. 32; *Or Same'ach, Chametz UMatzah* 4:3; responsa *Emek She'elah*, in the *hashmatos* to *Orach Chaim*, secs. 2,3; responsa *Chelkas Yoav, Orach Chaim*, sec. 15; *Achiezer* part 3, secs. 1,2; *et. al.*

[78] *Mishnah*, beginning of *Beitzah.*

[79] *Gemara, ibid.* 7b.

[80] *Yoma* 74a.

[81] *Chacham Tzvi*, sec. 86.

[82] See *Yoma, loc. cit.*

[82*] See vol. I, "The Fast of the Tenth," p.215, concerning the various opinions as to the time defined as *achilas pras.*

[83] *Shaagas Aryeh*, sec. 81; and see responsa *Divrei Mordechai*, by Rav Mordechai of Malastovka, sec. 18, where the author writes at length to refute the argument of *Chacham Tzvi* and uphold that of *Shaagas Aryeh*.

[84] See above, fn. 42.

[85] *Mishnah, Makos* 23a.

[86] *Rambam, Chametz UMatzah* 1:3, based on *Tosefta, Makos*, ch. 4.

[87] *Rambam, loc. cit.*

[88] *Ibid.*

[89] *Pesachim* 85a.

[90] See *Mishneh LaMelech, loc. cit; Shaagas Aryeh*, secs. 80-82; *Or Same'ach, 1:3, et al.* And see the explanation cited above in the name of Rav Chaim Soloveitchik.

[91] *Pesachim* 6b.

[92] Beginning of ch. 3.

[93] 1:3.

[94] *Ibid.*

[95] *Menachos* 56b.

[96] *Pesachim* 42a.

[97] *Rambam* 4:8 [and *Maggid Mishneh* states that according to one interpretation of *Rambam*, even in cases where eating the *taaroves* does not constitute a transgression — for example, if one eats less than a *kazayis* during the time span of *achilas pras* (see *loc. cit.*, 1:6) — nevertheless one transgresses the prohibition of *bal yera'eh*]. *Tur* and *Shulchan Aruch*, 442.

[98] See *Pesachim* 35a.

[99] Sec. 42.

[100] *Pesachim* 43b.

[101] *Ibid.* 35b.

[102] *Ibid.*

[103] See *Rashi*, 35b, s.v. דמאי and s.v. טבול; *Shaagas Aryeh*, secs. 98, 99; *Chasam Sofer, Orach Chaim*, sec. 137; *et. al.*

[104] *Pesachim* 120a.

[105] *Ibid.*

[106] In this custom, incidentally, we find a meeting of opposites: "The *Baal Shem Tov* would eat a third meal (שָׁלוֹשׁ סְעוּדוֹת) on the final *Yom-Tov* day of Pesach" (from the Lubavitch calendar, *HaYom Yom*, Brooklyn, 5703 — 1943, p. 47).

[107] *Maaseh Rav*, sec. 185; and see *Chasam Sofer, Yoreh De'ah*, sec. 191; responsa *Meshiv Davar*, by *Netziv, Yoreh De'ah, sec. 77; responsa Zecher Yehosef*, sec. 178; *Sdei Chemed, Chametz UMatzah*, sec. 14, os 10;

responsa of *Maharsham*, part 1, sec. 209; *et. al.*

[108] See the sources just mentioned.

[109] Sec. 453.

[110] On this whole subject [of the different types of flour for *matzah*] see *Pesachim* 40a and the commentaries of the *Rishonim* there; *Tur* and *Shulchan Aruch* and their commentaries, sec. 453.

[111] *Bava Kamma* 45b.

[112] Responsa of *Ridbaz*, sec. 13.

[113] Beginning of *Chullin*.

[114] *Sho'el UMeshiv*, first edition, part 3, sec. 87, and second edition, part 3, secs. 84 and 182. And see responsa *Shaarei De'ah*, part 1, sec, 181, where the author supports this line of reasoning.

[115] *Pesachim* 48b.

[116] 42a.

[117] 46a; *Tur* and *Shulchan Aruch* 459.

[118] 42a. For the detailed laws concerning the water, see *Tur* and *Shulchan Aruch*, 455.

[119] *Gemara, loc. cit.; Tur* and *Shulchan Aruch*, 459.

[120] 48a; *Tur* and *Shulchan Aruch*, 456.

[121] *Mishnah Berurah, loc. cit;* and see *Beis Yosef* and *Magen Avraham.*

[122] *Tur* and *Shulchan Aruch*, 461.

[123] *Rama, loc. cit.*, para. 5.

[124] See *Tur, Shulchan Aruch* and their commentaries, 462.

[125] *Tur* and *Shulchan Aruch*, 460.

[126] See *ibid.*, and their commentaries.

[127] *Ibid.*, para. 20.

[128] *Mishnah Berurah* in the name of *Maharil* and *Pri Chadash.*

[129] *Shibolei HaLeket*, sec. 211.

[130] See *Tur* and *Shulchan Aruch*, sec. 455.

[131] Sec. 35.

[132] *Chametz UMatzah*, sec. 10; and see also *Archos Chaim*, sec. 453 and the works cited there; and in responsa *Zecher Yehosef*, sec. 133.

[133] Sec. 6.

[134] Concerning this controversy, see a detailed discussion in *Sdei Chemed, Chametz UMatzah*, sec. 13.

[135] See responsa *Maharsham* of Brezzan, part 2, p. 16; responsa *Machazeh Avraham*, by Rav A.M. Steinberg of Brodi, secs. 103-105; *Nefesh Chayah*, by Rav R. Margolios, sec. 560.

מְכִירַת חָמֵץ ‏&

The Sale of Chametz

In this chapter our author deals with the problem that faces those that have businesses which necessitate their holding considerable quantities of chametz when Pesach comes; in fact, it affects every one of us to a lesser or larger degree every year. There have unfortunately always been some people who have used this halachah of selling the chametz to a non-Jew as a means of claiming that the Rabbis devised a "legal fiction" in order to cope with a problematic situation. That nothing could be further from the truth is evident to anyone who peruses the vast number of responsa to be found in halachic literature concerning people who forgot to sell their chametz in time or who received consignments of chametz goods during Pesach. For whilst the authorities to whom these questions were addressed constantly bore in mind the principle that "Torah is mindful of the property of Israel," not infrequently their answer is that the chametz had to be destroyed, often involving considerable expense. Obviously, the Rabbis would not have required destruction of property for the sake of a "legal fiction."

The permission to sell chametz reminds one of the custom of eating cholent on Shabbos. Now those "modern" people who reject this custom have always been treated in traditional circles with a certain degree of suspicion. It may be that there are many who are unaware that this is not some quaint European or chassidic custom. Indeed, one of the Rishonim — Rabbeinu Zerachyah, the author of Sefer HaMaor — writes as follows: "And anyone who refuses to eat 'warm food' (i.e., 'food put away on Erev Shabbos, such as cholent') should be closely watched, since it could be that he does not accept the ruling of the Rabbis that this is permitted."

It seems clear, then, that anyone who would consider an established practice as firmly rooted in the Halachah as the selling of chametz, and describe it as "a rabbinic subterfuge," has likewise placed himself in this category.

Among the elements which comprise the unique experience of the days before Pesach, the selling of *chametz* to a non-Jew occupies an important place. Ample space is likewise given to this topic in the halachic literature, especially in works of responsa. There is a certain historical value, as well, in seeing how this practice has taken hold and developed throughout the centuries. It will be worthwhile, then, to take time to examine this selling of *chametz*: to trace its sources and roots, the factors that have influenced it, the varying conditions under which it was practiced, and its halachic status.

A Straight-forward Sale The sale of *chametz* has passed through various transformations before arriving at its present form. Its original roots strike far back into ancient soil. Since *chametz* is Scripturally forbidden on Pesach and is subject to the prohibitions of *bal yera'eh* and *bal yematzeh* (see *Exodus* 13:7 and 12:19, and see previous chapters), there has always been the need to "dispose of" any *chametz* which may remain in one's possession before Pesach. If these leftovers were small in quantity, then the mitzvah of *You shall cause to cease* (תַּשְׁבִּיתוּ; *ibid.* 12:15; and see previous chapter) was performed on them by means of *biur chametz*, the destruction of *chametz*. If, on the other hand, a large quantity was involved, the *chametz* was sold to a non-Jew. This sale was straightforward; it consisted of actual selling. The first traces of this method of selling are to be found in a *mishnah*. "As long as it is permissible to eat [*chametz*], one may feed it to a domestic or wild animal or bird or sell it to a non-Jew."[1] *Beis Shammai* and *Beis Hillel* disagree about the time limit within which one may sell to a non-Jew. According to *Beis Shammai*, one may not sell unless the non-Jew has time to eat the *chametz* before Pesach.[2]

The selling referred to here is the ordinary transaction used for the sale of merchandise. It was required that the non-Jew actually buy and the Jew actually sell. The disagreement between *Beis Hillel* and *Beis Shammai* [does not involve anything unusual in the nature of the sale itself, but] follows the same lines as their disagreement over the time-limit within which one may sell merchandise to a non-Jew on *erev Shabbos*.[3] [There, the problem is that the non-Jew may need to use an animal to carry the merchandise away. This is a type of work *(mechamer)* which is forbidden to a Jew on *Shabbos*, and therefore one is also forbidden to tell a non-Jew to do it for him on *Shabbos. Beis Shammai* requires that the sale take place only if the non-Jew has time to do this labor on Friday, so as to avoid even the appearance that he is performing it for the Jew on *Shabbos;* while *Beis Hillel* does not follow this stringency.] Just as the sale on *erev Shabbos* is an ordinary commercial transaction, so too this selling of *chametz.* It is likewise to an ordinary commercial transaction that the *Gemara* refers in the following passage.[4] "It is related that a certain man left sacks full of *chametz* in the care of Yochanan Chakukaa. Mice tore the sacks and the *chametz* was continually leaking out. [Rabbi Yochanan Chakukaa] came before "Rabbi" [Yehudah HaNasi, in order to ask whether he should sell the *chametz* immediately to minimize the loss, or wait on the chance that the owner might appear before Pesach to claim his property; for the day was *erev* Pesach]. The first hour [of the morning] he told him to wait; the second hour — to wait; the third hour — to wait; the fourth hour — to wait; at the fifth hour [after which *chametz* may no longer be sold but must be destroyed] he told him, 'Go out and sell it in the marketplace.' " And this was the form of the sale of *chametz* at the period — selling "in the marketplace."

It is for this reason that we find in the Mishnah and Talmud neither legal details nor halachic debate about the means or the proper procedure for selling *chametz.* The relation between Jew and non-Jew with regard to *chametz* stimulates halachic discussion only in relation to the laws of *mashkon,* items left as security on a loan. Here the question is to what extent a Jew is to be considered the "owner" of *chametz* which a non-Jew has left with him — or which he has left with a non-Jew — as a *mashkon.* To these laws, which involve cases arising only infrequently and irregularly, a whole passage of *Gemara*[5] is devoted; while the sale of *chametz,* which occurs every Pesach, is mentioned only in passing.

How is it that this practice evolved from a definite and actual sale to one which is purely a legality, where the Jew neither takes the money nor the non-Jew the *chametz,* but the entire requirement is satisfied by some act which indicates legal transfer of ownership [such as the signing and delivery of a document]? It would be reasonable to suppose that a period of transition was involved. And this is in fact the case. During this period the sale was indeed an ordinary transaction, the seller taking the money and the buyer, the *chametz;* but the difference was that the Jew would sell to a non-Jew whom he

The Transition

knew and with whom he was on good terms, so that he could depend on him to sell the *chametz* back after Pesach.

The basis for such a sale is found as early as *Tosefta*.[6] "If a Jew and a non-Jew are travelling on a ship, and the Jew has *chametz* in his possession,° he may sell it to the non-Jew or give it as a gift, and then acquire it back from him after Pesach — but only if he had given it to the non-Jew unconditionally (מַתָּנָה גְמוּרָה)." In this case the phrase, "... and then acquire it back from him after Pesach" means that the Jew may do so even if his original intention at the time of the sale was to re-acquire it afterwards. We see, however, that this type of sale is mentioned only in connection with unusual circumstances — "If a Jew and a non-Jew are traveling on a ship ..." This implies that for on who was in his normal home surroundings there was no need for this type of sale. The standard practice was to attempt to eat before Pesach that which could be eaten, to estimate how much could not be eaten and to sell this while there was still time, and to destroy on *erev* Pesach whatever remnant was left uneaten and unsold. Thus the commandments of *bal yera'eh* and *bal yematzeh*, *It shall not be seen by you* and *It shall not be found in your houses*, were taken in their straightforward meaning.

A second *halachah* mentioned by *Tosefta* in the same place must be understood in the same light. "A Jew is permitted to say to a non-Jew, 'Rather than purchasing a hundred [*dinars'*] worth, purchase two hundreds' worth in case I have need of it and come and buy it from you after Pesach.' " Here, too, the reference is certainly to an unusual circumstance rather than a regular practice. It is reasonable to interpret this *Tosefta* as does Rabbeinu Manoach,[7] who writes, "For example, if a Jew and a non-Jew wish to set sail on a ship on *erev* Pesach, and thus the Jew, because of the restrictions of Pesach, cannot purchase among his supplies for the journey the *chametz* he will need after Pesach; he says to the non-Jew, 'Rather than purchasing a hundred *dinars'* worth of supplies for yourself for the journey, come and purchase two hundreds' worth for my needs and for your own.' "

According to this interpretation, there is no reference at all here to the Jew's selling his *chametz*. But even if we follow the interpretation of the other *Rishonim*, who understand this *Tosefta* as meaning that the Jew sells his *chametz* to the non-Jew, saying "... in case I have need of it ..." the reference is

___

° [It is obvious that we are talking of foods which the Jew will require for his needs after Pesach; thus he cannot be said to sell it without intending to re-acquire it after Pesach. — *Ed.*]

still to unusual circumstances, along the lines of the previous law (that of "traveling on a ship").

If He does not Adopt a Pretense

Even more than this — according to *Behag* and certain other *Rishonim*, the correct version of this *Tosefta* is one which concludes with the words, "... but only if he does not adopt a pretense" (שֶׁלֹּא יַעֲרִים). This phrase is interpreted, by Rav Amram Gaon and by a commentary attributed to *Ritva*, as implying that "If, however, he is engaging in pretense, *in that it is his regular practice every year to sell* [*his chametz*] *to a non-Jew before Pesach*, he is penalized"[8] [by being required to destroy the *chametz* after Pesach]. What clearer proof could there be that this sale had not yet become a standard practice!

It is true that *Beis Yosef*[9] raises objections to this interpretation. *(Beis Yosef* assumes that the conclusion, "... but only if he does not adopt a pretense" is not part of the quote from *Tosefta*, but rather an added comment on the part of the author of *Behag.)* He writes, "I do not understand this statement; for one is permitted to give it to the non-Jew as a gift and then re-acquire it after Pesach, and nothing could be more a 'pretense' (הַעֲרָמָה) than that; and nevertheless it is permissible since he removes [the *chametz*] from his possession completely." In attempting to explain the statement of *Behag, Beis Yosef* writes, "It is possible that the stipulation 'that he should not adopt a pretense' means that the gift or sale should not be conditional" (עַל תְּנַאי). Nevertheless we see that even *Beis Yosef* is careful to include the requirement that "he removes [the *chametz*] from his possession completely."

The author of *Chasam Sofer*[10] explains more fully why *Beis Yosef* regards the sale described by *Tosefta* as completely permissible and not involving any undue *haaramah*, pretense. *(Chasam Sofer* understood the objection to *Behag* — "I do not understand this statement" — as being a citation quoted by *Beis Yosef* from Rabbeinu Yerucham; but this is not the case; the objection was raised by *Beis Yosef* himself.) *Chasam Sofer* writes, "The explanation of this statement is that the *haaramah* involved in this kind of sale is entirely permissible on the Scriptural level without any doubt, for the sale is accomplished by one of the ways of transferring property *(kinyanim)* which are valid for a non-Jew. And in spite of the fact that both parties to the sale know that they wish the *chametz* to return to the Jewish owner after Pesach, nevertheless at the time of the sale it is actually sold, and the buyer has the right to eat the *chametz*, to donate it for sacred use, or to destroy it, without arousing any protest; it is just that the non-Jew is friendly to the Jew (אוֹהֲבוֹ) and does not do any of these things, but keeps the *chametz* until after Pesach and sells it back. Therefore the practice is completely permissible without any doubt ... and one may even say explicitly to the non-Jew, 'If you still have the *chametz* after Pesach and you wish to sell it then, it is all but certain that I will buy it from you at its market value.' "

An Established Custom This same law mentioned by *Tosefta* as relating to unusual circumstances serves later as the basis for a regular arrangement and established custom. The passage is cited by a large number of *Rishonim*. It would seem that these authorities understood the circumstance of "traveling on a ship" as an instance where "the Sages chose to speak in terms of current conditions" (דִּבְּרוּ חֲכָמִים בְּהוֹוֶה). That is, they did not intend to indicate that this type of transaction is prohibited under normal circumstances, but simply that there was no need for it. The conditions of life were such that it was possible to arrange things beforehand so that when Pesach arrived no *chametz* would be left in one's possession. When conditions changed, people became accustomed to performing this sale on a regular basis. Already in the time of *Tur*[11] we find that in citing this law the author does not mention the circumstance of "traveling on a ship." The same is true of *Shulchan Aruch*,[12] except that the author is careful to use the following phrasing: "If one sells it or gives it to a non-Jew *outside of one's house*, even though the Jew is acquainted with the non-Jew and knows that he will not touch [the *chametz*] at all, but will keep it for him until after Pesach and then give it back to him — the transaction is permissible, as long as the *chametz* is orginally given to the non-Jew unconditionally ..." (The commentaries explain that the phrase "outside of one's house" means not only that the non-Jew may not be a member of one's household, but that the *chametz* itself must be removed from the house.)[13]

Such a sale is in fact in no way defective. The object is removed from the possession of the seller not only formally, but also physically. Likewise, the intention on the part of the seller is to accomplish an unconditional gift (מַתָּנָה גְמוּרָה) or sale (מְכִירָה גְמוּרָה). The only difference between this and any other sale is one of knowledge. The one selling or giving the *chametz* knows that the non-Jew will sell or give it back. But this knowledge in no way mars or interferes with the legal validity of the sale.

There was no difficulty in removing the *chametz* from the precincts of the Jew to those of the non-Jew. For, after all, what was the *chametz* involved here? Grain and flour, even though not guarded for the sake of Pesach, are not classified as *chametz*. In fact, under conditions of extraordinary difficulty (בְּשַׁעַת הַדְּחָק) one may even bake *matzah* using "flour from the marketplace" (קֶמַח מִן הַשּׁוּק), which has not been specially guarded against contact with moisture, and rely on the opinion which holds that it is sufficient to guard the *matzah* from the time of kneading.[14] What, then, was the *chametz* that had to be disposed of? Ordinary bread and *gluskaos* (white rolls), a small amount of spirits made from fermented grain, and occasionally a small amount of grain concerning which one had clear knowledge that it had fermented. All these things are easily transported from one place to another.

In later times, however, such transporting became an impossibility. In Europe, it came about that the majority of Jewish businesses, both wholesale and retail, depended on stocks of spiritous beverages (יַיִן שָׂרָף — י"ש) made from fermented grain; and it was not possible to move such stocks from one place to another [because of the quantities involved and the special storage conditions needed].° Thus it became necessary to sell the *chametz* without moving it from its present location.

Sale Without Delivery

The first mention of this type of sale as a fixed practice is found in the commentary of *Bach* on the *Shulchan Aruch*, and there we find as well the reason for this development. "... In this country where the majority of the business done is in *yayin seraf*, distilled beverages, and, especially for those who derive their income from an *arenda*, government concession, it is impossible to sell their stock to a non-Jew outside of their house, it is proper in such cases to permit one to sell to a non-Jew all the *chametz* in a room, and to sell the room itself to the non-Jew ..."[15] *Bach* goes on to explain by which *kinyanim* one may sell the room, and that the key should be handed over to the non-Jew, and similar details. Subsequent authorities — *Taz, Magen Avraham,* and others — upheld the ruling of *Bach.* They gave clear and well-founded proofs from the Talmud and the *Rishonim* that strictly according to the law there is no objection even if the Jew merely sets aside a special area of his home in which to store the *chametz* owned by the

°[To these problems one had to add the likelihood that a considerable quantity would be drunk by the purchaser and his friends! — *Ed.*]

non-Jew; all the more so is such a sale permissible when the room is actually sold along with the *chametz*.

It is likewise reasonable to assume that with commercial quantities of *chametz* such as *yash* (*yayin saraf*) — and especially when "the majority of businesses" were based on this (distilleries, inns, and so on) — it was difficult for each businessman to find a non-Jew who was willing and able to pay for the *chametz* in full. Hence it was necessary to find a device — and obviously it had to be a device which was halachically effective in removing any problem of *bal yera'eh* and *bal yematzeh* — to deal with the problem of payment for the *chametz*. The device was found — the seller would receive a deposit (עֵרָבוֹן, or *zhidatik*), and the balance of the price would take the form of a loan to the purchaser for a stated time period after Pesach. This type of *kinyan* is explained in the Talmud.[16]

The Bill of Sale Now that the outward form of the sale had taken on the coloration of *haaramah*, i.e., pretense or circumvention, the transaction began to be reinforced by the writing of a bill of sale. Strictly from the legal standpoint movable goods (מְטַלְטְלִין) cannot be transferred from one owner to another by a bill of sale alone. Nevertheless, the writing of such a document was seen as advantageous for three reasons. (1) The transaction would not be regarded as a mere jest or object of ridicule, since the non-Jewish purchaser would have a written and signed bill of sale.[17] (2) The room itself, being real estate (קַרְקַע) rather than movable goods, can legally be sold by means of a document. (3) Since according to the non-Jewish law movable goods may be purchased by means of a document alone, this in turn helps to make the *kinyan* valid even according to the Torah, through the law of *situmta*; the latter being an expression to denote a *kinyan* whose validity derives from the fact that it is the accustomed method of accomplishing a transaction among businessmen.

In responsa *Shivas Tzion*[18] the author records the text of a bill of sale prepared by his father, the author of *Noda BiYehudah*, in conjunction with the latter's *beis din* in Prague. This document is written in Hebrew letters, but in the German language. The wording is intended to effect the renting (not selling) of the rooms and the selling of the *chametz* (with the emphasis on "grain and spiritous drink"). The *chametz* is sold by means of money (through the acceptance of a deposit and the conversion of the balance of the price into a loan), and through *kinyan-agav*, the sale of "movables as an accompaniment to real estate" (מְטַלְטְלִין אַגַּב קַרְקַע). By this method, each individual owner of *chametz* sold his stock separately. Such forms for bills of sale were also printed in the *Haggadah* of Pesach.

The validity of these bills of sale in the civil (non-Jewish) law was put in question because of the fact that the usual stamp taxes were not paid on them. *Chasam Sofer* writes, "When the Gaon, Rav Baruch Frankel, *zatzal*, head of the *beis din* in Lipnik, was still living, it once happened that slanderers put it into the ear of the government ministers that the Jews were selling their *chametz* using bills of sale that did not bear the stamp (שְׁטֶעמְפֶּל) of his royal excellency the Kaiser. And when the matter was brought before the beneficence of his royal excellency the Kaiser, he declared that it was common knowledge that this was not a commercial affair but a religious one, and therefore did not require the official stamp [indicating payment of taxes]. This gave rise to a certain amount of doubt in the mind of the aforementioned Gaon, *zatzal*, since it implied that perhaps by the civil law the bill of sale had no legal validity. But to my mind it does not seem that there is any cause for doubt, for the document is a valid one, both by Jewish law — since if the non-Jewish purchaser goes to a Torah court to claim the merchandise it will be awarded to him — and by the civil law; except that if the purchaser were to turn to the civil courts he would first have to stamp the contract; it is only that his royal excellency the Kaiser in his generosity and honesty has declared that he does not wish to impose the yoke of the tax on this type of transaction since the sole purpose of both buyer and seller is to avoid the prohibition of *chametz*."[19]

The format for a bill of sale printed in the *siddur* of *Baal HaTanya* likewise includes the words, "Permission is granted (to the purchaser) to translate this document into the Russian language in official form (עַל נְיָיר הָאַרְבַּא״וו) in any place of jurisdiction of his royal excellency the Czar, and to pay the required imposition of his royal excellency the Czar to give this document the legal force of a contract made according to the laws and conventions of the royal government, both as concerns the renting of the aforementioned rooms and as concerns the sale of the aforementioned *chametz*."

Rav Chaim of Sanz (the son-in-law and disciple of Rav Baruch of Lipnik) takes a different approach in explaining the validity of the sale. "We go according to our own law, whether this results in stringency or leniency (בֵּין לְהַחְמִיר

בֵּין לְהָקֵל), and this of necessity must be so, for no document of any kind written according to their law can be of any use in this [matter of selling *chametz* before Pesach], for it is a clearly established law among them that a sale of this type, performed for the sake of satisfying a religious requirement is no sale at all; therefore no official stamp of theirs is needed [to make the transaction valid], and all the procedures of the civil courts cannot strengthen this sale. This being the case, what is our sale if it has no validity by their law? Rather, we must certainly say that we have only the law determined for us by the Torah. Therefore it makes no difference whatever whether we write [the bill of sale] in German or in the holy tongue."[20] He goes on to add that it is better not to write it in German, since "In our region, especially among Torah scholars, they are not acquainted with the German language at all," and hence its use could lead to difficulties and mishaps due to improper phrasing of the document.

A case occurred in which a Jew sold his *chametz* to a non-Jew by means of a civil notary. A halachic query concerning the validity of such a sale in terms of making the merchandise kosher after Pesach was addressed to the author of *Shaarei De'ah*[21] and he replied that this type of sale was even worse than one which satisfied Torah, but not civil, law. If, declared the author, the man had sold his *chametz* by a *kinyan* that was valid according to the Torah, we would not be concerned by the fact that it had no validity in civil law; but since the *kinyan* used has no legal [Torah] validity, and we rely entirely upon their law, then it is necessary that the transaction follow their law in every detail; and by their law this type of sale is mere *haaramah*. (The ruling, all the same, was to permit the *chametz* after the fact, but for different reasons.)

Selling Chametz and Livestock In addition to the trade in grain and *yash*, it was also common to make a business of fattening oxen and other livestock on *chametz*, mainly the by-products of the grain used by distilleries. This led to a more difficult question than that of selling *chametz*. On the one hand, if the animals remained unfed for the eight days of the festival, they would be greatly weakened and heavy financial loss would result. On the other hand, if a non-Jew feeds *chametz* on Pesach to animals owned by a Jew, the "pretense" is extremely conspicuous.

One great scholar, the author of *Tevuos Shor*, in his *chiddushim*, *Bechor Shor* (Tractate *Pesachim*) relates that "In this city (L'vov?), the principal commercial activity was the manufacture of *yash* and beer from *chametz*, and the by-products were used for fattening livestock, either for milking or for slaughter. When the Pesach season arrived, even though all sold their *chametz* to non-Jews as was the custom, nevertheless not one of them avoided difficulty by selling their livestock as well, so that they could be fed *chametz*. [Consequently the animals could not be fed during the festival week, and] the deleterious effect on the livestock was great for a number of weeks after Pesach, until they finally regained their strength." However, this stringent practice did not long remain in effect. The author notes that "Certain contemporary writers have suggested that it is permissible to sell the animals to a non-Jew before Pesach, along with the amount of *chametz* they would normally be expected to consume; this is done in the same way as the sale of *chametz*. The animals thus eat *chametz* all throughout Pesach, and afterwards [the Jewish owner] buys them back from the non-Jew. But this is something which I have never seen in my whole life ..."

The author goes on to level criticism against this innovative custom. In his opinion, it is definitely forbidden. The whole device of selling *chametz*, he argues, is only *haaramah*, "For the buyer is someone who never purchases [such quantities of *chametz*] and as for the seller, this is not his normal way of selling, and in most cases the purchaser is a poor man; yet, as the custom now stands, he purchases several hundred *guldens'* worth of *chametz*." However, the author states, since on the Scriptural level it is sufficient to annul the importance of the *chametz* mentally, while the requirement to physically destroy it is Rabbinic, it follows that the whole prohibition circumvented by the sale of *chametz* is a Rabbinic one — and for a Rabbinic prohibition *haaramah* is permissible. This, however, is not the case when it comes to feeding *chametz* on Pesach to livestock owned by a Jew; for here the prohibition [i.e., deriving benefit from *chametz* during Pesach] is a Scriptural one, so that *haaramah* is not valid.

This ruling by the author of *Tevuos Shor* made a great stir in the halachic literature. The author was widely known as a gaon and a holy person, and his opinion was not to be treated lightly. All the same — his conclusion did not gain acceptance. He was surrounded on all sides by numbers of counter-arguments from other halachic authorities. To give a few examples: (1) Even with the ordinary sale of *chametz*, the prohibition circumvented is not Rabbinic but Scriptural; for the *chametz* sold to a non-Jew is never included in the mental nullification *(bitul)* that satisfies the Scriptural requirement.

Hence there is no difference between this *chametz* (sold for the feeding of livestock) and any other. (2) The opponents of *Tevuos Shor* prove that *haaramah* is valid even for a Scriptural prohibition,° as long as there is no defect in the transaction used to accomplish the *kinyan*. (3) The sale of *chametz* is not to be defined as *haaramah* at all; for the seller truly agrees that if the non-Jew pays the entire debt undertaken as a loan, the sale will be valid; and the mere fact that the seller knows that this will not in fact happen, and that the non-Jew will sell the merchandise back to him, does not make the term *haaramah* applicable here.[22]

Subsidiary Problems The validity of the sale of *chametz* finds expression as well in subsidiary problems which have nothing to do with the prohibition of *chametz* on Pesach. We may consider two examples — one from *Yoreh De'ah*, the division of *Shulchan Aruch* that deals mainly with permitted and prohibited food; and the other from *Choshen Mishpat*, the division that primarily deals with non-criminal adversary proceedings.

The first question involves instances where one sells cooking vessels which had contained *chametz*. The law in general is that cooking or eating vessels bought from a non-Jew must be immersed in a *mikvah* before use; does this law apply to these *chametz* vessels when they are bought back from the non-Jew?[23] A number of *Acharonim* rule that it is advisable not to sell the vessels at all, so that there will be no need to immerse them afterwards.[24] [Since the vessels, which are not used during the festival, are not themselves *chametz*, but at the most may have absorbed the taste of *chametz* into their walls, there is no prohibition against owning them on Pesach. — *Ed.*]

The second question involves the possibility that a man might sell his *chametz* in the customary manner and then die during Pesach, leaving sons, one of whom is entitled to the inheritance rights of the first-born *(bechor)*. Does the *bechor* inherit a double portion of the *chametz* which is bought back after Pesach? There are two possible arguments against this. First, there is the talmudic principle that "the *bechor* does not receive a double portion of things which are due to be acquired by the estate, but only of those things already owned by it" (אֵין הַבְּכוֹר נוֹטֵל פִּי שְׁנַיִם בְּרָאוּי כְּבְמוּחְזָק)[25] and with this *chametz* it is as if it were purchased by the estate after Pesach.

°[Thus we are allowed to sell to a non-Jew an animal that is about to give birth to a first-born *(bechor)*, in order to avoid the inconveniences involved should the animal give birth to a male, even though the non-Jew knows that the Jew will buy the animal and its offspring back.— *Ed.*]

Or, second, it is as if the *chametz* were received from the non-Jew as a debt which had been owed to the father; and again there is a talmudic rule that the *bechor* does not receive a double portion from a repaid loan.[26]

A major innovation in the arrangements for the sale of *chametz* was introduced by the Rav of Liadi, *Baal HaTanya*, who formulated a precisely worded bill of sale for *chametz* and included it in his *Siddur*. From there this form was also cited in the author's own *Shulchan Aruch*, at the end of the section on *Hilchos Pesach*. This bill of sale is introduced by the statement, "If it should occur to anyone to think that the sale of *chametz* [involves only] a Rabbinic commandment *(midivrei sofrim)*, in accordance with the practice that each person nullifies his *chametz* and declares, 'May all the *chametz* be annulled and ownerless ...' — any such assumption is a mistake, for the *chametz* which is sold is not included in that which is nullified and pronounced ownerless ..." The innovation on the part of *Baal HaTanya* is the assertion that the practice of converting a portion of the total price into a loan is invalid — "and for this problem there is no other solution, if one wishes to sell on credit, than to make use of another Jewish person as an intermediary, so that the one who owns the *chametz* should have absolutely no dealings with the non-Jewish buyer, and the latter should owe nothing at all to the owner of the *chametz*, but rather to the third party, who himself has never owned the *chametz* in question." The principle suggested is that another Jew must act as guarantor and contractor (עָרֵב קַבְּלָן) for the non-Jew.

Baal HaTanya's Innovation

The Rav, *Baal HaTanya*, does not in fact explain why it is that converting the balance of the price into a loan is not a valid procedure, even though its validity would seem to be indicated by a basic reading of the Gemara in *Bava Metzia* [see footnote 16 above]. However, the Rav's brother, Rav Y. L. of Yanovitch,[27] and his grandson, the author of *Tzemach Tzedek*,[28] do provide the explanation. It would seem that according to the interpretation of a number of *Rishonim*, as cited in *Shitah Mekubetzes*, the conversion of the balance of the price into a loan is invalid if the seller "goes out looking for the money" (עָיֵיל וּנְפִיק אֲזוּזֵי); [that is, by pressing for payment of the loan the seller reveals that he was not satisfied to sell by means of a loan, and hence the sale is invalid. For this reason, it would seem, the Rav requires that the seller have no direct dealings with the buyer, so that it cannot come about that he is "going out looking for the money." — Ed.].

The Rav himself also hinted at these sources in writing, "It is known in circles conversant with these matters that many of the works of the *Rishonim* had not yet been published in the days of the *Acharonim* [of the generation of] *Taz* and *Magen Avraham* ... it is quite evident that parts of *Shitah Mekubetzes* on a number of tractates, and similar material [is included in this category]."

The innovation of *Baal HaTanya* was put into practice in a number of communities. Of course, this goes without saying as regards *Chabad* chassidim. Such communities naturally accepted and fulfilled the modification immediately, treating it as unquestionable law. But even in communities where the "Chabadnicks" were not in the majority, if nevertheless individual chassidim lived there they made every possible effort to ensure that the local Rav, even if he were a non-chassid *(misnagged)*, would arrange the sale by means of an intermediary *(arev-kablan)*. (Concerning the entire subject of how the sale came to be carried out by the Rav of the city, see below.) The local Rav, for his part, ordinarily would raise no objection to the request of the chassidim. Why should he object? Even if he himself did not agree that an *arev-kablan* was necessary, still "if it does not help, it will not hurt either." But even in many localities where there were no Chabad chassidim at all, the custom of using an *arev-kablan* was instituted. This amendment by the Rav finds an echo, too, in works of responsa. Among these, some authors take a critical stance and others uphold the validity of the amendment.[29] Incidentally, in Jerusalem and Tel Aviv the custom is to follow this amendment of *Baal HaTanya*. And even when the Gaon Rav A. Y. Kook [in circumstances of extreme hardship] instituted the "selling" of farm lands to a non-Jew in order to allow agricultural work during the *Shmitah* or sabbatical year, he included in the arrangement the use of an *arev-kablan*.[30]

A Multitude of Questions This initial period of the sale of *chametz* as a legality — in which the *chametz* was not removed from its place nor the full amount of money received from the purchaser — lasted, one may estimate, about two hundred fifty years; from the time of Bach, who is the first to refer to this type of sale as a permanent institution, and who died in the year 5400 (1640), until the first half of the seventh century of the sixth millennium by the Jewish reckoning; for by then the sale of *chametz* had begun to enter into the subsequent period, that of the comprehensive sale. During this period of two and a half centuries the halachic queries, stimulated by various types of cases where some aspect of the sale was not in order, were extremely numerous. This would seem inevitable by the very nature of the matter. Since "each one's Torah was in his own hands," every individual selling his *chametz* on his own, and since the sale was not a simple concrete transaction, it was natural that it did not always go off smoothly from the halachic standpoint. One man forgets to affix his signature to the bill of sale (it is interesting to note that, judging from the large number of questions about this problem, this seemingly odd occurrence was quite common); another sells his *chametz* during the sixth hour on *erev* Pesach [the sale at this point being Rabbinically invalid but Scripturally valid]; yet another neglects to sell or rent the room in which the *chametz* is stored; and so on — the possible entanglements are endless. To such cases we must add those involving laymen and the ignorant, where through lack of knowledge it sometimes happened that the sale took on ridiculous forms. The author of *Magen Avraham*[31] had already found it necessary to warn: "'... but not like the masses, who declare, 'I hereby sell to you the key of the room,' for this is no transaction at all, and even after the fact (בְּדִיעֲבַד) the *chametz* remains forbidden [and must be destroyed after Pesach], since it was never sold at all."

As a result, an excellent idea was raised at the beginning of the seventh century [i.e., the 5600's, or around 1840]: a comprehensive sale of *chametz* would be instituted, involving all the members of the community, and arranged directly by, or under the supervision of, the *beis-din* of the city. The *dayanim* would know, of course, how to arrange all the details according to the requirements of the *Halachah*, and in this manner the entire congregation would be saved from the danger of violating the Scriptural prohibitions of *bal yera'eh* and *bal yematzeh*. The comprehensive sale found expression originally in one of two forms: (1) The residents of the city would sell their *chametz* to the Rav or to the *beis-din* and the latter would sell it to a non-Jew; °(2) The Rav or *beis-din*

The Comprehensive Sale

° [An interesting point is made by a contemporary author in *Moadim U'Zmanim* regarding the custom of paying the Rav who sells the *chametz* — a payment which many people think of as merely a gift to the Rav. We have a rule that when we are dealing with an אָסוּר מִדְּאוֹרַיְיתָא we do not rely on the assumption that someone appointed to fulfill the task has in fact done so. Thus, when we appoint the Rav as our representative to rid us of a possible אָסוּר מִדְּאוֹרַיְיתָא by selling our *chametz*, should we rely on his having done so? Perhaps we ought to visit the Rav on Erev Pesach and enquire if in fact he has sold the *chametz*? However if we pay him for it the Rav is in fact 'employed' by us for the purpose of selling the *chametz* and we can therefore rightly assume that he has fulfilled his undertaking. Thus we see that like all Jewish customs (even when it is not immediately apparent), this custom too is based on a sound halachic principle. — Ed.]

would be made the legal agents (שְׁלוּחִים) of the residents, through a special document of authorization (שְׁטַר הַרְשָׁאָה), in which they gave power-of-attorney to these authorities to sell all their *chametz* to whomever the authorities chose. In the course of time the first form, that of a double sale,° disappeared, and the form involving the *harshaah* or power-of-attorney became accepted throughout all the lands of Israel's dispersion.

It was not without difficulty that the comprehensive method of sale — *mechirah clallis* — became accepted. A number of great *rabbanim* were among those who rose up in opposition to it. This innovation, which in truth entails a great improvement over the previous state of affairs, was perceived by some as a *pirtzah*, a breakdown of the law. They regarded it as making the *haaramah* excessively recognizable. Rav Yosef Shaul Natansohn writes: "On *erev Shabbos Kodesh, parashas Metzora,* the sixth of Nissan, 5616 (1856), a responsum reached me from the city of Zborov; the subject is the sale of *chametz.* The author of the responsum, previously the Rav of the city and presently Head of the *beis din* in Betchuch, Rav Avraham Tumim, gives a ruling which has in fact already taken root as the local custom: to sell, by means of one appointed agent, all the *chametz* belonging to the merchants of the city and the inn-keepers and so on; and that Rav instituted the custom of writing a *harshaah* in the name of the appointed agent; this document is signed by all the residents of the city and the surrounding villages, and the agent then sells to a non-Jew ..."[32] The author writes at length to nullify this custom. In his opinion, there is no substance to such a sale. The basis of his objection, however, is extremely frail. He claims that since the sale of *chametz* is in any case a *haaramah*, the law of appointing an agent or proxy (דִּין שְׁלִיחוּת) does not apply to it. Wherefore, one may ask, and why not? No matter what approach we take (מִמָּה נַפְשָׁךְ), this argument does not hold up. If this sale has halachic validity — and in fact it certainly does! — then it may be performed by means of an agent like any other transaction. And if one asserts that the sale does not have halachic validity — then that is equally true even if no agent is employed.

In any case, we do learn two things from this responsum. (1) By the year 5616 the custom of selling all the *chametz* of the city by means of one agent had already "taken root" in Zborov. (2) In 5616, in the great Jewish city of L'vov, this

° [I.e., from the owner to the Rav and from the Rav to the non-Jew. — *Ed.*]

custom was not yet in force.

In Rumania, Rav Aharon Moshe of Yasi most emphatically opposed the idea of the *mechirah clallis*. His grandson, Rav A. Sh. P. Taubes, published a sizeable monograph by his grandfather Rav Aharon Moshe "concerning the new innovation, fabricated out of whole cloth, of performing a *mechirah clallis* for the sale of *chametz*, whereby one man purchases all the leavened products in the city ... and I have already made known in public that this innovation is of no substance, and that I have not heard that this custom has been adopted in any of the communities where great and renowned scholars are in authority."[33] The author goes on to argue at great length against the ruling of Rav Shlomo Kluger of Brodi. *Rashak* replied to the monograph of *Ra'am*, and the author in turn presents counter-arguments upholding the opinion of his grandfather (in the year 5645 — 1885!). In the end, the custom became accepted in Rumania as elsewhere. In the work *She'elas Shalom*[34] by the Rav of Botishan, another grandson of *Ra'am*, we already find the custom referred to as an established fact. The author finds it distressing — "this development seems very bad to me" — but what is to be done? "In any case it is wise to ensure that those appointed as agents are well-known personages of knowledge and intelligence who will understand what to do, so that everything will be carried out according to the *Halachah*."

In Lithuania, it seems, the new custom was accepted without opposition and with no difficulty. Rav Shmuel HaLevi, secretary [of the community] and *dayan* (סָפְרָא — סוּ"ד וְדַיָּינָא) of Bialistok, writes in his responsa, *Bigdei Yesha*:[35] "I have seen fit to explain that which I instituted in the city of Bialistok, that the sale of *chametz* should be done by means of the court of justice (בֵּד"צ), as is known to all ..."[36] And further, "My friend, Rav ... halachic authority and head of the *beis din* in the city of Zablodowa has written to me requesting that I send him the format of the bill of sale for *chametz* by means of the *beis din;* a format which I wrote and instituted here in our congregation of Bialistok ..."[37]

In the work *Reshis Bikurim*[38] by Rav Betzalel HaKohen, *zal,* the chief of the *rabbanim* of Vilna, there is likewise a format for the *harshaah* used in the *mechirah clallis.*[39] In Russia, too, the custom became established at approximately this same period.

The bill-of-sale devised by *Baal HaTanya* for the sale of *chametz* was intended for the individual, rather than the comprehensive, sale [since the latter had not yet been introduced in his time], but in responsa *Tzemach Tzedek*[40] we find two responsa on this subject: one concerning "a city where the local halachic authority is appointed as agent for selling the *chametz*,"[41] and another "in the matter of the sale of *chametz* whereby one Jewish man purchases all the *chametz* from the entire city and then sells all of it to a non-Jew."[42] Thus both methods of carrying out the *mechirah clallis* were presented for his opinion, and he upheld both. In responsa *Be'er Yitzchak* by Rav Yitzchak Elchanan, *zal*,[43] the author speaks of "the *beis din* which is appointed for the transaction of the sale of *chametz*" as a familiar custom. This work was published in the year 5618 (1858), when the author was still Rav of Navardok.

Causes of Doubt The principle causes of doubt which gave rise to opposition against the *mechirah clallis* (in its second form, that involving the *harshaah)* are the following. (1) According to *Mekor Chaim*,[44] an agent does not have the power to sign his name to a bill of sale for the person he represents. (2) According to a number of the *Rishonim*, the main valid means of sale to a non-Jew is by means of money [that is, no matter what the total price may be, the seller must receive at least a minimal coin — *perutah* — in cash, and this is what makes the *kinyan* valid]. When the *chametz* of an entire city is sold to a non-Jew in return for the receipt of a deposit, it may be that the deposit is not large enough so that each resident will receive a *perutah's* worth. Hence, it may be that according to these *Rishonim* the sale would not be valid.

In answer to the first problem, that of the signature, the reply given is that the difficulty can be overcome if the *harshaah*, containing the signatures of all the owners of *chametz*, is attached to the bill-of-sale.[45] And this indeed is the procedure; along with the bill of sale, the Rabbi hands over to the non-Jew the *harshaah* with all its signatures. Moreover, the basic claim of *Mekor Chaim* — that the signature of the appointed agent is not by itself effective — has been discussed by some *Acharonim*, who conclude that the correctness of this assertion is not entirely clear.[46]

As for the second problem — that the money deposited may not be sufficient to ensure that each of the sellers receives at least a *perutah* — some authorities have replied that the requirement that each seller receive a *perutah* does not apply to this kind of transaction; for the matter is discussed in the *Gemara* not in terms of sales of merchandise, but in terms of marriage. In Tractate *Kiddushin*[47] the Talmud asks, "[If one father should say to another,] 'Your two daughters are hereby married to my two sons for a *perutah*,' what is the ruling?" [In marriage, as in sales of merchandise, the transaction is validated by the giving of an object of value which must be worth at least a *perutah*. In the case discussed, the fathers are empowered to perform the marriage transaction of their sons and daughters; hence the two marriages can be accomplished through one transaction between the fathers. The point of doubt raised by the *Gemara* is whether the minimum requirement of a *perutah* applies to the transaction as a whole (and therefore it is valid), or whether it applies to each of the two marriages (in which case this transaction is invalid, since for each bride there is only half a *perutah*). In the words of the Talmud,] "Do we look at the transaction in terms of the giver and receiver [of the *perutah*, i.e., the two fathers], in which case there is [the minimum necessary] money? Or do we look at it in terms of them [i.e., the brides] in which case there is not [the required minimum] money?" [Here the two brides, through the agency of the father, are as it were partners, giving themselves in marriage by means of a single shared *perutah*. The Talmud expresses doubt as to whether such a transaction is valid. Hence one might conclude that any transaction involving partners (for example, the comprehensive sale of *chametz*) is of doubtful validity if those who must be given money receive less than a *perutah* each.

The reply is, however, that the Talmud intended to express doubt only regarding the transaction of marriage. The difference is that in marriage, the brides can be "acquired" only as two separate individuals; the concept of partnership does not apply; each bride must be acquired on her own. This is not the case when a buyer purchases two items (from partners) with a single *perutah*. If, for example, a buyer purchases two cows or two fields, he looks at them not in terms of their individuality, but in terms of their total worth; if one cow or field were worth as much as the two, he could equally well purchase the one in the same way as he purchased the two. (This of course is not the case with two men "acquiring" two women in marriage.) Thus the fact that the *Gemara* raises doubts about a marriage transaction does not mean that the same doubts would arise in the case of two partners who wish to sell two lots of *chametz* with one *perutah*; in the latter case we would certainly view the transaction as a whole, and the *perutah* would be sufficient.[48]

Others solve the problem a different way. [The deposit given is, after all, only a part of the total price; that total is equal to, or more than, the actual worth of the *chametz*, and] the balance not given as a deposit is converted into a loan. These authorities point out that according to many *Rishinom* this loan obligation undertaken by the non-Jew is itself considered "money";[49] hence each seller certainly receives more than a *perutah*.

Variations in Custom

The *mechirah clallis* has by now been accepted in all communities. There are variations of custom, however, with regard to various details. Some follow the practice of writing the *harshaah* as a general power-of-attorney over all the kinds of *chametz* existing in the possession of the signers; they do not specify which kinds of *chametz* are being sold by each individual. Likewise they refer in general to all the rooms and places where the *chametz* is stored, without specifically identifying each room and its contents. But those who wish to be especially meticulous (הַמְהַדְּרִין) are accustomed to draw up a detailed list which specifies the *chametz* of each of the signers, and gives the exact location where it is stored.

Some follow the custom of writing the bill of sale not only in Hebrew but also in the local language. Others — and these are the majority — hold that a document in Hebrew alone is sufficient. Of the variances in custom with regard to the appointment of an *arev-kablan*, a Jewish intermediary who serves as guarantor and contractor for the non-Jew, we have already spoken. One aspect of the sale is common to all, and that is the use, for "maximum security," of many different methods of *kinyan*: the transaction is validated by means of money (קִנְיָן כֶּסֶף); as an adjunct to the sale of real estate (קִנְיָן אַגַּב); by *chalipin* (קִנְיָן סוּדָר; see below, *Ruth*, p. 292); by means of a document (שְׁטָר); and by means of a hand-clap (תְּקִיעַת בַּף).

Four Eras

In surveying the various transformations through which the sale of *chametz* has gone — and without taking into account certain variations in detail which do not constitute basic differences — we have seen that four definite eras in the history of this sale may be distinguished: (1) ordinary, actual sale; (2) complete sale (involving the removal of the *chametz* to the precincts of the purchaser and payment of the full amount of money), but with the intention of re-acquiring the *chametz* from the non-Jew after Pesach, this possibility having been hinted at previous to the sale; (3) a purely legalistic sale, performed by each individual owner of *chametz*; (4) the *mechirah clallis* through the rabbi or *beis din*, in the manner which has now been accepted throughout the entire Dispersion of Israel.

NOTES

[1] *Pesachim* 21a.

[2] *Tosefta, Pesachim,* ch. 1, cited in the Babylonian Talmud, *Shabbos* 18b, and in *Pesachim, loc. cit.,* and in the *Yerushalmi, Pesachim,* ch. 2.

[3] And see the *mishnah* in *Shabbos* 17b.

[4] *Pesachim* 13a.

[5] *Ibid.* 30, 31.

[6] *Pesachim,* ch. 2.

[7] See Rav Sh. Liberman in *Tosefes Rishonim.*

[8] See *Tosefes Rishonim, loc. cit.*

[9] 448.

[10] *Orach Chaim,* sec. 103.

[11] *Loc. cit.*

[12] *Loc. cit.,* para. 3.

[13] *Magen Avraham;* and *Taz,* too, holds this interpretation.

[14] See above, p. 81.

[15] *Bach,* 448.

[16] *Bava Metzia* 77b.

[17] There is a source for this idea in the *Rishonim:* Concerning *Kesubos* 56a, in the matter of a woman who writes a document to her husband stating that she has received a hundred *zuz* of her *kesubah, Shitah Mekubetzes* states that even though ordinarily forgiveness of a debt *(mechilah)* does not require a document, an oral statement being sufficient, nevertheless in this case where the *mechilah* is only *haaramah,* a document is necessary; and see responsa *Shaarei De'ah,* part 1, sec. 5.

[18] Sec. 11.

[19] *Chasam Sofer, Orach Chaim* 113.

[20] Responsa *Divrei Chaim,* part 2, sec. 37.

[21] Part 1, sec. 8.

[22] See *Chasam Sofer, Orach Chaim,* sec. 62; *Mekor Chaim,* sec. 448; *Magen HaElef, loc. cit.; Nishmas Adam, she'alah* 8; responsa *Oneg Yom-Tov,* sec. 28; responsa *Mayim Chaim, Orach Chaim,* sec. 8; *Sdei Chemed, Chametz UMatzah,* sec. 9. *os* 3, and the works cited there; *Archos Chaim,* 448.21, and the works cited there.

[23] See *Tur* and *Shulchan Aruch, Yoreh De'ah* 120.

[24] Responsa *Shivas Tzion,* sec. 11; *Chasam Sofer,* sec. 109; *Chachmas Adam, klal* 73; *Atzei Levonah, Yoreh De'ah,* sec. 120; *et. al.* And see *Shaar HaKolel,* by Rav A.D. Lavaut, on the text of the document of sale of the Rav, *Baal HaTanya* in his *Siddur (os* 17).

[25] *Bava Basra* 125b.

[26] See responsa *Tiferes Yosef, Orach Chaim,* sec. 30; *Sho'el UMeshiv,* first ed., part 1, sec. 211; *et. al.* Both these authors write at length to prove that in this case the firstborn son inherits a double portion of the *chametz.*

[27] *She'eris Yehudah, Orach Chaim,* sec. 10.

[28] In his responsa, *Orach Chaim,* secs. 45 and 48, and in the part entitled *Piskei Dinim, Orach Chaim,* sec. 448.

[29] See *Sdei Chemed, Chametz UMatzah,* sec. 60, and *Maadanei Shmuel,* 114.16, and the works cited by these two authors.

[30] See *Mishpat Kohen,* p. 360.

[31] 448, para. 4.

[32] *Sho'el Umeshiv,* second ed., part 2, sec. 7.

[33] Responsa *Ori VeYishi* (Levov, 5646 — 1886), sec. 121.

[34] Second ed. (Levov, 5645 — 1885), sec. 91.

[35] *Vilna,* 5604 (1844).

[36] Sec. 2.

[37] Sec. 4.

[38] *Vilna,* 5629 (1869).

[39] And see, in responsa *Divrei Malkiel,* part 2, secs. 22-24, a detailed *shtar harshaah,* a detailed *shtar mechirah klallis,* and a full explanation of all the details of the texts of both documents. The text of a *harshaah* for the sale of *chametz* was also printed at the end of the work *Nachalas Shiva,* but Rav A.D. Levaut, in *Shaar HaKolel,* correctly observes that this document was not formulated by the author of *Nachalas Shiva,*

and contains "several things which are in contradiction to the *Halachah*."

[40] The author died on the thirteenth of Nissan, 5626 (1866).

[41] Sec. 46.

[42] Sec. 48.

[43] Sec. 1.

[44] 448, para. 8.

[45] See responsa *Divrei Nechemiah, Orach Chaim*, sec. 35; responsa *Reshis Bikurim*, sec. 5; responsa *Bigdei Yesha*, sec. 4; *Shaar HaKolel*, on *Siddur Torah Or, os* 11; *et. al.*

[46] See responsa *Bigdei Yesha, loc. cit.*; responsa *Chelkas Yoav, Orach Chaim*, sec. 22; *et. al.*

[47] *Kiddushin* 7b.

[48] Responsa *Chelkas Yoav, loc. cit.* And see *She'ilas David*, by Rav David Friedman of Carlin, *Ishus*, part 1, ch. 3, sec. 137; both these authors cite the *Yerushalmi, Kesubos* 5:1: "A man may acquire two items of real estate for the equivalent of a *prutah*, but a man may not acquire two wives for the equivalent of a *prutah*."

[49] See *Sdei Chemed*, sec. 9, *os* 6; responsa *Devar Avraham*, part 1, sec. 39; responsa *Divrei Malkiel*, part 4, sec. 24, *os* 56, and 58; *et. al.* The author of *Devar Avraham* deals in especially great depth with this concept of a money obligation. He also uses the concept to interpret the *mishnah* in *Gitin* 41a which states, "If a person is half slave and half free ... we compel his owner to free him and he writes him a *shtar* for half his worth ..." This means, says the author, that it is by writing him the *shtar* for half his worth that the owner frees him, for the obligation is considered like money, and a non-Jewish slave goes free by means of money. It should be noted, however, that in the same *Gemara*, 45a, in the case of the slave who escaped from outside *Eretz Yisrael* to *Eretz Yisrael*, it is stated: "Let a *shtar* be written to you for his worth, and you write him a bill of release." Here it is explicit that the *shtar* of financial obligation by itself does not accomplish the release.

קְטְנִיּוֹת בְּפֶסַח &

Kitnios on Pesach

The Talmud tells us (Tractate Yevamos 20a) that it is not enough to abstain from those things which the Torah explicitly forbade us, for HaShem has commanded us to be a holy nation. Indeed, one who defies this rule is not only disqualified from being called holy: he is in fact called a sinner. At any rate, to qualify for inclusion in the holy congregation, the condition is laid down: "Sanctify yourself by refraining even from such things as are allowed" — if indulgence in these things could lead even remotely to the realm of that which is forbidden.

In the Halachah we often encounter debates as to whether certain actions do or do not entail punishment. If the decision is against punishment we say the offender is patur. There are likewise questions as to whether certain items are forbidden or permitted. If the decision is that a particular item is permitted, halachic language says the item is mutar. Making a play on the similarity of these two words to the Yiddish for "father" (fatter) and "mother" (mutter), a well-loved chassidic Rebbe of the pre-war era, Rabbi Yisrael Hager of Vizhnitz זצ"ל, explained the proximity of two verses in Leviticus (19:2 and 19:3). The first verse commands us to be holy; the next, to fear our father and mother. With this in mind the Rebbe would jocularly say: "Always be afraid of doing something objectionable, even if by strictly legalistic criteria you may be fatter (patur), and beware of enjoying anything doubtful, even if technically it qualifies as mutter (mutar)."

Pesach can be said to be the supreme example of how Am Yisrael has rejected anything whose permissibility could be questioned and debated — even if the answer of the letter of the law is patur or mutar. The prohibition against eating kitnios on Pesach is but one such case which, as the author explains in this chapter, all Ashkenazi Jewry has in the course of time accepted as binding.

T he problem of *kitnios*° has been a topic of discussion in the literature of *Halachah* for the past seven hundred years. The problem has given rise to much debate, concerning both the essential question — whether there is any reason at all to forbid the eating of *kitnios* on Pesach — and resultant issues (food products made from *kitnios*, the use of *kitnios* in times of special difficulty — שְׁעַת הַדְּחָק — and others).

No Possibility of Chametz

The *Halachah* has determined that concerning *kitnios* themselves there is no possibility whatsoever of their becoming *chametz* — and on this point no one has ever disagreed. It is the five species referred to as "grain' *(dagan)* which can be used to fulfill the obligation of *matzah*, and it is they which can become forbidden as *chametz*. This linkage between *chametz* and *matzah* is derived by the Talmud from a verse. "The Torah says, *Do not eat chametz with (the Pesach sacrifice); for seven days you shall eat matzos with it* (לֹא תֹאכַל עָלָיו חָמֵץ שִׁבְעַת יָמִים תֹּאכַל עָלָיו מַצּוֹת): *Deuteronomy* 16:3). [This teaches us that] things which are capable of fermentation *(chimutz)* may be used by a person to fulfill the obligation of *matzah*; this excludes those things (rice, millet) which are not capable of fermentation, but of rotting *(sirchon)*."[1] Rambam[2] explains the law in further detail. "The prohibition of *chametz* on Pesach involves only the five kinds of *dagan* — but *kitnios*, such as rice, millet, beans, lentils, and the like cannot be *chametz*; rather, even if one kneads rice flour or the like in boiling water and covers it with a cloth until it swells up like dough which has fermented (הֶחְמִיץ), this is permitted for eating [on Pesach], for this is not *chimutz*, but *sirchon*." Rabbi Yochanan ben Nuri, it is true, holds that rice is a species of *dagan*, but his opinion is rejected as *Halachah* and the Talmud tells us that "there is no one who takes this opinion of Rabbi Yochanan ben Nuri into account for practical purposes."[3]

Early Sources for the Prohibition

The earliest source for the prohibition of *kitnios* is found in *Semak (Sefer Mitzvos Katan)* by *Ri* of Corbeil. Not that he was the first to deduce a new prohibition; rather, he records a fact: "The people have been accustomed to prohibit [*kitnios* on Pesach] since the days of the early Sages." *Semak* was

° [The term "grain" (דָּגָן) in *Halachah* is restricted to five species: wheat, barley, spelt, oats, and rye (חִיטִים, שְׁעוֹרִים, כּוּסְמִין, שִׁיבּוֹלֶת שׁוּעָל, וְשִׁיפוֹן). All other edible seeds, except those that grow on trees, are included in the term *kitnios* (קַטְנִיוֹת). Thus the term includes, for example, rice and millet; beans, peas, lentils, and peanuts; sesame, sunflower seeds, and corn. — *Ed.*]

written in the first half of the first century of the sixth millennium[4] [around 1240] and already at that time this prohibition was an ancient custom, although not one accepted unanimously. These are the author's words.[5] "Concerning *kitnios* such as beans, rice, lentils and the like, our rabbis have practiced a general prohibition against eating them on Pesach. And it seems to me that I have heard concerning [the type of beans called] *pulim* that they should not be cooked on Pesach except in water which is already boiling when they are placed in the pot; though there are great rabbis who are accustomed to permit them. My teacher, Rabbeinu Yechiel, was accustomed to eat *pul halavan*, white *pulim*, called Poiche [in medieval French], and he also used to cite great rabbis as affirming this custom; as proof he noted that even as regards rice, which Rabbi Yochanan ben Nuri considers a species of *dagan* with respect to *chimutz*, the Talmud states that there is no one who takes this opinion of Rabbi Yochanan ben Nuri into account for practical purposes. However, it is very difficult to permit a thing which the people have treated as a prohibition from the days of the early Sages; for on the face of it they did not institute this prohibition because of any danger of actual *chimutz*, for they would not have erred in a matter with which every schoolchild is familiar, as explicitly stated in Tractate *Pesachim* — namely, that only the five kinds of *dagan* are capable of *chimutz*. Therefore it seems to me that the prohibition must be upheld, and that *kitnios* should be forbidden on Pesach. And this, not because of actual *chimutz*, for it is an error to claim this; rather, the reason for the prohibition is a precautionary decree *(gezarah)*; for since *kitnios* are used to make cooked dishes (מַעֲשֵׂה קְדֵרָה הוּא) and *dagan* is likewise used to make cooked dishes; and since *kitnios* are harvested in a way similar to the harvesting and piling up of *dagan* (מִידֵי דְּמִידְּגַן הוּא) ... and also there are places where the people are in the habit of making bread from *kitnios* as from the five kinds of *dagan* — therefore those who are not well-versed in Torah could come to confuse the two [types of food, and make the error of eating one of the five types of *dagan* on Pesach because of its similarity to *kitnios*]; and they are not similar to the vegetables [i.e., those things eaten as leaves, stems, roots, or fruit rather than seeds] ... and it is a proper custom to refrain from all species of *kitnios*, as I have explained ... Despite the fact that the Talmud permits rice [on Pesach], that was only in those days, when all were expert in the laws of forbidden and permitted things; but now in these latter generations it is certainly necessary to enact a precautionary *gezerah* ... and it should be forbidden even to put them into water which is already boiling, lest people draw the conclusion that cold water is also permitted."

The author of *Mordechai*, who was the brother-in-law of the author of *Semak*, cites his words. " ... Indeed, my brother-in-law, Rav Yitzchak of Corbeil, has written in *Sefer Mitzvos Katan* which he composed ..." (At this point *Mordechai* cites *Semak* from the words "it seems to me that the prohibition must be upheld ..." to the end of the passage). *Mordechai* then concludes: "And Rabbeinu Baruch and Rabbeinu Shimshon of Evreux did not eat *kitnios* on Pesach, but Rabbi Yechiel of Paris was accustomed to eat *pul halavan*, which is called Poiche."[6]

Beis Yosef[7] cites *Semak*, not from the original, but from a quotation thereof in *Hagahos Maimonios*[8], and with the addition of one futher explanation: "And it also sometimes happens that produce [of the five kinds] becomes mixed in with [*kitnios*] and it is impossible to sort through it properly." This problem of the mixing of produce is also recorded by *Tur*[9] in the name of "those who forbid it" (יֵשׁ אוֹסְרִין), but this author concludes: "This is an excessive stringency and is not the custom." And in *Toldos Adam VeChavah* by Rabbeinu Yerucham[10] we read, "And the practice followed by some, not to eat rice and species of *kitnios* cooked on Pesach, is an erroneous custom (מִנְהָג שְׁטוּת); the only explanation is that they have chosen to be strict with themselves, and I do not know why." *Beis Yosef* states, "There are none who take this opinion into account, *except for the Ashkenazim*" [the Jewry of the region of Germany]. This informs us that by the time of *Beis Yosef* the custom had already been generally accepted among Ashkenazic Jewry.

"We ...
Follow
the
Stringent
Custom"

In *Darkei Moshe*, by *Rama*, this author adds to the words of *Beis Yosef*, "And we the inhabitants of the Ashkenazic region follow the stringent custom." And even earlier than this we find a record, in the work of *Maharil* (d. 5187 — 1427) of the firm establishment of this prohibition in the land of Ashkenaz. *Maharil*, of course, is the foundation and pillar of our knowledge of the religious life and milieu of the Ashkenazim. And in his *Hilchos Pesach* he cites *Maharash* (i.e., Rav Shalom of Austria, his teacher): "*Maharash* states that by a rabbinic decree (*gezerah*) *kitnios* of all kinds are forbidden for cooking on Pesach, in spite of the fact that it is only the five kinds of *dagan* which ferment and become *chametz* ... and a person should not say to himself that since this is not a Scriptural prohibition it need not be taken into account; for whenever the Sages make a decree, he who violates it is worthy of the death penalty and furthermore, is in violation of the Scriptural commandment, *You shall not stray from the thing which they shall instruct you* (לֹא תָסוּר מִן הַדָּבָר אֲשֶׁר יַגִּידוּ לְךָ; *Deuteronomy* 17:11).° Likewise, one should not say, 'The custom in this place is to permit these things,' for [the custom of permitting them] is an erroneous one ... When the prohibition of a thing is widespread within a certain region and someone within that region claims that in his particular locality the prohibition was not adopted, [it is appropriate to apply the verse,] *the mouth shall be closed up of those who speak falseness* (יִסָּכֵר פִּי דוֹבְרֵי שָׁקֶר; *Psalms* 63:12). And even if one attributes his position to a sage, it is vanity and falseness that that 'prophet' has spoken, and if the sage were there he himself would refute the deceit and vanity and throw it back in his face."

To such an extent was this prohibition accepted, that it was possible for a question like the following to deserve the attention of one of the great early *poskim*, *Ri* Isserlin (d. 5220 — 1460), author of *Trumas HaDeshen*. This authority was asked about "produce in the category of *kitnios*, which is not of the five kinds [of *dagan*], upon which water has fallen, and which almost certainly has fermented (literally, 'become *chametz*') — whether it is permissible *to keep it in one's possession* on Pesach, or not?"[11] The reply is that keeping it in one's possession is permitted — in the author's words, "They [the Sephardim] permit eating it and we should not permit keeping it in one's possession?"

A second statement in this same responsum provides more evidence of the extent to which this prohibition had become an ingrained assumption. The *posek* rules that "If a seed of one of the kinds of *kitnios* is found in the pot or in the cooked food, we do not at all follow a strict line by declaring the food forbidden; we do not even forbid it for eating [let alone for other uses] — for the *gezerah* which prohibits a mixture containing even a tiny amount of forbidden substance [rather than setting a minimum percentage below which the prohibition does not apply] affects only produce in the category of the five kinds."

The opinions of Rav Yosef Caro and Rav Moshe Isserles have already been cited above from their works, *Beis Yosef* and *Darkei Moshe*. These same two authorities give their

° [See appendix to vol. II of the present work, p. 336. — *Ed.*]

positions expression as fixed *Halachah* in *Shulchan Aruch*.[12] The *Mechaber* (Rav Yosef Caro) states, "Rice and the other types of *kitnios* are not capable of becoming *chametz*, and it is permissible to use them as the ingredients of cooked dishes [on Pesach]" — on which *Rama* (Rav Moshe Isserles comments, "But there are those who forbid this, and the custom in Ashkenaz is to be stringent, *and one should not deviate from the custom.*"

A
Source
in the
Talmud

All the *Acharonim* cite it as a given fact, without elaboration, that the Ashkenazic custom is to forbid *kitnios*. It is interesting that the only exception, who does not rest satisfied to cite the *halachah* as a custom, but searches out a source for it in the Talmud, is a Sephardic authority, *Pri Chadash*. The source he finds is in Tractate *Pesachim*[13] where we find that Rava objects to the custom of allowing flour to be stirred into a pot on Pesach, even with flour made from lentils[14] in "a place where there are many slaves" who tend to be negligent about prohibitions.[15]°

Strong
Opposition

Strong words against the custom of prohibiting *kitnios* are found in responsa *Besamim Rosh*, attributed to Rabbeinu Asher, or *Rosh*.[16] This work states that "This [custom] is an outlandish thing, for the matter is explicitly permitted in the *Gemara*, and we are informed of no *beis din* in any place which ever enacted a decree in the matter." "We should not search out reasons and justifications for something which a part [of the people have done], not eating [*kitnios*] in certain communities." The work also contains the following strange speculation. "It is likely that it is due to the expulsions and the [resultant] confusions *(bilbulim,* i.e., the intermixing and disorientation of previously stable communities)" that this custom arose, for "In the first expulsion, that of *Monzon,* there was also a small community of Karaites amongst them; these [apostates] were expelled and were ensconced among us by going with us in the expulsion, and they did not recognize any distinction between one kind of bread and another, believing that all types [of seeds used for making flour] produce *chametz.*" The passage concludes: "Those who follow this stringency are destined to answer to judgment." However, as is known, charges of being a forgery have been leveled against this work, the claim being that it was actually the product of Rav Saul Levin, who had come under the

° [Since if you allow them flour made of lentils they will next do it with actual flour. — *Ed.*]

influence of the *maskilim* of the "Berlin enlightenment." These charges were verified, and hence the book is studied only in terms of its contents, but not in terms of its attributed authorship.

One of the great *Acharonim*, however, Rav Yaakov Emden, also came out with harsh words against the prohibition of *kitnios*. In his work, *Mor UKetzia*[17] he writes, "I can testify concerning my father and teacher, the Gaon, *zatzal (Chacham Tzvi)* how greatly this *tzaddik* was distressed by this [custom]. Every year at the festival of *matzos* he would grumble, saying 'If I had the strength I would annul this inferior custom, which by its very strictness leads to laxity (that is, those who follow the custom are forced to bake a large amount of *matzos* and hence are not sufficiently careful in the baking) ... therefore I declare, May my portion be with him who annuls this custom of refraining from eating *kitnios*. Would that the great men of the generation in this region would agree with me — I am ready to be included as an accessory in the mitzvah [of annulling this custom].' "

A Consensus of "Complete Validity"

"Would that they agree with me — " but not only did they not agree with *Chacham Tzvi* but quite the contrary, all the great Torah scholars who dealt with the problem of *kitnios* granted complete validity to the prohibition.[18] The journal, *Jahrbuch der Judische Literarischen Gesellschaft*,[19] published a declaration from the city of Furth in the year 5570 (1810) concerning "the bad tidings which have been heard in recent times here in our community — whoever hears [such tidings] should stop up both ears — to the effect that a few men occupying chairs of judgment in a certain country have risen up and broken through the fence made by the early Sages, and which has been practiced and accepted by the majority of the Exile. These men have placed a stumbling block in the way by permitting the eating of rice and millet and all species of *kitnios* on the *Yom-Tov* of Pesach. Woe to the ears who hear this! ... The whole land of Greater Poland and Lesser Poland, the land of Lithuania, the lands of Bohemia and Moravia, and the entire land of Ashkenaz [Germany], as well as every place where *Ashkenazim* dwell, have practiced and accepted upon themselves the aforementioned prohibition for the past four hundred years (here the declaration is less than precise; the history of the prohibition goes back even further; see above), and on this matter the prohibition remains in force forever, and there is no way to make it permissible ... and "whoever breaks down a fence, a snake shall bite him" (see *Ecclesiastes*

10:8) — for the serpent of the Sages there is no antidote" (see *Shabbos* 110a).

In the year 5601 (1841) there appeared a pamphlet entitled *Ashru Chamutz* (lit., "verify fermentation"), in which the author demands that the halachic authorities nullify the prohibition against *kitnios*. By way of reply, Rav Shmuel Freund, "judge and *posek* in the city of Prague" (דַּיָן וּמוֹ"צ בק"ק פְּרָאג), published the pamphlet *Keren Shmuel*, in which he demonstrates at length that no one has the authority to make these prohibited items *(kitnios)* permissible.

The Products of Kitnios: Oil

The products of *kitnios* — principally, oil — are also included within the prohibition. This may be inferred from a ruling given by *Trumas HaDeshen*.[20] This author gives permission *to kindle lights* by means of oil from *kitnios*, since the custom of prohibiting these products applies only to eating them, but not to deriving benefit from them. The author does mention, however, that "it seems to me that there is a general custom to prohibit the use of oils from *kitnios* for the kindling of lights on Pesach."

Maharil finds it necessary to warn against suspending above the dining table a candelabrum that contains the oil of *kitnios* — lest some of the oil fall into the food. On the other hand, *Rama*, in both *Darkei Moshe* and *Shulchan Aruch*, permits such a candlebrum over the table, explaining that there is no problem even if some of the oil should fall into the food, since there was never any *gezerah* against mixtures containing *kitnios (taaroves kitnios)*, but only against *kitnios* [and their products] themselves. In responsa *Tzemach Tzedek*[21] the author writes, "In order to make things easier for the poor in difficult times, one should be lenient in the matter of making oil from species of *kitnios*, if this is done in such a way that the *kitnios* are placed in a hot oven before being moistened for grinding (i.e., before *lesisah* — לְתִיתָה), and if the oven used is very hot, to the point that the *kitnios* are as if baked." (The author brings proof from the *Gemara* that, once baked, even flour of the five kinds of *dagan* is no longer capable of becoming *chametz*.)

In *Marcheshes*[22] there is a long discussion of "the seeds called 'Razen' and whether or not it is permissible to make oil from them on Pesach." This species, the author justly argues, is not the same as what the Mishnah calls *sumsumin* (שׁוּמְשׁוּמִין), even though such a possibility might be suggested by the fact that the latter name seems to derive from the word "sun" (שֶׁמֶשׁ), while Razen, too, whose structure and appearance are sunlike, is referred to by names containing the word "sun" in both German *(Sonnenblume)* and Russian. The author is not correct, however, in "proving" that Razen is identical to what the Mishnah calls *Shoshanas HaMelech*. Linguistic researchers — Kohut, Low, and others — prove that *Shoshanas HaMelech* of the Mishnah is the flower called אנמנה in modern Hebrew [anemone in English], and that "sunlikeness" plays no part in the name of that plant.

With regard to the oil, *Marcheshes* permits its use on two conditions: first, that the seeds be scalded (חֲלִיטָה) before grinding; and second, that they be searched for any seeds of other kinds which may be mixed in with them (the purpose being, of course, to eliminate any admixture of *dagan*). Under these conditions, neither of the two reasons for prohibiting the oil of *kitnios* exists. The problem of confusing *kitnios* with *dagan* is eliminated, for this would do no harm since strictly according to the law even *dagan* may be used for making oil if scalded beforehand. And the problem of a possible admixture of *dagan* is eliminated also, by the careful searching of the grain — and in addition, by the precaution of producing the oil only before Pesach, since with a mixture produced before Pesach, any *chametz* which may accidentally have entered into it is considered nullified if it constitutes less than one-sixtieth of the total.[23] The author writes at length to establish a general principle concerning oil made from *kitnios:* Since the entire prohibition of *kitnios* is derived purely from the fact that it is a long-standing and universally accepted custom (among Ashkenazim), it has the legal force of a vow, or *neder*. And the law is that if one makes a *neder* not to eat a certain kind of fruit, a liquid made from that fruit is still permissible to him. The only reason, then, why the oil of *kitnios* is prohibited is the problem of possible admixture of *dagan*. Hence the two precautionary measures — careful searching to eliminate seeds of *dagan*, and preparing the oil before Pesach — are sufficient to make the oil permissible.

If the author of *Marcheshes* thus advised in general that the oil of *kitnios*, properly prepared, could be used on Pesach, the Gaon Rav Avraham Yitzchak Kook gave a direct ruling along the same lines during the time of his rabbinate in Jaffa, with regard to sesame oil. The permission granted by Rav Kook involved broader precautions than that of *Marcheshes*. Rather than simply stipulating the scalding of the seeds, Rav Kook ruled that they must be guarded against all contact with water; and not only that, but the machinery which produced the oil operated in such a way that it was incapable of functioning except in complete absence of moisture. Nevertheless, this permission caused an uproar in Jerusalem. The "court of justice (בַּד״ץ) of all of the congregations of the Ashkenazim — *Perushim* and *Chassidim* — in Jerusalem, may it be rebuilt and established" launched protests and forbade the oil. Under the auspices of "the oil-press of the brothers Breslau of Jaffa" a booklet was published with the title, "Monograph on the Subject of the Permission Granted for Oil Made from Dry Sesame, not Moistened before Grinding, and Guarded for the sake of Pesach." This work presents the replies of Rav Kook to the aforementioned court of justice *(Badatz)* of Jerusalem; it establishes in detail the underlying reasons for the permission.

"Yash" In responsa *Be'er Yitzchak*,[24] the author replies to a query about *yash* (יֵין שָׂרוּף, spiritous liquor) made from a type of *kitnios* referred to as "*retshke*, which is also called *grika* (buckwheat)." The author permits this drink on condition that the seeds are searched for *dagan* before Pesach. Any problem of *taaroves* is thus eliminated by the fact that the *chametz* would be nullified if it is less than one-sixtieth of the total; and there is a rule that "Once one liquid has become subsumed (and hence nullified) within another liquid, it cannot later become significant again"° — לַח בְּלַח אֵינוֹ חוֹזֵר וְנִיעוֹר. In dealing with the second problem, that of confusing *kitnios* with *dagan* (i.e., the possibility that someone observing the use of liquor made from these seeds might come to make liquor from the five kinds of grain), this author introduces a novel halachic principle. In Tractate *Sukkah*[25] it is explained that when the Sages make a decree to prevent possible wrong conclusions, the decree does not apply if some positive action is taken to make it clear that the person understands the underlying principle. [The case in *Sukkah* has to do with the *gezerah* against using wide boards for the roof of the *sukkah*. Since these resemble the ceiling of a house, someone might be led to think that sitting in the house is as good as sitting in the *sukkah*, not realizing that a *sukkah* is valid only if the roof is expressly made to serve as the roof of a *sukkah*. The Talmud explains that if one takes some positive action, such as removing one of the wide boards of

° [If *chametz* is indistinguishably mixed with non-*chametz*, and is less than one-sixtieth of the total, the *chametz* is considered nullified. This is true, however, only if the mixture came about before Pesach. The same kind of mixture, if produced during Pesach, would be prohibited, since even the tiniest quantity of *chametz* cannot be considered nullified during the festival. Our rule tells us that a small amount (less than 1/60) of *chametz* which was subsumed and nullified in a mixture before Pesach does not become halachically significant again even when the festival arrives. — *Ed.*]

his (unplastered) ceiling and then replacing it for the sake of the *sukkah*, thus demonstrating that he understands the necessary prerequisite, the *gezerah* does not apply.]

Here, too, the careful searching of the seeds and the practice of making the liquor only before Pesach are positive actions which prove that the underlying principle is understood; thus here, too, the *gezerah* against *kitnios* and their products does not apply.

In responsa *Emek Halachah* by Rav Zev Wolf of Zetl,[26] the author writes at great length to permit *yash* made from "*grika*" and concludes: "Let a suffering people drink and forget its poverty and take pleasure in *Hashem* and rejoice in Him.'

An issue all its own is the question of baking *matzos* from the flour of *kitnios*. It seems like a strange vision, but it is nonetheless true that there were times and instances when pious men of devout deeds, fearing lest not enough care was used in the preparation of their *matzos*, would take the "especially meticulous" (הידור) measure of baking *matzos* from the flour of *cosemes (grika* in Yiddish), since this cannot become *chametz*. It never occurred to them that this might involve violation of the *gezerah* against *kitnios*. But we find in the works of responsa that *grika* was considered as possibly falling in the category of *kitnios*, and that stringency was advised.

In responsa *Maamar Mordechai*[27] the author is asked whether, in a year of high prices, it is permissible to make *matzos* from *kukurizen kemach*, corn flour, which is a kind of *kitnios*. It would seem at first glance that if these are baked with all the precautions applied to real *matzos*, what problem could arise? Someone might be led to do the same with real *matzos*? Let him do so as much as he likes! The author, however, rules otherwise. "How could it enter the mind of my distinguished correspondent to break through a fence established by the *Rishonim*; and what [difference does it make] even if the species of *kitnios* and *kukurizen kemach* are used to make *matzos*? Is it not certain that one type of flour will come to be confused with another? ... and people should not be lenient in this matter by saying, 'But we make these *matzos* before Pesach and they are guarded during the baking according to all the regulations applying to *matzos* made from the five kinds, and if so, how could anyone be led into error?' On the contrary, it is for this very reason that this is forbidden; for since all are scholars and know that the Torah

Matzos from Kitnios

says that these species involve no danger of *chametz* whatsoever, therefore they will come to be lenient with them, using them to make [*matzos*] even during Pesach; and flour certainly can become confused with flour — the result will be that they will do the same with flour of the five kinds." (But, after all is said and done, what harm is there in this?)

Likewise, in the responsa of *Mahariaz* (Rav Yekusiel Asher Zalman Enzel Zausmer) of Stry[28] the author raises much clamor against those who wished to rule that it is permissible to eat "a cooked dish made from *kemach kukuruz*, or bread baked with this same flour — even if they are baked before Pesach." This author, however, does not state explicitly that the prohibition applies as well to baking such flour in the form of *matzos*, according to all the laws governing the making of *matzos* from wheat flour — though from his words it would seem likely that he, too, prohibits the use of corn flour even in this way.

Chasam Sofer[29] likewise is asked about a year of high prices and hunger, when "a certain scholar in that city brought forth the idea of making *matzos* from the flour of Turkish wheat (i.e., corn) ... and they would bake *matzos* [from corn flour] with all the precise precautions taken when making *matzos* [from wheat or other *dagan*]." *Chasam Sofer* proves at length that this species (corn) is not a type of *dagan* but rather a type of *kitnios* and "Therefore, if we are to permit the making of *matzos* from these aforementioned חִיטֵי תּוֹגַרְמָה (corn kernels), it should in any case be done according to all the *halachos* of *matzah* and all the statutes [regulating the baking of *matzah* on] Pesach — the kneading must be done with water which has stood overnight (מַיִם שֶׁלָּנוּ), and only with cold water, without salt, and in a place fit for the baking of actual *matzos*, with all the details of their preparation." But the author goes on to require that a special mark of distinction (הֶכֵּר) be made to ensure that people will not mistakenly attempt to use these *matzos* to fulfill the mitzvah of eating *matzah* on the first night of Pesach.

Chasam Sofer originates a further stringency. He states that if the corn flour should become mixed with a small amount of wheat flour or the dough thereof, there is danger that the dough of *kitnios* will prevent the heat of the oven from completely reaching the wheat dough, so that it will not be properly baked and may become actual *chametz*. Hence he warns that at the time of grinding the corn flour, the mills must be cleaned of all wheat flour.[30]

The author of *Chayei Adam*[31] states it as a simple fact that "it is, however, permissible to grind and bake *(kitnios)* in the form of *matzos*, and to eat them." And we have already mentioned the innovation of *Be'er Yitzchak*, concerning the performance of a "positive action" which shows that the person understands the reason for the *gezerah*. On this basis, *Be'er Yitzchak*[32] goes even further then our other authorities in the matter of *matzos* made from *kitnios*. "For this reason," he writes, "there is no objection to the custom followed by all (!), to bake *matzos* from *retshke* [buckwheat] if the seeds are carefully searched for seeds of *dagan* before Pesach. And at the time of baking *one need not be concerned to bake them in the same manner as matzos of wheat ...*" — this, because the sorting and grinding before Pesach constitute the necessary "positive action" which makes the *gezerah* against *kitnios* inapplicable.[33]

All that has been discussed up to now applies in normal times. But what is the law concerning *kitnios* בְּשָׁעַת הַדְּחָק, in times of distress — famine or drought? The author of *Chayei Adam* states simply that *"Bishe'as hadechak* when a person manages only with difficulty to have food to eat, it is permissible to cook *kitnios* and the like." But the matter is not so simple. Whenever times of distress, *she'as hadechak*, actually occurred, the sages of the generation had to grapple with the problem in depth.

In Times of Distress

Nishmas Adam[34] records that "I have heard that in the city of Furth, in the year 5531-32 (1771-2), when there was a great famine in Ashkenaz, a *beis din* was convened and they gave permission to eat *bulbes*, which are called *erdeppel* (potatoes); for in the German region (Ashkenaz) they also do not eat *bulbes*, since in that area flour is made from them; and they also permitted *kitnios*, but not the species of *gropen* (groats) [since the latter more closely resemble the five kinds of *daggan*].

In the year 5570 (1810), there was another period of *she'as hadechak* in the state of Westphalia in Germany, and the Consistory gave permission to eat *kitnios* on Pesach. It is to this year that Maharatz Chayos refers in *Minchas Kenaos:*[35] "It was thirty years ago that a Rav Leib, *zal*, head of the *beis din* of Kassel in the state of Westphalia, along with the other rabbis of Ashkenaz, permitted the eating of *kitnios* during Pesach at a time of high prices; it was a time of emergency, and Rav Zev Heidenheim published a special essay on this matter. However, many great scholars of that time — among them, the great rabbis of the *beis din* of Prague, Rav Elazar

Flekeles, *zal*, and Rav Shmuel Landau, *zal*, rose up to annul the ruling of those authorities ...'' Maharatz Chayos goes on to argue that it is not within our power to annul this prohibition of *kitnios*, even in *she'as hadechak*. It was this granting of permission in Westphalia which prompted the declaration from Furth, cited above, about ''bad tidings.''[36] A similar declaration was also published in Prague, as recorded in responsa *Teshuvah MeAhavah* by Rav Elazar Flekeles.[37] His responsum is from the year 5570 (1810). He argues at great length that no *beis din* in the world has the power to annul this prohibition which has been established as custom ''in all the cities of Germany, France, Greater and Lesser Poland, Lithuania, Russia, Bohemia, Hungary, Moravia, and Silesia ...'' His conclusion is that ''Even if they were to convene the *beis din* of [the Prophet] Samuel the Ramatite, and Elijah the Prophet and his *beis din*, and all the great scholars of Israel together with them, they would not, in my humble opinion, have the power to permit rice and the species of *kitnios* on Pesach.''

In *Chasam Sofer*,[38] too, we find a responsum from that same year (5570) ''concerning the Consistory of the state of Westphalia, who sought to uproot established *halachos* taught us by our ancestors and rabbis, namely, the custom of forbidding the species of *kitnios*.'' But *Chasam Sofer* does not set forth to the fray with weapons of thunder and lightning — on the contrary, ''Since they have permitted this thing, perhaps they know for what reason they permitted it, and we must judge them with a presumption of merit, for it may be that their eyes beheld the emergence of many pitfalls through the baking of thick *matzos* ... and if it was for this reason that they acted, then it is well that they acted; however, they should have cautioned that the *kitnios* must be put into water which is already boiling ... But — הָא לְהוּ וְהָא לָן — 'that is their [ruling], and this is ours' — For us, where thank God we have no need of this precaution, it is clear that these species are not to be permitted.'' After demonstrating at great length that there is no way for these things to be permitted, he concludes: ''And this with the understanding that no inferences are to be drawn whatsoever concerning the people of Westphalia, for I have no authority in that matter.''

Among those who explicitly rule on the side of stringency even in *she'as hadechak* and for the needs of a specific time are *Tzemach Tzedek, Maamar Mordechai, Riaz Enzel*,[39] and others.

On the other hand, we have responsum of *Maharim* Padvah of Brisk[40] "in the matter of those who have asked me to permit them this year, 5613 (1853) on the festival of Pesach to eat *beblich* (beans), which is a species of *kitnios* — the custom of prohibition has already been established in this land, and they ask whether it is in our power to permit this at a time of distress and a year of hunger when the poor can barely find food to eat ..." His opinion is that "In a matter which was instituted as a fence (סְיָיג) [against infringement of a given *halachah*] or for the sake of self-restraint (פְּרִישׁוּת), we have no power to permit it decisively and to nullify the *gezerah* entirely. However, in a situation where permission is necessary in accordance with the conditions of the times (חַיֵי שָׁעָה) — (those who instituted the prohibition) did not have in mind to include such a situation in it at all." His proofs are drawn, among others, from the *mishnah* which states, "The poor may be fed *demai*,"[41] and that which states, "Four things were exempted from prohibition in the camp."[42] [The first of these two *mishnayos* informs us that when the Sages prohibited eating *demai*, produce about which we are not certain that the Levite's portion has been taken out, they did not include the poor in their prohibition. The second lists four other Rabbinic laws from which exemption was made for the special circumstances of an army camp on the move in time of war. In both *mishnayos*, the point is, according to the author, that in framing their original decree the Sages had in mind from the outset that exemption would be made for certain special circumstances. — *Ed.*] The author goes even further. "If we permit these things for the poor but not for the rich, we shall eliminate for [the poor] the joy of *Yom-Tov*, for they will think [concerning the food they are eating] 'there is something forbidden about this.'" Therefore *Maharim* Padvah's position is that these foods should be permitted for everyone, both rich and poor, under these circumstances.

The issue is likewise considered by the author of *Divrei Malkiel*,[43] who writes a responsum "concerning the fact that this year (5640 — 1880) prices have risen very high and it is difficult to acquire even potatoes; and for this reason the authorities in a number of places have permitted eating *kitnios* on Pesach. Here, too, I have been requested to permit them this ..." On the one hand, this author criticizes at length the position of *Maharim* of Brisk — "Far be it from us to assert, as he does, that the *gezeros* of the Sages were given to be subject to the judgment of the [current] *beis din* according to the needs of the time." A number of proofs for this point are

Two Rationales for Permission

brought from the *Gemara* and from the *poskim.* On the other hand, this author, too, permits *kitnios* at *she'as hadechak* — but he gives the permission a different halachic basis. The Talmud tells us that a person is released from a vow he has made if circumstances beyond his control prevent him from fulfilling it — נְדְרֵי אוֹנְסִין מוּתָּרִים. Now, the binding authority of an established custom is derived halachically from the fact that the custom is regarded as a vow undertaken by the community. If so, the rules relating to a custom should not be any more strict than those of an actual vow. [That is, a custom, too, should be regarded as no longer binding if circumstances make its fulfillment impossible.] The author concludes: "Since the entire basis of the permission is the aspect of compulsion and distress, therefore the permission can apply only to the poor who suffer distress, and not to the rich ... but *Maharim,* who extends the permission even to the rich, does so on the basis of his own way of understanding this issue; namely, that the sages of each generation have the power to make adjustments in the Rabbinic decree itself, according to need. But according to what I have already written, that far be it from us to tamper with the decree itself, and the only justification for granting permission is in cases of compulsion by circumstances beyond one's control, hence no permission can be granted except to those who are in such circumstances. And in truth, in the light of what has been related to us, the decision of the Gaon, *Maharim,* was a very good one in his time, which was a period of terribly high prices, and also a time when 'there was not a penny' in people's pockets. It must certainly be that the *tzaddik* realized that there were many people who would be too embarrassed to publicize their poverty [by taking advantage of a permission granted only to the poor] ... therefore he robed himself in garments of *tzedakah* and commanded that all should eat [*kitnios*], for at that time there was a question of life and death (פִּיקוּחַ נֶפֶשׁ) involved. But in our time, in a year like this when, thank God, we have not arrived at such a stage, God forbid ... certainly permission should be granted to the poor alone, and not to others; and every man should weigh in his own soul whether or not he has reached the point that he is suffering distress in this matter."[45]

A Recent Instance

Mishnah Berurah writes in brief, "It is known that the sages of the generations several times have permitted [*kitnios*] in times of drought." However, he requires that one should follow the stipulation of *Chasam Sofer* — to scald the *kitnios* in boiling water. The chief rabbinate of *Eretz Yisrael* likewise put this ruling into practice and required scalding *(chalitah)* in the *she'as hadechak* of the year 5702 (1942).

NOTES

[1] *Pesachim* 35a.

[2] *Chametz Umatzah* 5:1.

[3] See *Pesachim, loc. cit.* and 114b.

[4] See *Hilchos Shmitah* and *Hilchos Gerushin* in that work.

[5] Sec. 222.

[6] *Pesachim,* ch. 2, sec. 588.

[7] 453.

[8] I do not find this citation in our current editions of *Hagahos Maimonios.*

[9] 453.

[10] *Nesiv* 4, part 3.

[11] Sec. 113.

[12] 453.

[13] 40b.

[14] See *Tosafos,* 40b, in the name of *Aruch.*

[15] And see *Beur HaGra,* para. 4.

[16] Sec. 348.

[17] 453.

[18] See responsa of *Maharatz Chayos, Maamar Minchas Kena'us,* where the author writes at length to refute all the arguments of Rav Yavetz and to prove that "Once a custom has been universally adopted it has completely the same status with us as a Torah law and there is no possibility of anulling it." And see also: *Chasam Sofer, Orach Chaim,* sec. 122; responsa *Tzemach Tzedek,* by the Rebbe of Lubavitch, *Orach Chaim,* sec. 56; responsa *Maamar Mordechai,* by Rav M.Z. Etting, sec. 32. All these authorities write at length in support of the prohibition. And see *Shaarei Teshuvah,* 453.1.

[19] Frankfurt am Main, 1909.

[20] Sec. 113.

[21] Sec. 56.

[22] *Orach Chaim,* sec. 3.

[23] See above, p. 62.

[24] *Orach Chaim,* sec. 11.

[25] 15a.

[26] Sec. 134.

[27] Sec. 32.

[28] Sec. 71.

[29] Sec. 121.

[30] And see responsa *Binyan Tzion HaChadashos,* sec. 6, where the author raises objections to this stringency of *Chasam Sofer.*

[31] *Klal* 126.

[32] Sec. 11.

[33] See below, p. 117.

[34] Sec. 20.

[35] Pub. 5609 (1949).

[36] See below, p. 117.

[37] Sec. 259.

[38] Sec. 122.

[39] In the sections cited above.

[40] Sec. 48.

[41] *Demai* 3:1.

[42] *Eruvin* 17a.

[43] Part 1, sec. 28.

[44] *Nedarim* 27a.

[45] See also: *Sho'el UMeshiv,* second ed., part 4, sec. 128; *Amudei Esh,* by Rav. Y. Eizenstein, *Klal* 8, sec. 4; *Sdei Chemed, Chametz UMatzah,* sec. 6; *Maadanei Shmuel,* sec. 117; *et. al.*

הַסֵּדֶר ‏‮⳨‬

The Seder

The greatness of Am Yisrael has always lain in the ability to defy our enemies who, as we read in the Haggadah, have arisen in every generation to destroy us. This determination to survive is amply demonstrated during the Seder, when we celebrate our first redemption from an implacable enemy.

A careful reading of the story of our sojourn in Egypt shows that the main fury of the oppressors was directed against our children. First they tried to destroy our forefathers' family life, fearing "lest they multiply"; as we say in the Haggadah, " 'And He saw our misery' — this refers to the disruption of their family life." Next the edict went out to the midwives: "When you deliver the Hebrew women you must look at the birthstool; if the infant is a boy, you shall kill it" (Exodus 1:16). When this too did not succeed, the next step followed: "Pharaoh then commanded all his people, saying, Every boy who is born you shall cast into the Nile" (Exodus 1:22). The Midrash tells us moreover that if the required quota of bricks was not filled, Jewish children were inserted into the walls instead, and when Pharaoh became leprous, Jewish children were slaughtered to provide baths for him.

More than at any other festival, therefore, we express our defiant insistence to survive by doing all in our power throughout the whole of the Seder to attract the attention of our children to the story of this first redemption. This begins from its very first word, when on the family's return from the synagogue the child who is appointed as the evening's master of ceremonies gives the command: "Kadesh!" and explains, "When Father comes home from shul he recites Kiddush." So too throughout the whole of the Seder, we fulfill the mitzvah properly only when we "tell our sons." They who were the main targets singled out for destruction are our main cause for celebration and hope.

The crowning gem of the festival of Pesach — the *seder* night — holds an important place in the literature of the *Halachah*. This is not only because of the distinction between this night and the other days with respect to that mitzvah which in our time is the main one of the festival — the eating of *matzah* (an optional mitzvah all other days and obligatory on this night) — but also because of all those *halachos*, both Scriptural and Rabbinic, which belong exclusively to this night and in which the remaining days have no part. In the Talmudic sources — the Mishnah, *Tosefta*, and the Babylonian and Jerusalem Talmuds — most of the laws of the *seder* are concentrated within the chapter of Tractate *Pesachim* called *Arvei Pesachim* [Pesach Eve]. In the writings of the *poskim* and in works of responsa, these laws appear within *Hilchos Pesach*.

In setting out to examine the main *halachos* that distinguish the seder night of Pesach, we may save ourselves the labor of determining the proper order for such a discussion. For at the beginning of any Passover *Haggadah* we shall find ready-made an order which has been established and in continual use since the days of the *Rishonim*. We are speaking, of course, of the mnemonic which sets forth the main events of the *seder*: *Kadesh, URechatz*, it begins — "Sanctify [the day], and then wash" [hands for the preliminary appetizer, the *carpas*] ... Not that this is the only mnemonic for the order of the Pesach feast. A number of such devices were composed. *Abudraham* cites no less than six different ones.[1] But the version which has been accepted throughout the whole of Jewry is that beginning, *Kadesh, URechatz*. (Some attribute the authorship of this mnemonic to *Rashi*, while others state that it was composed by one of the *Baalei HaTosafos*.)[2] We, too, shall follow in its footsteps.

At the head of this entire order stands the *ke'arah*, the *seder* plate. The *ke'arah* is not mentioned in the Mishnah and Talmud; instead, we find the expression, "They bring him"[3] [*matzah, chazeres, charoses*, and two cooked items ... indicating that these things were brought in by someone rather than placed on the table from the beginning]. Nor is the *ke'arah* mentioned in the literature of the *Geonim*. We do find reference to it, however, as early as the *Rishonim*[4] and in *Shulchan Aruch*.[5] The items to be set out in the *ke'arah* are *matzos, maror, charoses*, a vegetable, and two cooked foods.[6] These items are themselves the subject of established *halachos.* The first four are discussed below.[7] The two cooked foods, the source for which is found in the Mishnah,[8] serve the purpose of commemoration — they symbolize the *Pesach* and *Chagigah* sacrifices,[9] the latter being the festival offering sacrificed on the fourteenth of Nissan along with the *Pesach* sacrifice.[10]

In the *Gemara* there is a difference of opinion about the identity of the two cooked items. The custom adopted is that one of them is meat from the part of the animal called *zroa* (זְרוֹעַ, lit., "arm") — this is an allusion to the verse, *And I shall redeem you with an outstretched arm* (וְגָאַלְתִּי אֶתְכֶם בִּזְרוֹעַ נְטוּיָה; *Exodus* 6:6) — while the second is an egg. The Aramaic for "egg" is בֵּיעָה, which is similar to the Aramaic for "want" בָּעָא; hence the egg alludes to the phrase, דְּבָעָא רַחֲמָנָא לְמִיפְרַק יָתְנָא — "The merciful One *wanted* to redeem us."[11] By a strict interpretation of the custom the *zroa* ought to be roasted, as a reminder of the *Pesach* sacrifice which by law could only be roasted; and it is forbidden to eat the *zroa* on the *seder* night, since the rule is that we may not eat roasted meat on the *seder* night of Pesach.°[12] The practice, however, is not to be strict about the requirement of roasting the *zroa*, and there are those who cook it in liquid; some even maintain that it is preferable to cook it this way, so as to avoid any appearance of the transgression of *kadashim bachutz*, that is, of an actual sacrifice slaughtered outside the *Beis HaMikdash.*[13] As for the egg, the custom is either to cook or roast it,[13*] and to eat it[14] on the *seder* night.

In determining how to arrange all the items on the *ke'arah*, some are guided by the principle that "One should not pass by one mitzvah for another" — אֵין מַעֲבִירִין עַל הַמִּצְוֹת. Hence they arrange the items in such a way that the item to be eaten first is the nearest and the easiest to reach [so that one is never reaching "past" one mitzvah to fulfill another].[15] The more common custom is to follow the arrangement determined by the *Ari.* This takes the form of two inverted triangles [corresponding to the vowel, *segol* — ֶ]. The upper triangle consists of the *zroa* on the right, the egg on the left, and the *maror* below and between them. The second triangle, consisting of *charoses, carpas,* and *chazeres* (i.e., the *maror* used for the mitzvah of *korech;* see below), corresponds to the upper triangle: the *charoses* beneath the *zroa,* the *carpas* beneath the egg, and the *chazeres* beneath the *maror.* And all these rest atop the three *matzos* reserved for the *ke'arah.*[16]

° [People might confuse the roast meat with a sacrifice *(korban),* which of course could only be brought in the *Beis HaMikdash. — Ed.*]

Yet a third custom for the arrangement of the *ke'arah* is that of *Gra*,[17] and there are those who follow it.

And now that the *ke'arah* is arranged — let us proceed to the *seder*, according to its sequence.

Kadesh To the extent that the *Kiddush* of Pesach is simply another example of the *Kiddush* always recited on *Yom-Tov*, it is, in the view of *Magid Mishneh*,[18] entirely a Rabbinic mitzvah. (This is in contrast to *Shabbos*, where the obligation to recite *Kiddush* is of Scriptural force, while the requirement to do so over a cup of wine is Rabbinic.) *Magen Avraham*[19] rules in accordance with this opinion, and all the *Acharonim* follow suit.[20]

There are, however, several halachic points connected with the *Kiddush* of Pesach night that do not apply to the regular *Kiddush* of *Shabbos* and *Yom-Tov*. The first of these points has to do with the time; this *Kiddush* must neither be put forward nor delayed. It is interesting to note that although the prohibition against delaying the *Kiddush* is set forth in a *baraisa* in the *Gemara*, while that against moving it forward appears only in the later *poskim*, nevertheless the latter is more important, and a more serious violation, than the former. Performing the *Kiddush* late does not invalidate the mitzvah; it is just that the best way of doing it (לְכַתְּחִילָה) is not to delay. Performing the *Kiddush* too early, on the other hand, invalidates the mitzvah even after the fact (בְּדִיעֲבַד).

The reason why the *Kiddush* must not be delayed is so that the children will not fall asleep. The source of this law in the *Gemara*,[21] and likewise *Tur* and *Shulchan Aruch*[22] refer to this problem in terms of eating — "The table should be set before dark in order *to eat* as soon as it gets dark ... for it is a mitzvah *to eat* as soon as possible for the sake of the children ... " But it goes without saying that it is impossible to eat without first performing *Kiddush*. The Rav, *Baal HaTanya*, succeeded in phrasing this law with great precision: " ... in order *to begin the seder* as soon as it gets dark ... for it is a mitzvah *to begin the seder* as soon as possible ... " The reason for this requirement is obvious — the questions asked by the children and the response, which fulfills the commandment of *And you shall tell your son* (וְהִגַּדְתָּ לְבִנְךָ; *Exodus* 13:8) come before the eating.[23] And as for the *Kiddush* — that, of course, is what is meant by "to begin the *seder*."

What, then, is the putting-ahead of the *Kiddush* which invalidates it even after the fact (בְּדִיעֲבַד)? On *Shabbos* and *Yom-Tov* it is a mitzvah to "add from the non-sacred to the sacred," that is, to begin the holy day somewhat before dark; and the *Yom-Tov* of Pesach is no exception. During this *tosefes*, or added period before dark, it is possible to perform *Kiddush* for *Shabbos* or *Yom-Tov*. But here, Pesach *is* an exception. If one puts ahead the *Kiddush* to the time of the *tosefes*, one has not fulfilled the obligation at all. The reason is that the cup of wine drunk at *Kiddush* is one of the Four Cups which the Sages decreed must be drunk during the *seder*. Now, these Four Cups, like all the special laws and the extraordinary procedures instituted by the Sages for the *seder* night, are connected with the Scriptural mitzvah of eating *matzah*. The latter mitzvah is in turn connected by the Torah to the eating of the *Pesach* sacrifice, of which it is written, *And they shall eat the meat* [of the *Pesach* sacrifice] *on this night* (וְאָכְלוּ אֶת הַבָּשָׂר בַּלַּיְלָה הַזֶּה; *Exodus* 12:8). We see, then, that the *Pesach* sacrifice, and hence the *matzah* may be eaten only at night; and the same is true of all the Rabbinic decrees of the *seder* — they must be performed when it is actually night. Concerning the *matzah* itself, this requirement had already been noted by the *Rishonim*.[24] But concerning the wine of *Kiddush*, mention of this law is found in *Trumas HaDeshen*,[25] who is cited by *Beis Yosef*[26] and all subsequent *poskim*.

Rav Meir Michl Rabinovich, in *HaMeir LaOlam*, provides a fine and detailed explanation why there should be a difference, with reference to the *tosefes*, between the Pesach sacrifice, *matzah* and *maror* on the one hand, and the *Kiddush* of *Shabbos* and *Yom-Tov* on the other. In essence, he explains that the halachic effect of the *tosefes* is not to give the added period of day the status of night, but rather to extend the sanctity of the evening which is about to enter so that it applies to part of the preceding afternoon. The *Kiddush* of *Shabbos* is not specifically dependent upon the night, but rather on the sanctity of *Shabbos* in general — as we see from the fact that if one does not perform *Kiddush* at night, one is obligated to perform it during the day. Thus, since the sanctity of *Shabbos* has been extended to the *tosefes*, it is possible to perform *Kiddush* then, even though it is daytime. This is not the case with the *Pesach* sacrifice, the *matzah* and the *maror*, mitzvos which can be performed only at nighttime.[27]

The issue of time — late and early — is not the only issue differentiating the *Kiddush* of Pesach from that of other sacred days. There is a difference also with regard to the minimum amount of wine which must be drunk. The

difference applies to all the Four Cups, and hence to the
Kiddush cup, which is the first of the Four. As regards the size
of the cup itself, this is the same for the Four Cups as for the
Kiddush of *Shabbos* and *Yom-Tov* — a *reviis*, one-fourth of a
log. For the ordinary *Kiddush*, however, one may fulfill the
obligation by drinking, not the entire cup, but simply the
majority of it; this is the amount called *kemelo lugmav*, "a
cheekful"; and it is sufficient to drink *kemelo lugmav* even if
the cup is a large one whose capacity is several times the
minimum of a *reviis*. As regards Pesach, there is disagreement
among the *Rishonim* about whether the same holds true.
Ramban rules that Pesach is an exception, and that the entire
cup must be drunk. *Ran* and others by contrast maintain that
on Pesach, as at other times, the majority of a *reviis* — i.e.,
kemelo lugmav — is sufficient.[28] Both these positions are
cited in *Shulchan Aruch*. The *Acharonim* have decided that
the second opinion is the principal one.[29]

As for the precise measure of a *reviis*, the Talmud states
that it is the amount of liquid which fills a square cup whose
base measures two finger-widths by two,[30] and whose height
is two finger-widths plus a half plus a fifth[31] [i.e., 2 and 7/10
fingerwidths].

The *Kiddush* of Pesach is exceptional in yet another way.
On Pesach one cannot fulfill the mitzvah, as on other days, by
listening [and answering amen] to another person's recitation
of the blessings. For by doing so, one does indeed fulfill the
mitzvah of *Kiddush* [i.e., the recitation of the blessings over a
cup of wine], but one does not fulfill the obligation of
drinking the wine.[32] [That is, the recitation of the blessings
may be performed on behalf of another, but not the drinking
of the wine.] This leads us to a fundamental point. In an
ordinary *Kiddush*, the essence of the mitzvah is the
sanctification, that is, the blessing "... Who sanctifies
Shabbos (or the appropriate *Yom-Tov*)." It is just that the
Sages decreed that this blessing must be recited over a cup of
wine. Pesach is different, for the essence of the mitzvah
includes not only the blessing of sanctification, but also the
drinking of the wine.

The wording of the *Kiddush* is similar to that of the other
Yamim Tovim with references at the appropriate points to
"the festival of *matzos*" (חַג הַמַּצּוֹת) and "the season of our
freedom" (זְמַן חֵרוּתֵנוּ). The *Siddur* of Rav Saadiah Gaon
mentions an "expanded" version of the *Kiddush* which
"many of our colleagues" recite; and the Gaon affirms that "it
is permissible to recite it." It reads, "... Who sanctified us

from amongst all the peoples and exalted us from amongst all the tongues, chose us and magnified us, favored us and glorified us; set us apart from all the nations, caused us to inherit a desirable land ..." — it is quite a lengthy version. In the *Haggadah* entitled *Zachrenu LeChaim* (Livorno, 5635-1875) this same "long version of the *Kiddush*" is printed, with the note that "it is the custom to recite it in the city of Djerba and in certain other places," and two different expositions of its meaning are printed with it.

As mentioned, the cup of wine over which *Kiddush* is recited is the first of the Four Cups which, by a decree of the Sages, we drink on Pesach night. A number of explanations for this decree have been given. It is said that the Four Cups correspond to the four expressions of redemption that *HaShem* used when telling Moshe that the time had come for *Bnei Yisrael* to be taken out of Egypt — *And I shall take them out* ... (וְהוֹצֵאתִי); *and I shall save them* ... (וְהִצַּלְתִּי); *and I shall redeem them* ... (וְגָאַלְתִּי); *and I shall take them* ... (וְלָקַחְתִּי) *(Exodus* 6:6-7); that they correspond to the four kingdoms in which Israel have been in bondage; to the four cups of retribution which the Holy One, Blessed Be He, will cause the nations of the world to drink; to the four cups of consolation which the Holy One, Blessed Be He, will cause Israel to drink; to the four times the word "cup" (כּוֹס) is used in the passage in *Genesis,* ch. 40, about the dream of Pharaoh's butler (שַׂר הַמַּשְׁקִים)[33] — this last, "because in the dream of Pharaoh's butler Joseph the *tzaddik* was given a forehint of the Redemption."[34]

And although this mitzvah is of Rabbinic origin, some of the conditions attached to it are even stronger than those associated with Scriptural mitzvos. A person is required, for example, to sell his clothes, to borrow, or to hire himself out in order to purchase this wine;[34*] he is also required to go from door to door requesting charity, if necessary, in order to meet this obligation of the Four Cups.[35] In distributing funds to the poor, those in charge of charity may not give less than what is needed for the Four Cups.[36] And even one for whom wine is harmful must exert himself and drink.[37] The Talmud relates that Rabbi Yehudah the son of Rabbi Ila'i would drink the Four Cups and then would bind up his temples from Pesach until Shavuos because of the pain of headache.[38] Further, even though women are normally exempt from mitzvos dependent upon time, and this is such a mitzvah, nevertheless in this case they, too, are obligated; the reason is that they, too, were involved in the miracle.[39] This reason is interpreted to mean either that *Bnei Israel* were redeemed as a reward for righteous women of that generation;[40] or that the women, too, were in exile in Egypt and were redeemed.[41]

The *Geonim* are the first to mention yet another law that indicates the extraordinary importance of this commandment: On the Rabbinic level, they write, one who fails to drink the Four Cups is liable to a lashing.[42]

The *Geonim* also devoted extensive discussion to the type of wine with which one may fulfill the mitzvah. They state that if grape wine is unavailable one may make an acceptable substitute by soaking raisins in water; but the mitzvah cannot be fulfilled with other alcoholic beverages (מִינֵי שֵׁכָר).[43]°
It is a mitzvah to try to obtain red wine (unless it happens that white wine is of higher quality).[44] This is derived from the verse, *Do not look upon wine when it is red* (אַל תֵּרֶא יַיִן כִּי יִתְאַדָּם; *Proverbs* 23:31) — this verse is a warning against succumbing to the attractiveness of wine; hence we see that redness makes wine especially attractive.[45] It is also said that the red color is a reminder of the blood of Israel, whom Pharaoh slaughtered.[46] (*Taz*, the author of this second explanation, goes on to say that "Nowadays we refrain from using red wine because of the blood libels to which we are subject in our present sinful condition.")[47]°

One law, to which much discussion is devoted in the halachic writings of the *Acharonim*, is not mentioned at all by their predecessors the *poskim* "in its place," i.e., among the laws of Pesach. The main source of this law is in the *Talmud*

°[The foulest of all the libels and falsehoods raised against our people is that of killing for ritual purposes. The Talmud (*Berachos* 8:2) tells a story of an attempt to involve Rav Papa in a charge of murdering a child. Although the Talmud does not specifically state that this had a religious connotation, no doubt had the attempt succeeded such a linkage would have been 'discovered'. Josephus, though on many matters a partisan and unreliable historical witness, can be believed when he states that already in the first century C.E. the Greeks claimed that the service in the *Beis HaMikdash* included ritual murder!

In the main these libels had the same ingredients. A Christian would disappear near Pesach time; sometimes one would be deliberately killed by the would-be accusers. The local Jews would be accused of having killed the missing person or the 'discovered victim' in order to use the blood in the making of *matzos* or to make the wine red (hence the remark of Taz). The accused Jews would be jailed and tortured until they 'confessed'; they would then be put to death and their property confiscated.

The shameful distinction of the first recorded libel belongs to the city of Norwich in England in the year 1144. Some twenty-seven years later in 1171 the Jewish community of Blois in France was charged with this foul libel and burned at the stake.

In spite of repeated declarations by some of the highest Christian religious authorities, including Pope Vincent IV (1247) and Clement XIV (1757) that 'Jewish law forbade the thing they were accused of' these accusations have persisted throughout the generations. The two most famous cases in modern history were the Tissa-Eisler case in Hungary (1882) and the Beilis case in Kiev, Russia (1913).

It goes without saying that Nazi Germany and present Neo-Nazis, may their names be blotted out, made great use of, and continue to make use of, this detestable lie. — *Ed.*]

Yerushalmi, Tractate Shabbos;[48] it is mentioned again in Tractate Shekalim,[49] and referred to a third time in Pesachim.[50] "Is it possible," the Yerushalmi asks, "to fulfill the mitzvah with wine of sheviis [the sabbatical year during which the Land must be given a rest from agricultural work]? Rabbi Hoshiyah teaches: 'The mitzvah may be fulfilled with wine of sheviis.' " Numerous suggestions have been given by the Acharonim as to the meaning of the Yerushalmi's query, "Is it possible to fulfill the mitzvah ... ?" One such suggestion is based on the fact that the produce of the sabbatical year is not subject to private ownership but rather is available to anyone who wishes to eat it. Perhaps, then, the question of the Yerushalmi is whether or not the wine of the Four Cups, like the matzah we are commanded to eat, must be "your own" (לָכֶם). If so, wine of sheviis, which belongs to all, might not qualify to fulfill the mitzvah.

Another explanation is based on the law of biur, which requires that once a given type of produce is no longer found in the fields one must also eliminate it from one's possession. Thus each type of produce has its deadline for being used up (biur); after that deadline, any produce of that type which remains is forbidden not only for eating but for any benefit whatsoever. The question, then, might refer to wine which has passed its time of biur.

Again, the very eating of sheviis produce constitutes a mitzvah, for the Torah says, to eat it (לְאָכְלָה; Leviticus 25:6). And since the Four Cups are also a mitzvah, it might be that using sheviis wine for the Four Cups would violate the rule, "One should not perform mitzvos in bunches" (אֵין עוֹשִׂין מִצְווֹת חֲבִילוֹת חֲבִילוֹת); that is, one should not combine two mitzvos into one if they could have been performed separately.

Another possible explanation rests on the fact that wine which is invalid for libations on the Altar is also invalid for Kiddush; and the wine of sheviis cannot be used for libations (נְסָכִים).

Yet another line of reasoning reminds us that at the Pesach seder we must eat in a way that shows that we are in freedom; since only the poor are allowed to eat sheviis produce after the time of biur [and to be poor is a lack of freedom], using such wine for the Four Cups would not be "in the manner of free people" (דֶּרֶךְ חֵרוּת). And still more explanations have been offered.[51]

One must drink the Four Cups according to the procedure instituted by the Sages. The first cup must be drunk as part of

Kiddush; over the second cup the *Haggadah* is read; the third cup is used for the grace after meals *(birkas hamazon);* and over the fourth cup, *Hallel,* psalms of praise, is recited.[52] If one simply drinks the four cups one after the other, and not according to this procedure, one has not fulfilled the obligation.[53] Each one of the Four Cups is a mitzvah of its own.[54] Between the first and second cups one is permitted, according to the law, to drink other wine.[55] "Nevertheless, it is proper to take care not to drink [wine] between the first and second [cups] unless one has a very great need to do so; this is in order that one should not become intoxicated and thus be prevented from performing the *seder* and the reading of the *Haggadah.*"[56]

There is a major dispute in the *Gemara* concerning the proper order for performing *Kiddush* when Pesach falls on *motzaei Shabbos,* that is, when Pesach enters as *Shabbos* departs. A great many different opinions are given, each with its own mnemonic acronym. All these acronyms involve the same letters, but in a different order. י stands for wine (יַיִן) that is, the first blessing of *Kiddush,* " ... Who creates the fruit of the vine" (בּוֹרֵא פְּרִי הַגָּפֶן). ק stands for *kiddush* (קִידוּשׁ) i.e., its second blessing "... Who sanctifies Israel and the festivals" (מְקַדֵּשׁ יִשְׂרָאֵל וְהַזְּמַנִּים). נ stands for light (נֵר), referring to the candle used in the *havdalah* ceremony marking the transition from a higher to a lower level of holiness (*Shabbos* to *Yom-Tov);* this is the light over which one recites the blessing, " ... Who creates the lights of the fire" (בּוֹרֵא מְאוֹרֵי הָאֵשׁ). ה stands for *havdalah* (הַבְדָּלָה), that is, the blessing which begins " ... who makes a distinction between the sacred and the ordinary" (הַמַּבְדִּיל בֵּין קֹדֶשׁ לְחוֹל). Thus, one opinion holds that the correct order is that signified by the acronym, יקנ״ה; others prefer קני״ה, קינ״ה, נקי״ה, or ינה״ק, יהנ״ק, נהי״ק.[57]

The difference of opinion is settled by the *Halachah* in favor of יַקְנְהַ״ז (the final ז stands for *z'man,* lit., "time" — i.e., the blessing *shehecheyanu,* "... Who kept us alive and preserved us and caused us to reach this time").

Kadesh is the first act of the *seder* night which is subject to the requirement of "reclining" (הֲסֵיבָה). One is obligated to lean on the left side in the manner of free men for the drinking of the Four Cups, for the eating of *matzah,* for *korech* (see below), and for the eating of the *Afikoman.*[58]

URechatz

In essence, this mitzvah is not restricted only to Pesach night. It is a general rule that before eating food that is to be dipped in liquid one must perform *netilas yadayim*, the ritual washing of the hands — and the *carpas*, dipped in salt water and eaten immediately after *Kiddush*, is only one example of this rule. But in fact the *Gemara*[59] records this law not in a general discussion of *netilas yadayim*, but specifically in connection with *carpas*. The *poskim*, on the other hand, discuss the details of this law, — with the accompanying explanations, logical arguments, differences of opinion, and conclusions, — among the other laws of *netilas yadayim*.[60]

[The reason for this washing of the hands is to eliminate possible *tumah*, ritual impurity. Thus] the *Rishonim* debate whether or not this *netilas yadayim* is obligatory in our time, after the Destruction of the Temple, when the laws of ritual purity and impurity are not in use. Since the issue is disputed, it is generally agreed that no blessing should be recited over this *netilas yadayim* (although *Gra* rules that the blessing is required).

The custom of the people as a whole has been to ignore this law of performing *netilas yadayim* before eating a food dipped in liquid. Thus *Taz*[61] asks: "In what way is this night different from all others? — for on all other days of the year people do not observe this law, but when Pesach night arrives, they are meticulous about it. "And if the reason were that one wishes to purify oneself especially on this night — it would be more appropriate to exercise this extra vigilance during the ten days of *teshuva*." *Netziv*, in his *Haggadah* entitled *Imrei Shefer*, responds to this question of *Taz*. "It is no question at all," he writes; and he goes on to explain that on Pesach night we do a number of things to commemorate the Pesach sacrifice offered when the Temple was still standing — and this *netilah* is simply one more such commemoration.[62] [Hence we are careful about *tumah* as in Temple times.]

Carpas

The term *carpas* is not found in the Mishnah and *Gemara*, which refer only to *yerakos*, (vegetables) and *chazeres*.[63] The Talmud states that the *yerakos* must be dipped [and eaten] before the meal, and all the *Rishonim* explain that the reason for this is to cause the children to ask questions. In the words of *Rashi*, "in order that the child should take notice and ask; for it is not the normal habit of people to eat *yerek* before the meal."[64] *Carpas (petrushka*, parsley) is one species of *yerek*, and is mentioned by the *Rishonim*.° Some authorities explain that this vegetable in particular is to be preferred because its

---

° [There are authorities (including *Rashi* and *Maharil*) who identify *carpas* as celery. — *Ed.*]

name hints at the backbreaking labor (עֲבוֹדַת פֶּרֶךְ) which Israel had to perform in Egypt.[65] For by reading *carpas* in reverse we get ס׳ פֶּרֶךְ, i.e., the word for "backbreaking" preceded by the letter ס׳, which represents the number sixty [and the number of men of military age who went out of Egypt is sixty myriads, or six hundred thousand].

If one dips some vegetable other than *carpas* this does not, of course, invalidate the mitzvah; one may use any vegetable one chooses. There is a difference of opinion among the *Rishonim* about the substance into which the *carpas* is dipped. *Rambam* and others hold that the vegetable should be dipped in *charoses* while the majority of the *Rishonim* are of the opinion that vinegar or some other strong-tasting liquid should be used.[66] The custom is to dip in salt water.[67]

It is thanks to *carpas* that we find in the *Gemara*[68] one more passage on a topic of general application throughout the Talmud; namely, מִצְוֹת צְרִיכוֹת כַּוָּנָה — the question whether or not a mitzvah is valid if the act is performed without the intent of fulfilling the mitzvah. It may happen that the only vegetable available for dipping is one of the types which qualify for the subsequent mitzvah of eating *maror*. When the time arrives for eating *maror*, should one recite the blessing for this mitzvah, or not? On the one hand, one has already eaten *maror*; but on the other hand, when eating it one had no intent to fulfill this mitzvah, but rather to fulfill a different mitzvah, that of dipping a vegetable before the meal. Thus the question whether or not to recite the blessing depends on whether or not intent is an essential component of performing a mitzvah. If it is not, then one has already performed the mitzvah, though without intent, and hence the blessing would now be in vain. But if intent is essential to a mitzvah, then one has not yet performed this mitzvah, and the blessing is appropriate now.

Ultimately, the *Halachah* does not solve this particular problem in terms of whether or not mitzvos require intent. For the ruling is that, even if we accept the premise that "mitzvos require intent," nevertheless "once one has already filled his stomach with [this vegetable] one should not now pronounce the blessing ... concerning the eating of *maror*." What, then, should one do in such a case? The solution is to recite both blessings over the first act of eating — " ... Who creates the fruit of the earth" (בּוֹרֵא פְּרִי הָאֲדָמָה), and " ... concerning the eating of *maror* "(עַל אֲכִילַת מָרוֹר). Then when the time comes for the mitzvah of eating *maror*, one eats the vegetable again without a blessing. The time lapse is not considered a violation of the rule that prohibits any interruption between the blessing and the act, since at the very time of reciting the blessing one did eat a little of the *maror*.[69]

The *poskim* debate another question about the relationship between these two acts of eating a vegetable — the *carpas* before the meal and the *maror* during it. We know that normally we are not required to recite the blessing, "... Who creates the fruit of the earth" (בּוֹרֵא פְּרִי הָאֲדָמָה) over the *maror*. But why is this so? Is it because we have already recited this blessing over the *carpas*, and it applies to the *maror* (even if the *maror* is a different species) as well? Or is it because the *maror*, being an obligatory feature of the repast, falls in the category of "things necessary to the meal" (דְּבָרִים הַבָּאִים מֵחֲמַת הַסְּעוּדָה), and hence is exempted by the blessing over the bread (*matzah)?* This problem has practical consequences in cases where the blessing recited over the *carpas* cannot apply to the *maror;* for example, if the vegetable used for dipping was eaten raw, but is a type normally eaten cooked, so that the blessing required for it is not " ... the fruit of the earth," but "... by Whose word everything comes to be" (שֶׁהַכּל); or again, if one recites a concluding blessing (בְּרָכָה אַחֲרוֹנָה) after the *carpas,* so that the first blessing can no longer apply to subsequent items. [In such cases, there would be doubt as to whether or not " ... the fruit of the earth" should be recited over the *maror.* If it is the bread which makes the *maror* exempt, then here, too, it is exempt. But if the exemption depends upon the *carpas,* then in these cases a blessing over the *maror* would be necessary.] In order to eliminate any doubt as to whether a blessing " ... Who creates the fruit of the earth" is required for the *maror,* the *poskim* rule that it is best to eat less than the amount of *carpas* called *kazayis,* the volume equivalent of an olive — that is, less than the amount which necessitates a concluding blessing. And even if one ate a *kazayis* and recited the concluding blessing after it, all the same one should not recite " ... Who creates the fruit of the earth" over the *maror;* for the rule is, "In cases of doubt about a blessing, be lenient [i.e., omit the blessing]" — סָפֵק בְּרָכוֹת לְהָקֵל.[70]

Yachatz

The source for the *mitzvah* of *yachatz* — breaking one of the *matzos* over which the blessing for bread will later be recited — is found in Tractate *Berachos.*[71] "Rav Papa said: All agree that on Pesach one places a broken [*matzah*] with the whole one, [then recites the blessing, " ... Who brings forth bread from the earth"] and then breaks bread. What is the reason?

— because it is written, the bread of poverty" (לֶחֶם עֹנִי; see *Deuteronomy* 16:3). The exegesis itself is explained more fully in Tractate *Pesachim*.[72] "The Torah says, *the bread of poverty*, but it is written [without the letter *vav*] לֶחֶם עֹנִי [so that it could be read, 'the bread of a poor man (עָנִי)'] — just as the way of a poor man is to eat broken bread, here too [the mitzvah is to eat the bread] broken."

The *Rishonim* are in disagreement as to whether this "broken piece" *(perusah)* detracts or adds from the normal situation. *Rif* and *Rambam* hold that it detracts — in place of the *double bread* (לֶחֶם מִשְׁנֶה; *Exodus* 16:22) comprised of two whole loaves, this mitzvah involves one whole and one broken. *Tosafos, Rosh, Mordechai,* and others argue that the broken piece is in addition to the *lechem mishneh*, the two whole pieces.[73] Even earlier, in the days of the *Geonim*, there had already been considerable debate on the subject of the broken and the whole *matzah*.[74] This was one of the *chilukim*, the divergences of custom, between the inhabitants of Babylonia and *Eretz Yisrael*. *Bnei Bavel* followed the custom that when Pesach fell on *Shabbos*, two whole pieces and one broken one were used for the *seder*; *Bnei Eretz Yisrael* used one whole and one broken no matter whether Pesach fell on *Shabbos* or on a weekday.[75] The *Halachah* follows the view of *Tosafos* and the allied opinions: Two whole pieces and one broken one are used, whether on *Shabbos* or on a weekday. *(Gra follows the custom of Rif.)*

Why is it that the *matzah* is broken early in the *seder*, before the reading of the *Haggadah* and hence long before the blessing over the *matzah*? *Kol-Bo* writes: "the custom is to break [the *matzah*] before reading [the *Haggadah*], so as to be able to say over it, "This bread of affliction" (הָא לַחְמָא עַנְיָא) — 'Just as a poor man eats broken bread, here too [we eat the *matzah*] broken.' " (The same author cites further reasons here.) The Rav, *Baal HaTanya*, gives a fine explanation of this reason in his *Shulchan Aruch*.[76] Strictly according to the law, the *Haggadah* must be read over *matzah* which is fit for the performance of the mitzvah of eating *matzah*, as the Sages said [taking note of the words עֹנִי — poverty — and עוֹנֶה — to recite or reply]: "לֶחֶם עֹנִי — for many things are recited over it."[77]

And since it is with broken *matzah* that one must perform the mitzvah of eating *matzah*, it follows that the *Haggadah*, too, must be read over a broken piece.

The *Haggadah* [this word means, literally, "telling"], up to the   *Maggid*
end of the blessing " ... Who redeemed Israel" (גָּאַל יִשְׂרָאֵל) is
to be recited over the second of the Four Cups [that is, this cup
should be filled and ready to drink during the recitation of the
Haggadah].[78] The *Rishonim* are in disagreement as to
whether or not the blessing " ... Who creates the fruit of the
vine" (בּוֹרֵא פְּרִי הַגָּפֶן) should be recited over this second cup.
One position is that since, as the Talmud states, each of the
Four Cups constitutes a separate mitzvah,[79] a separate
blessing should be recited over each cup.[80] Others hold that
between the first and second cups one's attention essentially is
not distracted from the act of drinking wine (אֵין הֶיסַח הַדַּעַת),
and therefore the blessing recited over the first cup applies to
the second also.[81] Likewise, there is disagreement as to
whether or not a concluding blessing (בְּרָכָה אַחֲרוֹנָה) is recited
after each cup separately.[82] The Ashkenazic custom is to
recite *Borei pri hagafen* before each of the Four Cups;[83]
however, the custom concerning the concluding blessing is to
recite it only after drinking the fourth cup [with the intention
that the blessing apply to all four cups].[84]

To the *Haggadah* itself, its general principles and specific
features, we have devoted a separate chapter.[84*]

"One washed one's hands before the first 'dipping,' and one   *Rachtzah*
washes one's hands before the second 'dipping' " (i.e., before
the meal itself) — this is the rule given by Rav Chisda.[85] The
Gemara explains why the first *netilas yadayim*, for the *carpas*,
does not serve for the meal as well. "Since one must recite the
Haggadah and the *Hallel*, it may be that one's attention was
distracted" [from one's hands, and they touched something
which would necessitate washing them again before the meal].
From this statement of the Talmud the author of *Mordechai*
concludes that if, at the first *netilas yadayim*, one's intent was
to remain mindful of one's hands, and in fact one guarded
them from touching anything unclean, there is no need to
perform the second *netilah*. But *Beis Yosef* disagrees, asserting
that the second *netilah* has the status of a Rabbinic decree
(תַּקָּנַת חֲכָמִים). The *Acharonim* have ruled that if one is sure
that he has been mindful of his hands the whole time, he
should perform the second *netilah*, but without reciting the
blessing.[86]°

° [*Mishnah Berurah*, in *Biur Halachah* 475.1, s.v. יטול, rules that one should deliberately touch
something (e.g., one's shoes) which would cause the hands to require washing, thus ensuring
that the blessing is necessary. — *Ed.*]

Motzi Here we are discussing not the nature of and requirements for
Matzah the *matzah* itself, so that it should be qualified to be used for
the mitzvah;[87] rather, our subject is the blessings to be recited
and the nature of the act of eating. Two blessings precede the
eating of the *matzah: HaMotzi* (" ... Who brings forth bread
from the earth") and *al achilas matzah* (" ... Who has
sanctified us with His commandments and commanded us
concerning the eating of *matzah"*); of these, *HaMotzi* should
come first, in accordance with the principle that "When a
more frequent and a less frequent mitzvah° are both to be
performed, the more frequent comes first" — תָּדִיר וְשֶׁאֵינוֹ
תָּדִיר תָּדִיר קוֹדֶם.[88] The *Rishonim*, however, are in disagreement over a different issue. Some hold that the blessing
HaMotzi refers to the whole *matzah*, and *al achilas matzah*
to the broken one,[89] while others hold the reverse.[90] Both
sides agree, however, that one may not intend both blessings
to apply to the broken piece, because of the rule, "mitzvos
should not be performed in bunches" — אֵין עוֹשִׂין מִצְווֹת
חֲבִילוֹת חֲבִילוֹת — [meaning that a separate object, in our case
matzah, should be used for each mitzvah, i.e., each
blessing].[91] But a contrary opinion holds that this rule is not
applicable to blessings recited over beneficial experiences
(בִּרְכוֹת הַנֶּהֱנִין), and hence both blessings should indeed be
recited over the broken piece of *matzah*.[92]

In order to avoid any doubts about whether one is
peforming the mitzvah correctly, *Shulchan Aruch* and the
Acharonim rule that all three *matzos* — the broken one and the
two whole ones — should be held in hand when reciting the
two blessings. It would seem from the wording used by
Shulchan Aruch and by *Taz*, that all three *matzos* are to be
held the whole time that one recites the two blessings. But all
the *Acharonim* prescribe a somewhat different procedure.
While reciting *HaMotzi*, one holds all three *matzos* in hand
(the third *matzah,* on the bottom, is to fulfill the mitzvah of
lechem mishneh, the second loaf of bread which is always
required on *Shabbos* and *Yom-Tov*); but for *al achilas matzah*
one puts down the third *matzah* and recites the blessing over
the upper and the broken one.

As a result of this disagreement as to which blessing refers
to which piece of *matzah*, doubt arises concerning the act of
eating, as well; for the requirement to eat the full measure of a
kazayis of *matzah* applies to that piece (whichever it is) over
which *al achilas matzah* is recited. The reason is that the

° [The blessing *HaMotzi* is of course by far the more frequent, and hence has priority. — *Ed.*]

Torah commands the "eating" of *matzah*, and the minimum amount which qualifies as "eating" is always a *kazayis*.[93] [The blessing *HaMotzi*, on the other hand, must be pronounced even if one eats less than a *kazayis*. Thus] there is no requirement to eat a *kazayis* of that piece over which one recited *HaMotzi*.

The ruling handed down by *Shulchan Aruch* is that one should eat a *kazayis* of each *matzah* — a total of two *kezeisim*. All the *Acharonim* agree with this ruling — except that the author of *Mishnah Berurah* states that he finds this conclusion "extremely puzzling." In this author's opinion, all the conflicting opinions among the *Rishonim* would be satisfied as long as the combined amount eaten from both the broken and the whole piece adds up to a full *kazayis* — and this, not only after the fact, but even if one deliberately chooses (לְכַתְּחִילָה) to perform the mitzvah in this way.

A major point of dispute among the *Acharonim* concerns the case of one who has less than a whole *kazayis* of *matzah* available, or one who is ill and cannot eat a whole *kazayis*. We know that with regard to forbidden foods the *halachah* is that the eating of less than a *kazayis*, though not punishable, is Scripturally forbidden — that is, a transgression has been committed, though not enough food has been eaten to incur the prescribed punishment. What is the ruling, then, concerning one who eats less than a *kazayis* of *matzah*? Do we say that a mitzvah has been performed, though not enough food has been eaten to earn the full reward for that mitzvah? Or do we consider that the eating of less than the minimum amount constitutes no mitzvah at all?[94]

The third piece of *matzah*, which has remained whole, is used for the "*maror*, sandwich" *(korech)*,[95] so that all three of the pieces will have been used for a mitzvah.[96]

The piece with which one performs the mitzvah of *achilas matzah*, eating *matzah*, requires *heseibah*;[97] that is, one must recline on the left side while consuming that piece. If one eats it without *heseibah*, one has not fulfilled the commandment, and one must eat another *kazayis* with *heseibah*.[98] In such a case, the *Acharonim* agree, the blessing is not recited a second time.[99]

Maror

"In our time [after the Destruction], *matzah* is a Scriptural commandment; *maror*, Rabbinic" — this is the halachic conclusion reached by the Talmud.[100] The source for the commandment of eating *maror*, on the Scriptural level, is the verse *They shall eat [the Pesach sacrifice] with matzos and* maror (עַל מַצּוֹת וּמְרֹרִים יֹאכְלֻהוּ; *Numbers* 9:11). Hence, when there is no Temple and no Pesach sacrifice, this commandment does not apply. A different verse [see *Exodus* 12:18] provides us with the Scriptural obligation to eat *matzah* on Pesach even after the Destruction; but there is no such second verse for *maror*.

What are the species which may be used to fulfill the obligation of *maror?* — this question is discussed by the Mishnah and *Gemara*.[101] The conclusion reached is that the only valid species are those five (*chazeres, tamcha*, etc.) enumerated in the *mishnah* there — and in that same order of preference. Thus the most preferable of all is *chazeres* [romaine lettuce, called חַסָא in modern Hebrew and *salat* in Yiddish]. If one does not have *chazeres*, he should use *tamcha;* and so on, down the list. This same Talmud passage cites a *baraisa* which holds that any bitter herb, not just these five, qualifies as *chazeres*. Thus *Rama* and the *Acharonim* rule that if one does not have one of the five species which are valid for *maror*, one should use any bitter species, but without reciting the blessing *al achilas maror*.

The *poskim* and the works of responsa devote extensive discussion to the problem of the *shiur* — the minimum required amount — for the eating of *maror*. *Rosh*[102] writes that the reason why one must eat at least a *kazayis* of *maror* is that the blessing contains the words, " ... concerning the eating of *maror*" — and the minimum amount which halachically qualifies as "eating" is a *kazayis*. From this it may be inferred that in essence the mitzvah itself does not require a *kazayis* [it is only the blessing which necessitates that *shiur*]. This assumes that the phrase *They shall eat it* (יֹאכְלֻהוּ) in the above verse refers to the Pesach sacrifice but not to the *matzos and maror*.[103] By contrast, other *Rishonim* write that the reason for the requirement of a *kazayis* is the word, יֹאכְלֻהוּ — *they shall eat it* — in the verse.[104] The author of *Shaagas Aryeh*[105] argues at length against the conclusion of *Rosh*, adducing proofs that the essence of the mitzvah includes the *shiur* of *kazayis*. The *Acharonim* probe the issue in depth.[106]

One stringent ruling on the part of *Chavos Daas* caused a "storm" in the literature of the *Acharonim*. In his *Haggadah*, this author asserted that the obligation of *maror* cannot be fulfilled with *tamcha* (*chrein*, horseradish) if it is shredded or ground. The author backs his assertion with both a *Gemara* passage[107] and reasoning (he argues that the grinding and shredding dull the bitterness of the vegetable). This is an example of a "stringency which is beyond the capacity of the public"; for it is impossible to eat *chrein* when it is whole, and *chazeres* (lettuce) is not universally available. The *Acharonim* write at length to refute the opinion of *Chavos Daas*.[108] The responsa of *Maharsham*, in fact, discuss the opposite question — whether it is possible at all to fulfill the mitzvah with *chrein* when it is whole since this is not the normal way of eating it °.(כְּדֶרֶךְ אֲכִילָתוֹ)

Stolen *maror* — *maror hagazul* — is another topic debated by the *Acharonim*. The question whether or not one can fulfill the *mitzvah* with stolen *maror* depends on two issues: whether or not the disqualification known as "a mitzvah that comes about through a transgression" *(mitzvah habaah be-aveirah)* applies to Rabbinic mitzvos; and whether or not the Torah requires that the *matzah* and *maror* used to fulfill the mitzvah must be "one's own" (שֶׁלָּכֶם).[111]
The best way (לְכַתְּחִילָה) of performing the mitzvah of eating *maror* is that it should come after the eating of *matzah*; for, as *Rashbam* informs us, the order of words in the verse is significant — *with matzos and marorim* implies that the *matzah* comes first, and afterwards the *maror*.[112] After the fact, however (בְּדִיעֲבַד), the order is not essential, and the mitzvah is fulfilled even if one eats the *maror* before the *matzah*.[113] The blessing " ... Who creates the fruit of the earth" (בּוֹרֵא פְּרִי הָאֲדָמָה) is not recited over the *maror*.[114]

Essentially, the time for eating *maror* is dependent upon the time for eating the Pesach sacrifice; for the *Gemara* tells us that the juxtaposition of that sacrifice and the *matzah* and *maror* in the verse *They shall eat it with matzos and merorim* implies a connection between these three items in terms of the laws applying to them — [115] and from *Minchas Chinuch* we learn that this halachic linkage applies to the time of eating.[116] Nevertheless, in our time, when the eating of *maror* is a Rabbinic rather than a Scriptural mitzvah, it must be questioned whether the time limit for eating it is until dawn.[117] The *Acharonim* have written that it is best to eat the *maror* before midnight. And if this time limit has already passed, one should eat the *maror*, but without reciting the blessing.[118]

The eating of *maror* does not require *heseibah*, reclining, since the bitter vegetable is a reminder of slavery.[119] The *maror* vegetable must be dipped in *charoses* when eaten. Some

° [Because of these two divergent opinions there were and still are some who, wishing to be very exacting in the fulfillment of this mitzvah (מְהַדְרִין מִן הַמְּהַדְרִין), accepted both stringencies and ate both ground and unground *chrein*, arguing that especially a Rabbinic mitzvah requires *Mesiras Nefesh*, the willingness to undergo anything for the sake of the mitzvah! — *Ed.*]

commentators state that this is in order to overcome the toxins contained in *chazeres,* or that the purpose is to kill the worms found in it.[120] But others state that the *charoses* is itself a mitzvah, to commemorate [the self-sacrifice hinted at by the verse] *I roused thee under the apple tree (Song of Songs* 8:5) [this alludes to the determination of *Bnei Yisrael* to go on having children in spite of the murderous persecutions of the Egyptians — the women would give birth in the fields, under the trees. — *Ed.*]; the *charoses* is also a reminder of the mud used in making bricks for Pharaoh.[121] *Charoses* is made from species which have been used to symbolize Israel, such as apples, walnuts, pomegranates, and almonds; and it is flavored with spices, such as cinnamon and ginger *(zangvil),* which resemble the straw which our ancestors mixed with the mud.[122]

Women are obligated by the mitzvah of eating *maror* just as, on the Scriptural level, they are obligated to eat *matzah*[123] — for *matzah* and *maror* are mentioned by the verse in conjunction.[124] In our time, as well, women are obligated on the Rabbinic level, in the same way that they are obligated by all the mitzvos of the *seder* night — since they, too, were involved in the miracle.[125]

Korech Two separate passages in the Babylonian, and one in the Jerusalem Talmud, discuss the disagreement between Hillel and *Chachamim* as to whether or not, in the time of the Temple, the mitzvah of *maror* was performed by "joining" it *(krichah)* with *matzah.* These passages are in *Pesachim,,*[126] in *Zevachim,*[127], and (in the *Yerushalmi)* in *Challah.*[128] Underlying the disagreement is the question whether or not "mitzvos can annul each other." There is no clear-cut decision in the Talmud as to which opinion is the accepted one, and hence the ruling in the *Gemara* is that, in our time, one should recite separate blessings for the *matzah* and for the *maror* [and eat a *kazayis* separately], and afterwards eat both together in sandwich form *(krichah)* but without reciting a blessing. (This is what the *Haggadah* terms "a commemoration of the practice of Hillel in the *Mikdash".)*

The *Rishonim,* in turn, disagreed as to whether the practice of Hillel was to "join" the meat of the *Pesach* sacrifice, the *matzah* and the *maror* all together, or whether he ate the meat of the *Pesach* sacrifice separately and "joined" only the *matzah* and *maror.*[129] This dispute has practical consequences in our day in terms of the wording of that passage of the *Haggadah* beginning "This is what Hillel did ..." Depending upon which opinion of the *Rishonim* is accepted, the passage should read either " ... he would join the meat of the Pesach sacrifice, the *matzah* and the *maror* ..." or " ... he would join the *matzah* and the *maror* ..."[130]

The *maror* used in this sandwich or *korech* is also dipped in *charoses*; for Hillel, who used this *krichah* to perform the mitzvah of *maror*, used to dip the *maror* in *charoses*, and our practice is a commemoration of his.[131] But there are those who disagree with this ruling, since in our case we have already fulfilled the obligation of *charoses* with the previous *maror* which was eaten separately — nor would the problem of the toxins in the *chazeres* be a factor here, because the vegetable is eaten together with the *matzah*.[132] The *Acharonim* decide this dispute in favor of the opinion that the *maror* of the *korech* should be dipped in *charoses*.[133]

Concerning *heseibah*, too, there is disagreement with respect to *korech*. One opinion is that this mitzvah does not require *heseibah*;[134] but the ruling of the majority of *poskim* is that *heseibah* is necessary, for Hillel himself would recline while eating his *krichah*, since this "sandwich" was his way of performing the mitzvah of eating *matzah*.[135]

Differences of custom concerning the feast of Pesach night are cited by the Mishnah.[136] "In a community where the custom is to eat roasted meat on Pesach night, it is permissible to eat it; in a community where the custom is not to eat it, it is not permissible to eat it." The reason for the custom which forbids roasted meat is that we are commanded to prepare the *Pesach* sacrifice only by roasting, as indicated by the verse ... *but only roasted by fire* (כִּי אִם צְלִי אֵשׁ; *Exodus* 12:9). Thus, eating roasted meat might give the appearance of eating sacrificial meat outside the Temple [an offense punishable by *kares*, divine excision]. *Magen Avraham*, recording the custom of the Ashkenazic communities, writes: "In these lands it is not the custom to eat roasted meat,"[137] not even pan-roasted, i.e., cooked in a pan or pot without liquid.[138] But there is an opinion among the *Acharonim* which permits pan-roasted meat since this is different from the required method for the *Pesach* sacrifice, as expressed by the verse, *roasted by fire*[139] [i.e., roasted on a spit].

From the *Yerushalmi* we learn that in a locality where the custom is not to eat roasted meat, even beef or poultry — any kind of meat, in fact, which requires slaughtering — in spite of the fact that these types of animals are not valid for the *Pesach* sacrifice, are forbidden to be eaten roasted.[140] Roasted fish or

Shulchan Orech

roasted eggs, on the other hand, are permitted.[141] In fact, it is customary to eat eggs at this feast as a hint of mourning, because our calendar is constructed in such a way that the night of Tisha BeAv and the night of Pesach always fall on the same day of the week. A related reason for eating eggs is "as a reminder of [mourning for] the Destruction — for they used to offer up the Pesach sacrifice"[142] [and because of the Destruction we are unable to do so].

Incidentally, a number of responsa works record cases in which unlettered people would bring a sheep or a goat to the *shochet*, the ritual slaughterer, on *erev* Pesach, with the request that he slaughter for them their "*Pesach* sacrifice." They intended this term only as a flowery expression (מְלִיצָה). But the question arose whether this involves any danger of the transgression of slaughtering a sacrifice outside the Temple.[143]

During this feast, which takes place between the second and third of the Four Cups, it is permissible to drink wine.[144] "And a person should not eat or drink to great excess, so as not to eat the *afikoman* in a state of *achilah gassah* [when there is no longer any physical desire to ingest food], and lest one become intoxicated and fall asleep immediately."[145] These are the words of *Rama*. And the author of *Aruch HaShulchan* states, "The wise man has his eyes in his head and knows that this night is entirely holy, and performs the *seder* with great joy."[146]

Tzafon Afikoman — it is to this that the mnemonic *Tzafon* refers [because the custom is that, of the three pieces used for the mitzvah of eating *matzah*, the unused part of the broken piece is hidden away to be used for the *afikoman*] — is a word of Greek origin, meaning the pastries and delicacies eaten as dessert (קִינוּחַ) after a feast.[147] There are those who have "converted" the word to Hebrew/Aramaic, seeing in it the two words מָן and אֲפִיקוּ, lit., "they brought out the *manna*;" that is, 'they took out and served sweets.'[148]

The original and essential mention of *afikoman* is in a negative sense. The Mishnah tells us, "After [the eating of] the *Pesach* sacrifice, one may not add an *afikoman*."[149] That is to say, the feast of Pesach night may not be concluded with a dessert, or *afikoman*, since it is forbidden to eat anything after the meat of the *Pesach* sacrifice. In our time when there is no *Pesach* sacrifice, it is a matter of disagreement among the *Amoraim* whether or not one may "add an *afikoman*" after the *matzah*.[150] The *Halachah* is that one may not; one finishes the feast with a *kazayis* of *matzah*, after which one may not eat at all.[151] This final *kazayis* is considered either a reminder of the *matzah* that was eaten with the *Pesach* sacrifice,[152] or a reminder of the sacrifice itself, which had to be eaten on a full stomach (עַל הַשּׂוֹבַע), i.e., at the end of the meal.[153] In the course of time, the term *afikoman* came to be applied to this final piece of *matzah* itself,[154] the reason being, according to *Beis Yosef*, that after it no *afikoman* may be added.[155] The custom is that the preferred way (לְכַתְּחִילָה) of performing this mitzvah is to eat two *kezeisim*; one, as a reminder of the *Pesach* sacrifice, and the second as a reminder of the *matzah* that was eaten with the sacrifice.[156]

Rabbi Elazar ben Azaryah and Rabbi Akiva disagreed as to whether the *Pesach* sacrifice may be eaten only until midnight, or whether it may be eaten at any time of the night until dawn.[157] This disagreement has application for us as well, in connection with the time for eating the *afikoman*. It is true that not only the *afikoman*, but also the essential mitzvah of eating *matzah*, is linked to the time limit for eating the *Pesach* sacrifice.[158] However, since the *afikoman* comes later in the Pesach feast, this law is discussed by *Shulchan Aruch* in connection with it specifically. "One should take care to eat [the *afikoman*] before midnight (*chatzos*)."[159] From the wording, "one should take care," it may be inferred that this is not a clear-cut *halachah* [otherwise the phrase would have been, 'one must']. In fact, this is an issue disputed among the *Rishonim*. *Rambam* and others maintain that the *matzah* may be eaten throughout the night, while according to many other *Rishonim* the time limit is *chatzos*. The disagreement centers on two points: (1) whether the *Halachah* follows Rabbi Elazar ben Azaryah or Rabbi Akiva; (2) whether or not even according to Rabbi Akiva, who holds that on the Scriptural level the *Pesach* sacrifice may be eaten until dawn, there is in any case a Rabbinic "fence" (סְיָיג) or precautionary limitation of midnight [in order to "put distance between man and sin,"] as in the case of the time limit for reciting the *Shema* (see Mishnah *Berachos* 1:1).[160]

The *Rishonim* are divided as to whether or not it is permissible to drink after the *afikoman*. Some permit drinking, on the assumption that the drink does not remove the taste of *matzah* from the mouth.[161] Others forbid it, asserting that any drink except water does remove the taste of the *matzah*.[162]

The Torah tells us concerning the *Pesach* sacrifice, *It shall be eaten in one house* (בְּבַיִת אֶחָד יֵאָכֵל; *Exodus* 12:46).

"House" here is taken to mean "room", and hence the *halachah* is that one must remain in the same room the whole time of eating the sacrifice. And this same rule applies to the eating of the *afikoman*.[163] Even within the same room, one may not eat it at two different tables.[164] A corollary is that a person who falls asleep after beginning to eat the *afikoman* and then wakes up may not resume eating; for the sleep is considered an interruption (הֶפְסֵק) and if he were to begin eating again this would resemble the prohibition of eating the *afikoman* in two different places.[165]

Various customs are associated with the *afikoman*. One is to hide it under one's cushion until the time comes to eat it;[166] [as mentioned above] this is why the *afikoman* is called *tzafon*, the hidden. Another custom is that the children "steal" the *afikoman*, giving it back only in return for the promise of a gift.[167] And some follow the custom (at the end of the meal), before eating the *afikoman*, of taking it out wrapped in a cloth, hanging it over the shoulder as in a sling, and walking four cubits within the room while saying, "In this way our ancestors walked with their kneading troughs tied to their garments" (see *ibid*. 12:34).[168]

Barech Unlike the law for the rest of the year, on Pesach night the grace after meals, *Birkas HaMazon*, may only be recited over a cup of wine, and this is true even if *Birkas HaMazon* is recited separately by one or two individuals [as opposed to the group recitation, or *zimun*, when three or more men have eaten together]. This in fact is the third of the Four Cups. [It thus has independent status as a mitzvah, even without *Birkas HaMazon*,] but the Sages chose to link it with the mitzvah of the blessing.[169] Furthermore, *Tur* and *Shulchan Aruch* inform us that "It is a mitzvah to endeavor that the *Birkas HaMazon* be recited with *zimun*."[170] Though this law is mentioned in connection with *Birkas HaMazon*, its actual purpose is not for the sake of this blessing, but rather for the sake of the subsequent recitation of *Hallel*, to ensure that the lines beginning *Hodu* — "Give thanks to HASHEM" — will be recited responsively, between the reader and at least two others.[171] But *Netziv*, in his *Haggadah* entitled *Imrei Shefer*, cites evidence that for the sake of *Birkas HaMazon*, too, one should endeavor to arrange that there be a *zimun*. He points out that there is one hypothetical opinion in the *Gemara* (סָלְקָא דַעְתָּךְ) which holds that the Third Cup comes, not as a symbol of redemption and freedom, but simply because *Birkas HaMazon* requires a cup of wine. *Netziv* points out a difficulty in such a position. According to it, how can one explain the *mishnah* which states that even the poorest man of Israel, who depends upon charity, must be given enough so that he will have no less than four cups of wine for the Pesach *seder*? If indeed the third cup is only for the sake of *Birkas HaMazon*, then it would seem that the charity wardens need supply only three cups; for during the rest of the year, if a poor man cannot afford wine for *Birkas HaMazon*, the charity wardens are not required to supply it. Instead, he simply recited the blessing without wine. It would seem that he could do the same at the Pesach feast. But the answer must certainly be, asserts *Netziv*, that on Pesach this is impossible, since part of the mitzvah of the feast is to recite *Birkas HaMazon* with *zimun*.

Between the third and the fourth cups it is forbidden to drink wine,[172] lest one become intoxicated and be unable to finish the *seder*. But the wine which one drinks during the meal itself [i.e., between the second and third cups] does not cause intoxication.[173]

After *Birkas HaMazon* it is the custom to recite the passage beginning שְׁפוֹךְ חֲמָתְךָ — "Pour out Your wrath" — because one of the reasons for the Four Cups is that they correspond to the four cups [of retribution] which the Holy One, Blessed Be He, will in future time cause the idolatrous nations to drink.[174] According to the Vilna Gaon, a further reason for the recitation of *Shfoch Chamascha* is that the passage in the Hallel beginning לֹא לָנוּ — "Not to us give honor ..." speaks of the tribulations of the pre-Messianic era (חֶבְלֵי מָשִׁיחַ), of our subjugation to the kingdoms, and of the war of Gog and Magog.[175] *Or Zarua* gives another reason: Since we have mentioned the Egyptians several times, it is proper to curse them.[176] Before saying *Shfoch Chamascha* we open the door, to remember that this is *leil shimurim*, a night of protection;[177] and *Rama* tells us that by the merit of this faith, *Mashiach* will come and will pour out his wrath upon the idolators.[178]

Hallel, Nirtzah

The eating of the *Pesach* sacrifice must include the chanting of Hallel, psalms of praise — so we learn from a *mishnah* in *Pesachim*.[179] In the *Gemara*, this law is derived from a verse, *You shall have a song as on a night when the festival is sanctified* (הַשִּׁיר יִהְיֶה לָכֶם כְּלֵיל הִתְקַדֶּשׁ חָג; Isaiah 30:29) — "[This teaches us that] a night which is devoted to the festival requires *Hallel*." The special nature of the *Hallel* on Pesach night is not that of recitation (קְרִיאָה), but rather of song (שִׁירָה).[180]

The *Hallel* is divided into two parts — one part before the feast and one part after it. *HaManhig* points out that "Song is only chanted over wine," and explains that "The First Cup is enhanced by *Kiddush*, the Third Cup by *Birkas HaMazon*, the Fourth Cup, by *Hallel*. By what is the Second Cup enhanced? — for the *Haggadah* is simply the telling of a story [that is, it has no Scriptural or prophetic standing as do the blessings or the Psalms — *Ed.*] — hence it is necessary to chant part of the *Hallel* over the Second Cup."[181] *Levush* provides a different explanation. The part of the *Hallel* chanted before the feast speaks of the Exodus from Egypt ("When Israel went out from Egypt ..." — בְּצֵאת יִשְׂרָאֵל מִמִּצְרַיִם) and hence belongs with the *Haggadah*, while the second part of the *Hallel* speaks of other redemptions and of our destined Redemption; that is why it was set for after the feast.[182]

A *mishnah* records disagreement between *Beis Shammai* and *Beis Hillel* as to where the first part of the *Hallel* ends. "*Beis Shammai* say, until ... *the mother of children rejoices* (אֵם הַבָּנִים שְׂמֵחָה), and *Beis Hillel* say, until ... *He changes the flinty rock to a wellspring of water* (הַחַלָּמִישׁ לְמַעְיְנוֹ מָיִם)."[183] Another *mishnah* states that over the Fourth Cup we complete the *Hallel* and recite *birkas hashir*, "the blessing of the song."[184] The *Amoraim* are divided as to whether this phrase, *birkas hashir*, means the passage beginning יְהַלְלוּךְ — "all Your creations shall praise You ..." or the passage beginning נִשְׁמַת כָּל חַי — "The soul of every living thing will bless Your Name" — hence both passages are said. *Hallel HaGadol*, the Great *Hallel*, is also recited; this is chapter 136 of *Psalms* which begins, הוֹדוּ לַה' כִּי טוֹב — Give thanks to HASHEM, for [He] is good ..."[185] There are numerous opinions among the *poskim* concerning the correct wording of the closing blessing (*yishtabach*) which concludes this section of the Pesach feast, and also concerning the correct order of the passages beginning "All Your creatures shall praise You" (יְהַלְלוּךְ), "The soul of every living thing" (נִשְׁמַת כָּל חַי), and the closing blessing.[186]

During the period of the *Geonim* there was much debate over two questions: whether or not to recite the blessing "... Who has sanctified us by His commandments and commanded us to recite (or alternatively, "to complete") the *Hallel*;" and whether or not the *Hallel* [*HaGadol*] should be recited over a fifth cup of wine. Two reasons are given by those who oppose the recitation of the blessing before the chanting of *Hallel*. First, that [the blessing speaks of "reciting" the *Hallel*, and] this is not recitation, but rather song. Second, this *Hallel* is not chanted all at once, but rather divided into two parts, with an interruption between them.[187] *Tur*, after citing the various opinions about the blessing for the *Hallel*, writes that "In some communities the custom is for the congregation to recite the *Hallel* in the synagogue with a blessing so that it will be unnecessary to say a blessing over it during the reading of the *Haggadah* — and how good and pleasant (מַה טוֹב וּמַה נָּעִים) is this custom!" This practice has been adopted by the Sephardim and the chassidim. In *Eretz Yisrael* the custom was also accepted by that Ashkenazic group known as the *Perushim*.

The question about the fifth cup of wine depends upon which version of a *baraisa* (see *Pesachim* 118a) one accepts. The version in our current editions of the Talmud states, "Over the Fourth [Cup] one completes the *Hallel* and says *Hallel HaGadol*." But the version accepted by *Rif* reads, "Over the fifth [cup] one says *Hallel HaGadol*." The *Halachah* is that both *Hallels* are chanted over the Fourth Cup, not over a fifth cup.[188]

After the Fourth Cup one is not permitted to drink wine, nor any other drink except water, and this is for one of two reasons; either because further drinking might make one intoxicated and unable to continue telling of the Exodus (and the mitzvah of this telling is that it should continue "until sleep overcomes one"); or because further drinking would remove the taste of the *afikoman*[189] [which, as a commemoration of the *Pesach* sacrifice, should be the last taste remaining in one's mouth].

The custom is that on going to sleep after the *seder* one recites only the *Shema* and the blessing *hamapil* (" ... Who causes the bands of sleep to fall upon my eyes ..."), omitting the other passages normally recited before sleep as protection against harmful forces; for this is *leil shimurim*, a night of protection.[190] And in some places it is also customary not to lock the rooms in which people are sleeping, since " 'In Nissan they were redeemed and in Nissan they are destined to be redeemed' — and if the Prophet Eliyahu° comes on this

° [*Eliyahu HaNavi*, who will herald the coming of the righteous *Mashiach*, for which the month of Nissan is a propitious date, as the redemption from Egypt took place during that month, is thus given a special honor on this night. There is no doubt that his uncompromising and fearless stance in opposition to a wicked Sultan and a weak queen in one of Israel's most critical moments, when out of the whole nation very few did not bend their knee to Baal, earned him the love and reverence all Israel has since bestowed on him. His outraged rebuke fearlessly addressed to his king, *Have you murdered, and also taken possession?* (הֲרָצַחְתָּ וְגַם יָרָשְׁתָּ; *I Kings* 21:19), has echoed through the ages as a reproof to all evildoers. There is nothing in universal history to match the dramatic event described in the first book night, he should find an open door, and we should be able to go out quickly to greet him; and we believe in this, and for this faith we have great reward." For this same reason "it is customary to pour an extra cup of wine, beyond those needed for the participants in the feast; and it is called the cup of *Eliyahu HaNavi.*"[191]

We have completed the *seder* of Pesach as is prescribed by the *Halachah,* but by no means in all its rules and details. Rather we have recorded here a broad outline of the halachic elements of the *seder.*

---

of *Kings,* when before the whole nation the Prophet threw down his challenge: "*How long will you halt between two opinions? If HASHEM is God follow Him! but if Baal, follow him*" (עַד מָתַי אַתֶּם פֹּסְחִים עַל שְׁתֵּי הַסְּעִפִּים. אִם ה' הָאֱלֹקִים לְכוּ אַחֲרָיו; וְאִם הַבַּעַל לְכוּ אַחֲרָיו; *ibid.* 1t118:21). This event has been quoted as a possible explanation of the term תֵּיקוּ, an acronym for תִּשְׁבִּי יְתָרֵץ קוּשִׁיוֹת וּבַעֲיוֹת — The Tishbite (Eliyahu who came from Tishbi) will solve questions and problems — because he showed himself impatient of doubt and uncertainty and when he comes no unresolved problems will be left! The cry that has come down through the ages from Mount Carmel, *HASHEM, He is God!* (ה' הוּא הָאֱלֹקִים; *ibid.* v. 39), is timeless and will endure for all eternity. Rightly then do we on this night of nights pour a special cup for our honored guest, *Eliyahu HaNavi.* — Ed.]

[1] In *HaTzofeh*, 14 Nissan, 5702 (1942), Dr. Yom-Tov Levinski printed twelve different versions of mnemonics for the order of the *Seder*.

[2] See the *Haggadah* of Rav Reuven Margolios, p. 13; and Dr. Levinski, *HaTzofeh*, *loc. cit.*

[3] *Mishnah*, 114a.

[4] See *Tosafos* 101b, s.v. למה: *Shibolei HaLeket*, sec. 218: "A vessel or plate (קערה) is brought in ... "; *et. al.*

[5] 473.4.

[6] *Shulchan Aruch*, *loc. cit.*

[7] See below: *"Carpas," "Yachatz," "Maror," "Korech."*

[8] 114a.

[9] *Gemara*, 115b.

[10] *Rashi* and *Rashbam*.

[11] *Kol-Bo, Abudraham*, and others, in the name of the *Yerushalmi*; the statement is not found in our current editions of the *Yerushalmi*.

[12] *Tur* and *Shulchan Aruch*, 476, based on the *Rishonim*.

[13] See *Magen Avraham*, para. 8; *Taz* para. 4; *Aruch HaShulchan*, sec. 9.

[13*] *Rama*, 473.4.

[14] In the work, *Rambam and the Mechilta DeRashbi*, by Rav M.M. Kasher (New York, 5703 — 1943), p. 274, the author cites six reasons, gathered from the writings of the *Rishonim*, to explain why eggs are eaten Pesach night.

[15] *Maharil, Hilchos Pesach; Rama* and *Shulchan Aruch*, *loc. cit.*

[16] *Ba'er Heitev*, para. 8; *Shulchan Aruch HaRav*, sec. 26. And this is the arrangement adopted by the majority of *Haggados*.

[17] See *Maaseh Rav*, sec. 181.

[18] *Shabbos* 29:18.

[19] Sec. 271.

[20] However, in *Shitah Mekubetzes, Beitzah* 4b, it is stated that even the *Havdalah* of *Yom-Tov* is a Scriptural mitzvah. And see *Minchas Chinuch*, mitzvah 31.

[21] *Pesachim* 109a.

[22] 472.

[23] And see *Shaar HaTziun* in *Mishnah Berurah*.

[24] *Tosafos* and *Rosh*, beginning of *Arvei Pesachim*.

[25] 137.

[26] 472.

[27] And see vol. I, *Hoshana Rabba*, p. 330, concerning the *tosefes* of *Shmini Atzeres*.

[28] See *Beis Yosef* and *Darkei Moshe*, 472.

[29] See *Chok Yaakov, Shulchan Aruch HaRav, Chayei Adam, Mishnah Berurah, et. al.* The author of *Aruch HaShulchan* is the only one to hold that for "halachic purposes the principal opinion" is that of *Ramban*.

[30] *Pesachim* 109a.

[31] According to the calculations of Rav. A. Ch. Na'eh, in his work, *Shiurei Torah* (Jerusalem, 5703 — 1943, and 5707 — 1947), an *etzba* is equal to two centimeters, while the volume of a *revi'is* is 86.4 cubic cm.; this requires a vessel holding 86.4 grams of water. And for various opinions concerning this *shiur* see *Encyclopedia Talmudis*, s.v. *etzba*.

[32] *Shulchan Aruch HaRav*, 472:22; and see *Tosafos, Pesachim* 99b, and *Rosh* there, sec. 21; both *Rishonim* express doubt on this matter.

[33] *Yerushalmi, Pesachim* 10:1.

[34] *Pnei Moshe* on the *Yerushalmi*, *loc. cit.*; and see *Meiri, Pesachim* 108b.

[34*] *Rashbam, Pesachim* 99b; *Shulchan Aruch*, 472:13.

[35] See *Biur Halachah* in *Mishnah Berurah*, 656.

[36] *Mishnah*, 99b.

[37] *Shulchan Aruch*, *loc. cit.*

[38] *Nedarim* 49b.

[39] *Pesachim* 108b.

[40] *Rashi* and *Rashbam*, *loc. cit.*, based on *Sotah* 11b.

[41] *Tosafos*, *loc. cit.*

[42] *Otzar HaGeonim, Pesachim*, sec. 221.

[43] See *Otzar HaGeonim*, *loc. cit.*, 222-233. And see *Rama* in *Shulchan Aruch*, 483:2, and *Shulchan Aruch HaRav*, 472:27-9.

[44] *Tur* and *Shulchan Aruch*, 472.

[45] *Yerushalmi* 10:1.

[46] *Taz*, 472, para. 9. And see *Nazir* 38a where the *Gemara*, listing "five red things" (חמש סומקתא), includes among them the Four Cups of Pesach. And see *Roke'ach*, sec. 283, and the notes to *Machzor Vitri*, p. 274.

[47] *Taz. loc. cit.*

[48] 8:1.

[49] 3:1.

[50] 10:1.

[51] See the commentaries on the *Yerushalmi* on those pages; *Or Same'ach, Shabbos,* 29:14; *Mishmeres Habayis,* at the end of *Pe'as HaShulchan* on *Sheviis,* with the commentary of *Ridbaz,* p. 23 and 24; *HaYerushalmi Kipshuto* by Rav Sh. Liberman, p. 152; *Kalkeles Sheviis,* by Rav M. Chaskin, pp. 352-354; responsa *Keren Shlomo,* by Rav Sh. N. Kotler, secs. 88-91; and see the original commentary of Rav E.Y. Neimark in the periodical *Shaarei Tzion,* 5699 (1339), sec. 15; *et. al.*

[52] See below: "*Maggid*," "*Barech*," "*Hallel*."

[53] *Pesachim* 108b; *Shulchan Aruch* 472.8.

[54] *Pesachim* 110a. And see below, "*Maggid*," concerning whether or not the blessing "... Who creates the fruit of the vine" — (בּוֹרֵא פְּרִי הַגָּפֶן) is recited for each of the Four Cups. And see the disagreement between *Beis Yosef* and *Pri Chadash,* 484, concerning whether or not one fulfills the mitzvah if one drinks the Four Cups, not uninterruptedly, but with breaks in between, but nevertheless reads the *Haggadah* and the *Hallel* between the times of drinking [though not at the places indicated by the *Haggadah*]. And see *Biur Halachah* in *Mishnah Berurah,* 472.8.

[55] *Pesachim* 108a, with *Rashi* and *Rashbam.*

[56] *Shulchan Aruch* 473:3.

[57] *Pesachim* 103a. *Rashbam* there explains the reasons for each of the various opinions.

[58] For the detailed laws of *heseibah,* see the *Gemarah,* 108, and *Tur* and *Shulchan Aruch,* 472.

[59] *Pesachim* 115a.

[60] See *Tur* and *Shulchan Aruch, Orach Chaim* 158.

[61] 473:6.

[62] And see responsa *Eretz Tzvi,* by Rav A. Tz. Frommer, *Rosh Mesivta* of *Yeshivas Chachmei Lublin,* sec. 32, where the author expounds at length, bringing highly intricate arguments to justify the custom of performing *netilas yadayim* for the *carpas* on Pesach night, proving why it is more necessary to do this at that time than during the rest of the year. Incidentally, in the *Haggadah* of Rav Margolios, p. 17, the author explains this *netilas yadayim* simply by saying that it is a way of showing our freedom, since it is the way of free men to be careful about cleanliness in eating even a small amount. And this interpretation is surprising, for it runs counter to the *Gemara* and all the *poskim.*

[63] *Pesachim* 114 and 115.

[64] *Rashi,* 114a.

[65] *HaManhig,* p. 32, para. 60. And see *Maharil, Hilchos Haggadah.*

[66] See *Tur* and *Beis Yosef,* 473.

[67] And see in *Beis Yosef, loc. cit.,* an opinion cited as "I have found it written" (מָצָאתִי כָתוּב).

[68] 114b.

[69] *Ibid.* 115a, and *Tosafos, loc. cit. s.v.* מתקיף; *Shulchan Aruch* 475:2.

[70] See *Tosafos, loc. cit., s.v.* וְהָדָר; *Beis Yosef, Shulchan Aruch,* and their commentaries, 473.6.

[71] 39b.

[72] 115b.

[73] See *Tur* and *Beis Yosef,* 475.

[74] See *Otzar HaGeonim, Berachos, loc. cit.,* and *Pesachim, loc. cit.* And see Rav Sh. Albeck, in his notes on *Sefer HaEshkol,* pp. 59-61.

[75] See a detailed discussion of these customs in *Chiluf Minhagin Bein Bnei Eretz Yisrael UVein Bnei Bavel,* by Rav. B. M. Levine, pp. 46-48, and in *HaChilukim SheBein Anshei Mizrach UVnei Eretz Yisrael,* by Dr. Margolios, pp. 133-5. And see below, *When Pesach Falls on Shabbos.*

[76] 473.36.

[77] 115b.

[78] *Mishnah,* 116a; *Rambam,* 7:10.

[79] 110a.

[80] *Tur,* 474, in the name of Rav Sherira and Rav Hai; *Rif, Pesachim,* ch. 10; *Rambam,* 7:10. And see *Otzar HaGeonim,* 304-308.

[81] *Rosh* and *Tur,* and the *Mechaber* in *Shulchan Aruch,* 474.

[82] See *Machzor Vitri,* p. 276; *Otzar HaGeonim,* 310; *Tur,* in the name of Rabbeinu Chananel; *et. al.*

[83] *Rama* in *Shulchan Aruch, loc. cit.* And see *Beur HaGra* there.

[84] *Ibid.*

[84*] Below, *The Haggadah.*

[85] *Pesachim* 115b.

[86] *Shulchan Aruch HaRav,* 475.2; *Biur Halachah* in *Mishnah Berurah, loc. cit.;* and see *Aruch HaShulchan, loc. cit.*

[87] See above, p. 80.

[88] Or Zarua, part 2, sec. 256.

[89] Rosh, Pesachim ch. 10; Tur, 475. Concerning the law itself about the broken matzah, see below, "Yachatz."

[90] Tur, in the name of יֵשׁ אוֹמְרִים; and see Shibolei HaLeket on both opinions, sec. 218.

[91] Tosafos, Berachos 39b. And see Otzar HaGeonim, Pesachim, sec. 340.

[92] Tosafos, loc. cit., in the name of Rav Menachem of Vienna. [The reference to Vienna is almost certainly an error developed and perpetuated through successive printings of the Talmud; the authority is probably Rav Menachem of Toigni יוני or יואני) — Ed.] And see HaManhig, Hilchos Pesach, sec. 82.

[93] And see Shaagas Aryeh, sec. 100.

[94] See the works cited in Shaarei Teshuvah, end of sec. 475 and end of sec. 482; Sdei Chemed, Chametz UMatzah, sec. 14, os. 4; Archos Chaim, 475. And see also responsa Chelkas Yoav, Yoreh De'ah, sec. 9.

[95] See below, "Korech."

[96] Tur and Shulchan Aruch, 475.

[97] Pesachim 108a.

[98] Tur and Shulchan Aruch, 472:7.

[99] Rama, loc. cit.; and see Mishnah Berurah, loc. cit.

[100] 120a.

[101] 39a.

[102] Pesachim, ch. 10.

[103] Trumas HaDeshen, [Pesakim U]Kesavim, sec. 245.

[104] Yere'im HaShalem, sec. 94; and see above, p. 34.

[105] Sec. 100.

[106] See Chasam Sofer, sec. 140; Kesav Sofer, sec. 86; Emek Yehoshua, sec. 8; responsa Divrei Mordechai, sec. 48; Yeshuos Yaakov, sec. 475; Sho'el UMeshiv, sixth ed., sec. 10; responsa Toras Chesed, sec. 49; et. al.

[107] Berachos 39a: פרמינהו פרימי זוטי.

[108] See responsa Beis Ephraim, Orach Chaim, sec. 43; Nishmas Adam, sec. 33; Yeshuos Yaakov, 473; the Haggadah, Maaseh Yedei Yotzer, by Rav Sh. Kluger; et. al.

[109] Part 3, sec. 9.

[110] And see Chacham Tzvi, sec. 119.

[111] See Shaagas Aryeh, sec. 94; Kesav Sofer, sec. 98; Oneg Yom-Tov, sec. 39; Imrei Binah, Dinei Pesach, sec. 26; et. al.

[112] Rashbam, Pesachim 114a.

[113] Tosafos, 114a.

[114] See above, "Carpas."

[115] Pesachim, 120b.

[116] Minchas Chinuch, mitzvah 6.

[117] Concerning Hallel, see Tosafos, Megillah 21a.

[118] Pri Megadim, 477; Derech HaChaim, 123; and see responsa Binyan Shlomo, sec. 29.

[119] 108a, with Rashi and Rashbam.

[120] 115b, with Rashi, Rashbam, and Tosafos.

[121] 116a.

[122] Rama in Shulchan Aruch, 473.5, based on the Rishonim.

[123] See above, p. 78.

[124] Rashi, Pesachim 91b, s.v. לית ליה.

[125] Tur and Shulchan Aruch, 472.14. And see Beis Yosef there.

[126] 115a.

[127] 79a.

[128] 1:1. And see above, p. 34.

[129] See above, loc. cit.

[130] See the commentaries on Shulchan Aruch, 475.

[131] Rambam, Chametz UMatzah, 7:8; Or Zarua, part 2, sec. 256; Machzor Vitri, p. 282; Shulchan Aruch, 475.1.

[132] Hagahos Maimonios, in the name of Ri and Geonei Ashkenaz; Rama in Shulchan Aruch, loc. cit.

[133] Bach, Taz, Shulchan Aruch HaRav, and Aruch HaShulchan; et. al.

[134] Shibolei HaLeket, sec. 218; Roke'ach, sec. 283.

[135] HaManhig, 83; Or Zarua, part 2, sec. 257; Shulchan Aruch, 475; and all the Acharonim.

[136] Pesachim 53a.

[137] Magen Avraham, 476.

[138] Ibid.

[139] Aruch HaShulchan, 476.2.

[140] Yerushalmi, Pesachim 4:4; Shulchan Aruch, loc. cit., para. 2.

[141] Ibid.

[142] Rama, ibid. And see Rambam and the Mechilta DeRashbi, by Rav M.M. Kasher, p. 274, where the author gives six reasons, gathered from the writings of the Rishonim, to explain the custom of eating eggs on Pesach night.

[143] See *Chasam Sofer, Orach Chaim*, sec. 139; responsa *Tuv Taam VeDaas*, third ed., sec. 59; responsa *Machazeh Avraham*, sec. 116; *et. al.*

[144] *Mishnah, Pesachim* 117b, and *Rashbam* there.

[145] *Rama* in *Shulchan Aruch, loc. cit.*

[146] *Aruch HaShulchan*, end of sec. 476.

[147] See *Perush HaMishnayos* by *Rambam, Pesachim* 10:8, and *Aroch HaShalem, s.v.* אֲפִיקוֹמָן; *Tosefos Rabbi Akiva Eger* on *Mishnayos Pesachim, loc. cit.* in the name of the *Tishbi*.

[148] *Rashi* and *Rashbam, Pesachim* 119b.

[149] *Mishnah, Pesachim, loc. cit.*

[150] See *Pesachim* 119b.

[151] *Rambam, Chametz UMatzah* 8:9; *Tur* and *Shulchan Aruch*, 477, 478.

[152] *Rashi* and *Rashbam, loc. cit.* In their opinion, the essential mitzvah of eating *matzah* (מַצַּת חוֹבָה) is fulfilled by the *afikoman*.

[153] *Rosh, loc. cit.; Tur* and *Shulchan Aruch*, 478.1.

[154] See *Or Zarua*, part 2, sec. 256; *Shibolei HaLeket*, sec. 218; *HaManhig, Hilchos Pesach*, sec. 74; *et. al.* The term is likewise used by all the *Acharonim*.

[155] *Beis Yosef*, 478.

[156] *Maharil, Hilchos Pesach; Bach* and *Magen Avraham*, 477.

[157] See above, p. 36.

[158] *Pesachim* 120b: "In our time, if one eats *matzah* after *chatzos*, then according to Rabbi Elazar ben Azaryah one has not fulfilled the obligation." And see *Rashi, Rosh HaShanah* 20b, s.v. חצות.

[159] 477.

[160] For detailed discussions of this problem, see *Beis HaLevi*, part 1, sec. 34; *Or Same'ach, Chametz Umatzah* 6:1; *et. al.*

[161] *Tosafos, Pesachim* 117b.

[162] *Tosafos, loc. cit.* in the name of מְפָרְשִׁים; *Darkei Moshe*, 481, in the name of *Mahariv*. And see *Otzar HaGeonim, Pesachim*, sec. 358, and the commentaries on *Shulchan Aruch*, 478.

[163] *Tur* and *Rama, loc. cit.*

[164] *Magen Avraham, loc. cit.*

[165] *Rashbam*, 101a; *Tur* and *Shulchan Aruch, loc. cit.*

[166] The author of *Minhagei Yeshurun*, sec. 121, citing the author of *Amudei Or*, finds a hint of this custom in the Talmud: in *Berachos* 24a it is explained that placing something between the cushion and the chair is a customary way of guarding it (דֶּרֶךְ שְׁמִירָה); and since the Torah writes, *And you shall guard the matzos* (וּשְׁמַרְתֶּם אֶת הַמַּצּוֹת; *Exodus* 12:17), we hide the *afikoman* in the manner of a "guarded" thing.

[167] The author of *Chok Yaakov*, 472, para. 2, finds a hint of this custom, based on *Pesachim* 109a: "We snatch *matzah* on Pesach night, so that the children will not fall asleep."

[168] *Responsa of Maharshal*, sec. 88.

[169] *Pesachim* 117b: "[With] each one [of the Four Cups] a mitzvah is performed."

[170] *Tur* and *Shulchan Aruch*, 479.

[171] The source of this idea is in *Midrash Tehilim*.

[172] *Mishnah*, 117b.

[173] *Yerushalmi*, 10:6. And see *Rashbam* on the *mishnah*, 117b.

[174] *Ran, Pesachim*, beginning of ch. 10.

[175] *Beur HaGra*, 480.

[176] *Or Zarua*, sec. 256.

[177] *Ibid.*

[178] *Rama* in *Shulchan Aruch*, 480.

[179] 95a. And see above, p. 40.

[180] *Ran, Pesachim*, ch. 10, in the name of Rav Hai Gaon. And see *Otzar HaGeonim, Pesachim*, sec. 348.

[181] *HaManhig, Hilchos Pesach*, sec. 90.

[182] *Levush*, sec. 480. And see *Minhagim DeVei Rotenburg*, p. 25.

[183] 116b.

[184] *Mishnah*, 117b.

[185] 118a.

[186] See the *Rishonim* on *Pesachim*, 118a, and the commentaries on *Shulchan Aruch*, 480.

[187] See *Otzar HaGeonim*, 344-55; *Ran; Pesachim*, ch. 10; *et al.*

[188] See *Tur* and *Shulchan Aruch* and their commentaries, *loc. cit.*

[189] See *Tur* and *Shulchan Aruch, loc. cit.*

[190] *Maharil, Hilchos Pesach; Rama*, 481.2.

[191] *Maharil; Chok Yaakov* and *Shulchan Aruch HaRav*, 481.

ההַגָּדָה §

The Haggadah

There are no doubt more commentaries on the Haggadah of
Pesach than on almost any other area of our sacred literature.
A comparatively recent bibliography lists over 2700 editions of the
Haggadah since the advent of printing, many of them with new
commentaries. And just as every generation has its own problems
— for as we read in the Haggadah, "In every generation our
enemies rise against us to annihilate us," and it is only "the Holy
One, Blessed be He, Who saves us from their hands" — so every
generation produces fresh insights into this eternal story that we
retell every year.

A case in point is Zevach Pesach, a profound and moving
commentary by Don Yitzchak Abarbanel, who in addition to being
a supreme master in Torah was also the finance minister of the
Kingdom of Castile. The expulsion of the Jews from Spain in 1492
caused him, like many thousands of his brethren, to wander in
search of a new refuge, first in Naples where he succeeded in
partially rebuilding his life, only to flee again when the French
invaded the town. We hear of him briefly in Sicily, and later in
Corfu; until finally he completed his work on the Haggadah in
Venice.

Among the heartsearching questions Abarbanel asks is the one
that our People must have asked throughout the generations —
right to those of our own generation who "celebrated" the festival
of freedom in the extermination camps, and by our brethren who
celebrate Pesach under unspeakable conditions behind curtains of
iron and of oil. And that question is: Are we merely remembering
a historical event? For if so, what meaning has that event when
remembered under conditions that are as unspeakable as those of
ancient history?

Abarbanel's answer to this question rings true. The very fact that
even when most suppressed our People remember the miracle of
our redemption from Egypt is itself an assurance of the Geulah
Shlemah, the ultimate Redemption by our Righteous Mashiach.

The Haggadah, Abarbanel concludes, is not to be understoods a
mere story: the very secret of our future Redemption is hidden
therein.

On Pesach night at the *seder*, the *Haggadah* is the central feature; and it likewise holds a place of importance in the literature of *Halachah*. Fundamentally, the recitation of the *Haggadah* is neither a custom nor a Rabbinic decree, but rather a law of the highest order — a Scriptural commandment. The halachic literature examines the *Haggadah* in terms of several basic issues: the mitzvah; the blessing; the persons obligated; the time limits; and the wording.

The Mitzvah

To begin with the question of the mitzvah itself — as we have already mentioned, this is one of רמ״ח, the 248 positive Scriptural commandments. *Rambam* defines the mitzvah: " ... to tell about the miracles and wonders which were done for our ancestors in Egypt, on the night of the fifteenth of Nissan, as it is said, *Remember this day on which you went out from Egypt* (זָכוֹר אֶת הַיּוֹם הַזֶּה אֲשֶׁר יְצָאתֶם מִמִּצְרַיִם; *Exodus* 13:3); and as is said similarly, *Remember the day of Shabbos to sanctify it* (זָכוֹר אֶת יוֹם הַשַּׁבָּת לְקַדְּשׁוֹ; *ibid.* 20:8).[1]

Remember The fact that *Rambam* saw fit to cite the additional verse, *Remember the day of Shabbos,* has stimulated discussion by a number of scholars. What did *Rambam* wish to teach us by this addition; and what does the *Remember* of *Shabbos* tell us that we could not have learned from the *Remember* of Pesach?[2] In our own period, too, this addition by *Rambam* has occupied the attention of various authors.[3] One of the most likely suggestions is that *Rambam's* purpose was to deal with the question, How do we know that when the Torah commands us to *Remember this day,* it means that we should do so specifically *on* this day? It is in answer to this problem that *Rambam* writes, "as it is said similarly, *Remember the day of Shabbos to sanctify it:* for there, the expression, *to sanctify it* [*that is, to sanctify it* rather than some other day][4] tells us that it is on that very day itself that we are to "remember" it; and the same is true of the fifteenth of Nissan.[5]

A different solution also seems reasonable. The word, *Remember,* is vocalized in the Torah with a *kamatz* — זָכוֹר; this is the infinitive form of the verb; what leads us to interpret it as an imperative? Hence, *Rambam* cited the same word, with the same vocalization, in the verse about *Shabbos*; for there the expression, *to sanctify it* (לְקַדְּשׁוֹ) makes it clear that the Torah is not simply telling about events, but rather is giving a command.[6]

It must be noted, however, that this command to *Remember* is not the only source for this mitzvah. It has a second source, namely the verse, *And you shall tell your son* ... (וְהִגַּדְתָּ לְבִנְךָ; ibid. 13:8). The derivation of the commandment from this verse is found in *Mechilta DeRashbi*,[7] which states, "[From the verse,] *And it shall be, when your son asks you in the future* ... (וְהָיָה כִּי יִשְׁאָלְךָ בִנְךָ מָחָר לֵאמֹר; ibid. v. 14), one might conclude that if [your son] asks, you must tell him, and if not, you need not tell him. But we have the verse, *And you shall tell your son* — [This means, you shall tell him] even if he does not ask you. [From this verse] I learn only about the situation when one has a son — how do I know that one must tell about the Exodus even when alone with oneself, or to others [besides his son]? — from the verse, *And Moshe said to the People, 'Remember this day* ...' "[8] Thus it transpires that both verses are needed. From the verse, *And you shall tell your son* ... we would not know that there is a mitzvah even when one has no son; while from the verse, *Remember this day* ... we would not know the special mitzvah of relating the story of the Exodus to one's son.[9]

If it is true, then, that *Rambam* is careful to indicate that the time to "remember" the Exodus is the fifteenth of Nissan, this does not necessarily mean that this is the *only* time to do so. On the contrary, we are commanded to remember the Exodus every night of the year; this command is discussed in the Mishnah *(Berachos* 1:5) in a passage included in the *Haggadah* itself. "The Exodus from Egypt must be mentioned at night ... as it is said, ... *so that you shall remember the day of your going out from the land of Egypt all the days of your life* (לְמַעַן תִּזְכֹּר אֶת יוֹם צֵאתְךָ מֵאֶרֶץ מִצְרַיִם כֹּל יְמֵי חַיֶּיךָ; *Deuteronomy* 16:3) — *the days of your life* [would command us concerning] the days; *all the days of your life* includes the nights." This leads us to a fundamental question about the mitzvah of the *Haggadah*.° How is this night different from all other nights? In other words, what is the special quality of

To "Remember" Every Night

° [Incidentally, this is perhaps the right place to suggest that the four questions ought to be translated as an exclamation, "How different is this night!" rather than as a question as is traditional. We make great preparations and many changes so that our children should exclaim in wonder, "How different!" — and in the subsequent passages they enumerate the differences. — *Ed.*].

the mitzvah which is to be performed specifically on Pesach night?

A number of authors suggest solutions to this problem. *Minchas Chinuch* concludes that the distinguishing feature of the "remembering" on Pesach night is that it takes the form of a reply to one's son, or to someone else. Thus, if there is no one to whom to reply, then the mitzvah of "remembering" on Pesach night is indeed identical to that of any other night of the year. Most of the authors who deal with this problem, however, define the essential nature of the mitzvah on Pesach night as different from that for the rest of the year. The mitzvah during the rest of the year is simply to *mention* the Exodus, while on the this night the mitzvah consists of *telling* and *relating*, expanding on the story in detail and at length.[10]

On this basis, an ingenious interpretation has been provided for the passage in the *Haggadah* which states, "And even if we are all wise scholars ... it is still a mitzvah for us to tell about the going out of Egypt ... " In Tractate *Berachos*,[11] there is a passage describing how Rabbi Yehudah HaNasi, or "Rabbi," fulfilled the obligation of reciting the *Shema* as soon as evening arrived. Since he was teaching his students, and did not wish to interrupt, he would simply pass his hand before his face momentarily and perform the "acceptance of the yoke of the kingdom of heaven" contained in the first verse of the *Shema*. As for the mitzvah of mentioning the Exodus, rather than pausing to recite the third paragraph of the *Shema*, he was careful to teach one *halachah* (שְׁמַעְתָּא) every evening which contained reference in some way to the Exodus. This method, of course, was adequate only for the other days of the year, when the mitzvah consists simply of mentioning the going out from Egypt; it would not suffice for Pesach night, when the obligation is one of telling the story at length; here, an incidental reference by way of a lesson in *Halachah* would certainly not fulfill the mitzvah. This, then, is the meaning of the passage in the *Haggadah*. Even if we were all wise scholars, and all of us knew the Torah thoroughly — so that it would be possible for us to follow the practice of "Rabbi" and include the Exodus in a *Halachah* lesson — nevertheless, "it is still a mitzvah for us to *tell* about the going out from Egypt" — to tell, and not simply to mention.[12]

The Blessing

The question of a blessing over the *Haggadah* is discussed from two sides — positive and negative; that is, the blessing that is recited, and the one that is not; for the *Haggadah* has a blessing at the end — " ... Who redeemed us and redeemed our forefathers ..." (אֲשֶׁר גְּאָלָנוּ וְגָאַל אֶת אֲבוֹתֵינוּ) — but we do not recite a blessing when beginning it, as we do before performing many other mitzvos.

The Blessing That is ...

Concerning the blessing at the end of the *Haggadah*, there is a difference of opinion of *Tannaim*, as recorded in a *mishnah*. "One closes with redemption" (that is, one concludes the *Haggadah* with a blessing of redemption[13]). "Rabbi Tarfon says: ' ... Who redeemed us and redeemed our forefathers from Egypt,' and he does not close (אֵינוּ חוֹתֵם)" (that is, he does not conclude, "Blessed are You, *HASHEM*, Who redeemed Israel"). The *mishnah* continues, "Rabbi Akiva says: 'So may *HASHEM* our God and God of our fathers cause us to reach other seasons and festivals ... Blessed are You, *HASHEM*, Who redeemed Israel.' "[14] The opening statement in this *mishnah* (*Tanna kamma*) does not represent a third opinion besides that of Rabbi Tarfon and Rabbi Akiva; rather, there was an ancient *mishnah* which stated, "One closes with redemption," and Rabbi Tarfon and Rabbi Akiva differed over its interpretation.[15]

Rashbam explains the disagreement. According to Rabbi Tarfon, since the blessing consists only of one statement of gratitude, it is similar to a blessing over food or over the performance of a mitzvah, where the rule is that one begins with "Blessed are You ... " but does not close with "Blessed are You ..."[16] The *Halachah* in this instance follows Rabbi Akiva; and the wording of the *Haggadah* has been established accordingly.

... And The Blessing That Is Not

So much for the blessing that is; and what about the blessing that is not? Why do we not say, " ... Who sanctified us by His commandments and commanded us ..." over the telling of the *Haggadah*? this is a question discussed by both *Rishonim* and *Acharonim*. *Rosh* answers as follows: "You have asked why no blessing is recited over the telling of the *Haggadah*. The Holy One, Blessed be He, commanded us to do many things in commemoration of the going out from Egypt, and we do not recite a blessing over them. Examples are the setting aside of the first-born and the [celebration of] all the festivals (כָּל הַמּוֹעֲדִים). There is no need to mention, when setting aside the first-born, that we are doing so as a commemoration of the going out from Egypt; rather, the Holy One, Blessed be He, commanded us to do this act, and by so doing, we remember the going out from Egypt; similarly on the night of Pesach we have to remember יְצִיאַת מִצְרַיִם — this does not necessarily mean an oral telling, but rather, if someone asks, we explain it to him."[17] An objection has been raised: as stated before, we learn from a verse that even if there is no one to ask the question, one is obligated to tell the *Haggadah*.[18]

A different answer is provided in responsa *Besamim Rosh*,[19] a work which was attributed to *Rosh*. "It would not occur to anyone to recite a blessing for the recitation of blessings and praises; just as we do not recite, " ... Who sanctified us by His commandments and commanded us ..." before *Birkas HaMazon*, the grace after meals — and the *Haggadah* consists entirely of praise and glorification ..." This answer, too, is problematic; for we do say a blessing over the recitation of the *Hallel* even though it, too, consists entirely of praise and glorification.[19*]

Rabbeinu Yerucham[20] writes in the name of Rabbeinu Peretz: "We do not recite a blessing over the telling of the *Haggadah*, because in the *Kiddush* we have already said, 'a commemoration of the Exodus from Egypt.' " *Rashba*, on the other hand, explains, " ... because [the telling] has no minimum measure *(shiur)*; for one may fulfill the obligation with one utterance." The same objection is raised against both these explanations: Since the mitzvah consists of telling and relating at length, the obligation is fulfilled neither by the mention in *Kiddush* nor by a minimal utterance.[21]

One explanation offered by the *Acharonim* is that the *Haggadah* is concluded with the blessing, " ... Who redeemed Israel," and we never recite a blessing over a blessing.[22] To this the reply is given that for the reading of the Scroll of Esther we conclude with the blessing, " ... Who fights our fight," and nevertheless the Sages established a blessing to be recited at the beginning; for this does not constitute a blessing over the blessing of " ... Who fights our fight," but rather over the reading itself of the Scroll, which is the relating of a miracle — and if so, the same could be done for the *Haggadah*.[23]

In *Sefas Emes*, the Rebbe of Ger writes: " ... because even if we had not been commanded about this, of our own accord we would need to tell the story, as the Sages said, 'When a master sets a slave free and gives him silver and gold, [the slave] wishes to give thanks and praise.' "°[24] This is why there is no

---

° [Similarly, for example, we do not recite a blessing when fulfilling the commandment of honoring your father and mother because even if *Hashem* had not commanded us to do so our own senses would make us do so. — *Ed.*]

need for a blessing over this mitzvah.[25] Various *Acharonim* have written further about the blessing over the *Haggadah*.[26]

The Persons Obligated

As regards the persons obligated by the mitzvah of the *Women Haggadah*, there is much discussion of the question whether or not this is a commandment which obligates women. On the one hand, this is a positive mitzvah which must be performed at a set time (מִצְוַת עֲשֵׂה שֶׁהַזְּמַן גְּרָמָא) and women are exempt from all such mitzvos. On the other hand, the Torah did make an exception from this rule in obligating women for the related mitzvah of eating *matzah*. (As the Talmud explains, "Whoever is obligated not to eat *chametz*, is obligated to eat *matzah*.")[27] In another context, it is true, the Talmud cites the reasoning that "they, too, were included in the miracle;" but this is only a reason to include women in obligations of Rabbinic force, such as the drinking of the Four Cups of wine; it would not affect the question whether or not women are obligated by the positive Scriptural commandment of the *Haggadah*.[28]

Sefer HaChinuch states explicitly, "The mitzvah applies to both males and females." *Minchas Chinuch* objects at length to this statement. "I have in no way found any reason why women should be obligated." He goes on to prove from the wording of *Rambam* that women are not obligated by this mitzvah.

Tur and *Shulchan Aruch*[29] state as a general principle that for all the mitzvos to be performed on this night, women too are obligated. But they do not clarify whether the women's obligation to perform the mitzvah of the *Haggadah* is of Scriptural force (as the author of *Chinuch* maintains)° or whether the obligation derives from the reasoning of "they, too, were included in the miracle" — in which case the obligation is of Rabbinic status. The question has a practical consequence: our answer will determine whether or not a man's Scriptural obligation is fulfilled if a woman performs the mitzvah on his behalf by acting as the narrator while he listens.

° [*Rambam* in *Sefer HaMitzvos* (at the end of the list of positive commandments) lists sixty positive Scriptural commandments which an ordinary person may be expected to perform during his lifetime. Among these is the mitzvah of telling about the Exodus. *Rambam* further lists fourteen of the above sixty that do not apply to women. Our mitzvah is not included in the fourteen. Thus it would seem that *Rambam*, too, considers this mitzvah to apply to women. — Ed.]

The wording used by *Baal HaTanya* in *Shulchan Aruch HaRav* makes it clear that for all the mitzvos performed on that night the women's obligation is of Rabbinic force, on the basis of "they, too, were involved ..."; the exception is the eating of *matzah*, for which women are Scripturally obligated.[29*] In any case, *Rama* writes that "One should tell the *Haggadah* in a language understood by the women and children, or else explain the topics to them; and it was the practice of Rav Yaakov of London to tell the entire *Haggadah* in the local language so that the women and children would understand."[30] *Chayei Adam* writes: "Hence it is obligatory that the serving-woman, too, must sit at the table and hear the entire *Haggadah*; and if she needs to go out of the room to cook, in any case she is obligated to hear the *Kiddush*; and when [the one telling the *Haggadah*] arrives at the words, "Rabban Gamliel said, Whoever does not explain these three things has not fulfilled his obligation ... she must come in and hear, until after the Second Cup; for whoever does not explain these three things [or hear them explained on her behalf] has not fulfilled [her] obligation. And it is customary also to call her to hear [the passage about] the ten plagues that [*Hashem*] brought down upon the Egyptians, in order to relate how many miracles the Holy One, Blessed be He, did for Israel."[31]

One authority does indeed interpret this law about translating the *Haggadah* as stemming not from the fact that women are obligated by the mitzvah of the *Haggadah*, but rather from the obligation of the men; for the men are obligated to make known to the women the miracles and wonders of the going out from Egypt; and if they tell the *Haggadah* in a language the women do not understand, this does not qualify as "telling" or "making known."[32] However, others find this reasoning questionable, arguing to the contrary, that the necessity for translation stems from the obligation of the women themselves.[33]

The author of *Chayei Adam* gives an original proof for the idea that the women are obligated by the mitzvah of the *Haggadah*. The women are obligated to drink the Four Cups; and this mitzvah is only fulfilled if the cups are drunk in connection with the appropriate sections of the *Haggadah*;[34] hence the women are necessarily obligated by the *Haggadah*, in order to be able to drink the Four Cups in connection with it.[35]

Rav Shlomo HaKohen of Vilna produces an exegetical derivation of his own to show that the Torah obligates women in the mitzvah of the *Haggadah*. He notes that the commandment of telling about the Exodus and the prohibition against eating *chametz* are written in the same verse *(Remember this day on which you went out from Egypt ... and chametz shall not be eaten; Exodus 13:3);* this, says the author, constitutes a *hekesh,* an instance where the Torah has placed two things side by side in order to teach a *halachah* — in this case, the law to be derived is that "whoever is obligated not to eat *chametz* is likewise obligated to *remember this day.*"[36]

Children

From *Shulchan Aruch HaRav* we learn that once children are old enough to be taught (הִגִּיעוּ לְחִינוּךְ) — the Rav states that this is when "they have sufficient understanding to grasp what is told them about the going out from Egypt in the recitation of the *Haggadah*" — then, "it is proper to train them to hear the *Haggadah.*"[37] Thus it transpires that the commandment, *And you shall tell your son,* does not obligate the father alone. Just as, with all the mitzvos of the Torah, there is an obligation to train a child to perform them even before he or she comes of age and is legally obligated, here too there is an obligation to train the child to take part in the mitzvah.

The Blind

The obligation of a blind person (סוּמָא) is the subject of special discussion in the halachic literature on the *Haggadah.* In Tractate *Pesachim* we find, "Rav Acha bar Yaakov said, The *suma* is exempt from telling the *Haggadah.*" Rav Acha bar Yaakov's derivation of this law is based on the law about the *ben sorer umoreh,* the rebellious son. There, the verse says, *This son of ours ...* (בְּנֵנוּ זֶה; *Deuteronomy* 21:20). The Sages interpret the demonstrative pronoun, *This* (זֶה) as indicating the exclusion of blind parents from this law — "Since it says, *This,* it implies that they must identify him visually."[38] Rav Acha bar Yaakov explains, "Here [concerning Pesach] it is written *Because of this* (בַּעֲבוּר זֶה; *Exodus* 13:8), and there [concerning the rebellious son] it is written, *This son of ours* — Just as, there, a blind person is exempted, so also here, the blind person is exempted."[39] The Gemara, however, rejects the assertion of Rav Acha bar Yaakov. For Rav Yosef and Rav Sheshes, who were blind, not only recited the *Haggadah,* but did so on behalf of others. They held that the derivation suggested by Rav Acha bar Yaakov is invalid (אֵין זוֹ גְזֵרָה שָׁוָה) since the words, *because of this,* have a different purpose. "It is because of *matzah* and *maror* that the phrase is there" (*Rashbam:* "It is because of this that I eat *matzah* and *maror*, as a reminder of what [*Hashem*] did for me when I came out of Egypt").[40]

Although the exemption of the blind is rejected in terms of this specific derivation by Rav Acha bar Yaakov, nevertheless the issue depends on a more general disagreement; whether or not the blind are exempt from mitzvos altogether.[41] The author of *Mordechai*[42] in fact uses our *Gemara* passage to prove that the *Halachah* follows the view that the blind are obligated by mitzvos in general; for we see that Rav Acha felt that he needed a special exegesis (... *because of this* ...) to exempt the blind from the mitzvah of the *Haggadah*; and further we see that Rav Yosef and Rav Sheshes both told the *Haggadah* and did so on behalf of others.[43]

The Time

The time for the performance of this mitzvah is specified by the Torah: *And you shall tell your son on this day* ... In *Mechilta*[44] we read, "[From the words, *And you shall tell your son* ...] one might think that the telling should begin from the beginning of the month, Rosh Chodesh. But the Torah says, ... *on this day.* If *on this day*, perhaps one might think [the mitzvah should be performed] while it is still daytime (מִבְּעוֹד יוֹם); but the Torah says, ... *because of this*, [as if to say,] 'I command you to do this only at the time when *matzah* and *maror* are set before you.' "

During Tosefes Yom-Tov? It has been asked whether this mitzvah of the *Haggadah* may be performed during that period just before night which constitutes the *tosefes Yom-Tov*, the extra time taken from the ordinary day and added on to the entering sacred day; for we know that it is normally possible to fulfill the obligations of *Kiddush* and the evening prayer of *Yom-Tov* during this *tosefes* even though it is not yet actually night.

Rav Meir Michl Rabinowitz, one of the *geonim* of Vilna in his generation, has explained this issue clearly. He writes that just as the mitzvos of *matzah* and *maror* cannot be performed during the *tosefes*,[45] so too the *Haggadah*, which is connected to the time of *matzah* and *maror*, cannot be performed during the *tosefes*. He uses this fact, furthermore, to explicate the phrase of *Mechilta*, "Perhaps one might think [that the mitzvah should be performed] while it is still daytime." [Since *Mechilta* does not say, "during the day," but rather, "while it is still daytime,"] "this indicates that even according to the hypothetical position expressed by the words, 'one might think ...', the essential time for the mitzvah is at night; but the hypothesis was that one might begin 'while it is still daytime.' " And this, indeed, is the meaning of the passage in *Mechilta*, according to Rav Meir Michl: the topic is the period of the *tosefes*, the assumption being that the mitzvah of the *Haggadah* may be performed [or at least begun] during this time, as is the case [on other *Yamim Tovim*] with *Kiddush* and the evening prayer. But from the verse, ... *because of this*, the Talmud learns that "I command you to do this only at the time when *matzah* and *maror* are set before you" — and the time for these two mitzvos is only when it is actually night.[46]

This phrase, "at the time when *matzah* and *maror* are set before you" does not refer to a time period alone, but also to a concrete situation. That is, these items must actually be placed before the one who is reading the *Haggadah*. As the Talmud° says, the *matzah* is termed by the Torah, *lechem oni, the bread of affliction (Deuteronomy* 16:3), and this implies as well, "bread over which many things are recited *(onim)*."[47] And *Rashi* comments, "For the *Hallel* is chanted over it, and the *Haggadah* is told over it."[48]

If the time for performing the mitzvah of the *Haggadah* thus begins only when it is actually night, it remains to ask when the time for this mitzvah ends. It would seem at first glance that since the Torah indicates that the *Haggadah* is to be told "at the time when *matzah* and *maror* are set before you," its final time limit would depend upon that of *matzah* and *maror:* according to Rabbi Elazar ben Azaryah this would mean until midnight, and according to Rabbi Akiva, until dawn.[49] And this in fact is the conclusion adopted by one great authority;[50] furthermore, this author argues that the *Halachah*, regarding the *Pesach* sacrifice and the *Haggadah* as well, fixes their time limit at dawn. His proof is based on the talmudic story included in the *Haggadah* itself, relating how certain of the *Tannaim* were once sitting in Bnei-Brak and discussing the tale of the Exodus all through the night — even though one of those very *Tannaim* was Rabbi Elazar ben Azaryah. This, says our author, is proof that Rabbi Elazar conceded to the other *Tannaim* that the time limit for these mitzvos is dawn rather than midnight.[51] Other *Acharonim*, however, use this same story cited in the *Haggadah* as proof that even according to those who hold that the time limit for the eating of *matzah* is midnight, it is a mitzvah to tell about

The Time to Finish

° [The derivation here is based on the similarity between the words, עָנִי, "affliction," and עוֹנִים, "they answer" or "they say aloud." — Ed.]

the Exodus until morning. Some, in fact, interpret the whole sequence of the passage in this light. The *Haggadah* says, "And whoever goes to great lengths in telling about the Exodus is praiseworthy." That is, whoever "goes to great lengths" in that he continues telling of the Exodus even beyond the essential time of obligation, is praiseworthy; and has proof of this fact, "It once happened that Rabbi Eliezer and Rabbi Yehoshua and Rabbi Elazar ben Azaryah and Rabbi Akiva and Rabbi Tarfon were at the feast together in Bnei-Brak ... "[52]

The Wording

From   The wording of the *Haggadah* was established in very early
Temple generations. We have seen that Rabbi Akiva and Rabbi
Times   Tarfon, who lived at the time of the Destruction of the Temple, had a difference of opinion about a *mishnah* which was already ancient in their time, on the subject of the correct version of the Blessing of Redemption in the *Haggadah*.[53] Among the questions included in the passage, "How is this night different ... " as recorded in the Mishnah, one question obviously dates from the time when the Temple was still standing: "For on all other nights we eat meat either roasted, boiled, or cooked, and on this night, only roasted." Again the Rabban Gamliel who states that "whoever does not explain these three things on Pesach, has not fulfilled his obligation," was Rabban Gamliel the Elder, [who lived in the time of the Temple,] for when he spoke of the *Pesach* sacrifice he did not say, as we do, "The *Pesach* sacrifice which *our forefathers used to eat* ..."[54] but rather, "This *Pesach* sacrifice which we eat."

The wording of the passages beginning "in every generation ..." (בְּכָל דּוֹר וָדוֹר) and "Therefore we are obligated to give thanks ..." (לְפִיכָךְ) and the Blessing of Redemption ("... Who redeemed Israel" — גָּאַל יִשְׂרָאֵל) are all recorded in the Mishnah. And this, too, comes from the Mishnah: "One opens with [words of] discredit and closes with praise, expounding [the verses beginning] *an Aramean was destroying my father* (אֲרַמִּי אֹבֵד אָבִי; *Deut.* 25:5-8) until he completes the entire passage." Regarding this *mishnah* the *Amoraim* differed. "What is the meaning of 'discredit'? Rav said it refers to 'Originally our ancestors were idol-worshipers' (מִתְּחִלָּה עוֹבְדֵי עֲבוֹדָה זָרָה הָיוּ אֲבוֹתֵינוּ); Shmuel said it refers to 'We were slaves to Pharaoh' (עֲבָדִים הָיִינוּ)."[55]

Shulchan Aruch HaRav states that "the basic wording of the *Haggadah* as established by the Sages is obligatory upon all, from the beginning of 'We were slaves to Pharaoh,' (עֲבָדִים הָיִינוּ) until 'and whoever goes to great lengths ... is praiseworthy' (הֲרֵי זֶה מְשֻׁבָּח); and then from the beginning of 'Originally our ancestors were idol-worshipers (מִתְּחִלָּה עוֹבְדֵי עֲבוֹדָה זָרָה הָיוּ אֲבוֹתֵינוּ) until the end of the exposition of the verse, 'an Aramean was destroying my father' ... and then the passages beginning, 'The *Pesach* sacrifice which our forefathers used to eat ... This *matzah* ... This *maror* ... In every generation ... And He took us out from there ... Therefore we are obligated to give thanks ...' up to 'Blessed are you, HASHEM, Who redeemed Israel' (גָּאַל יִשְׂרָאֵל). All the rest of the *Haggadah* [is not an institution of the Sages, but rather] is the *minhag* [custom] practiced by all Israel from the first generations."[56] Rav Netronai Gaon has the following to say concerning those who recite the *Haggadah*, but omit the midrashic passages: "It goes without saying that they do not fulfill the obligation; rather, one who does this is an apostate (מִין) and his heart is in conflict with his people (חָלוּק לֵב), he denies the teachings of the Sages and treats contemptuously the words of the Mishnah and Talmud, and all communities are obligated to ostracize him and to segregate him from the Congregation of Israel, as it is written, *And he shall be segregated from the Congregation of the Exile* (וְהוּא יִבָּדֵל מִקְּהַל הַגּוֹלָה; *Ezra* 10:8) ... "[57]

The beginning of the *Haggadah* is the words, *Ha lachma anya,* "This bread of affliction." Or, as *Rambam* states, "The wording of the *Haggadah* used by Israel in the time of Exile is as follows: One begins over the Second Cup, saying, 'In haste they went out from Egypt. This bread of affliction ...' The conclusion of the *Haggadah* is the blessing, '... Who redeemed Israel.' " (The recitation of *Hallel* which follows is not part of the *Haggadah*, but is a mitzvah in its own right.) Even though after the Blessing of Redemption the *Haggadah* is essentially completed, still "a person is obligated to discuss the laws of the Pesach sacrifice and the going out from Egypt, and to tell about the miracles and wonders that the Holy One, Blessed be He, did for our forefathers [and to continue these discussions] until sleep overcomes him."[58]

Minor Variations

In general, all versions of the *Haggadah* — Ashkenazi, Sephardi, Yemenite, and so on — are essentially similar. At various points, however, we do find minor variations among the versions. One such variation is found in the Yemenite *Haggadah*, after the line, "If he had slain their firstborn but had not given us their wealth, it would have been enough (*dayeinu*)." At this point we find the following insertion. "And whence do we learn that He gave us their wealth? — because it is said, *And [the Egyptians] gave them what they requested, and they despoiled Egypt* (וַיַּשְׁאִלוּם וַיְנַצְּלוּ אֶת מִצְרַיִם; *Exodus* 12:36) — [The word, they despoiled — וַיְנַצְּלוּ — has the same root as "watery depth" — מְצוּלָה — this is a hint that] they made [Egypt] like a watery depth that is empty of fish. And why does the Torah value more highly (מְחַבֵּב) the spoils taken at the Red Sea than those taken in Egypt? — The reason is, that in Egypt [the children of Israel] took what was in the houses [of the Egyptians], while at the Red Sea, they took what had been in the treasure-houses; and this is what Scripture says in the verse, *The wings of the dove are covered with silver* (כַּנְפֵי יוֹנָה נֶחְפָּה בַכֶּסֶף; *Psalms* 68:14); this refers to the despoilment in Egypt. ... *And her limbs are engraved with yellow gold* (וְאֶבְרוֹתֶיהָ בִּירַקְרַק חָרוּץ; *ibid.*) — this refers to the despoilment at the Sea. *And you increased and grew great* (וַתִּרְבִּי וַתִּגְדְּלִי; *Ezekiel* 16:7; this is the despoilment in Egypt. *And you came in countless ornaments* (וַתָּבֹאִי בַּעֲדִי עֲדָיִים; *ibid.*) — this is the despoilment at the Sea. *We shall make for you necklaces of gold* (תּוֹרֵי זָהָב נַעֲשֶׂה לָּךְ; *Song of Songs* 1:11); this is the despoilment in Egypt. ... *with points of silver* (עִם נְקֻדּוֹת הַכָּסֶף; *ibid.*) — this is the despoilment at the Sea." The *Haggadah* then continues, "And if He had given us their wealth, but had not split the Sea for us ... "[59]

The Haggadah as Halachah

Many works discuss the text of the *Haggadah* from the halachic standpoint. For example, the Blessing of Redemption contains the phrase (referring to the future *Beis HaMikdash*), " ... *and there we shall eat from the offerings and from the Pesach sacrifices ...* " (וְנֹאכַל שָׁם מִן הַזְּבָחִים וּמִן הַפְּסָחִים), and the order of words here is deliberate; it would be incorrect to say, 'from the *Pesach* sacrifices and from the offerings.'[60] The reason is that the *Pesach* sacrifices must be eaten on a full stomach (עַל הַשּׂוֹבַע), and hence the offerings called *zevachim*, that is, "the festival-offering of the fourteenth of Nissan," are eaten first. Of course, if the fourteenth should happen to be *Shabbos*, in which case the *Pesach* sacrifice may be offered up, but not the *zevachim*, then on Pesach night, *motzaei Shabbos*, the *Pesach* sacrifice alone is eaten without any *zevachim*.° For

° [In the case referred to — that is, when Pesach falls on Sunday, so that *erev* Pesach is *Shabbos* — the only day on which a *zevach* could be brought before Pesach would be on Friday. But a *zevach* brought on Friday could not be eaten on *motzaei Shabbos*, for the maximum time during which a sacrifice may be eaten is two days and one night — viz., Friday, Friday night and *Shabbos*. — Ed.]

this reason certain authorities have written that on such a Pesach which falls on *motzaei Shabbos* the word-order should be, "and there we shall eat from the *Pesach* sacrifices and from the offerings;" in this case "the offerings" are the peace-offerings (שַׁלְמֵי חֲגִיגָה) which will be offered up the day after Pesach;[61] and indeed this reversal of wording on *motzaei Shabbos* is recorded in most current *Haggados*. However, in responsa *Knesses Yechezkel*[62] the author writes, "Pesach of the year 5487 (1727) occurred on *motzaei Shabbos* and I gave a public talk in which I referred to the statement of certain authorities who have written that on such a Pesach the wording should be, '... from the *Pesach* sacrifices and from the offerings,' since the festival-offerings cannot be sacrificed on *Shabbos*; and I pointed out that this is incorrect, for our prayer here is that *in the coming year*, we shall merit to eat these sacrifices — and in the coming year, Pesach will not fall on *motzaei Shabbos*." This author goes on to point out that even if it should happen that according to the calendar Pesach would fall on *motzaei Shabbos* the coming year also, it still would not be correct to reverse the normal wording; for our prayer is that we shall merit to eat the *Pesach* sacrifices when the *Beis HaMikdash* is rebuilt; and when that happens, the calendar will again be determined according to eye-witness reports of the new moon; so it is possible that Pesach will not fall on *motzaei Shabbos* after all. And it is interesting to note that Rav Yaakov Emden, who was the contemporary of the author of *Knesses Yechezkel* and was often his adversary in halachic controversy (בַּר פְּלוּגְתָּא), in this case concurs; he writes in his *Siddur* that the usual word order of the blessing "should not be changed on any occasion," not even on *motzaei Shabbos* — though the reason given by Rav Emden is a different one, namely, that the wording of the blessing should be in accordance with the majority of years.

Halachic commentaries on the *Haggadah* itself exist in great abundance, and in various forms: some present a straight-forward interpretation; others, ingenious commentary, probing talmudic analysis, or difficult problems and their solutions. Among the numerous commentaries which have been written on the *Haggadah*, there are those which are permeated from beginning to end with intricate halachic discourse. One such work, for example, entitled *Bris Mateh Moshe*,[63] contains one hundred and four double-columned pages filled with tremendous erudition, discussions far removed indeed from the simple meaning of the words. And there are other such communities, which, although they do not come under the category of simple paraphrasing of the text, are graced with the lightning-flashes of profound study.

Here we shall present a few examples of halachic commentary on the *Haggadah*.

Even If We Were All Learned

"And even if we were all sages, all men of understanding, all elders, all learned in Torah, it is a mitzvah for us to tell of the going out from Egypt; and whoever goes to great lengths in telling about the going out from Egypt, is to be praised." The Talmud states in Tractate *Makos* [64] that the act of cutting wood for the *sukkah* is not inherently a mitzvah, since if one were to find wood that is already cut, one would not cut more. The *Gemara* finds the implications of this statement problematic. It asks,[65] "Shall we say, then, that when a teacher chastises his students he is not performing a mitzvah, since if they were already learned it would not be a mitzvah?" The reply is, "There [in the case of the teacher], even if they are already learned it is a mitzvah, for it is written, *Correct your son and he will give you rest, and will provide pleasure to your soul* (יַסֵּר בִּנְךָ וִינִיחֶךָ וְיִתֵּן מַעֲדַנִּים לְנַפְשֶׁךָ; *Proverbs* 29:17). From this is it clear that were it not for the existence of a distinct and independent obligation, as reflected in the verse, there would indeed be no mitzvah to chastise students who are already learned. We may apply this line of reasoning to the mitzvah of the *Haggadah*. If one were to assume that the telling about the Exodus is purely for the sake of informing people about the meaning of the *Pesach* sacrifice, the *matzah*, and the *maror*, then it would follow that if the people already knew this information, there would be no mitzvah in the telling (as the Talmud says concerning the students: " ... if they were already learned, it would not be a mitzvah"). And even in cases where the people being told did not already know, the telling would be nothing more than a way of preparing them and making them fit to perform the mitzvos of eating *matzah* and *maror*; hence the rule, "whoever goes to great lengths, is to be praised," would be inappropriate [for there is no point in extending an act of preparation beyond the point where it has accomplished its purpose]. This is the meaning of the passage, "And even if we were all sages ... it is a mitzvah for us ... " — this comes to inform us that this telling about the Exodus is a distinct and independent mitzvah; and that is why it is appropriate to say, "whoever goes to great lengths, is to be praised." And as evidence that there is indeed a distinct and independent mitzvah, we are told, "It once happened that Rabbi Eliezer and Rabbi

Yehoshua ... were at the feast in Bnei Brak ..." — and among these Sages was Rabbi Elazar ben Azaryah, the proponent of the opinion that the time limit for the eating of *matzah* is midnight, and yet all the same they continued telling of the Exodus until dawn. Thus it is impossible to argue that this telling is simply a preparatory act for the eating of *matzah*; for they went on telling even after the time limit for the eating of *matzah* had passed.[66]

The above commentary concerns a *Haggadah* passage whose main contents are halachic in nature. There are other such passages in the *Haggadah*, setting forth basic laws and legal details — "The going out from Egypt must be mentioned at night;" "Rabban Gamliel used to say, whoever does not explain these three things ... ", and so on. Certain of these have already been the subject of comment in the course of this chapter. But even on those sections of the *Haggadah* which consist of narration or the description of miracles, innumerable explanations with a halachic bent have been written. The very opening words of the *Haggadah*, *Ha lachma anya* — "This bread of affliction" — may serve as an example.

Royal Food

Netziv[67] demonstrates, by citing the *Gemara*[68] and *Tosefta*[69] that leavened bread by itself is characterized as royal food. [The Talmud explains why the *kohanim* are allowed to add wine, oil or honey to their priestly portion of the *minchah*, or flour offering (i.e., bread), stating that this is the manner in which kings eat such food, and when the Torah characterizes the priestly portions as לְמָשְׁחָה *(Numbers* 18:8), this means "for greatness" (לִגְדוּלָה) — i.e., as symbols of royal service.] *Matzah*, on the other hand, is not characterized as royal food except when eaten with meat. *Netziv* further proves that on the very first Pesach, the one observed in Egypt on the night before the Exodus, the meat of the *Pesach* sacrifice was eaten separately from the *matzah*, in contrast with subsequent observation of the festival, where the obligation is to eat the meat and the *matzah* in conjunction, either as a sandwich (according to Hillel) or else the one immediately after the other (according to *Chachamim*). Thus we see that *matzah* only had the character of "the bread of affliction" on that very first Pesach and after the Destruction of the Temple [but when the Temple is standing and the meat of the *Pesach* sacrifice is eaten with the *matzah*, the latter becomes royal food]. This is why the text reads, "This bread of affliction which our forefathers ate *in the land of Egypt.*" (The passage *Ha lachma anya* was added to the *Haggadah* after the Destruction of the *Beis HaMikdash.)*°

Counting
the
Plagues
Sometimes a commentary does not alter our standard interpretation of the words of a passage, but simply explains those words in the light of a given *halachah*. What is it that underlines the difference of opinion between Rabbi Eliezer and Rabbi Akiva in the exposition of the verse, *He sent His fierce anger against them* (יְשַׁלַּח בָּם חֲרוֹן אַפּוֹ; *Psalms* 74:49)? For Rabbi Eliezer does not consider the words, *His fierce anger* to correspond to plagues; [rather, he begins his count only with the continuation of the verse:] *"Wrath* is one, *indignation,* two ... " But Rabbi Akiva includes the words *His fierce anger* within the plagues: *"His fierce anger is one; wrath,* two ... " *Gra* explains the difference in terms of a *mishnah* in Tractate *Mikvaos* (5:4) which records a disagreement among *Tannaim.* The disagreement concerns two categories of water; *mikvaos* are standing bodies of water and *neharos* (lit., "rivers"), are bodies of flowing water. The question is whether every sea in the world is classified in the category of *mikvaos,* or whether only the ocean, the Great Sea, comes under this category, while all other seas are considered *neharos.*

How is this *mishnah* connected to the *Haggadah?* The link is provided by a verse in *Chavakuk* which associates the words "fierce" and "anger" with *neharos,* and the word, "wrath" with the sea. *Has HaShem been fierce to the rivers, is Your anger against the rivers, is Your wrath against the sea?* (הֲבִנְהָרִים חָרָה ה' אִם בַּנְּהָרִים אַפֶּךָ אִם בַּיָּם עֶבְרָתֶךָ)[69*] If the seas are considered in the same category as rivers, in accordance with one opinion in the *mishnah,* then *fierce anger* and *wrath* are to be seen as one. But if the seas and the rivers are two separate categories, then likewise *fierce anger* is to be counted separately from *wrath.* [70]

Halachic
Eradication
And for a sample of an ingenious halachic exposition: The *Haggadah* tells us, "But Lavan sought to eradicate the whole [People]." Where do we find it recorded that Lavan sought this? In Tractate *Gitin*[71] we learn that if a man appoints a legal emissary, instructing him, "Go forth and act as my proxy in betrothing a woman to me," and the emissary subsequently dies, the man who sent him is forbidden to

---

° [We have in effect three periods. The first time matzah was eaten in Egypt when it was 'bread of affliction'; during the time that the *Beis HaMikdash* stood, when eaten with the meat of the *korban Pesach* it was 'royal food'; and since the Destruction, when it is again 'bread of affliction.' — *Ed.*]

marry any woman in the world. This is because a man may not marry both a woman and her near relative; and since this man does not know whom his emissary married to him before dying, it may be that any woman is the near relative of her to whom he is unknowingly betrothed. Now, Avraham had sent forth his servant, Eliezer, to betroth a woman to Yitzchak; and the Midrash tells us that Lavan wished to kill Eliezer — hence, if Lavan had succeeded, Yitzchak would have been forbidden to marry, and Avraham would have had no descendants.[72]

Various penetrating discussions have focused on the fifteen stanzas of the passage, *dayeinu* — "... it would have been enough for us." One of these concerns the line, "If He had slain their firstborn but had not given us their property, *dayeinu*." Our author interprets this line in terms of the talmudic principle, קָם לֵיה בִּדְרַבָּה מִינֵיה — lit., "He fulfills it with something greater than it" — meaning that if a person through one and the same act incurs both a death penalty and a financial obligation, the existence of the death penalty exempts him from the financial obligation. For example, if one were to light a fire in his neighbor's wheat field on *Shabbos*, the fact that he is liable to the death penalty for lighting a fire on *Shabbos* makes him exempt from the financial obligation of paying for the damage to the field. [Now, the Egyptians, by their enslavement of Israel and their murderous persecutions, incurred both a death penalty and a financial obligation in the form of unpaid wages.] But our principle would seem to dictate that having been punished by the death of the firstborn they should have been exempt from the financial penalty. The author, however, points to a passage in *Rashi*[73] where it is explained that our principle, *kam lei bederabbah minei*, means only that the court does not impose both the death penalty and the financial one; if, however, the party to whom the money is owed has already collected the debt, the court does not go so far as to take the money back. This, as it were, is the reason why the Holy One, Blessed be He, commanded that the Children of Israel should ask, *each man from his neighbor ... vessels of silver and vessels of gold* (אִישׁ מֵאֵת רֵעֵהוּ ... כְּלֵי כֶסֶף וּכְלֵי זָהָב); *Exodus* 11:2); since they had already collected these debts, they would have no obligation to return them. Now we can understand more fully the line, "If He had slain their firstborn but had not given us their property, *dayeinu*." It would have been enough for us — that is, it would have been all the law permitted us, on the basis of *kam lei bederabbah minei* — except for the fact that we were commanded to collect the property before the death penalty was executed.[74]

This, Too, is for the Good ...

Even verses of Scripture incorporated in the *Haggadah* receive halachic comment. In the passage beginning, "Originally our ancestors were idol-worshipers ... " we read the verse, *And I gave to Esau Mt. Seir as an inheritance, and Yaakov and his children went down to Egypt* (וָאֶתֵּן לְעֵשָׂו אֶת הַר שֵׂעִיר לָרֶשֶׁת אוֹתוֹ וְיַעֲקֹב וּבָנָיו יָרְדוּ מִצְרָיִם; *Joshua* 24:4). What need is there to tell about the inheritance of Esau? Rav Y.Z. Soloveitchik, Rav in Brisk (and later in Jerusalem), clarifies this point. We learn in Tractate *Nedarim*[75] that one who vows not to derive any benefit from "the seed of Avraham" may derive no benefit from a Jew, but may derive benefit from the members of other nations [even though many of them, too, are descended from Avraham, through Ishmael]. *Rambam*[76] writes that in the Torah the phrase "the seed of Avraham" refers only to the descendants of Yaakov, for it is written, *Because your seed will be a stranger in a land not their own* (כִּי גֵר יִהְיֶה זַרְעֲךָ בְּאֶרֶץ לֹא לָהֶם; *Genesis* 15:13), and this verse was fulfilled only by the seed of Yaakov. Thus we see that the covenant embodied in the verse, *I have given this land to your seed* (לְזַרְעֲךָ נָתַתִּי אֶת הָאָרֶץ הַזֹּאת; *ibid.* v. 18) is dependent upon the exile described in the verse, *in a land not their own*. For this reason the Torah states, *These are the chiefs of Edom, according to their settlements in the land of their possession, that is, Esau, the father of Edom, and Yaakov settled in the land of the wanderings of his father* (אֵלֶּה אַלּוּפֵי אֱדוֹם לְמֹשְׁבֹתָם בְּאֶרֶץ אֲחֻזָּתָם הוּא עֵשָׂו אֲבִי אֱדוֹם וַיֵּשֶׁב יַעֲקֹב בְּאֶרֶץ מְגוּרֵי אָבִיו; *ibid.* 36:43-37:1). That is, Esau settled in the land of his possession, while it was Yaakov who fulfilled the decree of exile. Our verse from the *Haggadah* is to be interpreted in this same sense. *And I gave to Esau Mt. Seir as an inheritance* — he sat in quiet complacency and did not go into exile — ... *and Yaakov and his children went down to Egypt* — It was they who fulfilled the verse, *Because your seed will be a stranger in a land not their own*: Hence, they alone are included in the verse, *I have given this land to your seed*. From this it will be seen that even the fact of Esau's receiving his inheritance is part of the story of the Redemption.

NOTES

[1] *Rambam, Chametz Umatzah* 7:1, And see: *Sefer HaMitzvos,* positive commandment 157; *Semag,* positive commandment 41; *Chinuch,* mitzvah 21.

[2] See *Yad Eitan, Chametz UMatzah, loc. cit.;* the notes of *Bnei Binyamin, loc. cit.; Or Sameach, loc. cit.;* the *Haggadah, Beis Yisrael,* by the Rav of Karelitz.

[3] See *Rambam and the Mechilta DeRashbi,* by Rav M.M. Kasher, p. 61; Rav M.L. Zakash, *Sinai,* 5706 (1946), issues 5-6.

[4] See *Pesachim* 106a, and *Rambam, Shabbos* 29:1.

[5] *The Haggadah Beis Yisrael.*

[6] Rav Zaks in *Sinai, loc. cit.*

[7] *Exodus* 13:3. This source is likewise cited in *Sefer HaMitzvos, Chinuch, et. al.*

[8] *Mechilta DeRashbi, loc. cit.*

[9] And see *Minchas Chinuch, parashas Bo.*

[10] See *Maharam Shik* on the 613 mitzvos; *Panim Yafos, Shemos* 13:8; the *Siddur* with the commentary of *Maharid* of Liadi; *Maaseh Nissim,* by the author of *Chavas Daas;* the *Haggadah, Imrei Shefer,* by *Netziv:* אָמַר רִ׳ אֶלְעָזָר בֶּן עֲזַרְיָה; *et. al.*

[11] 13b.

[12] See the *Haggadah, Nofes Tzufim,* by Rav M.N. Kahana.

[13] *Rashbam.*

[14] *Pesachim* 116b.

[15] See *Rashbam* and *Tosafos* there.

[16] And see *Pesachim* 105a with *Rashi.*

[17] In his response, *klal* 24, sec. 2.

[18] See *Mechilta DeRashbi,* cited above, and the *mishnah* in *Pesachim* 116a, and the *baraisa* cited by the *Gemara* there. And for a lengthy discussion of the responsum of *Rosh,* see the introduction to the *Haggadah, Beis Yisrael.*

[19] Sec. 196.

[19*] And see the *Haggadah, Yetzias Mitzrayim,* by Rav Tz. Kalisher, and the *Haggadah* of Rav Reuven Margolios.

[20] *Nesiv* 8, part 6.

[21] See the *Haggadah, Maaseh Nissim,* by the author of *Chavas Daas, et. al.*

[22] The *Haggadah, Maaseh Nissim.*

[23] See the *Haggadah* of Rav Tzvi Kalisher, *et. al.*

[24] *Pesachim* 116a.

[25] Vol. III, p. 63; and see *Klei Chemdah, Leviticus,* p. 282, where the author discusses the concept that no blessing is recited over a mitzvah which reason would dictate even if we were not commanded to do it (מִצְוָה שֶׁבְּכְלַיּוֹת).

[26] See *Pri Megadim,* 474; the *Haggadah, Maaseh Yedei Yotzer,* by Rav Shlomo Kluger; the *Haggadah, Birkas HaShir,* by Rav. A.L. Zunz; *Mekor HaBerachah,* by Rav Reuven Margolios; and the works cited in *Yalkut Yosef,* at the end of *Mekor HaBerachah.*

[27] *Pesachim* 43b.

[28] See *Tosafos, Pesachim* 108b.

[29] 472.

[29*] 472:25.

[30] *Rama* in *Shulchan Aruch* 473.6. And see *Kol-Bo, Pesach.*

[31] *Klal* 129.

[32] *Ikarei HaDat, Orach Chaim,* sec. 19, os 23, in the name of *Beis David.*

[33] See *Birkei Yosef,* 472, for a detailed discussion of this point.

[34] *Pesachim* 108b; *Shulchan Aruch* 472.8.

[35] *Klal* 129, *din* 12. And see *Tosafos, Sukkah* 38a, *s.v.* מִי. See also *Biur Halachah* in *Mishnah Berurah* 472.8.

[36] *Cheshek Shlomo* on *Pesachim* 116b. And it should be noted that according to the opinion of *Rashi, Sukkah* 31a, a *hekesh* is not the type of exegesis which one may use on one's own authority, but it may only be received as a tradition from Sinai. And even according to the opinion of *Tosafos* there, who disagrees with *Rashi,* it would seem that scholars after the Talmudic period do not employ the method of *hekesh* on their own authority.

[37] *Shulchan Aruch HaRav,* 472:25.

[38] *Rashbam.*

[39] *Pesachim* 116b.

[40] *Rashbam, ibid.*

[41] See *Bava Kama* 87a.

[42] *Megillah,* ch. 2.

[43] And see *Beis Yosef,* end of 473; responsa *Toras Chesed,* sec. 8; responsa *Edus BiYehosef,* sec. 9.

[44] *Parashas Bo,* and from there cited in the *Haggadah.*

[45] See above, p. 133.

[46] *HaMeir LaOlam*, p. 47.

[47] *Pesachim* 36a.

[48] *Rashi*. And see above, p. 142, where it is explained that for this reason the *matzah* is broken before the telling of the *Haggadah*.

[49] See *Pesachim* 120b. And see above, p. 151.

[50] Responsa *Mishkenos Yaakov*, *Orach Chaim*, sec. 121.

[51] *Ibid.*

[52] See *Emek Yehoshua*, part 2, sec. 11; the *Haggadah*, *Imrei Shefer*, *s.v.* וְכָל הַמַּרְבֶּה; responsa *Degel Reuven*, part 2, sec. 10.

[53] See above, p. 164.

[54] And see *Rambam*, *Chametz UMatzah* 8:4.

[55] 116a. And see the *Yerushalmi*, 10:5.

[56] 473:43.

[57] See *Otzar HaGeonim*, *Pesachim*, sec. 220; *Chagim UMoadim*, by Rav Y.L. HaKohen Fischman, second ed., pp. 181-90.

[58] *Shulchan Aruch* 481:2, based on *Tosefta*.

[59] This additional passage is also found in the *Siddur* of Rav Saadiah Gaon, Jerusalem, 5701 (1941).

[60] *Tosafos*, 116b, and the other *Rishonim*.

[61] *Bach*, *Taz*, and *Magen Avraham*, 473, in the name of *Mahariv*.

[62] *Orach Chaim*, sec. 23.

[63] Berlin, 5451 (1691).

[64] 8a.

[65] *Gemara*, *loc. cit.*

[66] *Emek Yehoshua*, part 2, sec. 11.

[67] The *Haggadah*, *Imrei Shefer*.

[68] *Sotah* 15a.

[69] *Zevachim* 75b, and *Bechoros* 27a.

[69*] *Chavakuk* 3:8.

[70] In his commentary on the *Haggadah*. And see *Hagahos HaRashash* on *Shemos Rabbah*, ch. 23.

[71] 64a.

[72] *Haggadas Mordechai*, by Rav M.G. Yaffe.

[73] *Bava Metzia* 92a.

[74] The *Haggadah*, *Birkas HaShir*, by Rav A.L. Zunz.

[75] 31a.

[76] *Perush HaMishnayos* on that *mishnah*.

פֶּסַח שֶׁחַל לִהְיוֹת בְּשַׁבָּת &§

When Pesach Falls on Shabbos

In Judges (ch. 8) we are told that Gideon, engaged in pursuit of the fleeing enemy, arrived with his band of warriors at a place called Sukkos. There the cowardly elders, not believing that his victory is final, refuse his request for bread with this taunt: "Are the hands of Zevach and Tzalmuna [the kings of Gideon's fleeing adversaries] in your hands now?" In other words, how do we know that the fortunes of war will not yet turn against you? Gideon brooks no nonsense: "Therefore when HASHEM will deliver Zevach and Tzalmuna into my hands I will tear your flesh with the thorns of the wilderness." The story goes on to tell of Gideon's victory and his return to keep his promise. Verse 14 thus relates how he captured a youth of Sukkos, who wrote down the names of 77 leading citizens of his town.

Now this simple fact is remarkable. Every nation has stories of heroic leaders and striking victories — but that some 3500 years ago a nameless youth hailing from an obscure provincial locality in the Jordan Valley should be able to write is surely one of the most remarkable statements in the Tanach. At a time when literacy, even in so-called civilized societies, was the exclusive prerogative of an extremely thin upper crust, a boy, probably a young shepherd, wrote down 77 names!

It was some 700 years ago that the halachic classic entitled Shibolei HaLeket *was written — yet the author, as quoted in the chapter before us, allows even an am haaretz, an uneducated member of Am Yisrael, to read the Haggadah of Pesach on Friday night, without fear that he will have to adjust the light in order to see better. His confident reasoning: "For there is no one in the world so unlettered that he is not somewhat familiar with the Haggadah, and through looking at it a little one is able to read, now from the book, now outside it." This was written in the thirteenth century, some two hundred years before the invention of printing, at a time when perhaps one percent of the general population was able to read. One is tempted to reword his sentence and say: "For there is no other people in the world of whom this could be said"; or as King David put it (I Chronicles 17:21), and as we repeat every Shabbos at the Minchah prayer, "And who is like Thy People Israel, a unique nation on the earth?"*

A Unique Halachic Territory

The halachic problems arising when Pesach falls on Shabbos do not form a unified topic dealt with in any one place in the literature. This is in contrast to the topic of *erev* Pesach, the day before Pesach, when it falls on *Shabbos*; for the latter does serve as the focal point of concentrated discussion. On *erev* Pesach, the confluence of the day's obligations with those of *Shabbos* engenders various halachic questions, some having to do with the slaughtering of the *Pesach* sacrifice and all the acts involved in offering it on the Altar (and hence these questions are of practical import only when the Temple is standing), and others — of practical import even in our own time — having to do with the search for *chametz* (בְּדִיקַת חָמֵץ), its destruction (בִּיעוּר), and the eating of the final *chametz* meal before Pesach. All these questions have no place when Pesach itself falls on *Shabbos*. Nevertheless, dispersed in various places throughout the Talmud and the works of the *poskim* there are discussions of a number of *halachos* which are of special concern when *Yom-Tov* Pesach falls on *Shabbos*. Nor are we referring here to those laws which apply in common to all the festivals when they occur on *Shabbos*. (These *halachos* form a group of their own, including such issues as the correct order of prayer; the wording of the blessing, " ... Who sanctifies the *Shabbos* and Israel and the festivals;"[1] the inclusion of a reference to *Yom-Tov* in the blessing over the *Haftarah* on *Shabbos* afternoon (in Talmudic times a *Haftarah* was read at *Minchah*, the afternoon prayer); and the blessing that ends, " ... Who sanctifies the *Shabbos*," recited aloud by the *sheliach tzibur*, the leader of the prayer [after the conclusion of the *Amidah* prayer on Friday night].[2] Rather, our subject is the unique halachic territory occupied by Pesach, as distinguished from other festivals, when it falls on *Shabbos*.

The night of *Shabbos*, the day of *Shabbos*, and the morrow — these are the three time periods discussed by the *Halachah* in connection with the festival of Pesach. The great majority of the laws discussed concern the first of these three periods — the night of *Shabbos* when this is also *leil haseder*, the night of the Pesach feast.

Roasting the Sacrifice

The roasting of the *Pesach* sacrifice is not part of the Temple service of this offering, but it is a necessary preparatory act for the mitzvah of eating the sacrifice; for the Torah tells us that it may be eaten *only roasted by fire* (כִּי אִם צְלִי אֵשׁ; *Exodus*

12:9).[3] And the principle time to perform this roasting is on Pesach night;[4] in any case, it is permissible to do the roasting that night. This is true, however, only when Pesach falls on a weekday, not when it falls on *Shabbos*. As the Mishnah tells us, "The roasting [of the *Pesach* sacrifice] and the rinsing out of its innards do not supersede *Shabbos*."[5] It is true that *Rashi* comments, "because it is possible [to do the roasting and rinsing out] after nightfall." From this comment it is evident that *Rashi* considers the *mishnah* to be speaking, not of Pesach that falls on *Shabbos*, but of *erev* Pesach that falls on *Shabbos*. But in fact the same principle applies to the problem of roasting when Pesach night itself coincides with *Shabbos*; here, too, the roasting does not supersede *Shabbos* — and for the same reason: it is possible to roast the sacrifice *before* nightfall. This is the meaning of a second *mishnah*, which states, "When *erev* Pesach falls on *erev Shabbos*, [the *tamid*, or daily offering] is slaughtered at six-and-a-half hours [of daylight]° (rather than seven-and-a-half, as is usually the case on *erev* Pesach), and is offered up at seven-and-a-half hours, and afterwards the *Pesach* [sacrifice is offered up.]"[6] The Talmud explains that the reason for performing the sacrifices one hour earlier is for the sake of "the roasting [of the *Pesach* sacrifice], which does not supersede *Shabbos*."[7] Performing the sacrifices earlier allows time to do the roasting while it is still day. Further details about this situation are provided by a *mishnah* in Tractate *Shabbos*. "It is permissible to suspend the *Pesach* sacrifice in the oven just before nightfall,"[8] so that the process of roasting will continue on its own after dark.[9] On any other *erev Shabbos* it would be forbidden to put meat over the fire for roasting unless there was still enough daytime for the roasting to take place before nightfall; this is a preventive enactment *(gezerah)*, lest one be tempted after dark to rake the coals in the oven in order to further the roasting process. However, this *gezerah* does not apply when Pesach falls on *Shabbos*, since "the people involved in offering a *Pesach* sacrifice *(bnei chavurah)* are meticulous [in the performance of mitzvos],"[10] for, as *Rashi* explains, those who band together to offer the *Pesach* sacrifice are engaged with sacred things connected with the Temple (עוֹסְקִים בְּקָדָשִׁים), and hence they are meticulous.[11]

This *halachah* about "suspending the *Pesach* sacrifice in the

°[The "hour" referred to here is equal to one-twelfth of the total time of daylight, and hence varies with the length of the days. At Pesach time, "six-and-a-half" and "seven-and-a-half" hours, are, respectively, about 12:30 p.m. and 1:30 p.m. — *Ed.*]

oven" constitutes one of the differences in practice between the Jewish communities of Babylonia and those of *Eretz Yisrael*. "The easterners [Jews of Babylonia] consider the oven permissible for this: they suspend the *Pesach* sacrifice in the oven just before nightfall; while the residents of *Eretz Yisrael* say: Set down [or "set aside"] the *Pesach* offering for it is a sacrifice and we are allowed to desecrate *Shabbos* for it."[12] This whole statement presents difficulties of interpretation; in particular, why should geographical differences play any role in customs connected with the *Pesach* sacrifice; since this is a mitzvah centered in the Temple in Jerusalem, why should the "easterners" have a different custom concerning it? Various explanations have been suggested. One which seems likely is that offered by Dr. Margolios, based on a variant version of the statement, found in the Qurquisani manuscript. This version reads: "The residents of Babylonia permit setting the pot in the oven before the beginning of *Shabbos* in order that it should cook on *Shabbos*, while the residents of *Eretz Yisrael* prohibit this practice." Thus, according to this version, the disagreement does not concern Pesach, but rather any *Shabbos*. In this light, the first version may be read as follows: "The easterners consider the oven permissible" — i.e., they consider it permissible on any *Shabbos* to set a pot in the oven in order that it should cook on *Shabbos* night. And their proof is, "from this:" from the fact that the *mishnah* states, "it is permissible to suspend the *Pesach* sacrifice in the oven just before nightfall ..." The residents of *Eretz Yisrael*, however, forbid setting the pot in the oven in order that it should cook on *Shabbos* night. They state, "Set aside the *Pesach*" — i.e., do not attempt to bring a proof from it, for it is a sacrifice for which we are allowed to desecrate *Shabbos*, and that is why the *gezerah* "lest one rake the coals" does not apply to it. (It is true that in the Talmud the permission to "suspend the *Pesach* sacrifice in the oven" is explained on a different basis, namely that those involved in the *Pesach* sacrifice are meticulous about mitzvos and therefore will not rake the coals; but it is no great wonder if in this context a different reason is given.)

The process of roasting the *Pesach* sacrifice just before *Shabbos* enters is the subject of a number of special laws mentioned in *Tosefta*[13] and in the *Yerushalmi*.[14] "One makes boards for [the oven] and one puts them on it in the daytime before *Shabbos*."[15] When Pesach falls on a weekday, if one should see that the heat in the oven is not sufficient one simply increases the fire; but on *Shabbos* night it is forbidden to add fuel to the fire; hence while it is still day one blocks up the mouth of the oven with boards in order to insulate the oven and keep the temperature high.[16] Another law stipulates that "one checks [the *Pesach* sacrifice] while it remains in the oven. If it is roasted, one removes it; if not, one waits until it is roasted." The reason is simple: if one tests the meat after taking it out of the oven, there is danger that one will find that it is not completely roasted, and then, since it is *Shabbos*, one would be unable to return the sacrifice to the oven to finish roasting.[17] Again: "According to Rabbi Yehudah, one may put the *Pesach* sacrifice back in the oven (on *Shabbos* night) if it is whole, but not if it has been cut up. Rabbi Yosei says, 'On *Shabbos*, in either case this is forbidden.' " The disagreement here has to do with a sacrifice which is already completely roasted, so that it is permissible to return it to the oven to prevent its cooling off;° but the fear is that doing so might lead to an error some other time. Relying on the fact that one may return the meat to the oven, one might put it in the oven just before dark, so that it would not become completely roasted before nightfall; and one might mistakenly think that in this case, too, returning the meat to the oven is permissible.[18]

To turn now to another mitzvah of eating, this one applicable to our own time — the commandment to eat *matzah* on the first night of Pesach, taken by itself, does not present any question of whether or not the laws of *Shabbos* are superseded. The act of eating involves no prohibition on *Shabbos*. But the question of superseding *Shabbos* does come up in terms of the preparatory acts (מַכְשִׁירִין) necessary for this mitzvah: baking and the like. On this issue, there is a difference of opinion among the *Tannaim*. The opinion of Rabbi Eliezer is that "*Matzah* and all its preparatory activities supersede *Shabbos*.[19] Rabbi Eliezer's conclusion is derived as follows. By an exegetical principle called *gezerah shavah*, i.e., the occurrence of an identical word in two disparate verses, we learn that certain similarities are to be drawn between the laws of *matzah* and those of the *sukkah*. Now the laws concerning the *sukkah* are themselves equated in certain respects with those concerning the *lulav*; and we know that the mitzvah of taking the *lulav* supersedes *Shabbos*, for the Torah writes that the *lulav* is to be taken *on the first day* (בַּיּוֹם הָרִאשׁוֹן; *Leviticus* 23:40). In the context of this verse, the word *day* is superfluous; it would have been sufficient to write, *on the*

Preparing the Matzah

° [We have a rule that this is not considered cooking since it is already cooked (אֵין בִּישׁוּל אַחַר בִּישׁוּל). — *Ed.*]

first. The word *day*, then, must be there for a different purpose: namely, to teach that this mitzvah is to be performed on any day, even on *Shabbos.* The same is true, then, for *matzah,* which has been exegetically equated with the *sukkah* and the *lulav.*[20]

Rabbi Eliezer's position raises a question. A *mishnah* in Tractate *Shabbos*[20*] indicates that the roasting of the *Pesach* sacrifice, as already mentioned, does not supersede *Shabbos.* Rabbi Eliezer is cited in that *mishnah* as disagreeing with certain elements of the *mishnah,* but on this point apparently he is in agreement. Why, then, does Rabbi Eliezer view the baking of the *matzah* as different from the roasting of the sacrifice, in that he forbids the latter and permits the former on *Shabbos?* The author of *Or Same'ach*[21] suggests an answer. In contrast to a rule stated by Rabbi Akiva, "If a type of work can be accomplished on *erev Shabbos,* it does not supersede *Shabbos*" (כָּל מְלָאכָה שֶׁאֶפְשָׁר לַעֲשׂוֹתָהּ מֵעֶרֶב שַׁבָּת דּוֹחָה הַשַּׁבָּת), Rabbi Eliezer maintains a different rule: Any mitzvah which is not already obligatory on *erev Shabbos* supersedes *Shabbos* (כָּל מִצְוָה שֶׁאֵינָה חִיּוּבָהּ מֵעֶרֶב שַׁבָּת דּוֹחָה שַׁבָּת). And this explains the difference between the *Pesach* sacrifice and *matzah.* The *Pesach* sacrifice may be eaten on Pesach night only by those who have designated themselves the previous day as a group for the purchase and slaughtering of the sacrifice. This means that the preparations and the obligation of the *Pesach* sacrifice already devolve upon a person the previous day, *erev* Pesach; hence when Pesach falls on *Shabbos,* one is obligated already on *erev Shabbos* to take care of all the preparatory activities which make it possible to eat the sacrifice on *Shabbos.* This is not the case with *matzah;* for with *matzah* the entire obligation begins only at nightfall. Thus, the sacrifice, whose obligation begins already on *erev* Pesach (in our case, *erev Shabbos*), does not supersede *Shabbos.* But *matzah,* whose obligation begins only at nightfall, supersedes *Shabbos.*

The *Halachah* does not follow the opinion of Rabbi Eliezer, but rather that of *Chachamim:* None of the preparatory acts of any mitzvah supersede *Shabbos.*[22]

Matzah used for a Transgression

If *matzah* has been used to violate *Shabbos,* in that one has taken it from the private to the public domain (מֵרְשׁוּת הַיָּחִיד לִרְשׁוּת הָרַבִּים), is this *matzah* still valid for the performance of the mitzvah, or is it valid as a "mitzvah which comes about through a transgression" *(mitzvah habaah be-averah)?* This problem is clarified in the *Talmud Yerushalmi.*[23] There a distinction is drawn between one who performs the mitzvah of a mourner by tearing his garment on *Shabbos* and one who attempts to perform the mitzvah of eating *matzah* with stolen *matzah*. In both cases, a trangression has been committed (it is forbidden to tear a garment on *Shabbos*). However, in the case of the mourner the *Yerushalmi* rules that in spite of the trangression, the mitzvah is valid, while in the case of the stolen *matzah* the mitzvah is not valid. The reason given is that "There the object itself [i.e., the *matzah*] is a transgression, whereas here it is the person who has transgressed." In support of this line of reasoning it is stated, "I say as follows: If one took *matzah* from the private to the public domain, [would anyone claim that] the *matzah* cannot be used for the obligation of Pesach?"

Thus we see that while stolen *matzah* cannot fulfill the obligation of Pesach, *matzah* taken from the private to the public domain can be used to fulfill the obligation. This latter distinction has been explained in a number of ways. *Korban HaEdah* interprets it on the basis of a principle suggested by *Tosafos*. The rule is that an act is not classified as a *mitzvah habaah be-averah* unless the transgression is necessary for the performance of the mitzvah, as in the case of stolen *matzah*, where if one had not stolen the *matzah* one would not perform the mitzvah with that particular *matzah*. [This is in contrast to the transgression of *hotzaah*. For one could have eaten that *matzah* even if one had not taken it from the private domain to the public domain.] *Beis Yosef*,[24] on the other hand, explains that the disqualification called *mitzvah habaah be-averah* applies only when the transgression takes effect on a specific object and is embodied in it; but not when the transgression is defined purely in terms of the actions of the person committing it. [Thus when one steals *matzah* the transgression remains a characteristic of the *matzah*; it remains "stolen *matzah*." This is not the case with the transgression of *hotzaah*. There is no such category as "taken-out *matzah*."]

A unique approach to this problem is found in *Shibolei HaLeket*.[25] This authority apparently understands the words in the *Yerushalmi*, about taking *matzah* from the private to the public domain, not as a question but as a statement. For he writes, in discussing a forbidden labor done by a non-Jew on behalf of a Jew: "... in spite of the fact that we read in the *Yerushalmi* (in the chapter called *HaOreg*) that *matzah* taken from the private to the public domain on *Shabbos* cannot be used to fulfill the obligation on Pesach, because of the rule about *mitzvah habaah be-averah* — this applies only when the transgression is done by a Jew; but in our case ... "[26]

As for the *Halachah*, the commentaries on *Shulchan Aruch*[27] rule that eating *matzah* with which this particular transgression *(hotzaah)* has been committed does not constitute a *mitzvah habaah be-averah.*[28]

Why no The transgression of taking *matzah* from the private to the
Gezerah? public domain serves not only as the basis for a specific legal problem as discussed above; it also leads to a more general question. We know that the Sages, in order to forestall the possibility of just such a transgression, forbade the performance of certain mitzvos on *Shabbos*. Thus, the *shofar* is not blown on *Shabbos*, nor is the *lulav* taken, "lest one carry it four cubits in the public domain." It is true that, regarding the *shofar*, the *Gemara* explains this preventive decree by saying that "All are obligated in blowing the *shofar*, while not all are experts in blowing the *shofar*; hence there is a decree, lest one should take it and go to an expert to learn, and carry it four cubits ..."[29] This reasoning would not seem to apply to the eating of *matzah*, since the act of eating does not require special expertise. But *Rashi* on Tractate *Sukkah,*[30] discussing the preventive decree about the *lulav*, writes that the expertise in that case is "to learn [the correct method of] waving [the *lulav*], or the blessing." If simply learning the correct wording of the blessing is considered sufficient impetus to go to an expert, then all the more so is there sufficient impetus regarding the *matzah*; for one needs to know not only the correct blessing over this mitzvah, but also the entire procedure for the *seder*, the Pesach feast. [Why, then, is there no *gezerah* prohibiting the eating of *matzah* when Pesach falls on *Shabbos*?]

This problem was put to the author of responsa *Sho'el UMeshiv,*[31] who found himself forced to construct a complex theoretical solution. The same question is also considered by *Netziv* in *Ha'amek She'elah*, his commentary on *She'iltos.*[32] He answers in these words: "The preventive decree *(gezerah)* [against reading the Scroll of Esther on *Shabbos*] was only enacted for the sake of the daytime reading, for on the mitzvah of the nighttime [reading] no *gezerah* was enacted, just as the *gezerah* of the type enacted for the *shofar* and the *lulav* was not applied to *matzah* and *maror*; the reason is that night is not so much a time when one leaves one's house."

To move now from "lest one carry" to "lest one tilt" — the *gezerah* "lest one carry it four cubits ... " is the subject of discussion among the *Acharonim;* the enactment "lest one tilt [the oil lamp]" is discussed by the *Rishonim.* On *Shabbos* night, it is forbidden to read by the light of an oil lamp, lest one tilt it in order to make the oil flow towards the wick, and thus become guilty of increasing a flame on *Shabbos.*[33] What, then, is the law concerning reading the *Haggadah* when Pesach night falls on *Shabbos?* This question is debated in *Sefer HaTrumah.* Even on an ordinary *Shabbos,* the prohibition against reading by an oil lamp applies only if one is alone; when two are reading together, it is assumed that the *gezerah* is not needed, since it is likely that if one attempts to tilt the lamp, his companion will remind him of the prohibition. The author of *HaTrumah* writes: "When Pesach night falls on *Shabbos,* and it is necessary to tell the *Haggadah* at the table, if one is alone he may not read [the *Haggadah*] from a book. And the prohibition is not relaxed when his wife looks on with him if she does not know how to read (in other words, if she *does* know how to read then the husband is permitted, as in the normal case of two who read together).[34] And if, by looking at the main headings, he knows how to finish outside the book (i.e., by heart), it is permitted."[35] This ruling is cited by other *Rishonim* as well.[36]

Shibolei HaLeket, however, citing his brother Rav Binyamin, disagrees with the author of *Sefer HaTrumah.* [*Trumah* means literally "sanctified produce," and] *Shibolei HaLeket* writes, "This particular batch of *Trumah* is slightly contaminated (הַתְּרוּמָה הַזֹאת מְדוּמַעַת בְּמִקְצָת) — what should a person do: nullify the commandment expressed by the verse, *And you shall tell your son* ... (וְהִגַּדְתָּ לְבִנְךָ; *Exodus* 13:8) for the sake of a [*gezerah*] 'lest one tilt [the lamp]?' " The author further argues, "The reading of the *Haggadah* from a book is of the nature of scanning main headings, for there is no one in the world so unlettered that he is not somewhat familiar with the *Haggadah,* and through looking at the book a little, one is able to read, now from the book, now outside it." *Shulchan Aruch*[37*] determines the *Halachah* in favor of the opinion of *Shibolei HaLeket,* and for the second reason: "There is no one so unlettered as not to be somewhat familiar [with the *Haggadah*]." In spite of the fact that *Shulchan Aruch* cites this as the reason for the ruling, *Pri Megadim* writes that one should rule leniently in this matter, and not nullify the mitzvah of the *Haggadah,* even in the case of a simple person who has never learned and cannot manage the *Haggadah* at all without a written text.[38] On the other hand, the work *Pesach Me'ubin*, by the author of *Knesses HaGedolah*, concludes that if one's wife does not know how to read, and one cannot recite the *Haggadah* with the aid of main headings, then reading it by the light of an oil lamp is forbidden, unless there is a second unlettered man present and the first says, "Watch me and protest [if I attempt to tilt the oil lamp], and say, 'Today is *Shabbos*, today is *Shabbos*.' "[39]

Charoses on Shabbos A *Shabbos*-linked problem arises in connection with *charoses*, the mixture of chopped apples, nuts and spices which symbolizes the mortar used in building for Pharaoh. Normally, a little wine is mixed with the *charoses* shortly before it is used, but "if [Pesach] falls on *Shabbos*, the liquid is added the previous afternoon."[40] The reason is that mixing the wine into the *charoses* is technically classified as "kneading," one of the main types of work forbidden on *Shabbos*. "And if one forgets to soften it (i.e., to add the liquid) while it is still day, he may soften it on *Shabbos* if he does so in a way different from the usual method (עַל יְדֵי שִׁינּוּי); that is, one puts the liquid in a vessel first, and afterwards puts the *charoses* into it; and one may mix it with one's finger, or pick up the vessel and shake it until the contents are mixed."[41] The point is that one should not do the mixing in the usual manner, with a spoon.[42]

Concerning the salt water in which the *carpas* is dipped we are likewise told, "If [Pesach] falls on *Shabbos*, one should prepare [the salt water] before *Shabbos*, and not make it on *Shabbos*." And "if one has not made it before *Shabbos*, one should make [only] a small amount of salt water."[43] This small amount is "only as much as is needed for the dipping alone; and since it is difficult to be so precise, one should make the salt water the previous day, and if one forgets [to do so], one should make a tiny amount on *Shabbos*."[44]

Incidentally, in my opinion it is to this law that we may trace the custom of Israel in many communities of the Dispersion that at the beginning of the feast on Pesach night the egg used during the *seder* is dipped in the salt water and eaten. Various explanations have been given for the eating of eggs on Pesach night.[45] But why are they eaten in salt water? The reason must be that when the festival falls on *Shabbos* it is forbidden by law to mix the salt into the water at night, except in the exact quantity needed for that meal; and even when the *Yom-Tov* does not fall on *Shabbos*, it is good to be strict and exercise care about this prohibition.[46] Thus eggs are eaten with salt water at this meal, making it possible to mix the salt water at night with no fear of violating *Shabbos* or *Yom-Tov* [since the salt water not needed for the *carpas* will be used for the eggs].

The Omission of "Me'ein Sheva"

Thus far we have discussed those *halachos* connected with prohibited types of labor on *Shabbos*. But when Pesach falls on *Shabbos* there are also special laws that are unrelated to any prohibition. One such law has to do with the evening prayer in the synagogue. The short recapitulation of the *Shabbos* evening prayer normally recited by the *chazzan*, called *me'ein sheva* and containing the passage, מָגֵן אָבוֹת, "Shield of the Fathers," is omitted when Pesach falls on *Shabbos*. *Tur* explains the omission. "*Baal Haltur* writes in the name of Rabbeinu Nissim that when [Pesach] falls on *Shabbos* one does not recite the blessing, *me'ein sheva*, for this passage was instituted for the sake of those who come late to the synagogue, to ensure that no harm befalls them (שֶׁלֹּא יַזִּיקוּם הַמַּזִּיקִים)." *Rashi's* commentary on the relevant *Gemara* passage states that "The synagogues in the talmudic period were not within the city ... but on *Shabbos* night the worshipers would come to the synagogue, and it was feared that some would not come on time, and would remain [alone in the unprotected outskirts of the city] after the prayer; hence the public prayer was lengthened [by the addition of the blessing *me'ein sheva*]."[47] But "on this occasion [Pesach night]," explains *Tur*, "there is no need [for this precaution], since it is *leil shimurim*, a night of protection."[48]

Abudraham indeed writes, " ... however, the custom is to recite it." But *Beis Yosef* concludes, " ... but the custom not to recite it has now become widely accepted," and this is how the same author records the law in his *Shulchan Aruch*, without citing any contrary opinion.[49]

An interesting and unexpected explanation for the omission of the blessing *me'ein sheva* when Pesach falls on *Shabbos* is suggested by the Gaon of Rogachov. He cites a statement of the *Talmud Yerushalmi*,[50] quoted by *Tosafos* in Tractate *Pesachim*,[51] to the effect that "It is the custom there [in Babylonia] in places where there is no wine [over which to recite *Kiddush* at home on *Shabbos* night] that the *sheliach tzibur* stands in his place at the head of the congregation and recites the blessing *me'ein sheva*, concluding with the words, " ... Who sanctifies the *Shabbos* (מְקַדֵּשׁ הַשַּׁבָּת) [in this way performing *Kiddush* on behalf of the congregation, since they are unable to do so over wine at home]." Thus we see that this blessing was essentially instituted for the sake of a place where there is no wine. But on Pesach that situation is inconceivable, for there is no Jew who does not have wine for *Kiddush* on this night. (In the words of the Mishnah, "For even the poorest man of Israel, [the charity wardens] should not give him less than four cups.") Hence there is no need for the blessing *me'ein sheva*.[52]

How
Many
Matzos?
According to a number of *Rishonim*, there is a difference between a Pesach which falls on *Shabbos* and one which falls on a weekday with regard to the *matzos* over which one recites the two blessings, " ... Who brings forth bread from the earth" (הַמּוֹצִיא) and " ... Who has sanctified us with His commandments and commanded us concerning the eating of *matzah*" (עַל אֲכִילַת מַצָּה). The Talmud states, "All agree that on Pesach one puts a broken piece of *matzah* with a whole one and recites the blessing. What is the reason for this? It is because the Torah writes ... *the bread of poverty* (לֶחֶם עֹנִי; *Deuteronomy* 16:3)."[53] The *Rishonim* disagree over the interpretation of this passage. Does it mean that the blessing is recited over one whole and one broken piece of *matzah*, or over two whole pieces and one broken?[54] Among the *Geonim*, some distinguish between one Pesach and another. When Pesach falls on a weekday, one whole and one broken *matzah* are used; and when it falls on *Shabbos*, two whole *matzos* and one broken.[55] These *Geonim*, according to Rav Shalom Albeck,[56] understand the *Gemara* in *Berachos*, cited above, in this light. For after the sentence, "All agree that on Pesach ... " the *Gemara* goes on to state, "On *Shabbos* a person is obligated to recite the blessing over two loaves." According to these *Geonim*, says Rav Albeck, the meaning is, "On *Shabbos* — i.e., on Pesach when it falls on *Shabbos* — a person is obligated to say the blessing over two loaves" — i.e., over two whole pieces of *matzah*, in addition to the broken piece. (All the commentaries on this *Gemara* passage, however, interpret it as referring to an ordinary *Shabbos*, not to Pesach.) This matter constituted one of the differences in custom between the Babylonian Jewish communities and those of *Eretz Yisrael*.[57]

On the day of Pesach, in contrast to the night, there are no laws at all which distinguish this festival from the others. Hence when Pesach and *Shabbos* coincide no new laws result, only those shared in common by Pesach and the other *Yamim Tovim* when they fall on *Shabbos* — changes in the wording of the prayers and in the blessings of the *Haftarah*.

However, outside *Eretz Yisrael*, where the "two days of *Yom-* *When* *Tov* of the exile" are observed, a question arises concerning *Se'udah* *se'udah shlishis*, the Third Meal of *Shabbos*, when the first *Shlishis* *Yom-Tov* day coincides with *Shabbos*. A *mishnah* in Tractate *is* *Pesachim* states, "On *erev* Pesach towards the time of the *Forbidden* Minchah service (from the tenth hour of daylight [i.e., about *Forbidden* 3:00 o'clock] onward), a person should not eat,"[58] so that he should have an appetite for the *matzah* that evening; for eating it with appetite constitutes a *hiddur*, enhancement of the mitzvah.[59] In the lands of Exile this law applies not only on *erev* Pesach, for the sake of the first *seder* night, but also on the first *Yom-Tov* day, for the sake of the second *seder*. [Thus the obligation not to eat in the latter part of the afternoon conflicts with the obligation to eat the Third Meal of *Shabbos*.] This conflict is resolved as follows by an authority cited by *Shaarei Teshuvah*. "It is written in *Igros HaRamaz*, regarding *se'udah shlishis* when the first day [of Pesach] falls on *Shabbos*, that it is preferable to refrain from acting (שֵׁב וְאַל תַּעֲשֶׂה עָדִיף; that is, not to eat *se'udah shlishis*), since for us this day follows the laws of *erev* Pesach, based on the doubt [which used to exist as to which day is actually Pesach] resulting in the two days of *Yom-Tov* of the exile; all the same, one should eat a little fruit, enough to enable one to recite [a concluding] blessing, but should not eat very much, because of the mitzvah of eating *matzah* with appetite on the night of the second *Yom-Tov*.[60]

The situation when the first *Yom-Tov* day of Pesach falls on *Refuting* *Shabbos* provided Rabbi Yochanan ben Zakkai with a basis *the* for refuting the opinion of the Sadducees (צְדוּקִים). This sect *Sadducees* rejected the traditional interpretation of the Torah which places Shavuos as the fiftieth day after Pesach. For the Torah states that the fifty-day count should begin *on the morrow of* *the Shabbos* (מִמָּחֳרַת הַשַּׁבָּת; *Leviticus* 23:15), and the word *Shabbos* is interpreted by the Sages as meaning the first *Yom-Tov* day of Pesach, which may also be termed a *Shabbos*, since it is a time of cessation of work. But the Sadducees interpreted the word *Shabbos* literally, as meaning the seventh day of the week (שַׁבַּת בְּרֵאשִׁית); thus they observed Shavuos as the fiftieth day after the *Shabbos* following Pesach. Rabbi Yochanan Ben Zakkai said to one of the elders of the Sadducees: "Fool! Is not our perfect Torah to be preferred to your idle chatter? One verse says, *You shall count fifty days* (תִּסְפְּרוּ חֲמִשִּׁים יוֹם; *ibid.* v. 16), and one verse says, *There shall be seven whole weeks* (שֶׁבַע שַׁבָּתוֹת תְּמִימֹת תִּהְיֶינָה; *ibid.* v. 15).

How can this be? The one verse speaks of the situation when *Yom-Tov* falls on *Shabbos;* the other, when *Yom-Tov* falls during the week.''[61] According to *Rashi,* the contradiction between the two verses is that the first verse indicates that the count should be one of days rather than weeks, while the second verse commands us to count weeks, and a week is only that which begins on Sunday and ends on *Shabbos.* The explanation given by Rabbi Yochanan ben Zakkai is that when the first *Yom-Tov* of Pesach falls on *Shabbos,* then the verse *seven whole weeks* is appropriate. And when the *Yom-Tov* falls during the week, then the verse *fifty days* is appropriate.

The author of *Sefer Haflaah* provides an ingenious interpretation of this same passage. According to the author, the contradiction is that seven weeks is equal to forty-nine days, and not fifty days. The explanation given by Rabbi Yochanan ben Zakkai is that when the first *Yom-Tov* day falls on *Shabbos,* then the verse, *fifty days,* is appropriate (the opposite of *Rashi's* interpretation); when *Yom-Tov* falls during the week, the verse, *seven weeks,* is applicable. How so? When the first day of Pesach falls on *Shabbos,* this means of course that the forty-ninth day of the count also falls on *Shabbos.* Now, the holiness of *Shabbos* is of a higher degree than that of *Yom-Tov;* both kinds of day require us to add an extra period of time, a *tosefes,* which is taken from the ordinary week and added to the holy day, and this *tosefes* is added not only at the beginning of the day, but also at the end of the day. Thus, when the forty-ninth day is *Shabbos,* it extends somewhat into the fiftieth day; that is, it extends into the *Yom-Tov* of Shavuos, since *Shabbos* has a greater holiness than *Yom-Tov.* But when the first day of Pesach occurs during the week, so that the forty-ninth day is likewise a weekday, with no *tosefes,* it follows that there are only *seven weeks,* i.e., forty-nine days, and no more.[62]

NOTES

[1] *Tosefta, Berachos,* ch. 3; *Beitzah* 17a.

[2] *Shabbos* 24a.

[3] According to *Tosafos* on *Beitzah* 27b, the act of roasting the Pesach sacrifice is also done "for the needs of the Altar" (צוֹרֶךְ גָבוֹהַ).

[4] See *Rashi, Pesachim* 41b, *s.v.* אֵין לִי, and *Maharsha* there. And see *Mechilta, Bo,* end of *parashah* 5; *Yerushalmi, Pesachim* 5:1;

HaYerushalmi KiPshuto, by Rav Liberman, p. 450.

[5] *Mishnah,* 65b.

[6] *Mishnah,* 58a.

[7] *Gemara, loc. cit.*

[8] *Ibid.,* 19b.

[9] *Rashi.*

[10] *Gemara,* 20a.

[11] *Rashi, Eruvin* 103a.

[12] For variant wordings, see *Otzar Chiluf Minhagim,* by Dr. Lewin, p. 22, and *HaChilukim Shebein Anshei Mizrach Uvnei Eretz Yisrael,* by Dr. Margolios, p. 77.

[13] *Pesachim,* ch. 7.

[14] *Shabbos* 1:11.

[15] *Tosefta, loc. cit.*

[16] *Chazon Yechezkel.*

[17] *Ibid.*

[18] See *Yerushalmi, Shabbos* 1:11, and *Minchas Bikurim* and *Chazon Yechezkel* on *Tosefta,* ch. 7. And see *Sifri, R'eh,* on the verse, *And you shall cook it and eat it* (וּבִשַּׁלְתָּ וְאָכַלְתָּ; *Deuteronomy* 16:7).

[19] *Shabbos* 131a.

[20] *Ibid.,* 131b.

[20*] 19b.

[21] *Korban Pesach* 1:18.

[22] *Shabbos* 131b; *Sukkah* 43a.

[23] *Shabbos* 13:3.

[24] *Bedek HaBayis* on *Yoreh De'ah,* 340.

[25] Sec. 369.

[26] See *HaYerushalmi KiPshuto,* by Rav Liberman, p. 178, where the author quotes the version of *Kuntres Acharon* [to *Yalkut Shimoni* on נ"י] and the latter's interpretation that the phrase is a statement rather than a question; Rav Liberman writes that "this is surprising," and does not cite *Shibolei HaLeket* which also interprets the phrase as a statement rather than a question.

[27] 454.

[28] See *Pri Chadash* there.

[29] *Rosh HaShanah* 29b, *et. al.*

[30] 42b.

[31] Fourth ed., part 1, sec. 5.

[32] *Vayakhel, She'ilta LePurim,* sec. 21.

[33] *Mishnah, Shabbos* 11a, with *Rashi.*

[34] See *Shabbos* 12b with *Rashi.*

[35] *Hilchos Shabbos,* sec. 219.

[36] See *Machzor Vitri,* p. 123; *Shibolei HaLeket,* sec. 64; *Or Zarua, Erev Shabbos* 32; *et. al.*

[37] The allusion is to *Sefer HaTrumah.*

[37*] 275.9.

[38] *Ibid., Mishbetzos,* para. 8.

[39] Secs. 256 and 257.

[40] *Magen Avraham* 473, para. 16, in the name of *Agudah.*

[41] *Shulchan Aruch HaRav,* para. 34.

[42] And see *Mishnah Berurah,* 321, para. 68, and *Ketzos HaShulchan,* by Rav. A. Ch. Na'eh, sec. 130, *os* 9.

[43] *Taz,* 463, para. 3; *Magen Avraham* there.

[44] *Shulchan Aruch HaRav,* para 19. His source is the *mishnah* on *Shabbos* 108b.

[45] See above, *The Seder,* footnote 14.

[46] See *Misgeres HaShulchan* 118, para. 4, based on *Taz* and *Shulchan Aruch HaRav,* 510.

[47] *Rashi, Shabbos* 24b.

[48] *Tur* 487.

[49] 487.1.

[50] *Berachos* 8:1.

[51] 106b, *s.v.* מקדש.

[52] *Tzafnas Paane'ach, Tefillah* 9:11. And see the author's explanation there of the connection between wine and this blessing.

[53] *Berachos* 39b.

[54] See above, p. 141.

[55] *Halachos Gedolos* (Warsaw ed.), p. 59; *Ritz Geos,* part 2, p. 103, in the name of Rav Netronai Gaon; *et. al.*

[56] In his notes on *Eshkol,* p. 60,

[57] See above, p. 142.

[58] *Mishnah, Pesachim* 99b.

[59] *Rashi.*

[60] *Shaarei Teshuvah* 471. And see *Pesach Me'ubin,* sec. 363.

[61] *Menachos* 65b.

[62] *Panim Yafos, parashas Emor.* And see below, *Shavuos: The Festival.*

❧ Omer

סְפִירַת הָעוֹמֶר

The Counting of the Omer

*In addition to his halachic works, our author also published
LaTorah VelaMoadim, which tests out thoughts and interpretations
on some of the mitzvos and halachos of the Torah. It is interesting
to read how he explains this commandment of HaShem that
requires each one of us to count "for yourself" (לָכֶם) the 49 days,
making seven full weeks, that prepare us for the day on which the
Torah is given.*

*There is a halachic principle that anything that is sold by count can
never be subsumed within another item, because the very fact that
it is counted proves its importance. By analogy we can learn
that during the seventy years that the Psalmist describes as our
lifespan (Psalms 90:10) — which are symbolically represented by
the seven weeks of the Omer — we must make every day of our
life count. No day that passes ever returns. Like the seven weeks of
the Omer, those seven decades have to be complete: if even one
day we forget to count we can continue the counting — but the
blessing is missing.*

*Rav Zevin develops this idea by explaining the reason why an
emphasis is laid on the word לָכֶם — "count for yourself." A cashier
who counts his employer's money may well be interested that
his figures tally, but he does not really lose sleep over whatever the
end result is. The baal habayis, however, the one whose money is
being counted, must of necessity know the end result in order to
be able to draw up a true profit and loss balance. If the count
shows a positive result, he is satisfied; if the result is negative he
becomes anxious, and considers how best to remedy the situation.*

*This, then, is why the Torah says, "Count for yourself," and why
the Talmud (Menachos 65b) explains that the counting of the
Omer has to be carried out by each individual for himself. For this
is our own account, our own individual balance sheet, which must
show a positive result to make us worthy of receiving the Torah at
the summation of our account.*

The laws governing how we count the forty-nine days between Pesach and Shavuos — that is, *hilchos sefiras
HaOmer* — do not occupy much space in the basic sources.
Two pages in the *Talmud;*[1] four *halachos* in *Mishneh
Torah;*[2] a single section in *Shulchan Aruch*[3] — that is all.
But within that small space a great deal is contained. The off-
shoots of these *halachos* branch out and flourish extensively
in works of commentary and responsa. Moreover, the
halachic problems connected with *sefiras HaOmer*, the
counting of the *Omer*, are weighty ones, both in their own
right and with regard to their implications for other areas of
Halachah.

In probing the various issues dealt with by the halachic
literature on the *sefirah*, we find, generally speaking, that it is
possible to classify them under the following main headings:
the obligation (הַחִיּוּב); the date (הַתַּאֲרִיךְ); the time (הַזְּמַן); the
continuity (הַהֶמְשֵׁךְ); the numbering (הַמִּנְיָן) the mode of
expression (הַדִּיבּוּר); the intent (הַכַּוָּנָה); the doubtful cases
(הַסְּפֵקוֹת); and the blessing (הַבְּרָכָה).

**The
Obligation**
What is the nature of this obligation? Essentially, it is based
on a Scriptural commandment: *And you shall count for
yourselves, from the morrow of the Shabbos, from the day
that you bring the waved Omer-offering* ... (וּסְפַרְתֶּם לָכֶם
מִמָּחֳרַת הַשַּׁבָּת מִיּוֹם הֲבִיאֲכֶם אֶת עֹמֶר הַתְּנוּפָה; *Leviticus* 23:15).
But in the Torah this counting is linked to the *Omer*-offering
in the Temple, as we see from this verse and from the
corresponding verse in *Deuteronomy* (16:9), which states that
the count is to begin ... *when the scythe is first put to the
standing grain* (מֵהָחֵל חֶרְמֵשׁ בַּקָּמָה), a phrase interpreted as
referring to the *Omer* of grain cut for the offering, since no
other grain may be eaten until the *Omer* offering is brought.
Thus the question must be asked, concerning our own time
when the Temple is no longer standing, whether the *sefirah*
remains a Scriptural obligation or whether it has become a
Rabbinic one.

On this question the *Rishonim* are divided. *Rambam*[4]
holds that this mitzvah is of Scriptural force in all places and
at all times. But the majority of the *Rishonim* are of the
opinion that in our time this mitzvah is of Rabbinic force.[5]
The source of this difference of opinion among the *Rishonim*
is a disagreement about the correct interpretation of the
Gemara in Tractate *Menachos.*[6] There, Abayye and "the

Sages of the school of Rav Ashi" hold that the mitzvah consists of counting the days and counting the weeks as well. Ameimar, on the other hand, counted the days only, explaining that the mitzvah is "a commemoration of the Temple." According to *Rambam*, those who disagree with Ameimar about the law — whether to count the days only, or both days and weeks — disagree with him also about the reason for the mitzvah. They hold that the *sefirah* is not a commemoration of the *Mikdash*, but rather a Scriptural mitzvah. (And according to *Rambam* the *Halachah* follows those who disagree with Ameimar.) According to the other *Rishonim*, this *Gemara* reflects no disagreement about the reason for the mitzvah. Both Ameimar and his opponents agree that it is a commemoration of the *Mikdash*. Their only point of difference is whether this commemoration should consist of counting days only, or both days and weeks.[7]

There is yet a third position among the *Rishonim:* that of Rabbeinu Yerucham.[8] According to him, counting the days is a Scriptural mitzvah even in our time, while counting the weeks is a Scriptural mitzvah only when the *Mikdash* is standing. The author of *Or Same'ach*[9] offers a fine explanation of this position, based on a *Gemara* passage in Tractate *Rosh HaShanah.*[10] There we learn a law concerning the sacrifices which must be offered up on the festival of Shavuos.° If these sacrifices are not offered at the correct time, on the day of the festival itself, then compensatory sacrifices (תַּשְׁלוּמִין) may be offered during the whole subsequent week. This is implied in the name "Shavuos," which means literally "weeks." The Talmud states that just as "The Torah commanded us to count the days and sanctify the *Atzeres*" [another name for Shavuos], so also it commanded us to count the weeks and sanctify the festival of Shavuos ("weeks") with respect to the compensatory sacrifices. Thus it is logical that since the festival day itself is observed even when the Temple is not standing, so also the counting of the days, which the Talmud relates to the festival day itself, should be a Scriptural mitzvah in all periods. And since the week of compensatory sacrifices, *tashlumin*, is observed only when the Temple is standing, the counting of the weeks, which the Talmud relates to these sacrifices, should be a Scriptural mitzvah only in Temple times.[11]

°[This refers of course to sacrifices brought by individuals to celebrate their being in the *Beis HaMikdash* (עוֹלַת רְאִיָה) and the *Yom-Tov* festival offerings offered on behalf of the public as a whole (חֲגִיגָה); the Temple sacrifices could of course neither be postponed nor compensated for.— *Ed.*]

Tur, Shulchan Aruch, and the Acharonim have determined the Halachah in accordance with the majority of the Rishonim: both aspects of the sefirah, the counting of the days and the counting of the weeks, in our time have Rabbinic rather than Scriptural status, serving as a commemoration of the Beis HaMikdash.

The
Date

The date of sefiras HaOmer, that is, the question when the count should begin, was a historic focus of dispute between our own tradition as transmitted by the Perushim (Pharisees) and the claims of the Tzadukim (Sadducees). In refuting the opinion of the Tzadukim, who claimed that the Shabbos referred to by the verse was not Yom-Tov Pesach but rather the first Sabbath day occurring after Pesach, many counter-proofs were given by the Tannaim. The same dispute was revived in the period of the Geonim, the antagonists this time being the Karaite sect, who took up the opinion of the Tzadukim regarding the first day of the sefirah. Again the Sages of Israel went forth, armed with a number of proofs, to uphold the Talmudic tradition.[12] In responsa Shemen HaMor, as cited in Bnei Yissachar,[13] it is suggested that this dispute explains why the Shabbos before Pesach is called Shabbas HaGadol, "the great Shabbos." This is to refute the opinion of the Tzadukim, who claimed that the term Shabbos can only mean Shabbas Bereishis, the Sabbath of Creation, i.e., the seventh day of the week. For in this week of Shabbas HaGadol we also have the first day of Pesach, which is likewise called "Shabbos" by the Torah. Hence the first of these two Shabbassos is distinguished as "the great Shabbos." Similarly we find in the Talmud[14] that the term klal gadol, "a great principle," implies the existence of a lesser principle.[15]

The
Time

The time for the counting of the Omer is at night. This law is derived in the Talmud, which states, "One might have thought [that the Torah commands us] to cut [the barley sheaf for the Omer], to count, and to bring [the offering] in the daytime. But the verse teaches, There shall be seven complete weeks (שֶׁבַע שַׁבָּתוֹת תְּמִימֹת תִּהְיֶינָה; Leviticus 23:15). When is it that you have seven complete weeks? — only when you begin to count in the evening."[16] [Otherwise the first week is not "complete," since one evening passed before the counting began. — Ed.] The phrase "in the evening" is basically interpreted to mean any time throughout the night. However, the poskim write that the best way to perform the mitzvah (לְבַתְּחִילָה) is to enhance it by counting at the very beginning of the evening.

A unique way of performing this mitzvah is mentioned in *Chilufei HaMinhagim*, which describes differences in custom between the Jewish communities of Babylonia and those of *Eretz Yisrael*. It is stated that the inhabitants of *Eretz Yisrael* counted the *Omer* both at night and in the daytime. This custom was preserved in modern times among the communities of Egypt; after the Morning Prayer they counted the *Omer* again.[17]

A different issue involving the time of the *Omer* count is debated among the *Rishonim*. If one forgets to count the *Omer* at night, and then remembers in the daytime, has he missed the opportunity to perform the mitzvah, or is it possible after the fact (בְּדִיעֲבָד) to count in the daytime? On this question there are three opinions among the *Rishonim*. (1) One who forgets to count at night may count in the daytime;[18] (2) he may not count;[19] (3) he may count in the daytime, but without the accompanying blessing (in accordance with the principle that "in cases of doubt about a blessing, one does not recite it" — סָפֵק בְּרָכוֹת לְהָקֵל).[20] The third opinion is the one cited as *Halachah* by *Shulchan Aruch*.[21]

This dispute is based on two *mishnayos* which contradict each other. One, in Tractate *Menachos*,[22] states: "The mitzvah [of the *Omer*] is to cut [the sheaf of barley from which the *Omer* offering is made] at night; if it is cut in the daytime, it is valid" (and if the cutting is valid in the daytime, then the counting is also, for the verse tells us that the counting should begin *when the scythe is first put to the standing grain* — see above). The conflicting *mishnah* is found in Tractate *Megillah*.[23] "The whole night is valid for the cutting of the *Omer*"[24] [implying that the daytime is not valid]. The three-way dispute among the *Rishonim* derives from the various ways of resolving the conflict between these two *mishnayos*.

Three of the great *Acharonim* are struck by the same question regarding these two *mishnayos* in relation to the *sefirah*. How can any conclusions about the counting of the *Omer* be derived from the *mishnah* in *Menachos* about the validity of cutting the sheaf "in the daytime"? For that *mishnah* is referring not only to the day of the sixteenth, but to the days before the sixteenth, as well — — and would anyone claim that the counting of the *Omer* may be validly performed during the days *before* the sixteenth?[25] To summarize the solution given by one of these scholars: When the *mishnah* states, "if it is cut in the daytime, it is valid," this does not refer to the validity of the offering; for even if the sheaf was not cut for the sake of the offering at all, the offering itself is still valid. The expression, "it is valid," then, means rather that the mitzvah of the cutting has been validly performed. Thus it transpires that the *mishnah* does after all refer only to the day of the sixteenth, and not the days before. The difference between these two times is that if the cutting is performed before the sixteenth, the offering is valid, but the mitzvah of cutting is not; while if the cutting is done on the day of the sixteenth, then according to this *mishnah* the mitzvah of cutting, as well as the offering, are both valid.[26] Thus the *mishnah* is indeed relevant to the question of counting the *Omer* on the day of the sixteenth.

The opinion of *Rambam* on this issue is a major topic in halachic literature. *Rambam* rules that if the sheaf is cut in the daytime, it is valid (and accordingly, if one does not count at night, he may count in the daytime). At the same time, he rules that the cutting of the *Omer* sheaf supersedes *Shabbos*. But in the *Gemara* it is explained that these two opinions are incompatible, and that those who hold the cutting to be valid in the daytime are of the opinion that it does not supersede *Shabbos*. Many scholarly analyses have been written in the attempt to reconcile these two seemingly contradictory rulings of *Rambam*.[27]

The The continuity of the *Omer* count is a concept stemming from
Continuity the Torah's use of the term, *complete* weeks (תְּמִימֹת). The *Gemara* itself derives no law from this term, *complete*, except for the requirement that the count must be done at night. But the author of *Behag* understands that all forty-nine days of the *sefirah* comprise one unified continuity, on the basis of the word, *complete*. This means that if one forgets to count the *Omer* for one entire day (including both night and daytime), then he may no longer count the succeeding days. In the period of the *Geonim* this opinion roused major debates. Its opponents claimed, "If one has eaten garlic and has strong breath, should he eat garlic again so that he shall have even stronger breath?"[28] [That is, if one has committed a transgression by failing to count the *Omer*, should one make matters worse by continuing not to count?] Furthermore, even if we assume that one has missed the opportunity of counting the days, why should he refrain from further counting and thus also miss the counting of the weeks?[29] And again: if all forty-nine days together comprise one single mitzvah, how

can it be that on each and every day we recite the blessing "... Who has sanctified us by His commandments and commanded us concerning the counting of the *Omer*"?[30] [If all forty-nine days are one mitzvah, then the blessing should be recited only once, at the beginning.] These are some of the objections raised by the *Geonim*. And *Tosafos*,[31] too, writes: "This idea [of one continuous mitzvah] is highly questionable and improbable." Likewise *Rosh*[32] writes in the name of *Ri* that each night of the count constitutes a separate mitzvah.

In dealing with this problem of the continuity of the count, some of the *Geonim* distinguish between the first day and the others. They rule that if one forgets to count on the first day, one may no longer perform the mitzvah on the remaining days; but if one skips any of the other days, this does not prevent him from continuing.[33] This compromise position, too, aroused opposition among the *Geonim*. In any case, the ruling given by *Shulchan Aruch* is that if one forgets to count, whether on the first day or any other, one counts on the remaining days without reciting the blessing.

A number of the *Acharonim* investigate the problem of a minor who becomes bar-mitzvah during the time of the *Omer* count. May he recite the blessing for the count, or do we rule that with regard to his obligation as an adult he cannot fulfill the requirement of "completeness"? The discussion of this question principally revolves around one general issue, namely, whether or not performing a mitzvah act constitutes valid fulfillment of that mitzvah if at the time of performing it one was not obligated to do so (was not בַּר חִיוּבָא).[34]

Exactly how does one accomplish the count? The Talmud states, "It is a mitzvah to count the days and a mitzvah to count the weeks."[35] The majority of the *Rishonim* hold that these are not two distinct mitzvos, but rather one mitzvah composed of two parts.[36] *Rambam* reinforces this conclusion by a comparison with the obligation devolving upon the Sanhedrin, or high court, to keep count of the fifty-year cycle culminating in the Jubilee Year *(yovel)*, a cycle which includes within it the *shmitah* or sabbatical year occuring every seven years. He writes: "Just as the *Beis Din* is obligated to count the years of the *yovel* year by year, *shmitah* by *shmitah*, likewise each and every one of us is obligated to count the days of the *Omer*, day by day and week by week ... and just as the commandment to count the years and the *shmitah* is one mitzvah, likewise *sefiras HaOmer* is one mitzvah ... and if [counting the] weeks were a separate mitzvah ... we would

The Numbering

recite two blessings, '... concerning the counting of the Omer' and '... concerning the counting of the weeks of the Omer.'[37]

Rabbeinu Yerucham,[38] on the other hand, is of the opinion that these are two separate mitzvos, and his statements on this subject imply that in the Temple period two blessings were in fact recited, one for the days and one for the weeks.

Even according to the majority opinion, the fact remains that this counting is a compound of two elements, and the correct procedure for combining them is a matter of disagreement among the Rishonim. According to one system, after the first week the total number of days is mentioned only once each week. Thus, at the end of the first week one says, "Today it is seven days, which are one week;" the next day one does not mention the sum total of days, saying only, "Today is one week and one day," and so on each day until the fourteenth day, when one says, "Today it is fourteen days, which are two weeks." On the next day, the fifteenth of the count, one says, "Today it is two weeks and one day," and so on until the end.[39]

Another system adopts the opposite procedure: the sum total of days is mentioned every day, while the total of weeks is mentioned only once a week (on day seven, fourteen, etc.).[40]

The practice which has been accepted is that mentioned by Rosh, Tur, and others. Both the days and the weeks are mentioned every day of the count. This still leaves a problem which is debated among the Acharonim. After the fact (בְּדִיעֲבָד), if one has counted only the days, without mentioning the weeks, has one fulfilled the mitzvah or not? Undoubtedly, if one has mentioned the weeks according to one of the two minority opinions mentioned above [i.e., either mentioning the week and day only, without the sum total of days, or else mentioning the weeks only once a week] this fulfills the mitzvah after the fact. But what if one does not mention the weeks at all? The Acharonim rule that in this case one should say the count again correctly, without saying the blessing.[41]

A major discussion among the Acharonim concerns the question of one who counts in terms of the Hebrew aleph-beis [which also constitutes a numbering system], rather than the names of the numbers; that is, instead of saying, "Today it is one day ... two days ... three days ..." he says, "Today is day aleph ... day beis ... day gimmel," and so on.[42] In this connection, it may be worthwhile to note a related discussion in Tzafnas Paane'ach.[43] That author contrasts the sprinkling of sacrificial blood on the curtain of the Sanctuary on Yom Kippur with the counting-off of animals when giving *maaser behemah*, the tithe of farm animals. On Yom Kippur, the High Priest counts with words: "one, two, three ..." while in tithing animals one counts with letters: "*aleph, beis, gimmel* ..."[44] The author explains that on Yom Kippur the count is with cardinal numbers, while for purposes of tithing the count is with ordinal numbers. According to this distinction, one would conclude that counting by means of the *aleph-beis* (ordinal numbers) would be inappropriate for the *Omer*.[45]

Halachah in general deals with many modes of expression: speech; thought; hearing the utterance of another person who speaks on one's behalf (שׁוֹמֵעַ כְּעוֹנֶה); and writing. All of these modes of expression are topics for discussion by the halachic literature on *sefiras HaOmer*. The essential way of performing the count is by speech.[46] The question whether or not the *Omer* has been counted if one does so by thought alone depends upon the outcome of a general disagreement in the *Gemara*:[47] whether "thought is equivalent to speech" (הַרְהוּר כְּדִיבּוּר) or not. In the *Gemara*, this issue is debated with regard to the mitzvah of reciting the *Shema*, and the conclusion for halachic purposes is that thought is "not equivalent to speech." Hence the author of *Pri Chadash* rules that here too, in the case of the *sefirah*, one cannot fulfill the mitzvah by thought alone.

The Mode of Expression

As to whether or not one can fulfill this mitzvah by listening to another person who is counting on one's behalf (שׁוֹמֵעַ כְּעוֹנֶה) — this is an issue over which the *poskim* disagree. A *baraisa* in Tractate *Menachos* states, "Our Sages teach that the verse, *And you shall count for yourselves ...* implies that there shall be a count for each and every person." *Levush* and *Chok Yaakov* interpret this as meaning that one person cannot perform this mitzvah on behalf of another. But *Pri Chadash* and others explain the *baraisa* differently, stating that its purpose is to prevent us from concluding that this mitzvah is the sole responsiblity of the *beis din*, like the counting of the years of the *shmitah* and *yovel* cycles. This mitzvah, by contrast, is intended for each individual. But this does not eliminate the possibility of fulfilling it through *shome'a ke'oneh*, listening to someone who speaks on one's behalf.[48]

The idea that the counting of the *Omer* might be accomplished through writing is the subject of an exchange of views between Rabbi Akiva Eger and his uncle, Rav Wolfe Eger. The exchange is recorded in the responsa of the former.[49] The principal arguments in this debate center about the disagreement among the *Acharonim* concerning vows and oaths made in writing.[50] With regard to the *sefirah* the problem is of very frequent occurrence, for in writing letters it is customary to write the day of the *Omer* count as part of the date. Thus the problem arises: If one has already written the count in a letter may one afterwards recite the blessing when counting the *Omer* by speech?° In this case, however, another factor enters in. The written count is defective in a different way, because it was not done with intent to perform the mitzvah.[51] And thus we arrive at our next topic regarding the *sefirah*: the question of the *kavanah*, or intent.

The The question of *kavanah* involves a wider problem: whether
Intention or not "mitzvos need *kevanah*," מִצְוֹות צְרִיכוֹת כַּוָּנָה — that is, whether or not a mitzvah is valid if the act was performed without the intent that it should constitute a mitzvah. *Shulchan Aruch*[52] rules that Scriptural mitzvos "need *kavanah*," but the question as regards Rabbinic mitzvos is left unanswered and remains a matter of disagreement among the *Acharonim*. In practice the problem arises quite regularly. One person asks another, "How many days are there in the count today?" And the other replies, without intending to perform the mitzvah, "Today is so and so many days of the *Omer*." Has the second person unwittingly performed the mitzvah, or may he still recite the blessing and count the *Omer*? The ruling given by *Shulchan Aruch* and the *Acharonim* was first stated by *Abudraham*: When asked what day of the *Omer* it is today, one should reply, "Yesterday was so and so many days of the *Omer*," for if one says today's count one may not afterwards count again with the blessing.

The question of *kavanah* comes into a discussion of a different law about the *sefirah*. The *poskim* state that if one is part of a congregation which is praying the Evening Prayer before it is actually night [it is possible to do so from *plag haminchah* on, that is, from about an hour and a quarter before sundown], and as part of the service the congregation count the *Omer*, one may count it with them without reciting the blessing, having in mind explicitly that one does not intend thereby to fulfill the mitzvah [since one prefers to do so

°[If the written count fulfilled the essential mitzvah, any subsequent blessing would be a "blessing in vain" (בְּרָכָה לְבַטָּלָה). — *Ed.*]

only when it is actually night]. In this way one may count the *Omer* afterwards at home, with the blessing.[53] What this means is that at the time of the first counting one makes a condition that if he remembers to count afterwards, he does not wish to fulfill the mitzvah with his present *sefirah;* and if he should forget to count later, then his intention is to fulfill the mitzvah with the present count.[54] The author of *Oneg Yom-Tov*[55] expresses strong reservations about the validity of such a condition. He draws a distinction between will *(ratzon)* and intent *(kavanah).* A condition is effective, this author claims, in cases where a person's will is necessary to bring about the desired legal effect (for example, in marriage, divorce, and the like); but not in cases where the requirement is only intent (an example is *chalitzah,* the ceremony by which a woman releases her brother-in-law from the obligation of levirate marriage). Thus, where the performance of a mitzvah is involved (requiring intent only and not will), a condition is ineffective, and the mitzvah is valid regardless of the condition.

The problem of *sefekos,* doubtful cases, like the problem of **The** *kavanah,* is essentially a general subject applicable to all **Doubts** mitzvos, not only to *sefiras HaOmer.* However, certain areas of this subject are unique to the *sefirah.* If we wish, we may divide into four categories the doubtful cases arising in the performance of this mitzvah. These are: doubts concerning the law; concerning the act; concerning the date; and concerning the time. Doubts concerning the law are very numerous; they include all the halachic disagreements mentioned above [e.g., whether or not it is valid to count in the daytime; whether or not the weeks must be mentioned every day, etc.]; in doubtful cases of this type, the ruling generally is to count, but without reciting the blessing. However, there are cases when different sources of doubt operate in combination. For example, if one forgot to count at night but counted in the daytime, what should he do on the remaining days of the *Omer?* Here, one doubt is compounded by a second (סְפֵק סְפֵקָא). First, there is the doubt as to whether or not the mitzvah is valid when performed in the daytime; if it is valid, then one has not skipped a day at all. Second, there is the doubt as to whether all forty-nine days are one continuous mitzvah, or each day is a separate mitzvah; if each day is a separate mitzvah, then skipping a day does not disqualify the count, so that one would still be permitted to continue on succeeding days. Thus the *poskim* have ruled that in this case on the succeeding days one counts with the blessing.[56]

Doubt about the act means that one does not remember whether or not he counted a given day. If the doubt arises while it is still that same day, one counts again without a blessing. If the doubt arises after that day has already passed, then again it is a case of *sefeik-sefeika* — compound doubt. The doubt as to whether or not he actually counted is compounded by the doubt as to whether missing a day disqualifies one from continuing. Hence in this case one continues to count with the blessing.[57]

How can doubt arise concerning the date? If a person is far from any Jewish community and does not know which day of the *sefirah* it is, the third or the fourth, for example, what should he do? At first glance it would seem that he should [recite the blessing once and] count both the third and the fourth day of the *Omer* and thus be certain that he performed the mitzvah, even though he does not know which count was the correct one. But the author of *Devar Avraham*[58] argues that in this case one should not recite the blessing at all. The author's reasoning is based on a basic definition: the very nature of the *sefirah*, he asserts, involves clear and definite knowledge that this is a certain day of the count. This, according to the author, explains the ruling of *Magen Avraham* that if one who does not understand Hebrew counts the *Omer* in Hebrew he has not fulfilled the mitzvah. Others have found this ruling puzzling. How is this mitzvah different from *Hallel, Kiddush*, and others, where the necessary words may be recited in Hebrew even if one does not understand the language? But our author explains that the other mitzvos consist of *recitation* (קְרִיאָה), whereas with the *Omer* the mitzvah is one of *counting* (סְפִירָה), which implies clear knowledge. The author uses this same basic principle to explain a statement of *Shitah Mekubetzes*[59] that with respect to the mitzvah of tithing animals (מַעֲשַׂר בְּהֵמָה) the usual laws allowing one in certain cases to rely on probability (רוֹב) do not apply. [For example, if an animal which is exempt from the tithe accidentally gets mixed in with many animals that are subject to the tithe, one may not give one of the animals as the tithe, relying on the probability that the one given will not be the exempt one.] For this, too, is a mitzvah involving counting, so that certain knowledge is required, not probability.[60] Again, the author applies this principle to answer a problem posed by the *Rishonim*. Because of doubt outside *Eretz Yisrael* as to which day is the actual date of a festival, two days are observed. Why, the *Rishonim* ask, is the same practice not applied to the *Omer* count [counting two days each day because of doubt]?[61]

[The answer, of course, is the same. Since the very concept of *sefirah* implies certainty, the mitzvah cannot be observed on the basis of doubt.]

Doubt regarding the time of the count arises at dusk (בֵּין הַשְׁמָשׁוֹת). During this time, one knows the correct count for the previous day and also for the coming day, but this period of dusk in essence is doubtful concerning the question to which day it belongs. *Tosafos, Rosh,* and others have written that in our time when the *sefirah* is a Rabbinic mitzvah it is permissible to count at dusk. (Nevertheless, according to *Shulchan Aruch*, "the scrupulous do not count until nightfall".) The same scholar quoted above, the author of *Devar Avraham*, draws a distinction between the doubt arising at dusk and that arising from lack of knowledge about the correct number to count. In the case of dusk, one is counting the coming day. The number assigned that day is clear and decisive; the only doubt is whether or not the time of obligation has yet arrived.

The blessing recited over the act of counting has attracted the **The** theoretical interest of the commentators more than the **Blessing** practical interest of the *poskim* (except for the question of doubt, where whether or not to recite the blessing becomes a practical problem). Why is a blessing recited over the *sefirah*, but not over the count of the *zav* or *zavah*, a man or woman who has had a ritually impure discharge and must count seven days before undergoing immersion for the sake of ritual purity? This question is discussed by *Tosafos*.[62] The answer suggested is that (in the case, for example, of a woman counting the days of menstrual purity), if she has a discharge of blood during the seven days, the count is annulled retroactively. [Thus, since we do not know if the count will stand, no blessing is pronounced.] (In the case of *shmitah* and *yovel*, *Tosafos* rules that the *Beis Din* in fact pronounce the blessing.) A different answer to the same question is given by *Sefer HaChinuch*.[63] According to this *Rishon*, the tradition given with the commandment of counting the days of impurity defines this mitzvah as one of paying attention (הַשְׁגָּחָה בְּלֵב) during the stated number of days to make sure that one remains in a state of purity; this is not an obligation of counting per se.[64] *Radbaz*[65] gives yet a third answer. The *sefiras HaOmer*, he says, is an obligatory commandment; the *zavah*, on the other hand, if she wishes to remain in a state of ritual impurity for the rest of her life, has the option to do so; hence no blessing is recited over her count.

The *Rishonim* consider a different question of a blessing over the *sefirah:* Why do we not recite *Shehecheyanu* — " ... Who has kept us alive and preserved us and caused us to arrive at this time" — as we do over every periodically recurring mitzvah? A number of answers have been given. One suggests that *Shehecheyanu* is not recited because in our day this mitzvah is of Rabbinic rather than Scriptural status. Another explains that *Shehecheyanu* is recited only over a mitzvah involving benefit or the commemoration of benefit, but *sefiras HaOmer* commemorates, not benefit, but grief over the destruction of the House of our aspiration. Yet other solutions have been proposed.[66]

Another question regarding the blessing is whether or not the *sheliach tzibur*, the one leading the prayer, may act as the representative of the congregation in reciting this blessing. *Rashba*[67] proves that not only is the procedure valid after the fact, but even when chosen deliberately (לְכַתְּחִילָה) it is acceptable; a person may have the blessing recited for him by the *sheliach tzibur* [after whom he answers amen] and thereupon count the *Omer* for himself. (As to whether listening to the utterance of a representative is valid for the counting itself, see above.) The *Acharonim* rule in accordance with the opinion of *Rashba;* nevertheless the custom is that after the blessing of the *sheliach tzibur* each person recites the blessing individually.

These are the halachic problems presented by the mitzvah of the *sefirah.* Here we have outlined these problems in terms of basic principles. From these branch out the many legal details and precise distinctions discussed by those who have devoted themselves to the mastery of *Halachah.*

NOTES

[1] *Menachos* 65b-66a.

[2] *Temidin UMusafin*, 7:22-25.

[3] *Orach Chaim* 489.

[4] End of ch. 7 in *Temidin Umasafin.*

[5] See *Biur Halachah* in *Mishnah Berurah*, where the author proves that a number of the *Rishonim* rule the same as *Rambam.*

[6] 66a.

[7] And see *Ran*, end of *Pesachim.*

[8] *Toldos Adam VeChavah, Nesiv* 5, part 4.

[9] *Temidin UMasafin* 7:22.

[10] 8a.

[11] And see *Sefas Emes*, by the Rebbe of Gur, on *Menachos, loc. cit.*, where the author holds the opposite: that the counting of the days is connected to the sacrifices, and the weeks, to the sanctity of the festival. See also *Ha'amek She'elah*, by Netziv, *She'ilta* 107, and responsa *Rashei Besamim*, sec. 27.

[12] See below: *Shavuos: The Festival.*

[13] *Nissan, maamar* 3.

[14] *Shabbos* 68a.

[15] And see *HaMidrash Vehamaaseh*, *parashas Acharei*, where the author originates this explanation on his own accord. See also *Toldos Chanuch*, by Rav Ch. H. Friedland, *parashas Emor*.

[16] *Toras Kohanim, Emor*, and the *sugya* in *Menachos*.

[17] And see *Chilukim Shebein Anshei Mizrach Uvnei Eretz Yisrael*, by Dr. Margolios, p. 167, and *Chagim UMoadim*, by Rav. Y.L. HaKohen Fischman, p. 192.

[18] *Halachos Gedolos, Hilchos Atzeres; Rambam, loc. cit., halachah* 23.

[19] Rabbeinu Tam in *Tosafos, Menachos* 66a; *Semag*, positive commandment 199. And see *Shibolei HaLeket*, sec. 234.

[20] *Rosh*, end of *Pesachim; Ran*, there; *Mordechai, Megillah*, ch. 2. *et. al.*

[21] 489.7.

[22] 71a.

[23] 20b.

[24] And see *Menachos* 72a: "Just as [those things whose mitzvah is specified for] the daytime are not [valid if done] at night, so also, if for the nighttime, not by day."

[25] See *Or Same'ach, Temidin UMusafin* 7:23; responsa *Oneg Yom-Tov*, sec. 43; *Sefas Emes* on *Menachos* 66.

[26] Responsa *Oneg Yom-Tov, loc. cit.* And see *Mishkenos Yaakov, Orach Chaim* 123; *Beis HaLevi*, part 1, sec. 38.

[27] See *Shach, Yoreh De'ah*, 262; *Tzon Kadashim, Menachos* 72b; responsa *Chacham Tzvi*, sec. 166; *Tiferes Yisrael* on *Mishnayos Menachos*, end of ch. 10; *Mishkenos Yaakov* and *Beis HaLevi, loc. cit.*; responsa *Ein Yitzchak, Orach Chaim*, sec. 15; *Zer Zahav* on *Sefer HaMachria*, sec. 18; responsa *Degel Reuven*, part 1, sec. 19; *et. al.*

[28] *Ritz Geos*, part 2, p. 109, in the name of Rav Kohen Tzedek and Rav Hai Gaon.

[29] *Ibid.*, in the name of Rav Hai. And see responsa *Beis HaLevi*, part 1, sec. 39, where the author suggests that one who forgets to count a certain day should, at the end of that week, count the number of weeks with a blessing, since this is a mitzvah which does not depend on the days. And this author did not see that Rav Hai Gaon had preceded him with this idea.

[30] *Shibolei HaLeket*, sec. 234, in a note taken from manuscript; *HaMachria*, sec. 29. And see *Pri Megadim* 489, *Eshel Avraham*, para. 13, where the author raises this

problem on his own accord, concluding that "it requires further study" (צָרִיךְ עִיוּן), not having seen that the *Rishonim* had preceded him in discussing the problem.

[31] *Menachos* 66a.

[32] End of *Pesachim*.

[33] Rav Yehudai and Rav Saadiah. See *Ran*, end of *Pesachim*, and *Tur*, 489; *Ritz Geos, loc. cit.; Shibolei HaLeket, loc. cit.* And for a lengthy explanation of the opinion of Rav Yehudai and Rav Saadiah, see the commentary of Rav Y. Perla on *Sefer HaMitzvos* by Rav Saadiah Gaon, part 1, positive commandment 51.

[34] See *Minchas Chinuch*, mitzvah 306; responsa *Kesav Sofer*, sec. 99; *Eretz Chemdah*, by Malbim, *parashas Emor; Nefesh Chayah*, by Rav R. Margolios, 489; responsa *Eretz Tzvi*, by the Rosh Yeshivah of *Yeshivas Chachmei Lublin*, sec. 17; *et. al.* The author of *Eretz Zvi* makes a suggestion which, characteristically, surprises by its brilliance. He points out that according to the *Gemara* in *Sanhedrin* 68b, on the topic of the rebellious son (בֵּן סוֹרֵר וּמוֹרֶה), were it not for a special verse exempting a rebellious son who is a minor, the minor would be liable to punishment, since the death penalty in this case is given, not for present crimes, but עַל שֵׁם סוֹפוֹ — because of the high probability that the boy will commit crimes when he gets older. The author suggests that the same principle would apply in a mitzvah of our type, i.e., *sefiras ha-omer*, which has relevance to the minor after he comes of age; here, too, he would be obligated to count, while still a minor, עַל שֵׁם סוֹפוֹ — because of the high probability that he will be obligated to count when he gets older (in our case, a few days older). Though the line of reasoning is brilliant, needless to say the halachic conclusion is arguable.

[35] *Menachos, loc. cit.*

[36] *Sefer HaMitzvos* of Rambam, positive commandment 161; *Chinuch*, mitzvah 306; *et al.*

[37] *Sefer HaMitzvos, loc. cit.*

[38] *Nesiv* 5, part 4.

[39] *Mordechai, Megillah*, in the name of Rabbeinu Ephraim; *Tur*, in the name of Avi HaEzri.

[40] *Baal HaMaor*, end of *Pesachim*.

[41] And see *Shaar HaTziun* in *Mishnah Berurah*, paras. 8 and 9.

[42] See *Get Pashut* 126, para. 73, and *Knesses HaGedolah, Orach Chaim* 489 (these

two sources hold that the mitzvah may be fulfilled in this manner), and *Pri Chadash, Orach Chaim, loc. cit.* (this author maintains that the mitzvah may not be fulfilled in this way); and see *Shaarei Teshuvah,* 489, para. 6.

[43] *Mahadura Tinyana,* p. 21.

[44] *Bechoros* 48b [as printed in the Talmud]. But it should be noted that in the *mishnah* as printed in the *Mishnayos* the counting for this mitzvah also is in numbers (אֶחָד, שְׁנַיִם, וכו׳) rather than letters.

[45] And see *She'elas Yavetz,* sec. 139, where the author, too, discusses whether the sprinklings on Yom Kippur may be counted by means of letters of the *aleph-beis.*

[46] *Netziv,* in *Haamek Davar, parashas Emor,* writes that in fact the commandment *And you shall count for yourselves* (וּסְפַרְתֶּם לָכֶם; *Leviticus* 23:15) refers to thought alone, as with the counting of the *zav* or *zavah;* while, as Rava teaches in *Menachos,* it is the repetition of the command — *You shall count fifty days* (תִּסְפְּרוּ חֲמִשִּׁים יוֹם; *ibid,* v. 16), which indicates that the count must be made orally as well. But I do not find that Rava, or anyone else, makes such a statement in *Menachos.* According to Rava, the repetition of the command is to teach us that we must count both days and weeks.

[47] *Berachos* 20b.

[48] And see *Biur Halachah* in *Mishnah Berurah,* sec. 1, where the author proves that this is the subject of a disagreement among the *Rishonim.* See also: *Hashlamas Divrei Nechemiah* on *Shulchan Aruch HaRav,* 651; *Chasam Sofer,* part 6, sec. 19.

[49] Secs. 29-32.

[50] See the works cited in *Pischei Teshuvah* on *Yoreh Deah,* sec. 236; responsa *Tzemach Tzedek,* by the Rebbe of Lubavitch, *Yoreh De'ah* 177 and 178; responsa of *Rim miGur, Yoreh De'ah,* secs. 13 and 14; responsa *Tiferes Yosef, Yoreh De'ah,* sec. 30; *et. al.*

[51] And see *Shaarei Teshuvah,* 489:6; *Chasam Sofer,* part 6, sec. 19; *Ikarei HaDat,* sec. 21, *os* 3.

[52] *Orach Chaim,* sec. 60.

[53] *Abudraham,* in the name of *Machzor Vitri* (and see the notes to *Machzor Vitri,* p. 301); *Shulchan Aruch,* para.3.

[54] *Abudraham.* And see *Taz,* para. 6, and *Magen Avraham,* para. 7.

[55] Sec. 3.

[56] See *Trumas HaDeshen,* sec. 37; *Shaar HaTziun* in *Mishnah Berurah,* para. 45.

[57] *Trumas HaDeshen, loc. cit.; Shulchan Aruch,* para. 8. And see responsa *Sho'el UMeshiv,* fourth ed., part 3, sec. 127, for a very lengthy discussion of the topic.

[58] Part 1; sec. 34.

[59] *Bava Metzia* 6b.

[60] And see responsa *Degel Reuven,* part 1, sec. 25.

[61] See *HaMaor HaKatan,* end of *Pesachim.*

[62] *Kesuvos* 72a, and *Menachos* 65b.

[63] Mitzvah 330.

[64] And see *Sidrei Taharah,* sec. 196, para. 18. The author of *Noda BiYehudah,* second ed., *Yoreh De'ah,* sec. 123, understands the solution offered by *Tosafos* as meaning the same as that offered by *Chinuch;* that is, since if the woman has a discharge during her count, the count is canceled, this means that the verse, *And she shall count for herself* (וְסָפְרָה לָהּ; *Leviticus* 15:28) is interpreted not as an actual counting but rather in the sense of paying attention to the passage of time and being careful to remain in a state of purity. However, the author of *Chok Yaakov,* 489:6, as well as the son of the author of *Noda BiYehudah* in his comment on his father's responsa, both understand *Tosafos* to mean that [the count is an actual one, but no blessing is recited because] if the woman has a discharge the count is canceled, and the blessing would be in vain (לְבַטָּלָה).

[65] Part 4, sec. 1102 (27). And see a similar idea in the commentary of *Ramban* on *parashas Emor,* at the verse, *And You shall count for yourselves* (וּסְפַרְתֶּם לָכֶם).

[66] See *HaMaor* and *Ran,* end of *Pesachim; Roke'ach,* sec. 371; responsa of *Rashba,* secs. 126 and 379; *et. al.* And see responsa *Yehudah Yaaleh, Orach Chaim,* secs. 154 and 155.

[67] In his responsa, sec. 126.

ל"ג בָּעוֹמֶר

Lag BaOmer

As the author points out, Lag BaOmer as a minor festival is somewhat clouded in mystery. Not only are we unsure of its reason, but unlike all other memorable days in the Jewish year, its name indicates neither the reason behind the festival (as, for instance, with Pesach, Sukkos, or Purim) nor its date (like Tu BiShvat, or the Tenth of Teves). The only indication of when the day occurs depends on the counting of the Omer, and if one were to forget or confuse this count the name would give no clue to the correct date.

There are many reasons given by our Sages for Lag BaOmer. One 19th-century authority who suggests that on this day we celebrate an event which took place at the very beginning of our history as a nation is the author of Chasam Sofer. This scholar dates the origins of the rejoicing connected with Lag BaOmer at the early stages of the wandering of our forefathers in the wilderness. The Torah tells us (Exodus 16:1): "And they journeyed from Elim, and all the congregation of the Children of Israel came to the Wilderness of Sin, which is between Elim and Sinai, on the fifteenth day of the second month after their departure from the land of Egypt." This was on the 15th of Iyar. On the 16th the people complained against Moshe and Aharon and all the elders, going as far as to say: "We wish we had died by the hand of God in the land of Egypt, when we sat by the fleshpots and ate our fill of bread" (Exodus 16:3). On the 17th of the month HaShem told Moshe that the manna — the bread from heaven — would begin to fall on the next day, the 18th of Iyar. This is the date of Lag BaOmer.

Thus on this day we are in fact celebrating the miracle of the manna — echoing the joy of our forefathers when for the first time they perceived this wonder. Since however the events preceding it do not reflect favorably on our ancestors, we make no direct reference to it.

The first known reference to Lag BaOmer° as a minor holiday (יוֹמָא דְפִגְרָא) is found in certain of the *Rishonim*. No
mention of this *halachah* is recorded in the geonic literature
except that one *Rishon (Meiri)* refers to it as a tradition
handed down by the *Geonim*. In *Meiri's* commentary, *Beis
HaBechirah*,[1] at the place where the Talmud tells about the
twelve thousand pairs of students of Rabbi Akiva who died
between Pesach and *Atzeres* (Shavuos),[2] the author relates,
"It is a tradition of the *Geonim, zal*, that on *Yom Lag BaOmer*
the deaths stopped, and that for this reason it is customary to
refrain from fasting on this day." It would seem that this is
our earliest source for this holiday.

Ending   *HaManhig*[3] states: "It is the custom in France and Provence
the   to marry from Lag BaOmer on [that is, to permit weddings,
Mourning   which are prohibited from Pesach until this date because of
mourning for the students of Rabbi Akiva]; and I have heard
in the name of Rav Zerachiah Rabbeinu HaLevi of Garonne
that it has been found written '... from Pesach until *pros
HaAtzeres* — and what is *Porsa(=pros)*? — it means 'half,'
[that is, half of the time period] that is taught in a *mishnah*,
'We ask concerning the laws of Pesach thirty days before
Pesach' — and half of that is 15 days; hence we forbid
weddings until 15 days before the *Atzeres*, and that is Lag
BaOmer.' "

In this passage from *HaManhig*, however, there is no
emphasis on the thirty-third day of the *Omer* as a special day
in itself. It is simply stated that from Lag BaOmer on, the
period of mourning ends. Not only this, but *Tashbetz*[4] cites
these words of Rav Zerachiah HaLevi and interprets them to
mean that the mourning ends after a small part of the *thirty-
fourth* day has passed; for there is a rule that מִקְצָת הַיּוֹם כְּכוּלוֹ
part of the day is counted as the whole day; and this leaves
fifteen days until *Atzeres* (that is from the thirty-fifth through
the forty-ninth, inclusive). According to this, "the reason why
they wrote [that the mourning stops on] the thirty-third day
rather than the thirty-fourth is because the mourning of the
thirty-fourth is not for the whole day." This is also the

°[The word, *omer* (עֹמֶר), is the name of a measure (one-tenth of an *ephah*) used for produce.
The *Omer* offering consisted of one *omer* of the first of the new harvest of barley, brought to
the *Beis HaMikdash* on the morrow of the first day of Pesach and waved in a prescribed
manner by the *kohen*. That day — the sixteenth of Nissan — is the beginning of the *Omer*-
count of forty-nine days culminating in Shavuos. The numerical value of the letters ל and ג
totals thirty-three — hence לַג בָּעֹמֶר, *Lag BaOmer*, thirty-third day of the *Omer*-count. —
Ed.]

opinion adopted by Rav Yosef Karo in *Beis Yosef*,[5] in the name of several *Rishonim*, and this is the ruling given by the same author in *Shulchan Aruch*.

On the other hand in *Maharil* we find (under "the days between Pesach and Shavuos"): "*Mahari* Segal said: 'Even though we find in the *Gemara* that the students of Rabbi Akiva died from Pesach until *Atzeres*, nevertheless we make a celebration on *Yom Lag BaOmer*, for they died only on those days on which we say *techinah* [i.e., *tachanun*, prayers for forgiveness, normally recited after the *Amidah* prayer, but omitted on *Shabbos* and festive occasions], while on those days when *techinah* is not recited they did not die. Now, if we subtract from the forty nine days of the [*Omer*-] count, the seven days of the [Pesach] festival, the three days of Rosh Chodesh — two for Iyar and one for Sivan — and the seven *Shabassos*, there remain thirty-two; hence, they died on only thirty-two days. Therefore, when those thirty-two days on which they died have finished, on the following day there is a celebration in commemoration of the event.' " Of course, "those thirty-two days on which they died" is not meant literally, for by this account it was not on the first thirty-two days that they died; all the same, in commemoration of the fact that the days of mourning are thirty-two in number, the thirty-third day of the *Omer* was made a day of *simchah*.[6]

In *Yuchsin*[7] a mnemonic phrase is given for the fact that on the eighteenth of Iyar it is again permissible to hold a wedding. The phrase is from a passage in *Pirkei Avos* (5:21) which sets forth the ages and stages of man's life. Among these are: בֶּן י״ח לְחֻפָּה — "At eighteen, the wedding canopy." The author records this mnemonic in the name of *Baal HaMichtam*. This implies that it is of ancient vintage, for *Michtam* is cited by the *Rishonim*.[8] And in *Minhagim* of Rav Aizik Tirna we read: "On the eighteenth of Iyar — that is, Lag BaOmer — [the prayers for forgiveness called] *nefilas apayim* are not recited the whole day, nor on the preceding evening; and also the [lines beginning] צִדְקָתְךָ, וְצִדְקָתְךָ, צִדְקָתְךָ are omitted when the seventeenth of Iyar falls on *Shabbos*." *Rama* rules similarly; for in the passage in *Shulchan Aruch* where Rav Yosef Karo states that "one should not have a haircut until the morning of the thirty-fourth day," *Rama* comments, "But in these lands this is not the custom;" Rather, one may have one's hair cut on the thirty-third, and on that day there is an increase "to some extent, of joy; and *tachanun* is not recited." Not only that, but "If [Lag BaOmer] falls on Sunday, it is customary to have a haircut on Friday, in honor of Shabbos."

The Acharonim discuss whether it is permissible to have a haircut on the night of Lag BaOmer before sunrise (הָנֵץ הַחַמָּה)[9] and in Orchos Chaim[10] on Orach Chaim it is stated that Baal Daas Kedoshim rules that if a wedding celebration is begun on Lag BaOmer during the day, it is permissible to continue the feast into the following night as well (i.e., the night of the thirty-fourth).

Two
Customs

The difference between the two opinions described above — those of Rav Yosef Karo and Rama — is not limited to the thirty-third day [which Rav Yosef Karo includes in the time of mourning, while Rama rules that it is a time of simchah]; rather, the difference of opinion affects the whole thirty-three day period of mourning, in terms of when it begins and ends. According to Rav Yosef Karo, the thirty-three days are counted from the second day of Pesach until the end of the thirty-third day of the Omer, and from the thirty-fourth day on it is permitted to have one's hair cut and to hold a wedding. According to Rama, haircuts and weddings are permitted until [and including the two days of] Rosh Chodesh Iyar; on the other hand, these prohibitions, once begun, continue until the festival of Shavuos, except for the day of Lag BaOmer itself. Thus, if we deduct from the forty-nine days of the count the first sixteen days (from the sixteenth of Nisan through the two days of Rosh Chodesh, inclusive), there remain thirty-three days of mourning. [Included within these thirty-three days is Lag BaOmer;] for that day we apply the rule, "part of a day is counted as the whole day." [The first part of the day — i.e., the beginning of the evening — is counted as a whole day of mourning, and from then on it is a time of celebration.]

However, as Rama writes, "Within one city, it should not be the practice that part of the people follow one of these customs and part of them, the other; for this would contradict the principle of לֹא תִתְגּוֹדְדוּ" [see Deuteronomy 14:1; there the phrase means literally, Do not make incisions in your flesh. But since the root of the verb can mean "group," the verse is also interpreted to mean, "Do not split into factions"]. "And," Rama continues, "all the more so is it prohibited to adopt the permissive aspects of both opinions." That is, one should not follow the practice of permitting haircuts and weddings through Rosh Chodesh Iyar, as allowed by Rama, and together with this follow the custom prescribed by Rav Yosef Karo and permit these activities from Lag BaOmer on; for these two leniencies are mutually contradictory, and it is concerning such mutually contradictory leniencies that the Talmud says, "[One who practices] the leniencies of *Beis Shammai* and the leniencies of *Beis Hillel* is a wicked man (רָשָׁע)."[11]

Some congregations have a custom of calculating the thirty-three days of mourning somewhat differently. They apply the prohibitions on the two days of Rosh Chodesh Iyar, but relax them during the "three days of limitation" (שְׁלוֹשֶׁת יְמֵי הַגְבָּלָה) leading up to Shavuos; but these three days are counted as two, for on the first of them the prohibitions are not relaxed until the morning, according to the rule, "part of a day is counted as the whole day."[12]

The Hilula

Lag BaOmer has another festive aspect: the rejoicing (הִילוּלָא) of Rabbi Shimon Bar Yochai. The commentary *Ateres Zekenim* on *Shulchan Aruch*[13] states: "It is the custom in *Eretz Yisrael* to go to the tomb of Rabbi Shimon Bar Yochai, *zal*, and of Rabbi Eliezer, his son, on the thirty-third day of the *Omer*. And Rav Avraham HaLevi testifies that he had a custom always to say the passage, נַחֵם [a passage of mourning recited on Tishah BeAv], in the blessing תִּשְׁכּוֹן (that is, the blessing which in the Sephardic rite begins תִּשְׁכּוֹן — "Dwell ..." — and in the Ashkenazic version, וְלִירוּשָׁלַיִם עִירְךָ — "Return to Jerusalem Your city ..." in the *Shemoneh-Esreh* Prayer). And once [when he did this on Lag BaOmer], when he had finished the prayer, Rav Yitzchak Luria, *zal*, said to him in the name of Rabbi Shimon Bar Yochai *(Rashbi)* who was buried there, that *Rashbi* had told him, 'Say to this man, why does he recite נַחֵם on the day of my joy? Therefore, he will soon be in consolation. And so it was, for his eldest son died. Thus we see that one should not recite *tachanun* on this day."[14]

The great student of *Arizal* and publisher of his works, Rav Chaim Vital, writes in *Pri Etz Chaim:*[15] "Concerning those who go to the tomb of *Rashbi* and Rabbi Eliezer his son in Meron on Lag BaOmer, I have seen my teacher, *zal*, these eight years going [each year] with his wife and family and he was there those three days. Further, Rav Y. S. [Rav Yonasan Seiges] testified to me that one year before I met [my teacher] he went there to [give his young son his first haircut] with feasting and joy on these days" (and again he cites the episode concerning the recitation of נַחֵם).[16]

Objections

The festivities on Lag BaOmer for the sake of the *hilula* of *Rashbi* — and in particular the *hadlakos*, the igniting of objects at the tomb in Meron — have aroused many objections. *Chasam Sofer* writes in his responsa:[17] "I know and I have also heard that nowadays the generations have improved and people come from afar seeking *HaShem* in the holy city of Safed on the day of Lag BaOmer, at the *hilula* of *Rashbi, zal.* And even though their entire intent is for the sake of heaven, and their reward is undoubtedly great, I would prefer to be one of those who refrain, so that I should not need to be there and deviate from their custom in their presence, and I should not want to join with them in this." The essential cause for doubt, according to this author, is that it is not correct "to institute a holiday (מוֹעֵד) on a day that is not the anniversary of a miracle and is not mentioned by the Talmud or the *poskim* anywhere in the literature, not even by an allusion or a hint. Rather, refraining from eulogy and fasting [on this day] is purely a custom, and the reason itself is not known to me." And after citing at length the justifications, according to the *Kabbalah*, for the observation of Lag BaOmer he concludes: "All the same, with regard to making it a day of celebration *(simchah)* and lighting of lights *(hadlakah)*, and especially in a designated place which becomes a focus of attention (תֵּל תַּלְפִּיּוֹת) towards which everyone turns — I do not know that it is permissible to do this."

An even stronger objection against this custom is voiced by the author of responsa *Sho'el UMeshiv:*[18] "Quite the contrary, for the death of a *tzaddik* and scholar one should fast; and we fast for the death of *tzaddikim;* and how can it be that a *Yom-Tov* should be celebrated over the death of our great teacher *Rashbi, zal* ... but in truth much could be said about the practice of burning clothes over [his tomb] on Lag BaOmer. This violates the prohibition of *bal tashchis* [against needless destruction of property]; and even for kings and princes [the Sages] did not relax this prohibition except for the coverings of the bier ... and in truth this [*hilula*] is the custom among them; and much could be said about it. But what can I do? For due to our many sins they will not listen to the voice of their teachers in this matter; and the Sages have already said, 'Just as it is a mitzvah to say a thing which will be heard [so also it is a mitzvah to refrain from speaking when one will not be listened to],' and especially in a matter which has become customary and which the masses consider the performance of a mitzvah, so that is difficult to refrain; for Israel are holy and desire the merit of mitzvos. But it is obvious that in the days of the *Ari* and the other *holy ones who are in the earth (Psalms* 16:2), what they did at the tomb of *Rashbi* was none other that Torah study, prayers, and supplications that through his death and through this day mercy would be awakened for Israel. And it is obvious that *Beis Yosef* and his circle would not have allowed people to behave in [the manner in which the celebrations are currently performed]; it was only after their time that the custom spread, and afterwards it was thought to be an ancient custom, and people were afraid of punishment, heaven forbid, if it were neglected. But I will stand as a guarantor for them that if they would take the same money and support the poor of Israel with it, this would be more to the liking of *Rashbi*, and would be 'a benefit to him, and a benefit to the world.' "

One of the great *Sephardi* scholars, as well, Rav Yosef ben Chaim Chazan (d. Jerusalem, 5580 — 1820), in his work *Chikrei Lev*[19] raises objections to the custom. "I have heard of a custom that in the holy city of Safed, may it be rebuilt and established, they ignite valuable items worth three and four hundred [coins] at the *hilula* of *Rashbi, zal,* by wrapping the items in oil [-soaked cloth] and lighting it. And I do not find any halachic justification for this, for it seems to violate the Rabbinic prohibition [against needless destruction,] *bal tashchis.* And I do not believe that the early sages followed this practice, unless the custom has recently become distorted in transmission; for even at the *simchas beis hasho'evah* nothing was burned except the outworn pants of the *kohanim*, and the belts of their priestly garments [see *The Joy of the Water-Drawing*, vol. I, p. 313]. And if [one were to attempt to justify this custom] on the basis of the fact that it is permitted to burn items for the death of kings, that is only for kings, and only at the time of their death ... and although I know of the greatness of *Rashbi, zal,* in the heavens above and on the earth — and who am I to speak in a matter which somewhat touches his honor — still, I know that he would not tolerate any flattery, and my heart tells me that he is not gratified by this [custom]."

And in responsa *Shem Aryeh:*[20] "I thought, 'I shall turn aside and behold this great spectacle,' why they make great celebrations over the tomb of the holy *Tanna, Rashbi,* and what is this great sound of tumult, that people come from the ends of the earth to rejoice there in his honor with great lights; and also this custom was founded by ancient and holy great men, and *Ari, zal,* went there on *Yom Lag BaOmer* to cut the hair of his son. All my life I have wondered about this. What is the purpose of this *simchah*? On the contrary, do we not find that it is proper to fast on the anniversary of the death of *tzaddikim*, ... and if it is possible that they did not wish to institute a fast on Lag BaOmer, since it is a day on which we do not recite *tachanun*, because on this day the pupils of Rabbi Akiva stopped dying, nevertheless what place is there for a great celebration of this kind? ... and thus I stood astonished and amazed at this thing for many years, and did not understand the meaning of it."

An After a lengthy discourse, this author suggests an original
Original explanation for the custom of rejoicing over the tomb of
Explanation Rashbi on Lag BaOmer. The explanation is based on the Talmud passage[21] which relates how the Roman authorities decreed that Rabbi Shimon Bar Yochai should die by the sword, and through a miracle the decree was annulled. Hence, a celebration is observed on the day on which he died through divine rather than human agency. And the reason why people go to the tomb on that day is that those executed by the authorities were not allowed to be buried; hence, the tomb is a sign of the miracle. This explanation of *Shem Aryeh* is brilliant, but somewhat tenuous. Still more tenuous is the author's interpretation of the word, *hilula*. In his opinion, "common opinion is mistaken about this," in understanding *hilula* to be a word for *simchah*, rejoicing. Rather, "it comes from the root of *hallel*, praise, for the honor of the deceased, to eulogize and praise him; for it is customary in eulogy to laud and praise [the deceased]."

This interpretation of *hilula* is not correct. It is indeed true that the derivation of the word is from the root of *hallel*, but the noun *hilula* undoubtedly refers to *simchah*, in particular a wedding celebration, as in אַגְרָא דְּבֵי הִילוּלָא מִילֵי[22] an expression of the Talmud which means [to paraphrase *Rashi*] that the reward to be earned at a wedding celebration is in rejoicing the bridegroom through words. Or again, עֲבֵיד הִילוּלָא לִבְרֵיה, "he held a wedding celebration for his son"[23] — and many similar passages. Likewise, the phrase "*hilula* of *Rashbi*" has the same meaning. This is a concept in Kabbalah, which draws a comparison between a wedding and the passing of a *tzaddik* to the highest heavens. In particular, the kabbalists draw this comparison concerning the *hilula* of *Rashbi*, for it is said that this world is of the nature of a betrothal, while the world-to-come is of the nature of a marriage,[24] since in this world the external aspects of Torah are shown to us, while in the world-to-come its inner secrets will be revealed;[25] hence for *Rashbi*, author of the *Zohar*, the work which revealed the inner secrets of the Torah, there was a light at his passing that resembled the light of the future world, of the nature of a marriage — *hilula*.[26]

As regards the doubts expressed by the authors of *Sho'el UMeshiv* and *Chikrei Lev* as to whether the *hadlakah* of clothing violates the prohibition of *bal tashchis*, an answer was given by the Rav of Safed, Rav Shmuel Heller (d. 5664 — 1904). The latter published a pamphlet entitled *Kevod Melachim* (Jerusalem, 5634 — 1874) which constituted, according to the title page, "a halachic ruling (פְּסָק דִּין) in the matter of the burning of expensive clothing at the *hilula* of *Rashbi* (may his merit defend us, amen)." Rav Heller refutes at great length the objections of those who had cast doubts on the custom of the *hilula*. (He does not mention the authorities cited above, but states, "A letter has reached us from a certain Torah scholar in the holy city of Jerusalem, may it be rebuilt and established, decrying and raising objections to the custom of burning very expensive clothes at the great *hilula* on Lag BaOmer in Meron, may it be rebuilt and established.")

The author states, "The Torah forbade [destruction of property] only when it is done in a wanton way (דֶּרֶךְ הַשְׁחָתָה), and when one has no reason for the action and receives no benefit except for the destruction itself" — this is the basis of his defense, for which he cites a great many proofs and supports. He concludes: "Every Torah scholar who understands and recognizes the greatness of the sanctity of the place and the day at the *hilula* on Lag BaOmer will realize that both these things (that is, the sorrow and the joy) are proper and are linked with each other like a woman to her sister. For it is impossible in this world to touch even the farthest edge of the true joy which emanates on this day, unless one contemplates and clothes oneself in fear and trembling and abnegates oneself ... and in accordance with the degree of self-abnegation and nothingness, and the annulment of the intervening veil, the gross material, to this same extent there will come inevitably and correspondingly an emanating light of joy, a divine joy ... whatever is done for his honor merits a very great reward, and I am troubled about the possible punishment of anyone who would raise objections against this. And I can testify in truth that in my youth I heard from the mouth of venerable rabbis of the Sephardim, whose fathers had seen and related to them that the holy rabbi, Rav Chaim ben Attar,° may his merit defend us, amen, was once

°[The reference is to the author of *Or HaChayim* on the Torah. — *Ed.*]

here for the *hilula* in the holy city of Safed, may it be rebuilt and established. When he went up to Meron and reached the bottom of the mountain where they ascend [to the tomb], he got down from his donkey and ascended the hill on his hands and knees; and the whole length of the way he bellowed like a beast of burden and exclaimed, 'How can I, a lowly creature, enter into the place of fire that gives forth tongues of flame ...' and at the time of the *hilula* he rejoiced with a very great joy, and he himself burned a number of expensive clothes in honor of *Rashbi*, may his merit defend us, amen; and also the elders of the Sephardim here know and have heard of this."

The *rabbanim* of Tiberias, too, in their reply to Rav Chaim Chizkiah Medini,[27] wrote a lengthy refutation of the assertions of *Sho'el UMeshiv* and argued in favor of the custom of *hadlakah*; however, they testified that if any of the participants "wishes to put an expensive garment on the fire, those in charge inform him that it is not proper to burn it in the fire; they dedicate [the garment for religious use] and sell it and distribute the proceeds among the poor in honor of the *Tzaddik*."

As to the claim of *Sho'el UMeshiv* that this custom was not practiced in the time of *Beis Yosef* and *Ari*, the *rabbanim* of Tiberias prove on the basis of a number of books that this is an ancient custom, and that the assertion of *Sho'el UMeshiv* is "the opposite of the tradition which we have heard, and it is known that our master *Beis Yosef* and the great men of his generation used to go up to Meron, to the burial place of *Rashbi*, and be glad and rejoice on his day of *hilula*."

It should be added that in the work *Shivchei Yerushalayim* (Livorno, 5545—1785), there are recorded the writings of a traveler of the year 5282 (1522), and there we find: "... On the fifteenth of Iyar a great caravan was formed in Meron; more than a thousand souls were there, for many came from Damascus with their wives and children, and most of the community of Safed, and the whole community of Levukim, which is a village near the cave where *Rashbi* and his son were hidden ... and there we passed two days and two nights (i.e., through the night of Lag BaOmer) — celebrating and rejoicing."

In the work, *Hilula DeRashbi*, by Rav Asher Zelig Margolies (Jerusalem, 5701—1941), the author cites a number of early sources confirming the custom of the pilgrimage to Meron and to the tomb of *Rashbi* (not only on Lag BaOmer). Rav Margolies puts his whole soul into his description of the *hilula* at Meron in our time.

"It is impossible to describe the greatness of the day of joy and *Joy* *exultation with trembling (Psalms* 2:11) which takes place in *Above* Meron on *Yom Lag BaOmer* — one can actually see that it is a *and* day of *simchah* for the upper worlds and the lower ... it is *Below* actually a *simchah* like that of the world-to-come. Some who are there sing out and rejoice, exult and delight in dances of holiness, with the joy of singing 'Bar Yochai' and other holy songs; others stand wrapped in sacred emotions, pouring out their souls in unceasing streams of tears near the holy burial sites of *Rashbi* and Rabbi Eliezer his son; elsewhere, garbed in prayer shawl and *tefillin*, men pray together; still others sit on the sacred floors and study the *Zohar* and the *Tikunim* and the *Idaros;* others pour out their souls in the recitation of psalms. Here and there, groups are seen with children, dancing and clapping, holding the little ones on their shoulders and giving the [three-year-olds with long locks] their first hair-cuts, distributing wine and heady *yash* and cakes, calling out *lechayim* and exchanging blessings — and the crowds dub these little children 'the bridegrooms of *Rashbi'* (חֲתָנִים דְּרַשְׁבִּ״י) — and group by group they sit down to friendly feasts in holy joy ...''

NOTES

[1] On *Yevamos,* p. 234.

[2] *Yevamos* 62b.

[3] 91b.

[4] Part 1, sec. 178.

[5] *Orach Chaim* 493.

[6] And see *Bach* and *Biur Halachah* of *Mishnah Berurah.*

[7] Warsaw ed., p. 36

[8] See *Shem HaGedolim,* part 2. secs. 40, 119.

[9] See *Mishnah Berurah,* paras. 10 and 11.

[10] 493.

[11] *Rosh HaShanah* 14b. And see responsa *Chasam Sofer, Orach Chaim,* sec. 142.

[12] See *Mishnah Berurah,* para. 15.

[13] 493.

[14] This story is cited in brief by *Magen Avraham,* para. 3.

[15] *Shaar Sefiras HaOmer,* ch. 7.

[16] And see *Mishnas Chassidim, maseches Iyyar;* the *Siddur* of *Rav Shabsai Rashkover, Sefiras HaOmer.* And see response *Divrei Nehemiah, Orach Chaim,* sec. 34.

[17] *Yoreh De'ah,* 233.

[18] Fifth ed., sec. 39

[19] Last ed., *Yoreh De'ah,* sec. 11.

[20] *Orach Chaim,* sec. 14.

[21] *Shabbos* 33b.

[22] *Berachos* 6b.

[23] *Ibid.,* 31a.

[24] *Shemos Rabbah,* ch. 15.

[25] See *Rashi,* beginning of *Song of Songs.*

[26] See a lengthy discussion of this matter in *Magen Avos,* by the Rebbe of Kapust, in part 7: "The Hilula of *Rashbi.*"

[27] *Sdei Chemed, Asifas Dinim, maareches Eretz Yisrael,* sec. 6.

❧ Shavuos

הֶחָג ‎

The Festival

Fifty days after our forefathers left the slavery of Egypt the purpose of their miraculous redemption was fulfilled: they were given the Torah.

The Exodus was accompanied by many other miraculous events. As the Torah tells us: "Has God ever done miracles, to go and bring one nation from the midst of another nation with such trials, signs, wonders, war, a mighty hand, an outstretched arm, and terrifying phenomena, as HASHEM your God did for you in Egypt before your very eyes?" (Deuteronomy 4:34). "Surely," argues Rabbi Levi Yitzchak of Berditchev, "the day after this ultimate miracle would appear to have been the logical time to give the Torah!"

But Rabbi Levi Yitzchak himself has an answer to this argument. "Quite the contrary," he explains. "It would then have seemed that the People of Israel accepted the Torah in gratitude for all those miracles. For this reason a period was deliberately allowed so that their ardor should cool. Indeed we are told that after leaving the sea and wandering for three days in the wilderness without finding water the people complained (Exodus 15:24). Thus, when they accepted the Torah it was because of their love for HaShem and His Torah, and not because of the miracles they had witnessed."

In this vein Rambam *(in Hilchos Yesodei HaTorah 8:1)* writes: "Israel did not believe in Moshe Rabbeinu because of the miracles that he performed ... Why then did they believe in him? Because when we stood at Mount Sinai it was we who saw — not that we were told that someone else had seen — the thunder and the lightning; it was our ears that heard — not that we were told that someone else had heard — the Voice of HaShem saying, 'Moshe! Moshe! Tell them thus and thus.' If therefore another prophet were to arise and perform signs and miracles and seek to deny the Torah of Moshe Rabbeinu we would not listen to him. We would know as a certainty that such signs and miracles were delusions. For the prophecies of Moshe are not based on miracles: we believe them because we saw with our own eyes and heard with our own ears just as he did. As the Torah says (Exodus 20:19), 'You saw that from the heavens I spoke to you.' "

A **Shavuos**, in comparison with other festivals, occupies a
modest place in the halachic literature. The experience of
the Jewish nation at Mt. Sinai, and the giving of the Torah,
have not been crystallized in the form of practical mitzvos
particular to those events. Sinai and the giving of the Torah
are related to the sanctity of this festival, to its essential value
and inner quality, but not to concrete *halachos* and fixed laws.
Perhaps this is in the nature of such things. That which
includes all does not stand in need of details; nor the root, in
need of branches. Be that as it may, the fact is that aside from
the prayers and the Torah reading, this day of the giving of
the Torah has no specific positive or negative commandments
— except, of course, the obligatory sacrifices of the day, which
are mitzvos applicable when the *Beis HaMikdash* is standing
(those sacrifices are the topic of the following chapter).

Of course there are the laws in effect on every *Yom-Tov*.
These — the mitzvos of joy *(simchah)*, rest *(shevisah)*, and
refraining from labor *(issur hamelachah)* — are explained in all
their details and fine points by the Talmud in *Beitzah* (a
tractate which the early Sages referred to by the name "*Yom-
Tov*"), and by *Shulchan Aruch* in its sections on *Hilchos
Yom-Tov*. But there are no separate *halachos* of Shavuos, as
there are *hilchos* Pesach and *hilchos sukkah*. All the *halachos*
of Shavuos are contained within a single section in *Shulchan
Aruch*,[1] the *siman* called "The Order of Prayer for the
Festival of Shavuos." And this *siman* itself is subsumed
within "*Hilchos* Pesach."

The
Debate
with the
Sadducees

On the other hand, there is one detail wherein the festival of
Shavuos engages the attention of the halachic literature more
than all the other festivals. To call it "one detail" is in fact not
the correct expression. This is not a detail, but rather the
essence of the festival, that is, the very day itself. For unlike
all the other festivals, whose date is fixed by the Torah, the
date of this "festival of the first-fruits" is not explicitly stated
by Scripture. Rather, the festival is linked to a different time:
seven *Shabassos* "*from the day after the Shabbos*" (מִמָּחֳרַת
הַשַּׁבָּת; *Leviticus* 23:15). As we know, the disputed
interpretation of these words, *from the day after the Shabbos*,
was the main rock of contention between the Sadducees and
the Pharisees (הַצְּדוּקִים וְהַפְּרוּשִׁים) in the time of the Second
Temple. This same dispute made its appearance again in the
period of the *Geonim*, this time because of the Karaites, who

took up the contention of the Sadducees that the count of seven weeks leading up to Shavuos should begin the day after the *Shabbos Bereishis*, the regular weekly *Shabbos*, following Pesach. *Sifra*[2] and the Talmud[3] record many proofs of the *Tannaim* to refute the opinion of the Sadducees. The *Geonim*, too, as well as the *Rishonim*, devoted much effort to upholding our tradition that *from the day after the Shabbos* means the day after the first *Yom-Tov* of Pesach. Not only that, but even in our present era of the *Acharonim*, when there is no longer any trace in daily life of this dispute with the Sadducees and the Karaites, a number of great scholars have seen fit to bring forth supplementary proofs for our tradition.

Here we shall indicate, by way of illustration, three proofs: one from the era of the *Tannaim*, one from the days of the *Rishonim*, and one from the *Acharonim*.

"... When the Boethusians (בַּיְתוּסִין) claimed that *Atzeres* [i.e., Shavuos] comes [always] after *Shabbos*, Rabban Yochanan ben Zakkai encountered them and said to them: 'Fools, whence do you derive this?' And there was not a single man to answer him, except for one old man who began to prate at him ... [Rabban Yochanan ben Zakkai] said to him: 'Fool, is not our whole and perfect Torah to be preferred to your vain talk? One verse says *You shall count fifty days* (תִּסְפְּרוּ חֲמִשִּׁים יוֹם; *ibid.* v. 16 — Rashi: "This implies days, not weeks"); while another verse says, *They shall be seven whole weeks* (שֶׁבַע שַׁבָּתוֹת תְּמִימֹת תִּהְיֶינָה; *ibid.* v. 15 — "and the term 'weeks' applies only to those which begin the day after *Shabbos* and end on *Shabbos"*). How can this be? [The answer is that] the second phrase refers to a year when *Yom-Tov* [Pesach] falls on *Shabbos* ("for in that case the day after it is the day after *Shabbos*, which is the day of the *Omer* offering when the count begins, and this is when the phrase *seven weeks* applies"); the other phrase refers to those years when *Yom-Tov* falls on a weekday' " ("This is the situation referred to by the phrase, *fifty days*, and not complete weeks").[4] This argument is the first of a series of proofs given by the *Tannaim*.[5]

From the period of the *Rishonim*, we may consider the proof given by *Rambam*. "We learn from our tradition (מִפִּי הַשְּׁמוּעָה) that [the *Shabbos* mentioned in the verse] is not *Shabbos*, but *Yom-Tov*, and this has been accepted always by the prophets and the Sanhedrin of every generation, for they would wave the *Omer* on the sixteenth of Nissan, whether it falls on a weekday or on *Shabbos*. Now, it says in the Torah: *And you shall not eat bread, nor parched grain, nor raw grain until that very day* (וְלֶחֶם וְקָלִי וְכַרְמֶל לֹא תֹאכְלוּ עַד עֶצֶם הַיּוֹם הַזֶּה; *ibid*. v. 14)." [This is the prohibition against eating *chadash*, the new crop of grain, until the *Omer* is offered up.] "And it is said (in the *Book of Joshua): And they ate from the produce of the land on the day after the Pesach, matzos and parched grain* (וַיֹּאכְלוּ מֵעֲבוּר הָאָרֶץ מִמָּחֳרַת הַפֶּסַח מַצּוֹת וְקָלוּי בְּעֶצֶם הַיּוֹם הַזֶּה).[6]" [Thus we see that the day of the *Omer* sacrifice, the beginning of the count, is the morrow of Pesach, not of *Shabbos*.] "And if you claim that that Pesach occurred on *Shabbos*, as the fools imagine — how could it be that the Torah would link the permission to eat *chadash* with something [Pesach] that was neither essential nor the determining factor, but merely coincidental? But rather, since the Torah links this matter with the day after the Pesach, it is clear that the day after the Pesach is the causal factor which makes the *chadash* permissible, and it makes no difference on which day of the week it falls."[7]

And for a proof from the era of *Acharonim*: "What is the meaning of the words, שֶׁבַע שַׁבָּתוֹת תְּמִימֹת — *seven complete weeks* (ibid. v. 15)? If we say that *from the day after the Shabbos* means *Shabbas Bereishis*, then there is no need for the former phrase. For since the Torah writes [that the count should continue] *until the day after the seventh Shabbos* (עַד מִמָּחֳרַת הַשַּׁבָּת הַשְּׁבִיעִת; ibid. v. 16), it is obvious that they are complete weeks. Rather, it must be that the phrase *seven complete weeks* refers to those years when *Yom-Tov* falls on a weekday. In that case, one might have thought it proper to apply the rule, מִקְצַת שָׁבוּעַ כְּכוּלּוֹ — "a part of a week is counted as a whole week"[8] — so that the second week would begin immediately after *Shabbos* [even though the first week had been only partial]. This is why the Torah writes *They shall be complete*, to ensure that we shall not consider the first week complete until seven days from the beginning of the *Omer*."[9] This proof is based on the plain meaning of the verses in question.

When was the Torah Given? If this discussion about the date of the festival is directed outward, against the opinion of the Sadducees, there is another talmudic debate regarding the time of the festival, a debate whose source is in the *Tannaim* and whose continuation extends to the works of the *Acharonim* and which constitutes an internal rather than an external debate, with practical consequences in the *Halachah* — in the laws of *niddah*, family purity. The focus of this debate is the question, When was the Torah given to Israel — on the sixth of Sivan or on the seventh?

On this question there is a difference of opinion between the *Chachamim* and Rabbi Yosei, and a lengthy *Gemara* passage[10] deals with the clarification of their disagreement. All agree that the Torah was given on *Shabbos*, and all agree that Israel came to the desert of Sinai on Rosh Chodesh Sivan. The difference of opinion concerns the number of days involved in the mitzvah of *perishah*, the separation of the men from their wives in preparation for receiving the Torah (וְקִדַּשְׁתָּם הַיּוֹם וּמָחָר; *and you shall be sanctified today and tomorrow — Exodus* 19:10). The *Chachamim* state that the *perishah* was for two days, while Rabbi Yosei says three days. The basis of this disagreement is the question, how long does the sperm remain viable? This matter has halachic consequences for our time as well, and in *Yoreh Deah*[11] the *Halachah* is determined according to the opinion of Rabbi Yosei.°

This ruling leads to a difficulty posed by *Magen Avraham.*[12] Why do we say in our prayers on Shavuos, [the sixth of Sivan] זְמַן מַתַּן תּוֹרָתֵנוּ — "the time of the giving of our Torah?" For according to the *Halachah* as determined in *Yoreh Deah*, it turns out that the seventh of Sivan was the day when the Torah was given. The same author asks another question. According to our calculations, it is evident that the Torah was given, not on the fiftieth day of the *Omer* count, but on the fifty-first; for the *Gemara* passage makes it clear that Israel went out from Egypt on a Thursday, and since the Torah was given on *Shabbos*, this would be on the fifty-first day. [Since the Exodus began on Thursday (Pesach), the *Omer* count began on Friday; the seven complete weeks of 49 days thus ended on Thursday. Two more days until Shabbos gives a total of 51. — *Ed.*] Why, then, do we observe the festival on the fiftieth day?

A great many authors have debated the solution to these two problems.[13] Among the answers to the first question, it

---

° [The disagreement between the *Chachamim* and Rabbi Yosei concerns the length of time that the sperm of a man remains viable within a woman's body. For as long as the sperm remains viable, its re-emission from the woman's body (an event which can occur without her knowledge) would put her in a state of ritual impurity (*Tumah*), which would be inappropriate for the giving of the Torah. The *Chachamim* are of the opinion that the period is two days; Rabbi Yosei, three. Thereafter, the sperm is no longer considered viable and cannot cause *tumah* if emitted. This dispute, which is decided in favor of Rabbi Yosei, has practical consequences in our time for the laws of family purity *(niddah)*. It affects the length of the waiting period which must pass before the woman can begin counting the "seven days of purity" which precede immersion in the *mikveh*. (In practice, the custom endorsed by *Shulchan Aruch* is to wait five days after menstruation and then, if the flow has ceased, to begin counting the additional "seven days of purity.") — *Ed.*]

has been suggested that it is simply for the sake of extra carefulness in the matter of *niddah* that we follow the stringent opinion of Rabbi Yosei for that purpose, but in terms of basic *Halachah* we accept the opinion of *Chachamim*.[14] Concerning the second question, one answer given is that Scripture did not set the festival of Shavuos for a specific date of the month, nor for the day when the Torah was given. Rather, we are told to observe the festival on the fiftieth day of the *Omer*. For us, for whom Nissan is always a "full" month of thirty days and Iyar is always a "short" one of twenty-nine days, the fiftieth day falls on the sixth of Sivan. But the time of the Exodus, both Nissan and Iyar were "full" months, so that even though the Torah was given on the fifty-first day of the *Omer*, in that year also it was the sixth of Sivan. This is why we call the sixth of Sivan "the time of the giving of our Torah."[15]

A different solution, combined with an unconventional interpretation of the verses involved, is given by the author of *Oneg Yom-Tov*. The Torah mentions two counts: seven weeks, and fifty days. Both of these, asserts the author, are meant literally — seven weeks from the offering-up of the *Omer* (the sixteenth of Nissan); and fifty days from the first *Yom-Tov* of Pesach. Now, when the Torah says *fifty days*, it means fifty complete days. But in that first year when we went out from Egypt, the first *Yom-Tov* of Pesach was not a complete day; the festival was interrupted, for we were redeemed from Egypt on the morning of the fifteenth of Nissan — *on that very day* (בְּעֶצֶם הַיּוֹם הַזֶּה; *Exodus* 12:17).[16] Hence, it was necessary to celebrate the festival of Shavuos on the fifty-first day of the *Omer*, in order to fulfill the requirement of fifty complete days from Pesach. [The addition of an extra day would not affect the other requirement of seven *weeks* from the sixteenth of Nissan.] Thus we are correct in saying "the time of the giving of our Torah:" Now, as then, the day of the giving of the Torah is after fifty days from the first *Yom-Tov* of Pesach.[17]

This entire debate about the date of Shavuos is purely an academic one. It has no practical implications because for us, the day of the festival has been firmly established as the sixth of Sivan. This is true, however, only "for us," that is, for our era when the calendar is determined by calculation. But for those times when the calendar depends upon eye-witness testimony about the appearance of the new moon, there is a disagreement in the Talmud[18] about the very day of Shavuos itself in terms of its correct date; and this disagreement is not only theoretical, but practical. "Rabbi Shmayah taught: 'The *Atzeres* is sometimes five [i.e., the fifth of Sivan], sometimes six, and sometimes seven. How so? If both [months, i.e., Nissan and Iyar] are full — five; both short — seven; one full and one short — six.' " However, others *("acherim")* disagree with this *baraisa*, holding that of the two months, one is always full and one short — and hence the *Atzeres* is always on the sixth of Sivan. This whole passage is seen by some *Acharonim* as providing the key to the first problem posed by *Magen Avraham* — the question concerning the date of the festival. The answer is that, as we see from this *sugya*, Shavuos does not depend on a set day of the month at all, but rather on the fiftieth day of the *Omer*.

Another question that has arisen concerning the date of Shavuos has to do with the second day of *Yom-Tov* of the Diaspora. With the other *Yamim-Tovim*, this second day reflects the fact that at one time in history the communities of the Diaspora which could not be reached in time by messengers from Jerusalem were in doubt as to which day had been proclaimed Rosh Chodesh, and hence about which day was actually *Yom-Tov*. But why should the extra day of *Yom-Tov*, resulting from *sfeika deyoma*, "doubt about the day," apply to Shavuos? With this festival, there could never have been any doubt as to its date, not even in the era when Rosh Chodesh was determined by testimony; for once these distant communities knew which day Pesach had fallen on, they simply had to count the forty-nine days of the *Omer*, and the next day was undoubtedly Shavuos. An allusion to this fact is found in the wording of *Rambam*.[19] "And in order not to create differences between the festivals, the Sages decreed that every place which could not be reached by the messengers of Tishrei [because of the great distance from Jerusalem] would observe two days, *even the Yom-Tov of Atzeres*."

The Second Day of Shavuos

   Chasam Sofer[20] asks a question based on this fact. We know that in our time, when there is no longer any doubt in the Diaspora about the dates of the festivals, the two days of *Yom-Tov* continue to be observed because of the principle of מִנְהָג אֲבוֹתֵינוּ בְּיָדֵינוּ — "the tradition of our forefathers is in our hands," and we maintain it שֶׁמָּא יַחֲזוֹר הַדָּבָר לְקַלְקוּלוֹ — "lest the uncertain situation come about again." But we can see from the words of *Rambam* that in the case of Shavuos our forefathers themselves, in the era when Rosh Chodesh was determined by testimony, never observed the extra day because of an "uncertain situation," but rather, "in order not to create differences between the festivals." Why, then, should we in our era be bound in this case by the principles of "our forefathers' traditions ..." and "lest the uncertain situation come about again"? As a result of these considerations, *Chasam Sofer* reaches a conclusion which is the opposite of what one at first glance might have expected. He concludes that the extra day of *Yom-Tov* of Shavuos is more binding (חָמוּר יוֹתֵר) than that of the other *Yamim-Tovim*. Since from the very beginning, the second day of Shavuos in the Diaspora was not instituted because of doubt, but rather by a decree of the Sages, it is similar to the second day of Rosh HaShanah. There, too, the Sages instituted a decree — namely, that whenever "the witnesses arrive after *Minchah*, that day is to be treated as holy, and the next day, holy."[21] And there, too, in the case of Rosh HaShanah, the second day hence has greater severity than the second *Yom-Tov* day of other festivals.

What brought *Chasam Sofer* to discuss this matter was a pivotal halachic query which had stirred up a great dispute among the sages of the city of Brod. It happened that a certain man was terminally ill, and on the second day of *Yom-Tov* of Shavuos, when he felt that his final hour was approaching, he wished to release his wife with a divorce document, so that she would not be bound to his brother by the requirement of a levirate marriage. [The law of levirate marriage, or *yibum*, requires that if a man dies childless his brother must take the widow in marriage, or else release her through the ceremony called *chalitzah*. In our time, levirate marriage is very rare, especially in the western world, but *chalitzah* from the brother-in-law is nevertheless required before the woman can marry anyone else. — *Ed.*] In this case, it would have been very difficult for the woman ever to remarry, for the brother lived in a distant place, the city of Rome. A certain scholar was consulted and gave instructions that [in spite of the prohibition against writing on *Yom-Tov*] a divorce document be written on the second day of *Yom-Tov*, on the basis of *takanas agunah*, the extra leniency instituted by the Sages in order to prevent Jewish women from being unable to remarry. [The more usual meaning of *takanas agunah* is in reference to legal testimony. Normally, there are strict qualifications determining who may and may not be a valid witness. These qualifications are drastically relaxed when the testimony involved is that required to establish widowhood so that a woman can remarry. — *Ed.*]

The *gaon* Rav Shlomo Kluger, who was then the head of

the *beis-din* and also the *maggid* of the town, opposed the other scholar's ruling with all his authority. Afterwards, he addressed a query to *Chasam Sofer*, "in order that 'the voice of the woman's blood' should not cry out to me saying that I am guilty of her blood. I decided to present my arguments before his honor, the illustrious *gaon (Chasam Sofer)* to make known whether I ruled correctly or, heaven forbid, made an error. For all the sages of our holy community reinforced me in my ruling, except for ... etc." The "etc." was inserted in order to avoid damaging the honor of the Rav who was the "exception." But the personnel of the dispute have since become known without being revealed by *Chasam Sofer*. In the book *Shivah Einayim*[22] by *Maharshak* (Rav Shlomo Kluger) are recorded all the questions which were the subject of disagreement between the author and the communal Rabbi, Rav Elazar Landau; and among those questions this one also appears.

Rav Elazar Landau was one of the well-known *geonim* of his generation. His major work, *Yad HaMelech*, is to this day considered to reveal understanding and clear logic; and the author was the grandson of the author of *Noda BiYehudah*. The debates between Rav Landau and Rav Kluger were sharp ones. *Maharshak* did not always refrain from searing expressions of disapprobation. As to the substance of the questions, in most cases *Maharshak* won the agreement of the great scholars of the generation. On this subject, too — the writing of the divorce document on the second *Yom-Tov* of Shavuos — *Chasam Sofer* responded at great length, ruling against such permission and refuting all possible counter-arguments.

A final subject of halachic disagreement which may be mentioned here concerns *Akdamus*, the Aramaic poem which is read during the Morning Service on Shavuos. In previous times, the custom was to recite *Akdamus* after reading the first verse of the day's Torah reading *(In the third month ... —* בַּחֹדֶשׁ הַשְּׁלִישִׁי; *Exodus* 19:1). *Taz*[23] criticized this custom, for it is forbidden to interrupt the Torah reading. He concludes: "I have heard from nearby that outstanding *rabbanim* have instituted the custom of singing *Akdamus* before the *kohen* begins the blessing over the Torah reading, and this would be the proper custom for every community."

In responsa *Shaar Ephrayim*,[24] however, there is a long responsum on this subject addressed to "the holy community of Venice." A fierce controversy had been ignited there

Akdamus and the Torah Reading

between the Sephardi and the Ashkenazi Torah courts. The latter followed the custom of interrupting the Torah reading with the recitation of *Akdamus*, while the former were making a concerted effort to abolish this practice. The question directed to the author of *Shaar Ephrayim* concerned three things: עַל הַדִּין, עַל הָאֱמֶת וְעַל הַשָּׁלוֹם — "the judgment, the truth, and the peace." The first aspect, "the judgment," involved the question whether the western, Sephardi Torah court was qualified to pass verdict on a matter of this sort, since "someone suspect in a given matter cannot give valid testimony on that matter, and hence they certainly are disqualified, for according to their custom they have never recited *Akdamus* at all. And if they have the power to pass judgment on our customs, there will be nothing to stand in their way from doing whatever they devise, and in the future they will annul all our customs, since they are in the majority."

As for "the truth," the query was whether or not the ruling of the Sephardi *beis-din* was in fact halachically correct — "for I have sought out and found all the old [books of] customs and the early prayerbooks and have found them to be in accordance with our Ashkenazi custom which has always been practiced."

"The peace" meant: "To silence the disputations, for the quarrels have multiplied among men of stature."

The author of *Shaar Ephrayim* writes at great length to reply regarding all three aspects and he confirms and upholds the custom of reciting *Akdamus* at just that point, i.e., after reading the first verse of the Torah portion. But this ruling has not been accepted. Rather, it has become customary throughout nearly the entire Diaspora to recite *Akdamus* before the blessing over the Torah by the *kohen*. Even the great-grandson of the author of *Shaar Ephrayim*, Rav Yaakov Emden, writes in his *Siddur:* "... Heaven forbid that the Torah reading should be ·interrupted ... even though our respected grandfather, מַר אַבָּא רַבָּה הַגָּאוֹן הֶחָסִיד the *gaon* and chassid, author of *Shaar Ephrayim* went to great efforts in a responsum, and would gladly have pledged himself for this custom ... nevertheless I have not seen that אָבִי מוֹרִי הַגָּאוֹן חֲסִידָא קַדִּישָׁא, the holy devout man (he refers to his father, author of *Chacham Tzvi*) ever followed this practice."

Rav Yavetz makes a characteristic comment on the question recorded in *Shaar Ephrayim* about "someone suspected in a given matter ..." "If there is any room here for this kind of doubt," writes Rav Yavetz, "it certainly should apply to none other than our Ashkenazi brothers, who are suspect on this point, to interrupt all the blessings and the Torah readings; they have made every smooth place painful with the stones of *piutim* ..." All the same, as regards the *piut, Akdamus,* he does remark, "In my eyes, also, this important *piut* is precious; we, too, recite it" — but not to the extent of interrupting the reading of the Torah.

In the Mishnah and Talmud the festival of Shavuos is *The* called the "*Atzeres.*" [The word comes from the root meaning *Atzeres* "to stop," and hence also has the meaning of "culmination" and "assembly." — *Ed.*] In the Torah, this word is found only in reference to the seventh day of Pesach and to Shmini Atzeres, the eighth day of Sukkos; but not in reference to Shavuos. The earliest source for the word *Atzeres* in reference to Shavuos is in the Aramaic translation of the Torah, *Targum Onkelos.* For the verse, *And on the day of the first-fruits ... on your festival of weeks* (בְּשָׁבֻעֹתֵיכֶם ... הַבִּכּוּרִים וּבְיוֹם);[25] — Onkelos renders, בְּעֲצַרְתְּיכוֹן — "on your *Atzeres.*" This point is discussed in *Pesikta Zutra.* "Rabbi Tuviah ben Rabbi Eliezer, *zal,* said: 'I have reviewed all [those parts of the Torah dealing with] the festivals, and I have not found that the festival of Shavuos is called *Atzeres;* but our Sages of blessed memory everywhere call the festival of Shavuos *Atzeres;* and this is an expression found in the *Targum,* for Onkelos writes, בְּעֲצַרְתְּכוֹן."[26] *Pesikta Zutra,* however, does not clarify the reason for this.

Elsewhere, we find Shavuos referred to as "the *Atzeres* of Pesach." A *midrash* says, "It would have been proper for the *Atzeres* of Sukkos [i.e., Shmini Atzeres] to be fifty days away from that festival, just as the *Atzeres* of Pesach is fifty days away from it ... [27] From this we may conclude that Shavuos is called *Atzeres* because of its linkage with the festival of Pesach. [That is, just as Shmini Atzeres is the culmination of Sukkos, so Shavuos is the culmination of Pesach. — *Ed.*]

The *Tzaddik* of Berditchev,[28] in the book *Kedushas Levi,* writes: "I was asked in the country of Lithuania° why it is that the festival of Shavuos is called the *Atzeres* ... and I answered the question on three levels. The first is the level of the plain meaning (פְּשָׁט). It will be seen that on all the festivals there are two types of service of the Creator, Blessed Be He. The first type of service is the performance of the commandment relevant to the particular festival: on Pesach,

° [Where they always tried to 'catch out' Chassidic Rebbes. — *Ed.*]

the eating of *matzah*, and so on. The second type of service is the prohibition against doing work. But on the festival of Shavuos it is not thus; there is but one mitzvah, namely, that we are stopped (נֶעֱצָרִים) from the performance of work. And this is why it is called *Atzeres.*"[29]

***

Customs *of* Shavuos

Among the customs of Shavuos, we may mention the following:

It is customary to strew greenery in the synagogue and in the home, in commemoration of the joy of the giving of the Torah.[30] For herbage surrounded Mt. Sinai, as it is written: *Also the flocks and the herds shall not graze opposite that mountain* (גַּם הַצֹּאן וְהַבָּקָר אַל יִרְעוּ אֶל מוּל הָהָר הַהוּא).[30*] From this we see that there was herbage on which to graze.[31] And some have the custom of putting trees in the synagogue and the home, to remind us that on the *Atzeres* we are judged concerning the fruits of trees,[32] so that we may pray for a favorable judgment about them.[33] *Gra* annulled the custom of erecting trees, because of the commandment, *And you shall not go by their statutes* (וּבְחֻקֹּתֵיהֶם לֹא תֵלֵכוּ; *Leviticus* 18:3), for nowadays the gentiles put up trees on their festival.[34] But some write that this custom does not violate the prohibition against going "by their statutes," since we do this for a specific reason of our own.[35]

It is the custom to stay awake on the night of Shavuos and to be engaged in Torah study.[36] This matter is mentioned in the *Zohar.* "The pious ones of former times did not slumber on this night, and they would labor in the Torah and say, 'Let us go to the possession, the holy inheritance, for us and for our children in two worlds.' "[37] *Magen Avraham* gives an explanation for the custom. "Because [when the Torah was given at Sinai] Israel slept the whole night and the Holy One, Blessed Be He, had to wake them up, as the Midrash states. Therefore we must rectify this." And a set order of study for the night, *Tikkun Leil Shavuos*, has long been in use; it is compounded of Torah, the prophetic writings, the other Scriptures, Mishnah, Talmud, Zohar, and other sources. It is interesting to note that the author of *Chak Yaakov* writes: "The *Tikkun* was principally established only because of the unlettered who do not know how to study, and hence read the *Tikkun;*" but accomplished scholars should study Torah, concentrating on whatever material their heart desires.[38] In the Lithuanian *yeshivos* it was customary to study *Gemara,* and not to recite the *Tikkun*. All the same, a great many scholars follow the practice of reading the *Tikkun* on this night.

Another custom of Shavuos is to eat milk foods.[39] In various works a number of reasons have been given; one characterizes this as a commemoration of the *shtei halechem*, the two wheat loaves offered up on this festival in the *Beis HaMikdash*.[40] Another explanation points out that at the time of the giving of the Torah the people were informed of all the prohibitions in the entire Torah. Thus, improperly slaughtered meat became forbidden to them; and it was impossible that same day to properly slaughter, salt, and cook meat, and all this with new utensils, since the utensils previously in use were now forbidden [having been contaminated by non-kosher meat]. Hence it was necessary to eat milk foods.[41] And though we now eat such foods in commemoration of the original event, nevertheless we are reminded that "it is necessary to eat meat meals as well, for 'there is no joy without meat.' "[42]

One way in which the *halachah* for Shavuos is more stringent *Isru* than for the other *Yamim-Tovim* is in connection with the day *Chag* after the festival. A *mishnah* informs us in general that "It is forbidden [to deliver a eulogy] on *Shabbos* and *Yamim-Tovim*; before and after, it is permitted."[43] Thus, from the point of view of the essential law (מִצַּד הַדִּין) it is permissible to fast on the day before or after *Shabbos* or *Yom-Tov*; nevertheless it is customary to prohibit fasting on the day after a festival; and this day is called *Isru Chag*. [*Isru* comes from the root meaning "to tie";] the name is derived from the Talmudic dictum, "Whoever observes an *issur* for the festival ("a connection and continuation of the festival on the morrow") by eating and drinking — Scripture accounts it to him as if he had built the Altar and offered up a sacrifice on it, as it is said, *Bind the festival [offering] with cords unto the horns of the Altar*" (אִסְרוּ חַג בַּעֲבֹתִים עַד קַרְנוֹת הַמִּזְבֵּחַ; *Psalms* 118:27).[44] This custom of prohibiting fasting on Isru Chag also has a source in the *Talmud Yerushalmi*, where the day is called בְּרֵיהּ דְּמוֹעֲדָא, "the son of the festival."[45] *Isru Chag* of Shavuos, however, is distinguished from that of the other festivals, for here the prohibition against fasting is not only custom, but law.

This may be seen from the following Talmud passage. "It once happened, on the death of Alexa (*Tosefta* reads: Alexander) that all Israel gathered to mourn him; and Rabbi

Tarfon did not allow them to do so, because it was the day of sacrifices (יוֹם טָבוּחַ) of the *Atzeres.*"[46] One possible interpretation of this passage is that the term "the day of sacrifices" is based on the *halachah* that certain obligatory sacrifices of the pilgrim festivals cannot be offered up on *Yom-Tov* itself, since the labor involved in these offerings does not supersede *Yom-Tov.* Specifically, these sacrifices are *olas re'iyah,* the burnt-offering by which one fulfills the requirement to "be seen" in the *Beis HaMikdash* on each of the pilgrim festivals; and *shalmei chagigah,* the festival peace offerings. These two sacrifices are offered on behalf of the individual, rather than on behalf of the public as a whole, and this is why they do not supersede *Yom-Tov.* Since they cannot be sacrificed on *Yom-Tov* itself, at the festivals of Pesach and Sukkos they were sacrificed during *Chol HaMo'ed,* the Intermediate Days of the festival. At Shavuos, they were sacrificed the day after the festival, and hence that day was given somewhat the quality of a *Yom-Tov,* so that eulogy [and fasting] are forbidden. This prohibition applies in our time as well, even though for us it is not "the day of sacrifices" — for Rabbi Tarfon himself, like us, lived in the period after the Destruction of the Temple.[47]

Certain of the *Acharonim* have raised a major question on this subject. They point out that there is a *mishnah* which explains: "When *Atzeres* falls on the day before *Shabbos,* according to *Beis Shammai* the day of sacrifices comes after *Shabbos,* while according to *Beis Hillel* there is no day of sacrifices after *Shabbos;*" for according to *Beis Hillel olos re'iyah* and *shalmei chagigah* may be offered up on *Yom-Tov* itself, and therefore there is no "day of sacrifices" at all after the festival. And the *Halachah* is according to *Beis Hillel.*[48] [It would seem, then, that Rabbi Tarfon's prohibition against fasting, based on the idea that *olos re'iyah* and *shalmei chagigah* may not be offered on *Yom-Tov,* is not the *Halachah.*] This apparent contradiction was in fact dealt with by one of the *Rishonim* (whose commentary was not seen by the *Acharonim* who raised the question). *Tosefos Rid* states that *Beis Hillel* did not in fact intend to indicate that there is no "day of sacrifices" after Shavuos. Rather, "*Beis Hillel* said only that the day of sacrifices is not a necessity, since the people are permitted, if they wish, to offer up [*olos re'iyah* and *shalmei chagigah*] on *Yom-Tov.* But it is not possible for all Israel to have time to offer up these sacrifices on the first day [i.e., on *Yom-Tov* itself], and many people offer them on the second day [*Isru Chag*]. For this reason, it was considered a day of sacrifices, and eulogy [and fasting were] prohibited."[49]

NOTES

[1] 494.

[2] *Emor, parashasa* 10, ch. 12.

[3] *Menachos* 65-66.

[4] *Menachos, loc. cit.*

[5] *Ibid.* And see above, p. 196 for an interesting interpretation of the *baraisa* of Rabban Yochanan ben Zakkai, in the name of *Panim Yafos,* by the author of *Haflaah.*

[6] *Joshua* 5:11.

[7] *Temidin UMusafin* 7:11. And see *Ibn Ezra, Emor,* 23:11; *Rambam* and *Abarbanel,* there; *Kuzari, maamar* 3, ch. 41, and the commentary *Kol Yehudah* there. And see above, p. 11.

[8] Cf. *Pesachim* 4a, *et. al.:* "Part of the day counts as all of it" (מִקְצָת הַיּוֹם כְּכוּלוֹ).

[9] *Panim Yafos, Emor* 23:15.

[10] *Shabbos* 86-88.

[11] 196.

[12] 494.

[13] See *Chok Yaakov,* 494; *Ba'er Heitev, ibid.; Shulchan Aruch HaRav,* 474; responsa *Oneg Yom-Tov,* sec. 42; *et. al.*

[14] See *Magen Avraham, loc. cit.*

[15] See *Chok Yaakov* and *Shulchan Aruch HaRav, loc. cit.*

[16] *Berachos* 9a.

[17] It should be noted that this idea of *Oneg Yom-Tov* can be used to give a good interpretation of the argument of Rabbi Yosi Bar Rabbi Yehudah, against the position of the *Tzedokim,* as recorded in *Menachos.* Rabbi Yosi states, "The Torah says, *You shall count fifty days ...* (תִּסְפְּרוּ חֲמִשִּׁים יוֹם; *Leviticus* 23:16); and if you say [that the count begins] from the weekly Sabbath, then you will find that sometimes [Shavuos] is fifty one, sometimes fifty-two, fifty-three, fifty-four, fifty-five, or fifty-six [days from Pesach]." The commentators have raised the problem: What sort of refutation is this? For the *Tzedokim,* too, say that only fifty days are to be counted; but they begin the count after the Sabbath, rather than after Pesach. But according to the interpretation of *Oneg Yom-Tov,* the words of Rabbi Yosi are understandable. (And the comment of Rava there: "Perhaps the meaning is fifty days aside from these six [days which may come between Pesach and the Sabbath]" is likewise still understandable, for in any case "perhaps" this could be the Torah's meaning.

[18] *Rosh HaShanah* 6b.

[19] *Kiddush HaChodesh* 3:12.

[20] *Orach Chaim,* sec. 145.

[21] See vol. I, *Rosh HaShanah in Four Eras,* p. 80.

[22] *Lemburg,* 5624 (1864).

[23] 494, para. 1.

[24] Sec. 10.

[25] *Numbers* 28:26.

[26] *Ibid.*

[27] *Pesikta DeRav Kahana* (ed. Rav Sh. Buber), *piska* בְּיוֹם הַשְּׁמִינִי עֲצֶרֶת; *Shir HaShirim Rabbah, parashah* 7.

[28] *Parashas Naso, drush* for Shavuos.

[29] This same idea was expressed in *Chazon Yechezkel* on *Tosefta, Rosh HaShanah,* ch. 1, where the author adds that "it would seem that after the Destruction of the Temple, when *shtei halechem* ceased to be offered up, and the festival thus involved no special mitzvah aside from the fact of being *Yom-Tov,* the festival of Shavuos began to be called by the name *Atzeres* in Babylonia, since on that day one is 'prevented' (עָצוּר) only from doing work." And this is not correct; Shavuos was called *Atzeres* in Temple times as well, and in *Eretz Yisrael* (see *Mishnayos Sheviis* 1:1, and several other places). *Targum Onkelos,* too, who in *Numbers* 28:26 translated בִּשְׁבֻעֹתֵיכֶם as בְּעִצְרָתֵיכוֹן, i.e., *Atzeres* [though in *Exodus* 34:22 and *Deuteronomy* 16:10 he translates חַג שָׁבֻעֹת as חַגָּא דְשָׁבֻעַיָא, "the festival of Shavuos] was written in Temple times, as is proven by S. D. Luzzato in *Ohev Ger.*

[30] *Maharil, Hilchos Shavuos; Rama* in *Shulchan Aruch* 494.3.

[30*] *Exodus* 34:3.

[31] *Levush,* 494.1.

[32] See *Mishnayos Rosh HaShanah* 1:2.

[33] *Magen Avraham,* para. 5.

[34] See *Chayei Adam, klal* 131, and *Mishnah Berurah,* para. 10.

[35] See *Archos Chaim*, in the notes of *Maharsham*.

[36] *Magen Avraham, Chok Yaakov, et. al.*

[37] *Emor 95a.*

[38] 494, para. 1.

[39] *Hagahos Minhagim Tirna*, Shavuos; *Rama, Shulchan Aruch* 494.2.

[40] See below, at the end of *Shtei HaLechem.*

[41] *Sefer HaMatamim*, Shavuos, sec. 85; *Mishnah Berurah*, para. 12. And, it should be added, according to the statement of the *Gemara* that the Torah was given to Israel on *Shabbos* (see above, p. 235), by law it was impossible to slaughter animals that day.

[42] *Hagahos Minhagim Tirna, loc. cit.*

[43] *Taanis 17b.*

[44] *Sukkah 45b*, with *Rashi*. The custom is cited by *Rama*, 429; and see *Magen Avraham* and *Shulchan Aruch HaRav* there.

[45] *Yerushalmi, Avodah Zarah* 5:1. And see *Tosafos, Rosh HaShanah* 19b; *Shibolei HaLeket*, sec. 262. *Pnei Moshe* gives a different interpretation of בריה דמועדא, not having seen the interpretation of *Shibolei HaLeket, et. al.*

[46] *Chagigah* 18a. And see *Tosefta* there, end of ch. 2.

[47] *Tosefos Rid, Chagigah, loc. cit.; Shibolei HaLeket*, sec. 262; *Shulchan Aruch* 494.3.

[48] See *Magen Avraham*, 494; *Levush, ibid.; Hagahos Rabbi Akiva Eger, ibid.; Mishneh Lamelech, Klei HaMikdash* 6:9.

[49] *Tosefos Rid, Chagigah, loc. cit.* And see *Shulchan Aruch HaRav*, end of sec. 494.

שְׁתֵּי הַלֶּחֶם
The Two Loaves

The progressive order of divine service which began with the Omer of barley brought to the Beis HaMikdash on the second day of Pesach, setting in motion a nationwide count of 49 days, culminated in the offering of the Two Loaves on the fiftieth day, the festival of Shavuos. In fact, as the author points out in the chapter before us, so important was this offering considered that it gives Shavuos one of its alternative names, for the Torah refers to this Yom-Tov as the "festival of the First Fruit" (Chag HaBikkurim), an honor not granted to any other offering or sacrifice brought throughout the year.

A question thus arises. If the offering in the Beis HaMikdash is the essence of the festival, how do we, who are as yet unworthy of bringing this offering, celebrate today? A fitting answer can be found in Aruch HaShulchan (Orach Chaim 489:2,3): "Although nowadays we cannot bring this offering, one could say that the main reason for our counting the Omer is to prepare ourselves for the giving [and receiving] of the Torah. As the Midrash says: When Moshe Rabbeinu told the People, 'On this mountain you will serve HaShem,' the Children of Israel asked, 'Moshe our Teacher, when will this be?' So he told them, 'In fifty days' time.' And each one of them counted off these days. That is why our Sages told us too to count these days. Even in our era, when we have no Omer and no sacrifices, we count these days in joyful anticipation of the day the Torah is given, as did our forefathers in that time."

Aruch HaShulchan then continues: "HaShem commanded us to bring an offering of barley at the beginning of the count and of wheat at the end — to teach us that without Torah we are like animals, whose food is barley; and it is only when we are elevated by the Torah that we assume the attributes of a human being and can bring an offering of wheat. This is why the Torah commanded us to bring these offerings. The meaning and intention of the Omer period is thus to prepare us to receive the Torah, and this is a mitzvah that has application for our own days" — and, indeed, for all times.

The Essence of Shavuos

Shtei halechem,[1] the two loaves of wheat bread that are to be waved before the Altar on Shavuos, stand above the other offerings of this festival, and of the festivals in general, in that the whole essence of the festival of Shavuos is in relation to these loaves, and from them the festival takes its name — *Yom HaBikurim*, the day of the first-fruits. "The festival of Shavuos is called *Bikurei Ketzir Chitim*, the first-fruits of the wheat harvest, because of the *shtei halechem* which are the first of the meal offerings of wheat to come from the new crop *(chadash)*" — thus writes *Rashi* in his commentary on the verse, וּבְיוֹם הַבִּכּוּרִים בְּהַקְרִיבְכֶם מִנְחָה חֲדָשָׁה לה' בְּשָׁבֻעֹתֵיכֶם — *And on the day of the first-fruits, when you offer up a new meal offering to HASHEM on your festival of weeks ...*[1*] In his commentary on the Talmud,[2] *Rashi* gives this same interpretation to two other verses: *You shall observe for yourself the festival of Shavuos, the first-fruits of the wheat harvest* (וְחַג שָׁבֻעֹת תַּעֲשֶׂה לְךָ בִּכּוּרֵי קְצִיר חִטִּים);[3] *and the festival of the harvest, the first-fruits of your labors* (וְחַג הַקָּצִיר בִּכּוּרֵי מַעֲשֶׂיךָ).[4] That is to say: the *shtei halechem* are rightly called *bikurim*, first fruits, because they precede [at the Altar] the entire harvest of wheat and barley; they even precede what is also, in the more usual sense of the word, called *bikurim* — that is, the first-fruits of the seven types of produce which each individual land-owner is obligated to bring to the Temple when he gathers the harvest of his vineyard, orchard, and field.

It is true that *Rashi* writes elsewhere that it is these latter *bikurim*, of produce of the seven kinds, which give the festival its name; for *Atzeres*, or Shavuos, is the time when one may begin to bring these *bikurim* to the *Beis HaMikdash*.[5] And this second interpretation is the one applied by *Netziv* to the verse. *And on the day of the first-fruits ... Netziv* tells us: "The verse makes known three aspects of this day's sanctity. (1) *And on the day of the first-fruits ...* [That is, this festival marks the time when these first-fruits of all kinds may be brought to the Temple.] (2) *... when you offer up a new meal offering* [i.e., *shtei halechem*]. (3) *... on your festival of weeks* [the culmination of the period of counting seven weeks].[6] But in the final analysis, whichever interpretation of the term *bikurim* one adopts, the fact remains that the sanctity of this festival is tied to the *shtei halechem*. Even according to the second interpretation, although the two loaves are not the essence of the day's holiness, they are a basic attribute thereof; for the Torah describes the "day's sanctity" in terms of the bringing of the *new meal offering* — *shtei halechem.*

The terms *bikurim* and *minchah chadashah* (new meal offering) which are applied to the *shtei halechem* indicate both a mitzvah and a prohibition. It is a mitzvah that the *shtei halechem* should be baked from wheat of the new crop; and there is a prohibition against offering up any other meal offering from the *chadash* until the *shtei halechem* have been offered. This prohibition is expressed [in positive terms] by a *mishnah:* "The *Omer* [offering of barley on the second day of Pesach] made [the *chadash*] permissible in the rest of the country; *shtei halechem,* in the *Mikdash.*"[7] The *Omer,* however, brought about a change not only in the rest of the country, but in the *Beis HaMikdash* as well. "Before the *Omer,* one may not offer up [from the new crop] meal offerings or first-fruits or the meal-offering that accompanies an animal sacrifice *(minchas behemah);* and if one does offer them, they are invalid. Before the *shtei halechem,* one may not offer up those things; but if one does offer them, they are valid."[8]

One may pose a fundamental question about the prohibition of *chadash* in the *Beis HaMikdash* before the offering of *shtei halechem.* Is this the very same prohibition of *chadash* in effect until the offering of the *Omer,* except that then, before the *Omer,* the prohibition applied both to man and to the Altar, whereas after the *Omer* the new crop became permitted to man while remaining prohibited for the Altar? Or is the prohibition with regard to the Altar separate and independent, not deriving at all from the prohibition for man?

It would seem that this *chakirah,* or conceptual investigation, is of the type which characterizes the "modern study method" of the *yeshivos* of recent times. But in fact this is not so. The matter is discussed by one of the *Rishonim, Rashba* — or at least in a work of that period attributed to him[9] — and he explains at length that the *Tannaim* were in disagreement over the issue. The disagreement itself is recorded in *Sifri*[10] and in Tractate *Menachos*[11] in a revealing form. We are told that Rabbi Tarfon was sitting and grappling with the problem, "What is the difference between before the *Omer* and before *shtei halechem?* (That is, what accounts for the *halachah* that offerings from the new crop, before the *Omer* are invalid even post factum, while such offerings, if performed after the *Omer* but before the *shtei halechem,* are valid post factum?) Yehudah bar Nechemiah said before him: 'Not so! [That is, the *halachah* is not difficult to explain.] Surely it is reasonable that there should be a difference between the time before the *Omer*, when [the *chadash*] is not permitted at all in the ordinary world (אֵצֶל הֶדְיוֹט) and the time before *shtei halechem*, when [the *chadash*] is entirely permitted in the ordinary world.' Rabbi Tarfon was silent. Rabbi Yehudah ben Nechemiah's face shone ["he rejoiced" — *Rashi*]. Rabbi Akiva said to him: 'Yehudah, did your face shine when you refuted a Sage? I wonder whether you will be long-lived.' Rabbi Yehudah ben Rabbi Ilai said: 'That incident happened at *pras haPesach* ["two weeks before Pesach" — *Rashi*]. When I went up [to Jerusalem] for the *Atzeres*, I asked about him: Yehudah ben Nechemiah, where is he? They told me: He has died and is gone.' "

Rashba's
Chakirah

Rashba raises many problems in connection with this *baraisa*, and he resolves all of them by means of an original interpretation of the disagreement between Rabbi Tarfon and Rabbi Yehudah ben Nechemiah. Rabbi Tarfon holds that the prohibition of *chadash* in the *Beis HaMikdash* does not derive at all from the prohibition of *chadash* for the ordinary world. Rather, it is a special prohibition of its own. And this is why even certain things which are not forbidden to the ordinary world before the *Omer* — things such as wine and oil, which are not subject to the law of *chadash* — are nevertheless prohibited on the Altar before *shtei halechem*. Hence Rabbi Tarfon asked what difference there was in the *Mikdash* between the time before *shtei halechem* and the time before the *Omer*, such that meal offerings and *bikurim* should be valid post factum in the one period though invalid in the other. It is true that there is a law that only those foods which are permitted to the people of Israel may be offered on the Altar (as derived from *Ezekiel* 45:15, where it is implied that sacrifices must be מִמַּשְׁקֵה יִשְׂרָאֵל — *from the provisions of Israel*). Hence before the *Omer*, *chadash* for the altar is in effect subject to two prohibitions rather than one. All the same, the difference between two prohibitions and one cannot account for the post factum validity of the *chadash* after the *Omer*.

The reply of Rabbi Yehudah was that the prohibition of *chadash* for the Altar is identical with the prohibition of *chadash* before the *Omer*, except that after the *Omer* this prohibition becomes more lenient, in the sense that it is permitted for man though remaining forbidden for the Altar.

And since the force of the prohibition is thus lessened, it is reasonable that even on the Altar *chadash* should be valid post factum.[12]

"Rabbi Tarfon was silent"! What is the meaning of this silence? Did it indicate acquiescence or not? *Tosefos Yom-Tov*[13] demonstrates, both from the wording of the *sugya* and from rulings given by *Rambam*, that Rabbi Tarfon did not accept the reasoning of Rabbi Yehudah ben Nechemiah and did not change his position. Hence it must be asked, What of the problem posed by Rabbi Tarfon? The law, after all, is not rejected by the Talmud. The *halachah* remains that — although *chadash* should not be offered on the Altar before *shtei halechem* — if it *is* offered, it is invalid even post factum before the *Omer*, but valid after the *Omer*. And if the explanation of Rabbi Yehudah was not accepted by the Talmud, then what after all is the difference between these two periods? *Tosefos Yom-Tov* simply points out that even though the *mishnah* remains problematic in the Talmud, nevertheless the *Halachah* does not reject a given law simply because it results in difficult questions.

New light was thrown on this problem by the Rebbe of Ger in his work, *Sefas Emes*.[14] The Rebbe states that there is in fact no independent prohibition against offering up *chadash* on the Altar in the period before *shtei halechem*. For where is any such prohibition written in the Torah, comparable to the prohibition before the *Omer*, about which the Torah writes, *And you shall not eat bread nor parched grain nor raw grain* (וְלֶחֶם וְקָלִי וְכַרְמֶל לֹא תֹאכְלוּ עַד עֶצֶם הַיּוֹם הַזֶּה; *Leviticus* 23:14)? Thus we see that the Torah was concerned only to ensure that *shtei halechem* should be *a new meal offering* [not an old one] and it is for this reason alone that no other meal offering from the *chadash* should be offered before it. If in fact a meal offering from the *chadash* is offered up before the festival of Shavuos, this results in a defect and lack in *shtei halechem*, in that henceforward it cannot be called *a new meal offering*. And this is the whole extent of the prohibition — in the act of the premature offering itself there is no invalidity.

Beyond this, the Rebbe leans toward the conclusion ("it is possible") that if one meal offering has already been offered before *shtei halechem*, then afterwards it is altogether permitted (not only post factum,) to offer other meal offerings from the *chadash*; for in any case these additional *menachos* do not change the fact that there will be no *new meal offering* on Shavuos.[15]

Flour from the New Crop There is a disagreement among the *Tannaim* as to whether the requirement that *shtei halechem* be baked from flour of the new wheat crop is an essential prerequisite or only the preferred mitzvah. The *mishnah* states: "[The loaves] may only come from the *chadash*."[16] This implies that the requirement is indispensable. But the *Gemara* cites a *baraisa* to the contrary, stating "Our *mishnah* is not in agreement with the *Tanna* who teaches ... *shtei halechem* that come from the 'old' are valid, but one has omitted a mitzvah." And *Rambam* rules in accordance with the *baraisa*. "If they do not find *chadash*, they may bring ["old" grain] from the silo."[17]

An original interpretation of the *baraisa's* expression, "that come from the old" is offered by *Tzafnas Paane'ach*.[18] The meaning is that if a "new meal offering" has been offered before *shtei halechem*, thus rendering the offering of *shtei halechem* "old," nevertheless *shtei halechem* should be offered, as it is stated in *Toras Kohanim*:[19] "One might think that if [*shtei halechem*] have been preceded by something else (that is, another "new meal offering" offered before *shtei halechem*), the *shtei halechem* should not be offered. [But this is not so, for] the Torah says, *You shall sacrifice* (תַּקְרִיבוּ; *Leviticus* 2:12)."[20]°

Grain from Heaven Whence may the grain for the *shtei halechem* be brought? Based on the Torah's expression, — ... *from your places of settlement* (מִמּוֹשְׁבֹתֵיכֶם; *ibid.* 23:17) — the Sages deduce: "... but not from outside *Eretz Yisrael*."[21] The *Gemara* poses a question: "If wheat comes down from the clouds, may it be used for *shtei halechem*, or not? (According to *Rashi*, the *Gemara* refers to the possibility that "when the clouds drank from the ocean they swallowed up a ship loaded with wheat." *Tosafos* says it means that the wheat "came down in clouds miraculously.")°° The issue raised here by the *Gemara* is as follows. Did the Torah write, *from your places of settlement*, simply in order to exclude places outside *Eretz Yisrael*, in which case wheat from clouds would be permissible [since it is not from a foreign land]? Or did the Torah mean that the wheat positively must be from *Eretz Yisrael*, in which case wheat from the clouds would be invalid [since it is not from the Land]?[22]

°[According to this interpretation, the *shtei halechem* must in any case come from the new crop, but it may be "old" in the sense that it is not the very first crop to be offered up. — *Ed.*]

°°[See Vol. II, p. 57. — *Ed.*]

The author of *Tzafnas Paane'ach*[23] further explains this issue. Do the *shtei halechem* need to have the superior quality (מַעֲלָה) of *Eretz Yisrael*, or is the Torah's only concern that they should not have the defect (חִסָּרוֹן) of the other lands? The clouds in question have neither the *maalah* of *Eretz Yisrael* nor the *chisaron* of the other lands. Another great scholar explains the matter somewhat differently. Certainly, he says, *shtei halechem* must have the *kedushah*, holiness, of *Eretz Yisrael*. The question in the *Gemara* is whether or not the holiness of wheat which came down from heaven is similar to the holiness of wheat from *Eretz Yisrael*; since heaven, too, is a place of *kedushah*, and we know that "impure things do not come down from the heavens,"[24] it may be that this *kedushah*, too, is sufficient to make the wheat valid for *shtei halechem*.[25]

Great effort was involved in the preparation and baking of *shtei halechem*. *Rambam* explains: "How did they do this? they bring three *sa'in* of new wheat, and rub (שָׁפִין) and pound it (וּבוֹעֲטִין) in the same manner as the other meal offerings (that is, "three hundred rubbings and five hundred poundings: rub once and pound twice; rub twice and pound thrice"[26]); they grind the wheat to flour, and from this they sift two *esronim* of flour which has been sifted through twelve sifters."[27]

Making the Loaves

The correct procedure for kneading and baking *shtei halechem* is the subject of much interest and debate in the halachic literature. [The laws concerning *shtei halechem* are connected to those concerning *lechem hapanim*, the twelve loaves placed on the table before the Holy of Holies every *Shabbos* throughout the year.] A *mishnah* states: "The *shtei halechem* are kneaded one at a time and baked one at a time; the *lechem hapanim* are kneaded one at a time and baked two at a time."[28]

This law is derived from Torah verses. Concerning the *lechem hapanim*, it is written, *Each single loaf (chalah) shall be two esronim* (שְׁנֵי עֶשְׂרֹנִים יִהְיֶה הַחַלָּה הָאֶחָת; *Leviticus* 24:5). "This teaches us that they are to be kneaded singly. Whence do we know that the same is true of *shtei halechem*? From the term, *shall be*." [Since the verse could have stated simply, "Each loaf, two *esronim*," it is inferred that the extra term, *shall be* comes to teach an additional law; namely, the fact that this requirement applies also to *shtei halechem* — Ed.] "And whence do we know that they [the *lechem hapanim*] are baked two at a time? — because the verse says, *and you shall put them* (וְשַׂמְתָּ אוֹתָם; *ibid.* v. 6). [Here the verse changes from

singular to plural form — and the minimum plural is two.]
One might think, then, that the same is true of *shtei
halechem*? [Not so, for] the verse says אוֹתָם — *them*.[29] The
most economical way to write "and you shall put them" in
Hebrew would have been the inflected form, וְשַׂמְתָּם. Since the
Torah chooses to use the expanded form, וְשַׂמְתָּ אוֹתָם, an extra
law is inferred — in this case, the law that "two at a time"
applies only to *lechem hapanim*, but not to *shtei halechem*.[30]

Minchas Chinuch[31] writes that the prohibition against
baking *shtei halechem* two at a time applies only to baking the
two sacred loaves together; but to bake one loaf of the *shtei
halechem* together with another, non-holy loaf, is permissible.
The author of *Kreisi UFleisi* is of the same opinion.[32] The
author of *Tiferes Yaakov*[33] disagrees. He points out the
parallel with another talmudic derivation, this one involving
the red cow *(parah adumah)* whose ashes are used in the
purification of those who have been contaminated with the
tumah of corpses. The Torah writes, *And he shall slaughter it
(Numbers 19:3)*, and the Sages, again noting the expanded
form וְשָׁחַט אֹתָהּ rather than וּשְׁחָטָהּ, infer that the law is, "it,
but not another [with it]." And here, even if the second cow is
non-holy, it is forbidden to slaughter the two together.[34] It
must be, then, that likewise with the *shtei halechem* the
prohibition applies even when the second loaf is non-holy.
This proof of *Tiferes Yaakov* is not valid. For the prohibition
against baking *shtei halechem* two at a time is derived entirely
from the verse about *lechem hapanim*: namely, from the word
them (אוֹתָם), which comes to exclude *shtei halachem* from the
commandment of "two at a time." Hence, the negative
commandment about *shtei halechem* must correspond
precisely to the positive commandment about *lechem
hapanim*. And just as the positive commandment concerning
lechem hapanim is to bake together two of the twelve loaves
(and you shall put them; וְשַׂמְתָּ אוֹתָם*)*, and not one of the
twelve loaves together with a non-holy loaf, so also the
negative commandment concerning *shtei halechem* relates
only to the two holy loaves, and not to the joining of a holy
and a non-holy loaf.

*"Putting,"
or
Baking?* A surprising interpretation of the *mishnah's* phrase, "The
shtei halechem are ... baked one at a time" is found in *Keren
Orah*.[35] The author states that the concern of the Torah here
focuses only on the moment of putting the loaves into the
oven, and this is the meaning of the term "putting" (שִׂימָה) in
the verse, ... *and you shall put them*. Thus the meaning of the

commandment is that one should not put more than two of the lechem hapanim into the oven at one time, nor more than one at a time of the *shtei halechem;* but once the specified number of loaves (either one or two) has been put into the oven, the others may be put in as well [in the correct number each time], and all may be baked together. It is a matter of wonder that the author of *Keren Orah* did not bring support for this theory from the wording of *Toras Kohanim*,[36] where it is stated: "Whence do we know that [the loaves] should go into the oven (יֵרְדוּ לַתַּנוּר) two at a time? ... one might think that both loaves of the *shtei halechem* also go together into the oven ..." [The expression "go into the oven" in place of "are baked" would seem to strengthen the author's contention.] But the wording of the *mishnah,* "... and baked one at a time ... and baked two at a time ..." clearly indicates that the subject of this law is the baking and not only the moment of putting into the oven.

Even more surprising is the interpretation given by *Chazon Ish.*[37] "... baked one at a time," according to him, means *even* one at a time, but if it is desired, the two may be baked together! We have already seen that the other *Acharonim* do not understand the *mishnah* in this sense. And likewise this is not the plain meaning of the words of the *mishnah.* And this interpretation by *Chazon Ish* is refuted by a source of greater antiquity. In *Kiryas Sefer*, by *Mabit*,[38] it is stated explicitly that the *shtei halechem* should not be baked two at a time, but rather one at a time.

Concerning the rising of the dough there is a difference of opinion among the *Tannaim.* For we learn in a *mishnah,* "All the meal offerings brought in the Temple are *matzah,* except for the leavened bread of the thank-offering (תּוֹדָה) and the *shtei halechem,* which are *chametz.*" (In accordance with the verse, *They shall be baked as chametz* — חָמֵץ תֵּאָפֶינָה; *Leviticus* 23:17.) The *Tannaim* differ regarding the exact way in which the bread is caused to rise; that is, whether the leavening (sourdough) which causes the dough to rise is to be taken from that dough itself, or is to be brought from outside.] "Rabbi Meir says, one takes the leavening from the midst [of the dough which is being used to make the loaves]." *Rashi* explains: "From the midst of the *isaron* [of flour used] for the *todah* or the *shtei halechem* he would take out from that flour leavening, which he would knead a little after [that flour] had been measured; and he would re-insert this leavening into the flour, and it would rise of itself, and from this the rest of the dough would rise." The *mishnah* continues, "Rabbi Yehudah says, 'But this is not the preferred way (מִן הַמּוּבְחָר)." *Rashi* comments, "... for it does not rise well." Rather, in the opinion of Rabbi Yehudah, "One brings the leavening ("well-risen, from within the house") and puts it into the measure and fills up the measure."[39] *Rambam* rules in accordance with the opinion of Rabbi Yehudah.[40]

Place vs. Time In particular, the place and the time of the baking pose an important problem in understanding the Talmud. These two factors — place and time — here come into conflict. A *mishnah* states, "Both the *shtei halechem* and the *lechem hapanim* are kneaded and shaped outside and baked inside, and they do not supersede *Shabbos*."[41] On this the *Gemara* comments: "Rabbah said, 'A certain man has raised an ironclad objection; and who is the man? — Rav Sheshes ... [Since the *mishnah* says,] 'and they are baked inside' [the Temple, this implies that] the oven sanctifies [them]. [But since the *mishnah* says,] 'and they do not supersede *Shabbos*,' [this means that] they would be rendered invalid by remaining overnight (לִינָה)." For the law for all meal offerings, including the *lechem*, stipulates that once they have been sanctified by contact with one of the Temple implements, they then are rendered invalid if they are left overnight; and since they cannot be baked on *Shabbos*, because this mitzvah does not supersede *Shabbos*, they are baked the day before, *erev Shabbos*; hence they would have to remain overnight and would be rendered invalid. Rav Ashi in the *Gemara* offers a solution to the dilemma. "What is the meaning of 'inside'? — in the place of the *zerizin*, those who are swift and accurate in the performance of mitzvos." *Rashi* explains, "['Inside' does not mean] actually in the Temple precincts, but rather they are baked by *kohanim*, who are *zerizin*, so that the dough will not become *chametz*." The words of *Rashi* have been a cause of wonder to many "... so that the dough will not become *chametz*"? But the mitzvah of the *shtei halechem* is precisely that they should rise and become *chametz*! *Noda BiYehudah*[42] writes concerning the author of *Or Chadash*, who pointed out this problem in *Rashi*: "A certain man has raised an ironclad objection." *Noda BiYehudah* offers a somewhat far-fetched solution, "because of the gravity of the objection, in order that we should not leave the light of our eyes, *Rashi*, in the position of one who has made an error."[43]

Chasam Sofer[44] and Or Same'ach[45] both demonstrate, each in his own way, that the Talmud's "ironclad objection" was raised only regarding *lechem hapanim*, and not regarding *shtei halechem;* and regarding *lechem hapanim* [which is *matzah*] of course *Rashi* was perfectly correct in writing, "... so that the dough will not become *chametz.*"

The Talmud rejects the solution about *zerizin* offered by Rav Ashi, stating: "However, [the opinion] of Rav Ashi is incorrect" (בְּדוּתָא; or perhaps the proper word is בָּרוּתָא "rejected"). Thus there remains an unresolved contradiction between the place for baking the *lechem* ("within") and the time for doing so *(erev Shabbos).* *Tosafos* solves the contradiction by concluding that it is a "split" *mishnah,* compounded of two different opinions — "The one who taught this did not teach that" — that is, whoever holds that the loaves are baked "within" must hold that the baking supersedes *Shabbos;* while anyone who holds that the baking does not supersede *Shabbos* must hold that it is done outside [where the bread will not become sanctified by the oven].

Rambam, however, cites both laws as *Halachah:* the *lechem* is baked "within," and on *erev Shabbos.*[46] Here too, as is his wont, *Tosefos Yom-Tov* explains that "An objection raised by the *Gemara* is not grounds for rejecting a *mishnah* as *Halachah,* in spite of the fact that the objection is not refuted."[47] It goes without saying that a "simple" explanation of this sort is not sufficient for the seasoned warriors of the halachic battlefield. In this case, however, the problem is especially difficult. For there are two things to explain: the *Gemara,* and the opinion of *Rambam.* The better our explanation of *Rambam,* the more difficult it is to explain the *Gemara;* the question becomes, "If everything is so easy, then why is everything so hard?" — If there is no contradiction between the two laws cited by *Rambam,* then why does the *Gemara* characterize the objection as "tough as steel," and why did the *Gemara* itself not adopt the proposed solution? Thus it is necessary both to "rescue" *Rambam* and to explain the *Gemara.*

A great many intricate arguments have been written on this subject. Most of them are based on one of two foundations. (1) The problem depends on whether or not Temple implements have the effect of sanctifying objects they touch even when the time has not yet arrived for the mitzvah to be performed with those objects.[48] (2) The problem depends on whether or not Temple implements have the effect of sanctifying objects even though the person handling them does not wish the objects to become sanctified.[49] *Rambam* holds that, outside the time and against the wish of the person

"Rescuing" Rambam

handling them, Temple implements do not have the effect of sanctifying objects; hence, when the *shtei halechem* are baked on *erev Shabbos* they are not rendered invalid by staying overnight [since they are not yet sanctified]. The *Gemara sugya*, on the other hand, is written from the point of view of those who hold that the Temple implements do sanctify objects they touch, regardless of the time and regardless of the wishes of the person handling the objects. All the authorities who treat this problem prove conclusively, each in his own way, that *Rambam* in fact holds consistently to the opinion that the Temple implements sanctify objects only when it is time for the mitzvah to be performed, and only with the intent of the person performing the mitzvah.[50]

[The *Halachah* is, then, that *shtei halechem* do not supersede *Shabbos*.] And just as they do not supersede *Shabbos*, so also they do not supersede *Yom-Tov*. Thus the *mishnah* tells us, "*Shtei halechem* are eaten not less than the second [day, inclusive, from when they are baked] and not more than the third. How so? If they are baked on *erev Yom-Tov*, they are eaten on *Yom-Tov* [i.e.,] the second [day]. If *Yom-Tov* falls on the day after *Shabbos*, they are eaten on the third [day]."[51] The reason why the *lechem* may not be baked on *Shabbos* or *Yom-Tov* is based on the verse, ... *but that which is to be eaten by each person, that alone shall be done for you* (אַךְ אֲשֶׁר יֵאָכֵל לְכָל נֶפֶשׁ הוּא לְבַדּוֹ יֵעָשֶׂה לָכֶם; *Exodus* 12:16). From the term, *for you*, the Sages deduce an exclusion: "*For you*, but not for the Altar."[52] And even though the *shtei halechem* are eaten by *kohanim*, this does not put the baking of them in the permitted category of *maleches ochel nefesh*, the work necessary for a person's food. Similarly, the *shlamim* sacrifices resulting from vows and freewill offerings may not be sacrificed on *Yom-Tov*, even though their meat is eaten after the sacrifice,[53] for the fact that this meat is also for the needs of a person is overridden by the fact that it is intended mainly for the "needs" of the Altar.[54] The reason why the needs of the Altar are considered primary, overriding the needs of the person, is that the person is forbidden to derive any benefit from these sacrifices until the service on the Altar has been performed with them.[55]

Rabban Shimon ben Gamliel, in the name of Rabbi Shimon ben HaSgan, holds the contrary position, namely, that *shtei halechem* may be baked on *Yom-Tov*;[56] but the *Halachah* does not follow this opinion.[57]

A question asked by the author of *Kreisi UFleisi* has become well-known:[58] Why should the *shtei halechem* not be baked on *Yom-Tov*? Could they not be baked together with ordinary bread, on the grounds that the ordinary bread will thereby bake better, as the Talmud states, "[It is permitted for] a woman to fill the whole oven with bread, even though she needs only one loaf [since a full oven improves the flavor of the bread]"?[59] [Thus we see that bread which is not needed for *ochel nefesh* may be baked on *Yom-Tov* in this manner.] As a result of this question, the author concludes that רֵיחָא מִילְתָא — "odor is a thing" (of substance, i.e., has halachic effect), and that the odor of *shtei halechem*, entering the bread baked with them, would cause that bread, too, to be forbidden for ordinary use. This opinion serves as the subject of wide-ranging debate in several works.[60]

The Waving

The *shtei halechem* are not placed on the Altar; for it is to them that the verse refers, *The offerings of the first fruits, you shall offer them to HASHEM, but they shall not go up on the Altar* (קָרְבַּן רֵאשִׁית תַּקְרִיבוּ אֹתָם לַה' וְאֶל הַמִּזְבֵּחַ לֹא יַעֲלוּ *Leviticus* 2:12).[61] The service to be performed with the loaves is *tenufah*, waving, together with the two *kivsei atzeres*, the two sheep associated with *shtei halechem*. The loaves are waved before the Altar twice; once before the slaughtering of the two sheep and once after the slaughtering, when the loaves are waved together with the *chazeh* and *shok*, the breast and thigh, of the sheep.[62] The *shtei halechem* are eaten by the *kohanim*. The *Kohen Gadol*, High Priest, receives one loaf,[63] and the second loaf is divided among all twenty-four groups (*mishmeros*) of *kohanim*, for [even though during the rest of the year these groups serve in the *Beis Hamikdash* by turns,] the rule is that "on the festivals all the *mishmeros* are equal."[64] Both the loaves must be eaten either the same day they are waved or that night before midnight, like the meat of *kodshei kadashim*, the sacrifices of the highest order of sanctity.[65]

The distribution of the *shtei halechem* among the *kohanim* serves in the Talmud itself as the basis for discussion of a broad halachic topic. It is a well-known rule that תָּדִיר וְשֶׁאֵינוֹ תָּדִיר, תָּדִיר קוֹדֶם — the more frequent mitzvah takes precedence over the less frequent. But when the choice is between תָּדִיר the more frequent, and חוֹבַת הַיּוֹם, the "obligation of the day," which should come first? The example of such a problem given in the Talmud is the question which to recite first, *shehecheyanu* — "... Who has kept us alive ... and brought us to this time" [the more frequent blessing] or *leishev basukkah* — "... Who has sanctified us by His commandments and commanded us to dwell in the *sukkah*" [the obligation of the day]. The example discussed in the literature of the *poskim* is the question which should come first on Rosh HaShanah, a *bris milah*, circumcision, [the more frequent] or the sounding of the *shofar* [the obligation of the day].

A *sugya* in the Babylonian Talmud[66] debates this issue. One piece of evidence brought forward is a *mishnah* which states that when the *Atzeres* falls on *Shabbos*, so that it is necessary to distribute among the *kohanim* both *lechem hapanim*, which is *matzah*, and *shtei halechem*, which is *chametz*, "He says to him, 'Here is *matzah* for you; here is *chametz* for you.'" This would indicate that the more frequent mitzvah *(lechem hapanim)* takes precedence over the "obligation of the day" *(shtei halechem)*. However, the *Gemara* there cites a *baraisa* which contains a disagreement of *Tannaim* on this matter. In this *baraisa* Abba Shaul holds that the formula should be, "Here is *chametz* for you; here is *matzah* for you." The *poskim* deal extensively with this *sugya*. Their interest focuses on two aspects of the problem. One aspect is the conclusion in *Halachah*; for the issue has consequences in terms of practical halachic rulings. The other aspect is a "difficult *Rambam*" related to this *sugya*; for *Rambam* omits all mention of the law stated in the *mishnah*, "Here is *matzah* for you; here is *chametz* for you."[67]

An interesting proof based on *shtei halechem* is cited by one of the *Acharonim* in order to nullify a women's custom. The author was asked by a certain Rav concerning "A custom practiced by the women, that if they forget to remove the bread from the oven, and it stays there the whole night, they consider that the bread should not be eaten because of danger to health — Is this a valid consideration?" "In my humble opinion," the author replies, "There is no substance to this custom." His proof is drawn from the *lechem hapanim* and *shtei halechem*, which are baked on *erev Shabbos* or *erev Yom-Tov* and are not rendered invalid by remaining overnight. *Tosafos*[68] writes that the bread remains in the oven in order to preserve its heat until the morning; and if this involved a danger to health the *lechem* would be invalid, as we see in the *Talmud Yerushalmi, Sukkah*, where it is explained that an item which, for man, would involve a danger to health, is forbidden for use on the Altar.[69]

The Animal Sacrifices Together with *shtei halechem*, animal sacrifices were offered — those specified in *parashas Emor (Leviticus 23:18-20)*: one bull, two rams, and seven sheep. All these are *olos*, burnt-offerings. They are not a prerequisite for the *lechem,* nor is the *lechem* a prerequisite for them.[70] The exception to this lack of interdependence are the two *kivsei Atzeres* (sheep of *Atzeres)* which are peace-offerings on behalf of the public as a whole (שַׁלְמֵי צִיבּוּר), and the goat sacrificed as a sin-offering (חַטָּאת). Regarding the two sheep there is a disagreement of *Tannaim* as to whether they are the essential sacrifice, the *lechem* being an accompaniment, or whether the *lechem* is essential and the two sheep are the accompaniment.[71] This linkage between the two sheep and the *shtei halechem* is the subject of lengthy debate in several *sugyos* of the *Gemara.*

Concerning the sin-offering of a goat, a dispute has arisen over a matter of practical consequence, and in none other than our own era. How so? In our *Mussaf* prayers for *Yom-Tov* we mention, of course, the verses in *parashas Pinchas* commanding the "additional" *(mussafim)* sacrifices to be offered on the festivals (see *Numbers* ch. 28). At the end we add, "And their meal offering, and their libations ... and a goat to atone." This concluding passage is found in all prayerbooks, and is the same for all three pilgrim festivals, including *Shavuos.* At least, this was the case until *Baal HaTanya* wrote his *Siddur* and determined that for Shavuos the wording should be, "... and two goats to atone." The reason at first glance is obvious: besides the goat of the *mussaf* sacrifices there is also the goat which comes with *shtei halechem.* This innovation in the *siddur,* however, aroused opposition, for, some claim, if this change is to be made then why not also mention the other sacrifices which come with *shtei halechem?* The *Chabad* chassidim, of course, have adopted the wording of *Baal HaTanya* without reservation, and have even justified the Rav's version from the halachic standpoint.[72]

A Commemoration

In our day, we commemorate the *shtei halechem* — in the form of the custom to eat milk foods on Shavuos. A number of explanations have been suggested for this custom.[72*] *Rama* writes in *Shulchan Aruch:* "It seems to me that the reason is similar to that for the two cooked foods prepared for Pesach [e.g., a meat bone and roasted egg] in commemoration of the *Pesach* and *chagigah* sacrifices. Likewise, we eat a milk dish and [after the customary waiting period between milk and meat] a meat dish, so that it should be necessary to have two loaves of bread on the table ("since it is forbidden to eat meat and milk over the same loaf of bread" — *Magen Avraham*). For the table takes the place of the Altar, and in this way there is a commemoration of the *shtei halechem* which was offered up on *Yom HaBikurim."*[73] Adds *Magen Avraham:* "If so, then the two loaves should be of wheat, on the model of *shtei halechem."*

NOTES

[1] As *Tosafos* has pointed out, the word *lechem* is sometimes treated as the feminine gender: *And they shall give you two loaves of bread* (וְנָתְנוּ לְךָ שְׁתֵּי לֶחֶם; *I Samuel* 10:4). [The verse reads שְׁתֵּי which is feminine rather than שְׁנֵי in the masculine.] *Tosefos Yom-Tov* adds that on our own topic, too, *shtei halechem,* the Torah says, *From your settlements you shall bring two loaves of bread as a wave-offering* (and the word, *two,* modifying *loaves of bread,* is in the feminine form: מִמּוֹשְׁבֹתֵיכֶם תָּבִיאוּ לֶחֶם תְּנוּפָה שְׁתַּיִם; *Leviticus* 23:17). In this connection, there is an interesting debate over the verse, *His bread shall not be lacking* (וְלֹא יֶחְסַר לַחְמוֹ; *Isaiah* 51:14). *Tosafos* cites this verse as an example of *lechem* in the masculine gender. *Tosefos Yom-Tov* objects: "This is no proof at all, for the word יֶחְסַר (lacking) refers to the man; this is similar to the verse, *So that they shall lack bread and water* (לְמַעַן יַחְסְרוּ לֶחֶם וָמָיִם; *Ezekiel* 4:17) — and *Tosefos Yom-Tov* proceeds to cite numerous other examples for the use of *lechem* as a masculine noun. Other authorities have come to the defense of *Tosafos.* They argue: (a) If לֹא יֶחְסַר referred to the man, the verse would state לֹא יֶחְסַר לֶחֶם, as in *Ezekiel;* but since we find, not לֶחֶם but לַחְמוֹ, this shows that it is the *lechem* itself which "will not be lacking." For, as the Rebbe of Ger states in *Sefas Emes, Menachos* 94a, "The verse thereby states that the bread which is in the stomach is lacking." (b) In *Isaiah,* the vocalization of the letter י in this word יֶחְסַר is *segol,* while in *Ezekiel* the י in יַחְסְרוּ is vocalized with *pasach;* and this indicates that in *Isaiah* the "lacking" refers to the bread (*Ahavas Eisan* in *Mishnayos Vilna*).

[1*] *Numbers* 28:26.

[2] *Menachos* 84b.

[3] *Exodus* 34:22.

[4] *Ibid.* 23:16.

[5] See *Rashi, Sanhedrin* 11b, s.v. וְעַל פֵּירוֹת, and *Rashi's* commentary on the Torah, *Exodus* 23:16.

[6] *Ha'amek Davar, Numbers,* loc. cit.

[7] *Mishnah Menachos* 68b.

[8] *Ibid.*

[9] It has not yet been established with certainty who wrote the commentary known as *Chiddushei HaRashba* on *Menachos; Mishneh LaMelech* cites it as "The commentary on *Menachos* by an unidentified *Rishon."*

[10] *Numbers.*

[11] 68b.

[12] And see this same source for a lengthy explanation of the continuation of the *sugya,* based on this understanding. Incidentally, in the work, *Birkas HaAretz,* by Rav Y.L. Mashbaum (Warsaw, 5694-1934), sec. 2, the author on his own accord examines these two possible ways of understanding the prohibition of *chadash* on the Altar; and he, too, attempts to relate the two possibilities to the disagreement between Rabbi Tarfon and Rabbi Yehudah ben Nechemiah; but he rejects the thesis and concludes that according to both *Tannaim* the prohibition for the Altar is independent of that for the people. And the author did not see the statement of *Rashba.*

[13] *Mishnayos Menachos* 10:6.

[14] *Menachos,* loc. cit.

[15] And see *Tzafnas Paane'ach, Matnos Aniim,* p. 70, where the author discusses at great length whether *shtei halechem* actually make *chadash* permissible (מַתִּירִים) on the Altar, or whether it is simply a requirement that *shtei halechem* should be "first-fruits," preceding all other flour-offerings.

[16] *Menachos* 83b.

[17] *Temidin UMusafin* 8:2. And see *Isurei Mizbe'ach* 6:15, with *Kesef Mishneh* and *Lechem Mishneh.*

[18] *Matnos Aniim,* loc. cit.

[19] *Leviticus, parashasa* 12.

[20] But the wording of the *Gemara,* 'even from the silo," runs counter to the interpretation of *Tzafnas Paane'ach.*

[21] *Toras Kohanim, Emor,* ch. 12; *Menachos,* loc. cit.

[22] *Menachos* 69b.

[23] *Kila'im* 1:1.

[24] *Sanhedrin* 59b.

[25] Responsa *Chelkas Yoav, Yoreh De'ah,* sec. 33.

[26] *Menachos* 76a.

[27] *Rambam, Temidin UMusafin* 4:4, based on *Menachos* 76b.

[28] *Mishnah, Menachos* 94a.

[29] *Baraisa* in *Menachos, loc. cit.;* the source is in *Toras Kohanim Emor,* ch. 18, with a difference in wording.

[30] *Gemara, loc. cit.*

[31] Mitzvah 307.

[32] Sec. 108.

[33] In the large [*Yachin* and *Boaz*] edition of *Mishnayos* first published by Rom (Vilna), *Menachos,* end of ch. 10.

[34] *Chullin* 32a.

[35] *Menachos, loc. cit.*

[36] *Emor,* ch. 18.

[37] *Kadashim,* sec. 26.

[38] *Temedin UMusafin,* ch. 8.

[39] *Mishnah, Menachos* 52b.

[40] 8:9.

[41] *Mishnah,* 95b.

[42] First ed., *Orach Chaim,* sec. 15.

[43] And see the second edition, *Orach Chaim,* sec. 36.

[44] *Orach Chaim,* sec. 125.

[45] *Maaseh HaKorbanos* 7:3.

[46] *Temidin UMusafin* 8:7,8.

[47] Ch. 11, *mishnah* 2.

[48] See *Menachos* 100a.

[49] See *Sukkah* 50a.

[50] See *Birkas HaZevach, Menachos, loc. cit.; Sefas Emes,* ibid.; *Tiferes Yisrael* on *Mishnayos Menachos,* end of ch. 10; responsa *Noda BiShaarim,* end of part 2; *Chiddushei Chemdas Shlomo,* end of part 2; *Or Same'ach, Maaseh HaKorbanos* 7:3; *Levush Mordechai, Kadashim,* sec. 26; *Chazon Ish, Kadashim,* sec. 24, *et. al.*

[51] *Mishnah, Menachos* 100b.

[52] *Pesachim* 47a.

[53] *Beitzah* 22.

[54] *Tosafos, Beitzah* 27b.

[55] See *Tosafos, Pesachim* 5a.

[56] *Mishnah, Menachos, loc. cit.,* and *Pesachim* 47a.

[57] *Rambam, loc. cit., halachos* 8, 9.

[58] Sec. 108.

[59] *Beitzah* 17a.

[60] See *Taam HaMelech, Yom-Tov,* ch. 3; *Minchas Chinuch,* 307; responsa *Maharsham* of Brezzan, part 2, sec. 14, and in the *hashmatos; et. al.*

[61] *Rambam, Maaseh HaKorbanos* 12:3. And see *Toras Kohanim, Leviticus, parashah* 12, and *Rashi, Menachos,* 58a.

[62] Concerning the way in which the "waving" was performed, see *Menachos* 68a.

[63] *Yoma* 17b.

[64] *Sukkah* 55b.

[65] *Rambam,* 8:11.

[66] *Sukkah* 56a.

[67] See *Noda BiYehudah,* first ed., *Orach Chaim,* sec. 39; *Chiddushei Shas* (by the son of the author) at the end of *Sefer Haflaah;* responsa *Sho'el UMeshiv,* second ed., part 3, sec. 183; responsa *Divrei Malkiel,* part 1, sec. 17; *Marcheshes,* part 1, sec. 11; *Even HaAzel, Klei HaMikdash* 4:5, and in the *hashmatos; et. al.* And see vol. 1 p. 270 of the present work.

[68] *Chagigah* 26b.

[69] Responsa of *Maharsham* of Brezzan, part 2, sec. 8. And see vol. I, p. 309 of the present work.

[70] *Mishnah, Menachos* 45b.

[71] *Ibid.*

[72] See *Shaar HaKolel,* appended to the *Siddur, Toras Or,* ch. 43; *Beis Avraham,* by Rav Abale *Macherson* of Kherson, at the end of the work; responsa *Birkas Avraham,* by Rav A. Brodna, part 1.

[72*] See above, p. 243.

[73] 494.3.

עֲשֶׂרֶת הַדִּבְּרוֹת ‎⧽

The Ten Commandments

The high point in our celebration of the festival that commemorates the giving of the Torah by HaShem to His People is without doubt the solemn public reading of the Aseres HaDibros, the Ten Commandments engraved on the Tablets that Moshe Rabbeinu transmitted to Am Yisrael.

In deliberate detail the Torah describes both the preparations for this wondrous event and the awesome assembly at Mount Sinai. Both have received their due explanations by the Rabbis of all generations. For example, by way of preparation for the chapter before us — on the halachos peculiar to the Aseres HaDibros — we could ponder a comment by a chassidic gaon of the recent past. We find that HaShem told Moshe Rabbeinu: "Go to the People, and sanctify them today and tomorrow" (Exodus 19:10). Yet when Moshe spoke to the People he commanded them, "Prepare yourselves for three days" (ibid. v. 15). Rabbi Yosei explains, "Moshe added an extra day at his own discretion." On this Talmudic statement Rabbi Shlomo of Radomsk comments: Moshe Rabbeinu, even at that early stage of our acceptance of the Torah, wanted to teach that without the interpretation of the Sages, there can be no observance of the Torah. He therefore showed his authority by adding a day on his own accord, even though this entailed a delay of a whole day before the Torah was given — thus teaching all future generations what vast authority is vested in the Chachmei HaTorah, the Rabbis and Teachers of all the generations.

Each one of the Ten Commandments, whether positive or negative, individually occupies an important place in the literature of the *Halachah*. Three of them are distinguished by the fact that each is the subject of a whole tractate in the Mishnah and in the Jerusalem and Babylonian Talmuds: לֹא יִהְיֶה לְךָ — "*You shall not have other gods before Me*"° — is the subject of Tractate *Avodah Zarah*: לֹא תִשָּׂא — "*You shall not take the name of HASHEM your God in vain*" — is dealt with in Tractate *Shevuos*: and זָכוֹר — "*Remember the day of Shabbos to sanctify it*" — is the subject of Tractate *Shabbos*. Nevertheless, we do not find that the *Halachah* grants these ten mitzvos a special status purely because of the fact that they belong to *Aseres HaDibros*, the Ten Commandments. When the Talmud tells us that every Jew is "always under oath from Mt. Sinai" — that is, that the commandments have the character of an ongoing oath obligating all Israel — this refers equally to all six hundred thirteen [תרי"ג] commandments.[1] And this applies not only to the essential 613 mitzvos themselves, but also to the precise details of their proper performance; for, as the *midrash* tells us, "Just as [the laws of] *Shmitah* (the sabbatical year of rest for the land) were given with all their precise details at Mt. Sinai, so also all [the mitzvos] were given with all their precise details at Sinai."[2] It is true that concerning this cardinal principle the Talmud records a difference of opinion among the *Tannaim*. "Rabbi Yishmael says that the general principles were given on Sinai and the details in the Tent of Meeting (אֹהֶל מוֹעֵד); Rabbi Akiva says the general principles were given on Mt. Sinai and the details [too] were given at Sinai, and were repeated in the Tent of Meeting."[3] But according to both these opinions, all 613 mitzvos were given on Mt. Sinai, not just *Aseres HaDibros*. Some authorities find ways in which it is possible to derive and enumerate all 613 commandments within the Ten. A poem (אַזְהָרוֹת) for the Shavuos prayer service contains the lines: "I included within *Aseres HaDibros*, in My profound thought / Six hundred thirteen mitzvos, laws to be taught / Utterances of *HaShem*, in purity wrought."[4]

And yet it is interesting to note that each one of the Ten Commandments has some feature which gives it a unique and special status in the *Halachah*. While the pure fact that it is one of the Ten does not, as stated, give the mitzvah any

°[All verses cited in this chapter, unless otherwise indicated, will be found in the Ten Commandments, *Exodus* 20:2-14 and *Deuteronomy* 5:6-18. — Ed.]

inherent distinction as compared to the rest of the mitzvos, nevertheless each one of the Ten is found to have a special distinguishing quality in one respect or another. Not all the Ten are distinguished in the same manner or to the same extent. But in each one of them we see something which sets it apart from other commandments, even though this uniqueness cannot be attributed to its status as one of *Aseres HaDibros*. [In the following paragraphs we shall discuss the unique features of each of the Ten Commandments.]

אָנֹכִי — *I am HASHEM your God* — is considered by *Rambam* to be not simply a statement of fact, but a distinct positive commandment: "To know that there is a Prime Being Who causes the existence of all that exists ... and the knowledge of this fact is a positive commandment, as it is said, *I am HASHEM your God*.[5] *Rambam* states that this commandment is the basis for all others. It is "The foundation of the foundations and the supporting pillar of all wisdom,"[6] and in explaining this statement the author of *Chinuch* states: "This faith is the foundation of the religion, and whoever does not believe in this has denied the essence and has no portion or rights with Israel ... and if one is asked about this, one must answer, no matter who the questioner, that this is what one believes in one's heart; one may not profess any alternative belief, even under threat of death ..."[7]

Ramban, in his critical commentary on *Rambam's Sefer HaMitzvos*,[8] cites the opinion of the author of *Behag* that the verse, *I am HASHEM your God*, should not be enumerated as one of the 613 commandments. But this is not because the author of *Behag* in any way detracts from the importance of this verse; quite the contrary, his argument is that "The essence and root from which the mitzvos are derived should not be counted as one of them." *Ramban* himself takes the side of *Rambam* on this issue, but he does explain the reasoning of *Behag*. "The orders and the decrees are what should be counted, the instructions to do and not to do, but not the faith in the very existence of the Blessed One; for without such faith it is impossible even to conceive of a commandment."[9]

The verses beginning, לֹא יִהְיֶה לְךָ — *"You shall not have other gods before Me"* — in the opinion of *Rambam*, include four negative commandments. (1) לֹא יִהְיֶה לְךָ: that one should not believe in any god other than *HaShem* alone; (2) לֹא תַעֲשֶׂה לְךָ פֶסֶל — *'You shall not make for yourself a sculpted image'* —

that one should not make idols to worship; (3) לֹא תִשְׁתַּחֲוֶה לָהֶם — 'You shall not bow down to them' — that one should not bow down to idols; (4) וְלֹא תָעָבְדֵם — 'And you shall not serve them' — that one should not serve idols through the means by which the devotees of those particular idols serve them. (In the opinion of *Behag*, these verses contain only two commandments: *You shall not have other gods ...* and *You shall not make a sculpted image ...*)

Each of the negative commandments just enumerated includes a number of details, both fundamental and subsidiary. But the root of all these details is the prohibition against idol worship *(avodah zarah)*. The exceptional gravity of this prohibition in comparison with the other prohibitions of the Torah is openly stated by the Sages in a number of places; for one who professes belief in *avodah zarah* is as if he had denied the Torah in its entirety.[10] This principle is brought to light in connection with the Talmudic derivation of a different rule: "If the deliberate violation of a given sin incurs *kares*, divine excision of the soul, then its accidental violation incurs the obligation to bring a sin-offering *(chatas)*." This rule is derived from the verse, "*And if you err and violate all these commandments ...*" (וְכִי תִשְׁגּוּ וְלֹא תַעֲשׂוּ אֵת כָּל הַמִּצְוֹת הָאֵלֶּה; *Numbers* 15:22). The problem confronted by the Talmud is exactly which commandments are meant. The solution reasons, "Which mitzvah is it whose gravity is as all the other mitzvos? — it is *avodah zarah*."[11] (*Rashi:* "for whoever professes belief in it is as if he had denied the Torah in its entirety.")° Hence, a *mumar*, one who rejects a specific part of the Torah, having rejected the prohibition against idol worship is considered as if he had rejected the whole Torah, with the resulting legal consequences: an animal slaughtered by him [even though the slaughtering conforms to all the other requirements of the Torah] is not kosher;[12] it is permissible to loan money to him at interest;[13] one is not required to return lost property to him;[14] and so on.

There is yet another way in which the prohibition against idol worship is more severe than nearly all other commandments. It is one of the three transgressions in the avoidance of which a person is obligated to give up his life — "One should be killed rather than transgress."[15] In addition, this is one of the seven commandments which are obligatory for gentiles (בְּנֵי נֹחַ).[16]

°[The Talmud then goes on to state that *avodah zarah* is the example from which we learn that all sins punishable by *kares* require a *chatas* for their inadvertent violation. — *Ed.*]

לֹא תִשָּׂא — *You shall not take the name of HASHEM your God* לֹא תִשָּׂא
in vain — the prohibition against taking a false oath is likewise
a negative commandment of unique severity. Its exceptional
gravity is spelled out in *Tosefta*[17] and in the Babylonian
Talmud,[18] where we read of the warnings given to a litigant
who is about to undertake to swear an oath in the name of
HaShem. The particular oath in question is *shevuas
hadayanim*, the oath taken by someone who has been sued for
a financial obligation and denies part but not all of the debt.
"[Before administering] *shevuas hadayanim*, [the judges] say
to [the one about to take the oath]: "Be it known to you that
the whole world shuddered at the moment when the Holy
One, Blessed Be He, said on Mt. Sinai, *You shall not take the
name of HaShem your God in vain*. Furthermore, concerning
all other transgressions in the Torah it is said, *And He shall
cleanse (וְנַקֵּה)*, while concerning this it is said, *He shall not
cleanse (לֹא יְנַקֶּה* — see *Exodus* 34:7). For all other
transgressions in the Torah, punishment is exacted from the
transgressor; concerning this, from both the transgressor and
his family ... from both the transgressor and the entire world
... For all other transgressions in the Torah, if one has merit
one's judgment is suspended for two or three generations; but
concerning this transgression, punishment is exacted
immediately ... And we have learned [from Scripture] that
even things which cannot be ruined by fire and water can be
ruined by a false oath."

This idea that a false oath is a transgression of exceptional
gravity is cited as *Halachah* by the *poskim*.[19] Thus *Rambam*
states: "This sin is one of the most serious ... Even though it
incurs neither *kares* nor death at the hands of the earthly
court, it involves the desecration of the sacred Name, *a sin
greater than all other transgressions*."[19*] It is because of this
extreme severity that "the *Geonim* decreed that in our time
oaths should not be administered — neither those using the
Name itself, nor those using other appellations [such as "the
Merciful One," and the like] — so that the world should not
suffer ruin through those who might sin in this way."[20] Even
in the time of the Mishnah the Sages refrained from
administering oaths in the case of widows claiming the
financial benefits accruing to them from the estates of their
deceased husbands as stipulated in their *kesubos*; here, too,
the reason was that the punishment for a false oath is so
great.[21]

The extra severity of the punishment for a false oath also
has other halachic consequences. For example, even if the

court has reason to suspect that a litigant may perhaps have illegally taken someone else's property, this still does not justify suspecting that perhaps the person will swear a false oath. In the language of the Talmud, הֶחָשׁוּד עַל הַמָּמוֹן אֵינוֹ חָשׁוּד עַל הַשְּׁבוּעָה — "One who is financially suspect is not suspect with regard to oaths."[22] The explanation given is that people look upon an oath with more apprehension than upon thievery (gezelah).[23]

זָכוֹר זָכוֹר — Remember the day of Shabbos to sanctify it — consists of two mitzvos: a positive commandment ("To sanctify verbally the Shabbos day"), and a negative one ("You shall not do any work"). Halachically, the extraordinary importance of Shabbos consists of the fact that one who rejects this commandment to the extent of violating Shabbos in public is treated as if he had rejected the entire Torah.[24] Rashi explains that this is because "One who worships idols denies the Holy One, Blessed Be He; and one who desecrates Shabbos denies His deeds and testifies falsely that the Holy One, Blessed Be He, did not rest in the work of creating the world."

Rambam[25] states: "Each of these two, Shabbos and idol worship, is as weighty as all the other mitzvos combined; and Shabbos is the sign (אות) between the Holy One, Blessed Be He, and us forever. Therefore, [while] one who violates the other mitzvos is included in the wicked of Israel, one who desecrates Shabbos in public is like one who worships idols — and both of these [i.e., both a Jew who worships idols and a Jew who violates Shabbos in public] are [treated halachically] like idol worshipers [i.e., non-Jews] in every respect." There is extensive discussion among the poskim as to whether wine becomes forbidden if touched by one who rejects the mitzvah of Shabbos as is the case with wine touched by one who worships idols.[26] Another topic discussed is the definition of "in public" (בְּפַרְהֶסְיָא) with regard to desecration of Shabbos.[27] Likewise, various similar details are dealt with in the literature concerning this law that one who chooses to publicly violate Shabbos has the legal status of one who rejects the entire Torah.

כַּבֵּד The special status of the commandment, כַּבֵּד — Honor your father and your mother — is clarified by a baraisa in Tractate Kiddushin:[28] "Our Sages teach, 'It is said, Honor your father and your mother; and it is said, Honor HASHEM from your fortune (כַּבֵּד אֶת ה' מֵהוֹנֶךָ; Proverbs 3:9). Scripture thus equates [the commandment of] honoring father and mother with [that of] honoring the Omnipresent.' " And this is not a philosophical statement, an *aggadah;* rather, this has the full legal force of *Halachah.* Otherwise, it would not have been necessary for the Torah to inform us explicitly that if one's father commands one to desecrate *Shabbos,* one should not obey him. For, concerning the verse, *Each man shall fear his mother and father and you shall keep My Shabbasos; I am HASHEM* (אִישׁ אִמּוֹ וְאָבִיו תִּירָאוּ וְאֶת שַׁבְּתֹתַי תִּשְׁמֹרוּ אֲנִי ה'; *Leviticus* 19:3), the Sages explain that *Shabbos* was mentioned immediately after the mitzvah of fearing mother and father in order to tell us that a command of one's parents does not supersede a command of *HaShem,* since "All of you" — both parents and children — "are obligated to honor Me." Now, why should it be necessary for the Torah to spell out this point? After all, honoring father and mother is a positive commandment, while *Shabbos* is both a positive and a negative commandment; and we already have a rule in *Halachah* that a positive commandment does not supersede one which is both positive and negative. But since the Torah explicitly equates honoring father and mother with honoring *HaShem,* we might have reasoned that this is an exception to that rule, and that one would be obligated to obey one's father even in violation of a command of *HaShem.*[29] Thus, the explicit Torah passage is needed.

Even to so great an extent, then, does the special status of this commandment reach. Even when in conflict with *Shabbos,* which is as weighty as the whole Torah together, and is both a negative and positive commandment, and is punishable by stoning — if it were not for a specific verse in the Torah, the mitzvah of honoring father and mother would have taken precedence.[30]

As *Rambam* puts it, "Honoring father and mother is a major positive commandment, as is fearing father and mother. Scripture gives these mitzvos the same weight as honoring and fearing Him ... In the same way that [He] commanded us concerning honoring His name and fearing it, so too He commanded concerning honoring and fearing [one's parents]."[31]

לֹא תִרְצָח The gravity of the negative commandment, לֹא תִרְצָח — *You shall not murder* — is self-evident. It is one of the three mitzvos for which "One should be killed rather than transgress."[32] The Talmud explains why it is that, if ordered on pain of death to murder, one must give up one's own life rather than obey. "What evidence do you have that your blood is redder? — it may that the other man's blood is redder." *Rashi* interprets this to mean: "When the Torah states that one is permitted to violate any of the mitzvos in order to save a life, was this not because of the preciousness of the life of each person of Israel? But in this case, where either way, a person of Israel will be killed, there is no gain in one's violating the commandment of *You shall not murder:* 'A transgression is committed, and a life is lost.' "[33*] [Whereas, if one gives up one's own life, no transgression is committed and still only one life is lost.]

The name given this prohibition in the Torah is שְׁפִיכוּת דָּמִים, the spilling of blood. *Rambam* tells us, "There is nothing about which the Torah is so insistent as about *shfichus damim*, as it is said, *And you shall not pollute the Land ... for the blood pollutes the Land* (וְלֹא תַחֲנִיפוּ אֶת הָאָרֶץ ... כִּי הַדָּם הוּא יַחֲנִיף אֶת הָאָרֶץ; *Numbers* 35:33).[34] And in a *mishnah* we find: "Why is it that man was originally created as a single individual? — to teach you that he who destroys one life of Israel is considered by Scripture as if he had destroyed an entire world; and he who preserves one life of Israel is considered by Scripture as if he had preserved an entire world."[35] *Rambam* relates this talmudic dictum to the idea of "murder through inaction" (רְצִיחָה בְּשֵׁב וְאַל תַּעֲשֶׂה): "He who sees someone pursuing another man to kill him, and can save him but does not do so, has transgressed [the commandment] *You shall not stand by the blood of your fellow man* (לֹא תַעֲמֹד עַל דַּם רֵעֶךָ; *Leviticus* 19:16). And even though one does not receive a lashing for this prohibition, since it is one which does not involve an action, nevertheless it is a grave one, for 'He who destroys one life ...' "[36]

This concept of "murder through inaction" is found in the Mishnah in another context. The Torah tells us that if a man is found slain in the countryside, the Sages must measure to determine which is the city nearest to the corpse; and the elders of that city must perform the ritual of the *eglah arufah*, the beheading of a calf. During this ritual the elders are required to proclaim, *Our hands did not spill this blood and our eyes did not see* (יָדֵינוּ לֹא שָׁפְכוּ אֶת הַדָּם הַזֶּה וְעֵינֵינוּ לֹא רָאוּ; *Deuteronomy* 21:7). On this the Mishnah comments, "Could it enter our minds that the elders of the Torah court are murderers? Rather [the required proclamation means], 'It did not happen that he came into our hands and we sent him away without provisions; nor that we saw him and left him without someone to accompany him."[37] Thus it is clear that if they did see him and sent him away without food and company, it is as if they had spilled this blood with their own hands.

You shall not murder is one of the seven commandments incumbent upon the gentiles.[38]

לֹא תִנְאָף — *You shall not commit adultery* — refers to illicit relations with a married woman.[39] As part of the general prohibition of גִּלּוּי עֲרָיוֹת, forbidden relations, it is one of the three commandments for which "one must be killed rather than transgress." The Talmud tells us that the consequences of this transgression are "more ruinous for the world than [the sins of] the generation of the Flood," for it is in reference to these offenses that it is written, *Therefore shall the land mourn, and everyone that dwells in it shall languish, along with the wild beasts, and the birds of the sky; indeed, the fish of the sea shall also be taken away*[40] (עַל כֵּן תֶּאֱבַל הָאָרֶץ וְאֻמְלַל כָּל יוֹשֵׁב בָּהּ בְּחַיַּת הַשָּׂדֶה וּבְעוֹף הַשָּׁמָיִם וְגַם דְּגֵי הַיָּם יֵאָסֵפוּ; *Hosea* 4:3). [Here even the fish of the sea are subject to destruction, while in the Flood they remained alive. Furthermore, this is a transgression for which no atonement can be achieved even through repentance, for] concerning one who has relations with a married woman, thus making her forbidden to her husband, Scripture says, *That which is twisted cannot be made straight*[41] (מְעֻוָּת לֹא יוּכַל לִתְקֹן; *Ecclesiastes* 1:15). [Repentance for a sin against one's fellow man can only effect atonement if one first repairs the damage caused to the other person; here, where the woman can never live with her husband again, there is no way to restore the damage, and hence no possible atonement. — Ed.]

You shall not commit adultery is one of the seven commandments incumbent upon the gentiles.[42]

לֹא תִגְנֹב — *You shall not steal* — refers to kidnapping, i.e., stealing a person. The Sages base this fact on one of the thirteen principles of Scriptural exegesis; namely, "A matter which is modified by its context" (דָּבָר הַלָּמֵד מֵעִנְיָנוֹ). In this case, just as *You shall not murder* and *You shall not commit adultery* refer to sins punishable by death at the hands of the earthly court, so also it is inferred that *You shall not steal* refers to a sin punishable in this manner.[43]

This prohibition is unique in that the perpetrator incurs capital punishment (חֶנֶק) for a deed which, in one sense, never occurred. For the kidnapper does not incur the death penalty unless he makes use of the victim, even for a service worth less than a penny (פְּרוּטָה), and then sells him to someone else.

But such a sale has no validity whatsoever. Is it legally possible to sell a Jewish person? Rather, the Torah makes the kidnapper liable to the death penalty for the *action* of the [attempted] sale, even though from the legal standpoint such a sale has no validity.[44]

Rambam[45] writes that kidnapping is a [capital] transgression for a gentile, too (but for the *ben noach* this sin comes under the category of robbery[46]).

לֹא תַעֲנֶה   The prohibition of לֹא תַעֲנֶה — *You shall not give false testimony against your fellow man* — is more severe than other negative commandments, in that normally any negative commandment not involving a concrete action is not punishable by lashing. However, one who gives *false testimony* incurs a lashing, in spite of the fact that no concrete action is involved.[47] [For purposes of this rule, speech is not considered a concrete action — *Ed.*]

This prohibition is more severe in another way. Usually, violation of a prohibition is not punishable by a lashing unless the perpetrator had received prior warning; but for the violation of *false testimony*, prior warning is not required.[48]

[The two exceptional severities just discussed refer to punishment by the earthly court. But this transgression also brings down punishment from heaven.] Concerning the punishment at the hands of heaven it is written, *Clouds, and wind — but no rain: a man who glorifies himself giving out lies* (נְשִׂיאִים וְרוּחַ וְגֶשֶׁם אָיִן אִישׁ מִתְהַלֵּל בְּמַתַּת שָׁקֶר; *Proverbs* 25:14).[49] *Rashi* interprets: "Because of one who glorifies himself by giving out lies — i.e., those who give false testimony — the rains are stopped." Furthermore, on the verse, *A man who gives false testimony against his fellow is like a maul and sword and a sharpened arrow* (מֵפִיץ וְחֶרֶב וְחֵץ שָׁנוּן אִישׁ עֹנֶה בְרֵעֵהוּ עֵד שָׁקֶר; *ibid.* v. 18), *Rashi* explains: "Through the sin of false testimony, the plague (דֶּבֶר) comes." And on a different level, "False witnesses," the Talmud tells us, "are despised by those who hire them." The proof of this is drawn from the Scriptural account of the way in which Jezebel acquired the vineyard of Navot by having him convicted on false charges. In the letter in which she commands the hiring of lying witnesses, even she speaks of them in contemptuous terms. "As it is said, *And set two base fellows before him, and they shall testify against him, saying, you cursed God and the king* (וְהוֹשִׁיבוּ שְׁנַיִם אֲנָשִׁים בְּנֵי בְלִיַּעַל נֶגְדּוֹ וִיעִדֻהוּ לֵאמֹר בֵּרַכְתָּ אֱלֹהִים וָמֶלֶךְ; *I Kings* 21:10).[50] All these evil consequences of false testimony, though extra-legal, are mentioned as *Halachah;* for the *beis din*, before witnesses testify, is required to warn them about these forms of divine retribution. Thus *Rambam* writes: "[The judges are required to] warn [the witnesses] in front of everyone, and to inform them of the power of false testimony and the humiliation visited, both in this world and the next, upon one who gives such testimony."[51]

There is even one opinion — that of Rabbi Meir as interpreted by Rav Chisda — which attributes yet another great severity to the sin of false testimony. "If witnesses are threatened with death and told to sign [a document which they know to be] false, they must be killed rather than sign falsely."[52]

The commandment, לֹא תַחְמֹד — *You shall not covet* — is the subject of a disagreement among the *Rishonim.* According to *Rambam*, this prohibition is violated whether one takes the coveted object from its owner by force without payment, or whether one pays money for it; and no matter whether one pays for the object against the owner's will or whether he agrees to the sale. "Whoever covets the manservant or the maidservant, the house or the furnishings of one's fellow, or anything which it is possible to purchase from him, and exerts pressure on him (הִכְבִּיד עָלָיו) through friends, and implores him until he gets it from him — even if he pays a great amount of money for it — has violated a negative commandment, as it is said, *You shall not covet.*"[53] But according to *Ravad*, the prohibition is violated only when one takes the object from one's fellow against his will.[54] Both, however, agree that no transgression is committed until one takes the coveted item. "As in the passage where it is said, *You shall not covet the silver or gold that is on them, nor take it for yourself ...* (לֹא תַחְמֹד כֶּסֶף וְזָהָב עֲלֵיהֶם וְלָקַחְתָּ לָךְ; *Deuteronomy* 7:25) — [Here, too, in the ten commandments, the Torah means] a coveting which involves action."

Another disagreement among the *Rishonim* concerns the difference in vocabulary between the ten commandments as stated in *Exodus* and in *Deuteronomy*. In *Exodus*, only the word תַחְמֹד — covet — is used, while in *Deuteronomy* both this word and תִתְאַוֶּה — desire — appear. According to *Rambam, You shall not covet* and *You shall not desire* are two distinct prohibitions. "As soon as one thinks in his heart about how he can acquire that item, and is led astray in his heart on the matter, one has violated a negative commandment, as it is said, *You shall not desire* — and the

לֹא תַחְמֹד

word desire means in the heart alone."[55] But according to *Semag*, both these expressions refer to one and the same prohibition.

It is difficult to find, from a purely halachic standpoint, a feature of the commandment *You shall not covet* which makes it unique or preferred in comparison with other laws. From the moral standpoint, however, the extraordinary gravity of this prohibition is made clear by the *poskim*. As *Rambam* writes, "Desiring leads to coveting, and coveting leads to stealing; for if the owner does not wish to sell the object in spite of the fact that a high price is offered and in spite of imploring him through friends, then one will come to the point of stealing, as it is said, *And they covet fields, and take them by force* (וְחָמְדוּ שָׂדוֹת וְגָזָלוּ; *Micah* 2:2). And if the owner blocks one's way in order to save his property, or prevents one from stealing, one comes to the spilling of blood. Go and learn the lesson of the story of Achav and Navot"[56] (see *I Kings* ch. 21).

Bnei Noach, too, are obligated by this commandment, for it is a branch of the prohibition against stealing.[57]

The *Zohar* states, "It is taught, The last word of the ten commandments of the Torah is *You shall not covet the wife of your fellow man*, because this includes all [the commandments]; and one who covets the wife of another is as if he had transgressed the entire Torah.'"[58] And the Midrash tells us: "He who violates *You shall not covet* violates *I am HASHEM your God*."[59]

***

In the Prayers The reading of the Ten Commandments involves a number of issues discussed in the halachic literature. In Tractate *Tamid* we learn that the *kohanim* in the *Beis HaMikdash* used to read the Ten Commandments every morning before the recitation of *Shema Yisrael*.[60] An attempt was made to establish this morning reading of the Ten Commandments in the rest of the Land as well; but this was not allowed, "because of the grumblings of the apostates *(minin)*."[61] As *Rashi* explains — "so that they would not tell the uneducated that the rest of the Torah was not true, and cite as evidence the idea that they only read [each morning] that which the Holy One, Blessed Be He, said, and which they heard from His mouth at Sinai." A number of the *Amoraim* wished to re-institute the reading of *Aseres HaDibros* before *Shema Yisrael* but they were not permitted to do so for that same reason — the "grumblings of the *minin.*"[62] Similarly, we find in the *Talmud Yerushalmi:* "Strictly according to the law, *Aseres HaDibros* should be read every day; why, then, are they not read? — because of the claims of the *minin,* so that they should not say that these alone were given to Moshe on Sinai."[63]

Again in the time of *Rashba* there was an attempt to restore the custom of reading *Aseres HaDibros* in the communal prayer. In a responsum, *Rashba* writes: "You further ask what the law is concerning the saying of the Ten Commandments at the morning service in the synagogue, since there are people who wish to establish this custom for the public; is it proper to do so or not? The answer is that it is forbidden to do so ... and even though we learn in Tractate *Tamid* [that the *kohanim* did this in the *Beis HaMikdash*] ... the custom was annulled because of the grumblings of the *minin.*"[64]

Nevertheless, *Tur,*[65] and after him, Rav Yosef Caro in *Shulchan Aruch,*[66] write: "It is good to say (every day) *parashas HaAkeidah* (the binding of Yitzchak) and *parashas HaMan* (about the manna) and *Aseres HaDibros.*" The reasoning behind this ruling is that it was only for communal prayer that the Ten Commandments were removed from the service; while for the individual, on the contrary, "It is good to say them."[67] And *Maharshal*[68] writes in a responsum: "My custom is to say aloud [in public prayer] *Aseres HaDibros* before [the blessing for the morning Psalms,] *Baruch She-amar* ... the only thing that is forbidden is to establish [the reading of the Ten Commandments], like the reading of the *Shema,* in the blessings that begin with *Yotzer* [i.e., the blessings following *Barchu* that begin "... Who produces light and creates darkness ..."]; but as for saying [*Aseres HaDibros*] every morning for the honor of the Torah and for the honor of *HaShem* the Creator, since the Ten Commandments were engraved on the tablets in *the writing of God* (מִכְתַּב אֱלֹהִים; *Exodus* 32:16) — it is a great mitzvah to say them."

This distinction of *Maharshal* between saying *Aseres HaDibros* in the blessing called *Yotzer* and saying them elsewhere has not been accepted by the *Acharonim.* The law is that it is forbidden to recite the Ten Commandments as part of the communal prayer, whether included or not included in that blessing; only as an individual may one recite them.

A different distinction is proposed by the author of *Tevuos Shor.*[69] He distinguishes between the Talmudic era, when there were *minin,* and our own time when there are no *minin.*

The same author provides support for the practice of reading *Aseres HaDibros*, at least in the prayer of the individual. Concerning the verse, *This day HASHEM your God commands you to do these statutes and these judgments* (הַיּוֹם הַזֶּה ה' אֱלֹהֶיךָ מְצַוְּךָ; *Deuteronomy* 26:16), *Rashi* comments, "Every single day they should be in your eyes like new." And the author discovers that in *Tanchuma*, *parashas R'eh*, it is implied that "The basic meaning of the verse beginning *This day* ... is that it refers to the Ten Commandments."[70]

As the Torah Reading [If the reading of *Aseres HaDibros* as part of the daily morning prayer service is somewhat problematic, this is not the case with reading them as the Torah portion on special occasions.] At three times in the year the Ten Commandments are read as the communal Torah reading: on *Shabbos Yisro*, on *Shabbos Va-Eschanan* [for it is in these two weekly portions that the Ten Commandments appear in the Torah], and on Shavuos [the festival of the giving of the Torah]. And a special importance attaches to these readings. In the time of the Mishnah, as is known, it was not the practice that each person called to the Torah recited the blessing over reading it; rather, only the first and the last person called (הַפּוֹתֵחַ וְהַחוֹתֵם — "the one who begins and the one who concludes") recited a blessing. For the Ten Commandments, however, the one called to the Torah recited a blessing both at the beginning and at the end of the reading.[71] Further, it is the custom that the *chacham*, the most learned man of the community, be called up to the Torah for *Aseres HaDibros*.[72]

There is a difference in the cantillation of the Torah between the reading on the two *Shabbasos* and that on Shavuos. On the *Shabbasos* the melody for the reading is the טַעַם הַתַּחְתּוֹן, the "lower cantillation;" while on Shavuos טַעַם הָעֶלְיוֹן, the "upper cantillation" is used.[73] Other authorities rule that the difference in cantillation is not between *Shabbos* and Shavuos, but rather between public and individual reading; an individual by himself reads with *taam hatachton*, while *taam ha'elyon* is used for a public reading.[74] This latter ruling is the one followed in our day.

The essential difference between the two types of cantillation is that in the *taam hatachton* each verse is read as a separate unit, while in the *taam ha'elyon* the unit is not the verse but the commandment. Thus, in the *taam ha'elyon* the first two verses, *I am HASHEM your God ...* and *You shall not have other gods before Me ...* are read together as if they were one verse. (We are told that the people heard these two verses "from the mouth of the Almighty.") On the other hand, in this "upper" cantillation the commandments *You shall not murder, You shall not commit adultery*, etc., although all contained within one verse, are read as if they were separate verses. This in turn affects the vocalization of the words. Thus, in the *taam hatachton* the word תרצח is vocalized as usual with a *pasach* under the letter *tzaddi* (תִּרְצָח), while in the *taam ha'elyon* the *pasach* changes to a *kamatz*, as is appropriate for the syllable which ends a verse (תִּרְצָח). So, too, the letter ת in the words תרצח, תנאף, and תגנב is "soft," i.e., lacking a *dagesh* in the *taam hatachton*; but the ת is "hard," i.e., contains a *dagesh* in the *taam ha'elyon*, because it is separated from the preceding word (לא) by a pause in the cantillation (טִפְּחָא). And there are yet other changes resulting from the difference between the two cantillations.[75]

It is customary for the entire congregation to stand during the reading of *Aseres HaDibros*, whether in *parashas Yisro, parashas VaEschanan*, or at Shavuos. This practice, which has now spread almost throughout all Israel, is indeed an ancient custom, but at one time there were those who raised objections to it. Among the responsa of *Rambam*,[76] we find the following (from the Oxford manuscript): "A query concerning the people's standing during the reading of the Ten Commandments: One of the sages has commanded this, and there is another who forbids it. The latter cites as proof the fact that the Sages eliminated the reading of *Aseres HaDibros* [in the blessings preceding] *Shema Yisrael* because of the *minim*, who claimed that [these ten mitzvos] were in some way superior to the rest of the Torah. And this sage rules that if any man stands during the reading of the Ten Commandments from the Torah scroll, it is proper to reprimand him, for this act is a practice of the *minim* ... The other sage replies by pointing out that Israel, when they heard the utterance from the mouth of the Holy One, Blessed Be He, were standing, as it is said, *And they stood at the bottom of the mountain* (וַיִּתְיַצְּבוּ בְּתַחְתִּית הָהָר; *Exodus* 19:17). The reply to this is that [they stood] only in deference to *HaShem*, Blessed Be He ... and the fact that in Babylonia and the surrounding areas they used to stand [during this reading] is because the one called to the Torah was a sage or the head of the *yeshivah*, and it was for him that they stood; others who happened to see this custom were misled by what they saw." The arguments of the two sages were sent to *Rambam* with the request that he express his opinion. His reply agrees with the sage who forbids standing. "... In every place where the custom is to stand, it is proper to forbid them to do so, as [the practice] is detrimental to faith; for they may come to think that certain parts of the Torah are superior to other parts; and this is a very severe [error]; and it is fitting to close all doors that lead to this false belief. And in truth the claim of the other sage, that the inhabitants of Babylonia follow this custom, does not amount to anything; for if we see sick people we do not make a healthy man sick because of them, so that he should be like them; rather, we endeavor to heal the sick person so that he should be like the healthy one ... And it is not proper at all to give one part of the Torah superiority over another part."[77]

This same question concerning the practice of standing for the reading of *Aseres HaDibros* appears again in the responsa *Devar Shmuel*, by Rav S. Abuhav[78] (this author had not seen the responsum of *Rambam* just cited). Rav Abuhav supports the custom. He also provides an explanation for it. In reading *Aseres HaDibros*, he writes, it is as if we are welcoming the *Shechinah*, the divine Presence. And we see in the example of "the welcoming of our Father in heaven once each month" [i.e., the sanctification of the Creator of the moon — *kiddush levanah*] that "it must be recited standing."

Likewise, in responsa *Tov Ayin*, by *Chida*, the author answers a query which points out that there are those who object to the fact "that in a number of communities the people are accustomed to stand when the Ten Commandments are read." This author, too, upholds the custom. This is not a practice that would lead to "the grumblings of the *minim*," he argues, for "the entire Torah is read from the Torah scroll *Shabbos* after *Shabbos*, and likewise on this day ... and this is proof that [the entire Torah] is the truth; but they stand because these [mitzvos] are the foundation of the Torah, and were written on the tablets; and the Holy One, Blessed Be He, spoke them to all Israel, and the whole Nation trembled when the Holy One, Blessed Be He, uttered these things. Hence they wish to perform a kind of commemoration by standing when the Ten Commandments are read. *(Chida* does not cite the ruling of *Devar Shmuel.)* The author goes yet further. "Since the people are thus accustomed to stand all together for the Ten Commandments, it would seem that all are obligated to stand, and no one should remain seated ... otherwise, one might appear in the eyes of the multitude as if, God forbid, showing disrespect. Furthermore, the Sages have said that one should not sit among those who are standing."

[1] *Nedarim* 8a.

[2] *Sifra, BeHar.*

[3] *Chagigah* 6a.

[4] *Azharos* of Rav Saadiah Gaon, in his *Siddur* (Jerusalem, 5701 — 1941), p. 191. He, too, arranges the entire 613 mitzvos in the order in which they fit into the Ten Commandments. The authors of other *azharos*, composed especially for public recitation on Shavuos, did the same. And see *Targum Yonason, Exodus* 24:12: "From their tablets of stone there is a hint of the other Torah statements, and the six hundred thirteen commandments." See also *Midrash Rabbah, Naso,* where it is stated that the Ten Commandments contain 613 letters, corresponding to the 613 commandments.

[5] *Yesodei HaTorah* 1:1-6.

[6] *Ibid.*

[7] *Chinuch,* mitzvah 25.

[8] Mitzvah 1.

[9] And see the commentaries on *Sefer HaMitzvos,* who write at length on this disagreement between *Behag* and *Rambam.* The matter is also discussed at length by Medieval scholars in their philosophical works. And see *Tashbetz,* part 1, sec. 139, and the same author's work, *Zohar HaRakia,* sec. 11.

[10] *Sifri, BaMidbar* 15:22, and *Sifri, Devarim,* 11:28. And see *Nedarim* 25a, *et. al.*

[11] *Horios* 8a.

[12] *Chullin* 5a.

[13] *Yoreh De'ah* 159.

[14] *Choshen Mishpat* 266.

[15] *Sanhedrin* 74a, *et. al.*

[16] *Sanhedrin* 56b.

[17] *Sotah,* ch. 7.

[18] *Shevuos* 39a.

[19] *Rambam, Shevuos* 11:16; *Tur* and *Shulchan Aruch, Choshen Mishpat* 87:20.

[19*] *Rambam, loc. cit.,* 12:2.

[20] *Ravad,* in the *Hasagos, Shevuos* 11:13. And see *Shulchan Aruch, loc. cit.,* para. 19.

[21] *Gitin* 35a.

[22] *Bava Metzia* 5b.

[23] See *ibid.,* Rashi and Tosafos.

[24] *Chullin* 5a.

[25] *Shabbos* 30:15.

[26] See *Beis Yosef, Yoreh De'ah* 119, in the name of *Rashba;* responsa *Binyan Tzion HeChadashos,* sec. 23; responsa *She'ilas David,* by Rav David of Karlin, *Orach Chaim,* sec. 5 in *Hagah;* responsa *Elef HaMagen,* by Rav M.N. Rubenstein, part 2, sec. 41, *et. al.*

[27] See *Daas Torah, Hilchos Shechitah,* sec. 2, *os* 30; *et. al.*

[28] 30b, cited from *Sifra, Kedoshim.*

[29] *Bava Metzia* 32a.

[30] And see the *sugya* in *Yevamos* 6a, and *Tosafos* there.

[31] *Mamrim* 6:1.

[32] *Sanhedrin* 74a, *et. al.*

[33] *Ibid.*

[33*] *Rashi, Pesachim* 25b, and *Sanhedrin, loc. cit.*

[34] *Rambam, Rotze'ach* 1:4.

[35] *Sanhedrin* 37a.

[36] *Rotze'ach,* end of ch. 1.

[37] *Sotah* 45b.

[38] *Sanhedrin* 56b.

[39] *Sefer HaMitzvos,* negative commandment 347; *Chinuch,* mitzvah 35; *Rashi* on the Torah.

[40] *Kiddushin* 13a.

[41] *Chagigah* 9b.

[42] *Sanhedrin, loc. cit.*

[43] *Sanhedrin* 86a.

[44] *Bava Kama* 68b. And see *Minchas Chinuch,* mitzvah 36.

[45] *Melachim* 9:9.

[46] *Kesef Mishneh.* And see *Minchas Chinuch, loc. cit.*

[47] *Makos* 2b and 4b.

[48] *Ibid.* 4b.

[49] *Sanhedrin* 29a.

[50] *Ibid.*

[51] *Edus* 17:2.

[52] *Kesuvos* 19a. Rava there disagrees [with Rav Chisdah's interpretation of Rabbi Meir's words].

[53] *Rambam, Gezelah* 1:9.

[54] In the *Hasagos, ibid.*

[55] *Ibid.,* halachah 10.

[56] *Ibid.,* halachah 11; *Tur* and *Shulchan Aruch, Choshen Mishpat* 359.

[57] *Minchas Chinuch*, mitzvah 25.

[58] *Zohar, Leviticus* 78b.

[59] *Yalkus Reuveni, Yisro*, in the name of *HaPliah*.

[60] *Tamid* 5:1.

[61] *Berachos* 12a.

[62] *Ibid.*

[63] *Berachos* 1:5.

[64] Response of *Rashba*, part 1, sec. 184, and part 3, sec. 289.

[65] *Orach Chaim*, sec. 1.

[66] *Shulchan Aruch*, there.

[67] See *Beis Yosef* and *Rama* there.

[68] Sec. 64.

[69] *Chiddushei Bechor Shor* on *Berachos*.

[70] And see *Tov Ayin*, by *Chida*, sec. 10; *Artzos HaChaim*, by *Malbim*, sec. 1.

[71] *Yerushalmi, Megillah* 3:7.

[72] *Magen Avraham*, 428.

[73] *Ibid.*, 494.

[74] *Ibid.*

[75] And see a lengthy discussion of this matter in *Machatzis HaShekel*, and in *Biur Halachah* of *Mishnah Berurah* 494.

[76] Ed. Rav A. Ch. Friedman, sec. 46.

[77] And see there, in the *hosafos*, p. 359, for an expanded version of this responsum, from the Badahav manuscript.

[78] Sec. 276.

[79] Sec. 11.

רות

Ruth

Concerning the Scroll of Ruth the Midrash says: "This Megillah contains no laws regarding purity and impurity, nor laws of what is prohibited and what is permitted. Why then was it written? —In order to teach you the reward of those who do deeds of kindness." Many commentators point out that this may be why Ruth is read on the day HaShem gave us the Torah — to indicate that without deeds to match one's study of the Torah one has achieved nothing. As the Talmud says in this very connection (Tractate Yevamos 109b), "He that says that he has only Torah has not even Torah."

Shavuos is the festival that made us different from other nations. We do not seek after converts. In fact, in the story of Ruth, Naomi three times attempted to dissuade her daughters-in-law from leaving their alien faiths. Only after her third unsuccessful attempt did she accept the one who persisted in her determination to cleave to her. We find that in no fewer than forty-five places in the Torah are we commanded to "love the stranger in our midst." It is therefore fitting that on this day we should read of one who sincerely and with lovingkindness did likewise — and was privileged to have King David as her descendant.

❧ ❧ ❧

It is a good Jewish custom when completing the study of any part of the Torah to look for a connection with the beginning of that part. The introduction to the first chapter of this work quoted the author of Meshech Chochmah, who describes Yom-Tov as the day that binds the Jewish People to each other. When was that bond forged? — At that sublime moment when all of Am Yisrael stood before Mount Sinai to receive the Torah from HaShem. At that moment an unbreakable link was forged between the Torah of HaShem and the People of HaShem. And as long as Am Yisrael clings to the Torah which being the words of HaShem is eternal, Am Yisrael will share in that eternity.

The manner in which it is to be read, and whether or not to recite a blessing over it — these are the two main halachic issues involving the Book of *Ruth* as a scroll *(megillah)* in connection with the festival of Shavuos.

The *First* *Mention* The earliest mention of the custom of reading *Megillas Ruth* on Shavuos is found in Tractate *Sofrim*,°[1] which states: "The first half of *Ruth* [is read] on the night after the first *Yom-Tov* day of Shavuos; and [the scroll] is completed on the night following the second *Yom-Tov* day. Some say that for all [the scrolls read on Festivals; i.e. *Song of Songs, Ruth* and *Ecclesiastes*] the reading should begin on the *motzaei Shabbos* before [the appropriate festival], and this is the custom which the people have adopted; for no *halachah* becomes law until it has been established as a custom." Here, then, we have two different customs as to how the Scroll of *Ruth* is to be read on Shavuos — and both of them [since they split the reading into two halves on two separate nights] differ from the custom which has been adopted in our time.

The above source, Tractate *Sofrim*, is not in fact considered part of the Talmud. Thus *Rosh* notes: "The Talmud *Yerushalmi* is of higher authority than Tractate *Sofrim*, for Tractate *Sofrim* was written in more recent generations and is never cited by the Talmud."[2] The [great Eighteenth-Century Sephardic authority,] *Chida*[3] demonstrates that Tractate *Sofrim* was written in the days of the *Geonim*. Even so, in this passage we have a record of the custom of reading *Ruth* on Shavuos that dates back to an ancient period — that of the *Geonim*.

Another early record of this custom is found in *Yalkut Shimoni*:[4] "What is the relationship of *Ruth* to the *Atzeres* [i.e., Shavuos] such that it is read on the *Atzeres*, the time of the giving of the Torah? It is to teach you that the Torah is only acquired by means of suffering and poverty." As for the *poskim*, this custom is cited by *Abudraham, Maharil, Shulchan Aruch*,[5] *Levush*, and by all their successors. It is interesting to note that the source in Tractate *Sofrim* is not cited by the *poskim*. Perhaps the reason for this omission is the different procedure recorded there (that is, reading the scroll on the two nights after the *Yom-Tov* days or on the

° [*Sofrim* is one of the מַסֶּכְתּוֹת קְטַנּוֹת or Minor Tractates which, in many editions of the Talmud, are printed following *Seder Nezikin.* — Ed.]

motzaei Shabbos preceding the festival). The source in *Yalkut Shimoni* is cited by *Magen Avraham*.[6]

The brevity of the comment of *Rama* in *Shulchan Aruch* — "It is the custom to recite *Ruth* on Shavuos" — leaves an important question unanswered. Is it the custom to recite this *megillah* individually, each congregant on his own, or does the *sheliach tzibur* read from the *bimah*, as is the custom with *Megillas Esther*? However, in a different place *Rama* clarifies what he has here left unexplained. In his responsa[7] he is asked whether a blessing ("... Who sanctified us by His commandments and commanded us about the reading of the *megillah*") is obligatory in the case of *Megillas Ruth*. In the course of his reply he explains that it is customary that the only scrolls to be read publicly are *Eichah* and *Esther; the Song of Songs, Ruth,* and *Koheles* are to be read by each congregant individually. Therefore, no blessing is to be recited over the latter three, since the blessing over the reading of the scroll was only instituted as a matter of respect for the congregation (כְּבוֹד הַצִּבּוּר). [That is, the blessing lends dignity to the public setting, but is not necessary when the individual reads by himself. — *Ed.*] Thus we learn that the custom of *Rama* was to read *Megillas Ruth* individually.

It would appear that the same conclusion may be drawn from the phrasing of *Maharil:*[8] "*Megillas Ruth* is read on the second day [of the *Yom-Tov*] and *each one* first recites the blessing, '... concerning the reading of the *megillah*.' "

Yet another fact which may be learned from that same responsum of *Rama* is that the custom in his day was to read from printed *Chumashim*, and not from an actual scroll written on parchment in accordance with all the relevant laws; for this, too — the fact that the *megillah* is not read from a *kosher* scroll — is cited as a reason why no blessing is to be recited.

In our own time, four different customs are prevalent. (1) The *Four* members of the *edos hamizrach*, i.e., Asian and North African *Customs* Jewry, do not read the Scroll of *Ruth* at all in the synagogue at the time of the prayer service (and this is also the custom followed by *Chabad* chassidim, the chassidim of Kotsk-Gur, and others).° (2) The chassidim of Vohlin and Galicia, on the whole, follow the custom that before the Torah reading the whole congregation read the Scroll individually from

° [However, they read *Ruth* as part of *Tikun Leil Shavuos* during the first night of *Yom-Tov.* — *Ed.*]

Chumashim; outside Eretz Yisrael this is done on the second Yom-Tov day of Shavuos, and in Eretz Yisrael, on the festival day itself. (3) Communities which follow the customs known as nusach Ashkenaz (the Misnagdim or the Prushim) read the Scroll publicly, just as they read the Torah on Shabbos or Megillas Esther on Purim. If the congregation possesses a kosher Scroll written on parchment, the sheliach tzibur reads from it; otherwise, he reads from a Chumash. In either case, the sheliach tzibur does not recite a blessing over the reading. (4) "The Prushim in Eretz Yisrael instituted the custom of reading the megillah from a kosher parchment scroll and reciting the blessing, "... Who ... commanded us concerning the reading of the megillah' " [as well as Shehecheyanu, " ... Who kept us alive and preserved us and brought us to this time"]. In this practice the Prushim are following the ruling of Gra, the Gaon of Vilna.

The Blessing There is a whole body of halachic literature concerning this blessing which the Prushim, by their custom, recite over the megillah. Again, the source of the blessing is found in Tractate Sofrim; but this time, in a different place. The custom of reading Megillas Ruth on the Atzeres is mentioned at the end of the fourteenth chapter, while the blessing is mentioned at the beginning of that same chapter, and without connection to Shavuos. Thus we read there: "For Ruth and the Song of Songs, for Lamentations and for Megillas Esther one must recite, '... concerning the reading of the megillah,' even if they are written among the Writings [that is, even if they are not read from a separate scroll, but from one which contains other Books of Scripture]. One who reads from the Writings (Kesuvim) one should say, 'Blessed are You, HASHEM our God, King of the Universe, Who sanctified us with His commandments and commanded us to read the Kesuvim.' " And even though the poskim do not cite Tractate Sofrim as the source for the custom of reading the Scroll on the Atzeres, they do cite it as the source of the obligation to recite a blessing over the reading.[9] Rama, however, gives a lengthy proof in his responsa that in this matter we may not draw conclusions from Tractate Sofrim to apply to the customs of our own time, since there are a number of differences between the practice then and now. (Then the Scroll was read publicly; now, individually. Then it was read from a parchment scroll; now, from a Chumash; and so on.) And Rama rules accordingly in Shulchan Aruch:[10] no blessing should be recited.

On the other hand, the author of *Levush* argues at length against the opinion of *Rama* and rules that the blessing must be recited. *Taz* agrees with *Rama*, concluding: "Whoever recites a blessing over these *megillos* has uttered a wasted blessing (בְּרָכָה לְבַטָּלָה)." But *Magen Avraham* records that "*Levush* and *Bach* and *Minhagim* and *Mateh Moshe* have written that a blessing should be recited for all [the Scrolls] except *Koheles*, and this is the essential *halachah* according to the custom of our forefathers."

Beur HaGra at this same place in *Shulchan Aruch* writes that a blessing should be recited even for *Koheles*, and even if the *megillah* is not written as a scroll on parchment.

In connection with the claim of *Magen Avraham* that the recitation of the blessing is "the custom of our forefathers," note should be made of a passage in *Sefer Minhagim*, written by a pupil of *Maharam* of Rothenburg,[11] in the section on the customs of *Shabbos Chol Hamo'ed Pesach*, the *Shabbos* which falls during the Intermediate Days of the Pesach festival. Here we find: "After [the recitation of] *Hallel*, *Megillas Shir* [the *Song of Songs*] is read, preceded by the blessing, '... concerning the reading of the *megillah*,' recited with deliberation; and the same should be done for all the *megillos*, even for *Lamentations*." Thus, we see that the recitation of a blessing over the Scrolls was indeed an ancient custom in Ashkenaz, the region of Germany.

What, in fact, is the nature of the connection between *Ruth* and Shavuos? We have already seen the explanation offered by *Yalkut Shimoni*. *Abudraham* records two other explanations. One is that "[In the Scroll of *Ruth*] it is written, *At the beginning of the barley harvest* (בִּתְחִלַּת קְצִיר שְׂעֹרִים; *Ruth* 1:22), and [Shavuos] comes at the time of the harvest." The second explanation is that "Our forefathers received the Torah and entered into the Covenant only through circumcision and immersion and the offering of sacrifices" — that is, through the process of conversion — "And Ruth, too, was converted." A different reason is offered by *Levush*.[12] In *parashas Emor*, in the Torah passage which sets forth all the festivals, we read of the *shtei halechem*, the sacrifice of two loaves of bread offered on Shavuos, and immediately afterwards, *And when you reap the harvest of your land ... You shall leave* [parts of the harvest] *for the poor and for the stranger* (וּבְקֻצְרְכֶם אֶת קְצִיר אַרְצְכֶם ... לֶעָנִי וְלַגֵּר תַּעֲזֹב אֹתָם; *Leviticus* 23:22). Now, the commandment of this verse was fulfilled by Boaz, who said, *And let fall also some of the* *handfuls for her* (שֶׁל תָּשֹׁלּוּ לָהּ מִן הַצְּבָתִים; *Ruth* 2:16);° and *Ruth* was both poor and a stranger; hence we read *Ruth* on this very day.[13] The author of *Tevuos Shor* explains the connection in terms of the fact that King David was descended from Ruth. We know that David died on Shavuos,[13*] and we also know that the Holy One, Blessed Be He, sits, as it were, and counts out the years of the righteous day by day; hence it must be that David was also born on Shavuos [for each year of a *tzaddik's* life, including the last, is a complete year]. Therefore we read *Megillas Ruth*, in order to give the ancestry of David on the day of his birth.[14]

Ruth
the
Moabitess

If *Ruth*, the scroll, is a topic dealt with by the *Halachah*, so too is Ruth, the Moabitess. How can it be that she was accepted as a convert and allowed to marry into the Jewish people, when there is an explicit verse in the Torah which states, *Neither an Ammonite nor a Moabite shall come into the Nation of HASHEM ... forever* (לֹא יָבֹא עַמּוֹנִי וּמוֹאָבִי בִּקְהַל ה' ... עַד עוֹלָם; *Deuteronomy* 23:4)? And not only was Ruth found acceptable for conversion and marriage, but she even merited that from her would emerge the royal House of David. But the fact is that the *Halachah* interprets that verse as prohibiting "an Ammonite but not an Ammonitess; a Moabite but not a Moabitess." And the Talmudic discussion of this *halachah* is connected with the story of Ruth. The Scroll relates that when Boaz wished to negotiate with his relative as to which one of them would perform the levirate marriage with the widowed Ruth ... *And he took ten men of the elders of the city and he said, sit down here* (וַיִּקַּח עֲשָׂרָה אֲנָשִׁים מִזִּקְנֵי הָעִיר וַיֹּאמֶר שְׁבוּ פֹה; *Ruth* 4:2). Why did he want ten scholars to be present at this event? — for the sake of halachic discussion and to make it publicly known that the law refers to "a Moabite and not a Moabitess."[14*]

On the *mishnah* in *Yevamos*[15] which states: "An Ammonite and a Moabite are forbidden [to marry into the Nation] and the prohibition [applies to all the descendants of the convert] forever; but the females are permitted immediately [upon conversion]," we find a *Gemara* passage[15*] in which *Aggadah* and *Halachah* are closely interwoven. "Doeg the Edomite said (to King Saul), 'Before

---

° [The Torah's agricultural laws include various benefits for the poor. Among these, our verse in *Leviticus* mentions two. (1) The law of *pe'ah*, lit., "a corner," requires that when grain is harvested, part of the field must be left standing for the poor to take. (2) The law of *leket*, "gatherings," stipulates that if one or two stalks (but not more), should fall from the hand of the reaper, these stalks must be left for the poor to gather. It was this second law, *leket*, to which Boaz referred in saying, *Let fall ... — Ed.*].

you make inquiries about him [i.e., about David, after he had just slain Goliath] as to whether or not he is fit to marry the King's daughter° inquire first whether or not he is fit to marry into the congregation. Why? Because he comes from Ruth the Moabitess.' Avner said to him, 'We learn in a *mishnah:* An Ammonite and not an Ammonitess, a Moabite and not a Moabitess.' " Doeg now launches a series of challenges against this halachic conclusion. "If this is so, then [the verse, *Deuteronomy* 23:3, which forbids marriage with an illicit offspring, a *mamzer*, refers only to] a *mamzer*, and not a *mamzeress?*" Avner's answer is that in the case of *mamzer*, a specific exegesis informs us that the prohibition applies to both male and female, for "It is written, *mamzer*, implying *mum zar* [lit., "outlandish defect" — meaning that the prohibition includes all who are marred by the defect of being an illicit offspring, whether male or female]."

Doeg continues to challenge, "An Egyptian, and not an Egyptianess? [See *Deuteronomy* 23:8-9]." Avner at this point changes track, and instead of attempting to show how the verses cited by Doeg are exceptions to the rule, he attempts to show how the verse about the Ammonite and the Moabite is itself the exception. "This [verse] is different, for the reason behind it is explicitly stated: *Because of the fact that they did not meet you with bread and with water* (עַל דְּבַר אֲשֶׁר לֹא קִדְּמוּ אֶתְכֶם בַּלֶּחֶם וּבַמַּיִם; *Deuteronomy* 23:5). [Thus it is clear that the verse applies only to the men and not the women, since] it is normal for a man to meet [travelers] but it is not normal for a woman to meet them." To this argument, too, Doeg's reply is forthcoming. " 'The men should have met the men and the women should have met the women.' Avner had no reply. Immediately, *And the King said, you inquire whose son the youth is* (וַיֹּאמֶר הַמֶּלֶךְ שְׁאַל אַתָּה בֶּן מִי זֶה הָעָלֶם; *I Samuel* 17:56) — Why is it that previously he was referred to as a נַעַר and now he is referred to as an עֶלֶם? (Both words mean, "a youth".) [The change in vocabulary hints that] this is what the King said to Avner: 'The *halachah* has escaped you [נִתְעַלְּמָה, from the same root as עֶלֶם]. Go and inquire in the house of study.' He inquired. They told him: 'An Ammonite and not an Ammonitess, a Moabite and not a Moabitess.' Doeg challenged [those in the house of study] with the same series of objections. They had no reply. Doeg wished to make a proclamation about [David, to announce that he was forbidden to marry]."

° [This was the promise publicly made by Saul to whoever would kill the blaspheming Goliath. — *Ed.*]

What happened next, though not stated explicitly in the Book of *Samuel*, is hinted at, the Talmud explains, by an apparent discrepancy between two other Scriptural verses. "[In one place it is written,] *And Amasa the son of a man whose name was Yisra the Israelite* (וַעֲמָשָׂא בֶן אִישׁ וּשְׁמוֹ יִתְרָא הַיִּשְׂרְאֵלִי; *II Samuel* 17:25), [and in another place] it is written, *And the father of Amasa was Yeser the Ishmaelite* (וַאֲבִי עֲמָשָׂא יֶתֶר הַיִּשְׁמְעֵאלִי; *I Chronicles* 2:17). Rava said, 'This teaches us that [immediately Amasa] strapped on his sword like an Ishmaelite and declared, 'Whoever denies this *halachah* shall be stabbed by the sword. Thus I have received it from the Torah court of [the Prophet] Samuel the Ramasite: An Ammonite and not an Ammonitess, a Moabite and not a Moabitess.' "

Though Doeg may have found this a compelling argument, the Talmud itself is not yet satisfied. It continues, "This objection [of Doeg] is nonetheless difficult to answer." But two satisfactory answers are in fact produced, both in the form of verses which imply that the women would not have been expected to meet even the women, since the correct behavior for a woman is to remain within the home. "This is the explanation: *All the glory of the King's daughter is within* (כָּל כְּבוּדָה בַת מֶלֶךְ פְּנִימָה; *Psalms* 45:14). In the west [i.e., *Eretz Yisrael*] they said, — and some say it was Rabbi Yitzchak who said, —— 'The Torah states, *And they said to him, Where is Sarah your wife?* ... (וַיֹּאמְרוּ אֵלָיו אַיֵּה שָׂרָה אִשְׁתֶּךָ; *Genesis* 18:9). *Rashi* explains that the reference is to Avraham's reply, "*Behold in the tent* (הִנֵּה בָאֹהֶל; *ibid.*); for it is not usual for a woman to go out of her home.' "

Without intending it, *Maharsha* in discussing this Talmud passage implies the answer to a previously unresolved halachic problem. He asks about the passage: How could it ever have entered the mind of Doeg that Boaz might have married Ruth in violation of the Law? For the Sages tell us that Boaz was Ivtzan (one of the Judges) (see *Judges* 12:8-9), who served as the Judge and supreme legal authority of Israel for many years. How could it be that one of the Judges would publicly marry a person ineligible for marriage? The solution offered by *Maharsha* is as follows. In the commentary of *Rambam* on *parashas Vayeishev*, and likewise in *Bereishis Rabbah*, it is indicated that the law of levirate marriage, which states that if a man dies childless his brother is obligated to take the widow in marriage, originally was extended by custom to apply not only to the brother but to all male relatives. Furthermore, on the Scriptural level if it should happen that the widow is forbidden to the surviving relative by a negative commandment [i.e. a prohibition punishable by lashes but not *kares* — for example, if the widow were a divorcee from a previous marriage and the surviving relative is a *kohen*; or if the widow was a *mamzeress*], the positive commandment of performing the levirate marriage overrides the prohibition and the marriage is consummated.[16] It is only on the Rabbinic level that such a levirate marriage is prohibited. Now in the time of Boaz, explains *Maharsha*, this Rabbinic prohibition had not yet been enacted and hence, even if we assume that Doeg was correct and Ruth was forbidden for ordinary marriage, nevertheless the levirate marriage would be completely permissible in itself. In a case like this, however, even though the levirate marriage itself is permitted, any offspring resulting from such a union would be marred by the defect attaching to the mother, as we find in a *mishnah*, "Wherever there is a [valid] marriage [and yet that marriage nevertheless involves] a transgression, the offspring is affected by the defect."[17] Applying these laws to the case of Ruth, Doeg could argue that even though Boaz was permitted to take her in levirate marriage, nevertheless since she was forbidden for ordinary marriage, her descendants would be subject to that same prohibition, meaning that David would be forbidden to marry any woman of Israel. That prohibition does not exist, however, once we know that the law applies to "a Moabite and not a Moabitess" — for this means that Ruth herself was completely permissible for marriage.

From this discussion by *Maharsha* we thus learn incidentally that when the Sages point out that on the Scriptural level if a man is a non-*mamzer* and his brother's widow is a *mamzeress* he is obligated to perform the levirate marriage, this means nevertheless that the offspring of such a union is a *mamzer*. This very question is considered by the author of *Shaar HaMelech* (who makes no reference to the discussion by *Maharsha*),[18] and that author leaves the matter with the comment, "This requires further study" (צָרִיךְ עִיּוּן). The author of *Oneg Yom-Tov*[19] also discusses this same problem, and arrives at the opposite conclusion. "It is not reasonable to suppose that the law would permit the levirate marriage [with a *mamzeress*] and yet make the offspring a *mamzer*, thus increasing the possibility of *mamzerim*." (And this author cites neither *Shaar HaMelech*, who leaves the issue in doubt, nor *Maharsha*, who regards the opposite conclusion as self-evident.)[20]

* * *

Halachos Based on Megillas Ruth

On the verse, *May HASHEM treat you with lovingkindness as you have done with the dead and with me* (יַעַשׂ ה' עִמָּכֶם חֶסֶד כַּאֲשֶׁר עֲשִׂיתֶם עִם הַמֵּתִים וְעִמָּדִי; *Ruth* 1:8), *Yalkut Shimoni*[21] cites this *midrash*: "Rabbi Zeira said, This Scroll contains neither [laws of] ritual purity and impurity nor [laws of] that which is permitted and that which is forbidden. Why, then, was it written? To teach you the reward of those who do acts of lovingkindness (גּוֹמְלֵי חֲסָדִים)." On close examination we shall see, all the same, that several basic *halachos* are derived from various verses in the Scroll of *Ruth*.

Among these, there is one which is derived, not by way of hint nor abstruse exegesis, but from the straightforward meaning of an explicit verse in this *megillah*. And that is the law which establishes the method of *chalipin (kinyan sudar)* as a valid means of transferring property. *Now this was the custom in former time in Israel concerning redeeming and concerning exchanging, to establish any matter; a man pulled off his shoe, and gave it to his fellow; and this was the confirmation in Israel* (וְזֹאת לְפָנִים בְּיִשְׂרָאֵל עַל הַגְּאוּלָה וְעַל הַתְּמוּרָה לְקַיֵּם כָּל דָּבָר שָׁלַף אִישׁ נַעֲלוֹ וְנָתַן לְרֵעֵהוּ וְזֹאת הַתְּעוּדָה בְּיִשְׂרָאֵל; *ibid.* 4:7). [It is assumed that the shoe is only an example, and that other objects may be used instead. — Ed.]

This law of *chalipin* involves a number of details; and they, too, are derived from this verse. A *baraisa* cited in *Bava Metzia*[22] states, "Redeeming (גְּאוּלָה) means 'selling' as we see in the verse, *It shall not be redeemed* (לֹא יִגָּאֵל; *Leviticus* 27:33). Exchanging (תְּמוּרָה) means 'barter,' as we see in the verse, *He shall not exchange it, nor substitute [something else] for it* (לֹא יַחֲלִיפֶנּוּ וְלֹא יָמִיר אֹתוֹ; *ibid. v.* 10)." (The point of this *baraisa* is that *chalipin* is a valid method of transfer both for sales and for barter.)

Another detail concerns the phrase, *A man pulled off his shoe and gave it to his fellow*. The same *baraisa* cites this phrase and asks, "Who gave to whom? Boaz gave to the *go'el*. Rabbi Yehudah says: The *go'el* gave to Boaz." (The disagreement here concerns whether the *chalipin* ceremony should be performed with an item belonging to the buyer or to the seller, and the Talmud brings the *baraisa* as evidence that the *Tannaim* had already debated this very point.)

Yet another disagreement is that between Rav Nachman and Rav Sheshes, the former asserting that *chalipin* may be performed only with a *keli*, a utensil or item of clothing, while Rav Sheshes maintains that even an item of produce (פֵּירוֹת) may be used. Here, too, the disagreement is tied to the correct interpretation of our verse. "What is the reason behind the opinion of Rav Nachman? The verse says, *his shoe* — [this implies that it must be] a shoe [i.e., something in the same category as a shoe, which is a *keli*] and not something else [i.e., not something in a different category altogether such as produce]. What is the reasoning of Rav Sheshes? The verse says, *to establish any matter*." [Rav Sheshes understands the words *any matter* to refer to the object which may be used in the ceremony — it may be *any matter*, even produce.] "Does not Rav Nachman also acknowledge that the verse says *to establish any matter*? [Yes, but he understands the words *any matter* as referring to the object being sold], that is, 'to establish that *any matter* may be transferred by the ceremony of the shoe.' And does not Rav Sheshes also acknowledge that the verse says, *his shoe*? Rav Sheshes will say to you [that these words are written in order to clarify a different detail, namely], just as a shoe is a complete thing, so *chalipin* may be performed with any complete thing — thus excluding half a pomegranate or half a nut, to indicate that they may not be used."

The way that the law about *chalipin* is derived has broader implications which go beyond this law itself.

What is the meaning of the words, *This was the custom in former time in Israel?* Does it mean that this was a particular Rabbinic enactment relating specifically to the "transfer by means of a shoe," i.e., *chalipin*? Not at all. Here we have, not an instance where the custom ensues from a legal enactment, but just the opposite: the legal validity is determined as a result of the custom. This is the very nature of the law; it specifies that the transfer will be validated by whatever act is customarily used for such transactions. Thus the Talmud *Yerushalmi*[23] informs us, "At first they used to effect transactions by removing the shoe, and that is the meaning of the verse, *This was the custom in former time in Israel ...* Afterwards they changed to a method of transfer called *ketzatzah* (lit., cutting off). What was *ketzatzah*? When a man sold his ancestral holdings (שְׂדֵה אֲחֻזָּתוֹ), the relatives would bring a barrel and fill it with roasted grain and nuts; they would break it in front of the children and the children would gather up [the treats], and they would say, so-and-so is cut off from his holdings ... Afterwards they changed to transactions by means of money (כֶּסֶף), bills of sale (שְׁטָר), or some act of taking possession (חֲזָקָה)." Based on this passage in the *Yerushalmi*, the author of responsa *Devar Avraham*[24] demonstrates that any method of transfer customarily employed by the merchants (the general name for such methods being the talmudic term סִיטוּמְתָּא) constitutes a valid transaction on the Scriptural level just as does the method known as *chalipin*. [Thus *chalipin* is only one sub-category of the methods called *situmta*.] The source for this is the verse, *This was the custom in former time in Israel* [which implies that the law in this case follows the custom]. And the author sees this as the meaning of the connection between the opening and closing phrases of that verse. *And this was the custom in former time in Israel ... and this was the confirmation in Israel.* The first phrase describes the custom itself. The last phrase means, 'This is the testimony and the received tradition (the word תְּעוּדָה being used here as in *Isaiah* 8:16, צוּר תְּעוּדָה — *Bind up the testimony)* that the custom establishes the validity of the transaction.

Exegesis by the Poskim When studying the halachic works of the *poskim* — those who commented on the Talmud and, in case of conflicting opinions, determined which side to follow in practice — one does not usually expect to find these later authorities producing halachic decisions by direct interpretation of Scriptural verses, unless such derivations are based on some precedent in the *Amoraim* and the *Tannaim*. Yet it is precisely in connection with this verse about *chalipin* that we find innovative inferences on the part of the *poskim* — even including the most recent authorities, the *Acharonim*. The author of *Devar Avraham*, cited above, at least couches his exegesis in cautious language, stating that it is meant "by way of *derush*," that is, discursive rather than legal discussion. Not so with *Maharshadam*, who in his responsa[25] uses the verse to produce an original legal conclusion in opposition to that reached by Rabbeinu Tam. The latter holds that the method of transfer called *chalipin* is valid not only for transactions with Jews but also for those between Jews and non-Jews.[26] *Maharshadam* objects by pointing out that the verse states explicitly, "And this was the custom in former time *in Israel* ... And this was the confirmation *in Israel*." The author of *Pnei Yehoshua*,[27] too, questions the conclusion of Rabbeinu Tam, likewise basing his doubts on the expression, *in Israel* in our verse; *Pnei Yehoshua* concludes that the question "requires further study." He was preceded in this line of thought, as stated, by *Maharshadam*.[28]

The author of *HaMiknah*[29] similarly goes directly to the verse in *Ruth* to originate a halachic conclusion. He suggests that in the process of *chalipin* the purchaser himself must personally hand over the *sudar* (lit., "scarf," meaning the shoe, handkerchief, or other item being used to accomplish the sale), and that the transfer of ownership is invalid if someone else does the handing-over for him. This would mean that *chalipin* is different from other processes of acquisition which are also confirmed by an act of giving; e.g., the marriage ceremony or the acquisition of property by giving money; in these latter instances the acquisition is equally valid whether one personally gives the money or whether someone else gives it on one's behalf. That this is not true of *chalipin*, HaMiknah derives from the precise wording of the verse, which states, *A man shall pull off his shoe and give it to his fellow.*[30]

Elsewhere,[31] the same author, *HaMiknah*, discusses an assertion first made by *Rashba*, in connection with the law that if a man sells his hereditary property his relatives have the right to redeem it for him. There is an order of preference among the relatives so that, for example, an uncle takes precedence over a cousin. *Rashba* infers that if the uncle is not financially capable of redeeming the property, but the cousin is, the cousin is not permitted to redeem it [since the uncle has preference, but cannot exercise his right]. *HaMiknah* challenges this conclusion. "Do we not have an explicit verse at the end of *Ruth*, where Boaz says, *Naomi ... has sold a parcel of land which belonged to our relative Elimelech ... and if you do not redeem it ... I am after you* (חֶלְקַת הַשָּׂדֶה אֲשֶׁר לְאָחִינוּ לֶאֱלִימֶלֶךְ מָכְרָה ... וְאִם לֹא יִגְאַל ... וְאָנֹכִי אַחֲרֶיךָ *Ruth* 4:3,4). This implies that even if the first relative is living, nevertheless it is permissible for the second relative to redeem [the property]." The author then proceeds to an intricate discussion of how *Rashba* must have interpreted these verses.

The author of *Chiddushei HaRim*[32] attempts to derive from the verse, *... and give it to his fellow*, a hitherto undiscovered law. Just as, with the divorce process, the expression *he shall give* (וְנָתַן; *Deuteronomy* 24:1) implies that it is not sufficient to say, "Pick up your bill of divorce from the ground" [but rather, the bill of divorce must be placed directly in the woman's possession], likewise with *chalipin* the "giving" must be direct.° In this way *chalipin* is different from the acquisition of property by the "giving" of money; for there the focus is on the money as a thing of value

---

° [This is not meant to imply that a bill of divorce must be placed directly into the woman's hand, for the law is that it may be placed in her basket or into her courtyard, as long as it thus is given directly into her possession. The comparison with divorce simply implies that just as the term "give" entails certain restrictions on the proper manner of "giving" in divorce, so also certain restrictions are indicated by the same term in connection with *chalipin*. — *Ed.*]

(mamon), and the requirement is simply "that the *mamon* shall come into the possession [of the seller], and no significance is attached to the act of giving itself, as to the manner in which it is performed;" this is not so of *chalipin*, where the "giving" is not connected with the concept of *mamon*, as we see from the fact that the *chalipin* is validly performed even with an object of no legal value (less than a penny's worth).°

Chiddushei HaRim originates yet another conclusion about the details of *chalipin*.[33] "It is also possible," the author writes, "that since this method of acquisition is derived from the verse, ... *and give it to his fellow*, it is necessary that the 'giving,' in particular and not the receiving, be done with the purpose of effecting the acquisition [that is, the "giving" of the shoe or handkerchief effects the acquisition of the object being bought]; if so, it is not effective for the seller, to say ["I am receiving this handkerchief in order that you may acquire my property at such a price"]; it is only effective if the buyer [i.e, the one "giving" the handkerchief] is the one who expresses the purpose of the act."

In *Ketzos HaChoshen*[34] the author discusses an assertion of *Tosafos* to the effect that an item which is destined eventually to return to the seller cannot be sold by means of *chalipin*. *Ketzos* challenges this assertion directly on the basis of the verse. "The fact is that the very law of *chalipin* is derived from the passage about the *go'el* and Boaz ... *a man pulled off his shoe and gave it to his fellow*; and in that instance, the *go'el* [as the nearest relative of Elimelech] was heir to the field, and hence it was destined to return to him in the Jubilee year *(Yovel)*, for the incident took place at a time when the laws of *Yovel* were still in effect [and yet we see that the *go'el* transferred the rights to the field to Boaz by means of *chalipin*].

These laws of *chalipin* and their accessory details are connected with Megillas *Ruth*, but they have, of course, no special relevance to the festival of Shavuos. Yet it is interesting to note that the author of *Emek Yehoshua*, the

---

° [It should be borne in mind that the term "acquiring property by means of money" *(kinyan kesef)* does not mean that ownership is transferred when the seller receives the full price of the property in money. On the contrary, the legal transference of ownership may take place in spite of the fact that the seller has not yet received the full price of the property. Rather, the "money" referred to here is not the price of the property, but a legal method used to confirm the transfer of ownership. As such, the money may even be a minimal copper coin; its function is similar to that of the ring customarily given in marriage or the handkerchief used for *chalipin*, although, as mentioned in the text, the money or ring must have a minimum legal value, while the object used for *chalipin* may be of no appreciable value at all. — *Ed.*]

Gaon Rav Aizik of Slonim, in his work *Sefas HaNachal*[35] devotes his entire discourse on Shavuos to the verse, *Now this was the custom in former time in Israel* ... With great halachic erudition he presents many ingenious and original interpretations of the verse and of the Sages' comments thereon.

Two different *halachos*, unconnected with each other, are learned from *Megillas Ruth* in Tractate *Bava Basra*.[36] First, the Talmud states: "Our Sages teach, 'One may not leave *Eretz* [*Yisrael*] to go abroad unless [the price of wheat] has reached a *sela* for two *se'ah*.' Rabbi Shimon said, 'When is this true? — when one cannot easily find wheat (בִּזְמַן שֶׁאֵינוֹ מוֹצֵא לִקַּח). But if one has no difficulty in purchasing wheat, one may not leave even if the price [of wheat] has reached a *sela* for one *se'ah*. And thus Rabbi Shimon ben Yochai used to say: Elimelech, Machlon, and Chilyon were the greatest scholars of the generation and were the leaders of the generation. And why were they punished? — because they left *Eretz Yisrael* to go abroad [and they were punished for this even though it was a time of famine when the price of wheat was very high] — as it is said, *All the city was astir at their arrival, and they said, Is this Naomi?* (וַתֵּהֹם כָּל הָעִיר עֲלֵיהֶן וַתּאמַרְנָה הֲזֹאת נָעֳמִי; Ruth 1:19). Rabbi Yitzchak comments, 'What they said was: Have you seen what happened to Naomi, who left *Eretz Yisrael* to go abroad?' "[37]

Eretz Yisrael and ...

The second *halachah* is discussed as follows. "Rabba bar Rav Huna said in the name of Rav: 'Ivtzan is Boaz.' What does this mean? (*Rashi* explains the question. "What profit is there in this matter [of knowing that Boaz is identical with one of the Judges mentioned in the Book of *Judges*], and how do we learn about any mitzvah from this fact?") It is related to the statement of Rabba bar Rav Huna, who said, 'Boaz made a hundred and twenty feasts for his sons.' " ("And since he has said that Ivtzan is Boaz, and it is written of Boaz that he married Ruth, and this even though he already had many sons, we learn that though a man has taken a wife in his youth, he should take a wife in his old age, as did Ivtzan, i.e., Boaz" — *Rashi.*) [The fact that Boaz was not simply a rich man, but was the Judge of his generation, gives halachic significance to his actions. — *Ed.*]

... *a Mitzvah for Old Age*

The marriage of Boaz and Ruth serves as the source for a different *halachah*. "Whence do we know that [the blessings recited at a wedding] *Birkas Chasanim* [may be said only] in the presence of ten [men]? As it is said, *And he took ten men from the elders of the city and said, sit down here, and they sat down.*[37*] And here, again, the fact that "Ivtzan is Boaz" adds force to the *halachah.* The *Gemara* discusses whether the blessings are applicable at the marriage of a widow and widower, and it is demonstrated on the basis of the story of Boaz, "who was a widower who married a widow" [that the blessings are recited in such a case]. *(Rashi:* "For the Sage has said, 'Ivtzan is Boaz' and he already had thirty sons and thirty daughters").

Taz[39] uses the story of how Boaz and Ruth were married to draw an inference in connection with the law that if "a woman is urged to marry and she acquiesces" she must go through the seven-day waiting period associated with menstrual purity.[40]

[The conclusion of *Taz* is that since Ruth did not undergo such a waiting period, the law is a Rabbinic one enacted at a later date. — Ed.]

The Laws of Conversion Certain details of the process of conversion are derived in the *Gemara* from the conversion of Ruth. A *baraisa* cited in Tractate *Yevamos*[41] states, "We inform [the prospective convert] of a few of the less grave commandments and a few of the graver commandments ... and we do not overburden him with numerous mitzvos nor are we exacting with him in the fine details of the mitzvos." The *Gemara* comments, "Rav Elazar said, [On] what verse [is this based]? — as it is written, *And she saw that she was making an effort to go with her and she ceased speaking to her* (וַתֵּרֶא כִּי מִתְאַמֶּצֶת הִיא לָלֶכֶת אִתָּהּ וַתֶּחְדַּל לְדַבֵּר אֵלֶיהָ; *Ruth* 1:18). She said to her, 'We are prohibited [on *Shabbos* and *Yom-Tov* to go beyond the 2000 cubit boundary called] *techum Shabbos.'* [Ruth's reply was,] *'Where you walk, I shall walk'* (אֶל אֲשֶׁר תֵּלְכִי אֵלֵךְ; *ibid.* v. 16). 'We are forbidden to be in a closed room with someone of the opposite sex.' — *'Where you sleep, I shall sleep'* (וּבַאֲשֶׁר תָּלִינִי אָלִין; *ibid.*). 'We are commanded to obey six hundred thirteen mitzvos.' — *'Your people are my people'* (עַמֵּךְ עַמִּי; *ibid.*). 'Idol worship is forbidden us.' — *'Your God is my God'* (וֵאלֹקַיִךְ אֱלֹקָי; *ibid.*). Immediately, — *And she saw that she was making an effort to go with her, and she ceased speaking to her ...*"

On the basis of this concept that the verse is speaking of Ruth's conversion, a fine interpretation is handed down in the name of the Gaon of Vilna. In tractate *Bava Metzia*[42] it is related that the great *Amora,* Resh Lakish, had at one time been a highwayman, and Rabbi Yochanan brought him under the wings of the Torah. After having taken upon himself the yoke of the Torah, Resh Lakish attempted to leap across the Jordan River, as he had just previously done, and found that he could no longer do so, since, as *Rashi* explains, once he had taken upon himself the yoke of the Torah, his physical strength was diminished." The Gaon relates this to the story of Ruth. She, too, having wholeheartedly taken upon herself to convert, found her physical strength diminished, and she could no longer walk quickly as before. This is the meaning of the verse, *And she saw that she was making an effort to go ... and she ceased speaking to her.* When Naomi perceived that it was now an "effort" for Ruth to walk, she understood that her daughter-in-law had truly undertaken to convert.

There is even one *halachah* in the category of "Rabbinic decree" which is learned from this *megillah.* A *mishnah* at the end of Tractate *Berachos* tells us, "And the Sages decreed that one man greet another in the name of *HaShem,* as it is said, *And behold, Boaz came from Beis Lechem and he said to the reapers, HASHEM be with you, and they said to him, May HASHEM bless you* (וְהִנֵּה בֹעַז בָּא מִבֵּית לֶחֶם וַיֹּאמֶר לַקּוֹצְרִים ה׳ עִמָּכֶם עִמָּכֶם וַיֹּאמְרוּ לוֹ יְבָרֶכְךָ ה׳; *ibid.* 2:4).[43] And in Tractate *Makos*[44] this decree is counted as one of three things which were instituted by the earthly court and affirmed by enactment of the heavenly court. (As to the exact nature of this decree — whether it simply grants permission to use the name of *HaShem* in greeting one's fellow or whether it obligates one to do so, see two different interpretations cited by *Rashi* at that point in *Makos.* See also the commentary of *Gevuros Ari* there, where the author argues that the intent is only to grant permission.) *Rambam,* for some reason, omits mention of this *halachah.*[45]

And this, too, is *Halachah:* "*Wash, and anoint yourself and put on your clothes* (וְרָחַצְתְּ וָסַכְתְּ וְשַׂמְתְּ שִׂמְלֹתַיִךְ; *ibid.* 3:3). Was she, then, naked? Rather, these [clothes which Naomi told Ruth to put on] were her *Shabbos* garments. Based on this, Rabbi Chanina said, 'A person must have two sets of garments; one for the ordinary days and one for *Shabbos.* And thus did Rabbi Simlai teach to the public.'"[46]

Halachos of *derech eretz* — both proper ethical conduct and the improvement of character — are derived by the Sages from a number of verses in *Megillas Ruth.* For example, "*Behold, he is winnowing barley tonight in the threshing floor* (הִנֵּה הוּא זֹרֶה אֶת גֹּרֶן הַשְּׂעֹרִים; *ibid.* 3:2) — from this [and the subsequent verse, where Naomi tells Ruth to go to the threshing

Derech Eretz

floor and she will find Boaz sleeping there] we learn that a Torah scholar should not venture out alone at night."[47] [*Rashi* explains that this is why Naomi knew that if Boaz was winnowing the barley there at night, he would remain there to sleep, rather than returning to the city alone.] Again, *"And Boaz took ten men from the elders of the city [and said, sit down here, and they sat down]* (וַיִּקַּח עֲשָׂרָה אֲנָשִׁים מִזִּקְנֵי הָעִיר וַיֹּאמֶר שְׁבוּ פֹה וַיֵּשֵׁבוּ; *ibid.* 4:2) — from this we learn that the lesser scholar may not sit down until the greater gives him permission."[48] And there are other similar examples.

But if we wish to enter the realm of character traits and ethics, we are brought back to the fact that the whole essence of this wondrous *megillah* was written only "to teach you the reward of those who do acts of lovingkindness." "Come and see," invites *Midrash Ruth* in commenting on the verse, *HaShem will reward your actions ... in that you have come to take shelter beneath His wings* (יְשַׁלֵּם ה' פָּעֳלֵךְ ... אֲשֶׁר בָּאת לַחֲסוֹת תַּחַת כְּנָפָיו; *ibid.* 2:12). "How great is the strength of those who do acts of loving kindness! For they take shelter not in the shadow of the dawn, not in the shadow of the wings of the earth, not in the shadow of the wings of the sun, not in the shadow of the wings of the celestial creatures, not in the shadow of the wings of the cherubim, and not in the shadow of the wings of the seraphim, but in the shadow of Him at whose word the universe came into existence — as it is said, *How precious is Your lovingkindness, O God; and the sons of man take shelter in the shadow of Your wings"* (מַה יָּקָר חַסְדְּךָ אֱלֹקִים וּבְנֵי אָדָם בְּצֵל כְּנָפֶיךָ יֶחֱסָיוּן; *Psalms* 36:8).

NOTES

[1] Ch. 14.

[2] *Rosh, Hilchos Sefer Torah.*

[3] *Birkei Yosef,* 582, and *Ya'ir Ozen, maareches* 60, sec. 31.

[4] *Ruth, remez* 596.

[5] Sec. 490, in *Rama.*

[6] 490:8.

[7] Sec. 35.

[8] *Hilchos Shevuos.*

[9] See *Mordechai, Megillah,* ch. 1; *Abudraham; Hagahos Maimonios, Hilchos Tisha Be'Av, et. al.*

[9*] Sec. 35.

[10] 490.

[11] Jerusalem, 5698 (1938), p. 28.

[12] 494.

[13] And see the introduction to responsa *Chut HaMeshulash* for a detailed homiletic explanation of this custom.

[13*] See the *Yerushalmi, Chagigah* 2:3, and *Tosafos, Chagigah* 14a.

[14] *Bechor Shor, Bava Basra* 13b.

[14*] *Kesuvos* 7b.

[15] 76b.

[15*] *Ibid.*

[16] See *Yevamos* 20b.

[17] *Mishnah, Kiddushin* 66b.

[18] *Yibbum,* ch. 6.

[19] Sec. 121.

[20] And see *Avnei Miluim,* sec. 174; responsa *Beis Yitzchak, Yoreh De'ah, sec.* 167; *Achiezer,* part 1, sec. 4; et. al.

[21] *Ruth, remez* 601.

[22] 47a.

[23] *Kiddushin* 1:5.

[24] Part 1, sec. 1.

[25] *Choshen Mishpat,* sec. 59.

[26] See *Tosafos* on *Kiddushin* 3a, and the commentaries on *Shulchan Aruch, Choshen Mishpat* 123.

[27] *Kiddushin, loc. cit.*

[28] Concerning the problem raised by *Maharashdam,* see *Tumim,* sec. 123; *Aruch HaShulchan, ibid.; Imrei HaTzvi* on *Bava Kama,* in his *Chiddushim* on 70a. The author of *Imrei Tzvi* gives an original and ingenious interpretation of the verse וְזֹאת הַתְּעוּדָה.

[29] In his *Chiddushim* on *Kiddushin* 26b.

[30] *And see Chiddushei HaRim, Choshen Mishpat,* sec. 195, *os.* 13, where the author's opinion parallels that of *HaMiknah* with regard to this halachic insight and its derivation from the verse.

[31] In his *Chiddushim* on 21b.

[32] *Choshen Mishpat* 195:1.

[33] *Loc. cit., os.* 3.

[34] 195, para. 8.

[35] *Drush* 17 on the festival of *Shavuos.*

[36] 91a.

[37] And see *Rambam, Melachim* 5:9, where *Rambam* learns from the story of Machlon and Chilyon that even if grain is not readily available for purchase, it is an act of special piety *(midas chassidus)* not to leave *Eretz Yisrael.* As for the apparent contradiction between this opinion and the statement of Rabbi Shimon in the *Gemara,* see *Lechem Mishneh, ibid.,* and *Pe'as HaShulchan,* sec. 1, para. 24.

[37*] *Kesuvos* 7a and 7b. [And see the *Talmudic Encyclopedia,* s.v. *Birkas Chassanim,* vol. 4, p. 634, notes 37-48.]

[39] *Yoreh De'ah* 192.

[40] And see *ibid., Chavas Daas* and *Lechem VeSimlah,* the latter by Rav Sh. Ganzfried.

[41] 47a.

[42] 84a.

[43] *Mishnah,* end of *Berachos.*

[44] 23b.

[45] Rav Y. Pik, in *Omer HaShichechah,* lists all the omissions of *Rambam,* but this omission is omitted from the list.

[46] *Midrash Ruth.* And see *Shabbos* 113b.

[47] *Chullin* 91b. *Rambam,* in *De'os* 5:9, cites the law without giving the verse as the source.

[48] *Midrash Ruth.*

Glossary

Glossary

An asterisk refers the reader to an item appearing in this Glossary.
All non-English entries are Hebrew unless otherwise stated [Aram.=Aramaic; Yid.=Yiddish].

Acharon (אַחֲרוֹן; pl., *Acharonim):* a halachic authority of the period since the publication of *Shulchan Aruch* in the sixteenth century; (see also vol. II, p. 336)

achilah gassah (אֲכִילָה גַסָּה): eating beyond the point of complete satiety

achilas pras (אֲכִילַת פְּרָס), see *kedei achilas pras*

Adar (אֲדָר): the twelfth month. A leap-year has both *Adar Rishon* and *Adar Sheni,* the festival of Purim falling in the second

Additional Sacrifice, see *Musaf*

Additional Service, see *Musaf*

afikoman (אֲפִיקוֹמָן): the piece of **matzah* which is the last thing eaten at the **Pesach *Seder*

Afternoon Service, see *Minchah*

Aggadah, the (אַגָּדָה): the classical body of philosophical, ethical, poetic, and historical exposition of Scripture (see also vol. II, p. 333)

Akdamus (אַקְדָמוּת): poem recited during the Morning Service on **Shavuos*

amah (אַמָּה; pl., *amos):* cubit (approx. 1/2 m. or 1/2 yd.)

Amidah (עֲמִידָה; pl. *Amidos):* the "standing" prayer central to every service; also called *Shmoneh Esreh*

Amora (אָמוֹרָא; pl., *Amoraim;* Aram.): a post-Mishnaic authority cited in the **Gemara* (see also vol. II, p. 335)

Am Yisrael (עַם יִשְׂרָאֵל): the People of Israel

arev kablan (עָרֵב קַבְלָן): third party acting as a guarantor for a financial obligation, regardless of the involved party's ability or willingness to pay

Aseres HaDibros (עֲשֶׂרֶת הַדִּבְּרוֹת): the Ten Commandments

Ashkenaz (אַשְׁכְּנַז): medieval Hebrew name for the area now called Germany

Ashkenazi (אַשְׁכְּנַזִי): the Jewry of North, West, Central and Eastern Europe

Atzeres (עֲצֶרֶת; lit., "assembly"): alternative name for **Shavuos*

Av (אָב): the fifth month; the month in which both the First and Second **Beis HaMikdash* were destroyed

aveirah (עֲבֵרָה): transgression

avel (אָבֵל): bereaved person

avelus (אֲבֵלוּת): mourning

avodah zarah (עֲבוֹדָה זָרָה): idol-worship or the object thereof

bal tashchis (בַּל תַּשְׁחִית): the prohibition against needless destruction of property

bal yera'eh (בַּל יֵרָאֶה): the prohibition against having **chametz* which is (or can be) seen on **Pesach*

bal yimatzeh (בַּל יִמָּצֵא): the prohibition against having **chametz* in one's possession on **Pesach*

bamah (בָּמָה; pl., *bamos):* a local altar outside the precincts of the Tabernacle or Temple

bamah gedolah (בָּמָה גְדוֹלָה): the central, national Altar in the pre-Temple era prior to the erection of the sanctuary in Shiloh, and subsequent to its destruction

BaMeh Madlikin (בַּמֶּה מַדְלִיקִין): a chapter of **mishnayos* (the second of Tractate *Shabbos)* about the wicks and oils that may be used for **Shabbos* lights, and related subjects

baraisa (בָּרַיְיתָא; pl., *baraisos):* tannaitic statement not included in the **Mishnah*

bar chiyuva (בַּר חִיּוּבָא; *Aram):* person obliged to perform a particular **mitzvah*

Barchu (בָּרְכוּ; lit., "Let us bless!"): opening word of blessings preceding *Shema Yisrael* and Torah readings

Bar-Mitzvah (בַּר מִצְוָה): religious coming of age on a boy's thirteenth birthday

bechor (בְּכוֹר): first-born

bediavad (בְּדִיעֲבַד; Aram.): [legally valid or permitted only] after the fact

bedikah (בְּדִיקָה): see *bedikas chametz*

bedikas chametz (בְּדִיקַת חָמֵץ): the search for *chametz*, normally done the night before *Pesach

bein hashmashos (בֵּין הַשְּׁמָשׁוֹת): dusk

beis din (בֵּית דִּין): court of Jewish law

Beis HaBechirah (בֵּית הַבְּחִירָה; lit., "the House of [God's] choice"): the Temple or *Beis HaMikdash

Beis HaMikdash (בֵּית הַמִּקְדָּשׁ): the First or the Second Temple in Jerusalem

beis midrash (בֵּית מִדְרָשׁ): communal house of study

ben nechar (בֶּן נֵכָר; lit., "the son of an alien"): one who rejects the Torah

ben Noach (בֶּן נֹחַ): a non-Jew

berachah (בְּרָכָה; pl., *berachos*): a blessing

bikurim (בְּכּוּרִים): first-fruits

bimah (בִּימָה): platform in *Beis HaMikdash* or synagogue

Birkas HaMazon (בִּרְכַּת הַמָּזוֹן): blessings after a meal that included bread

bitul (בְּטוּל): see *bitul chametz*

bitul chametz (בְּטוּל חָמֵץ): the mental renunciation of one's *chametz*

biur (בְּעוּר): see *biur chametz*

biur chametz (בְּעוּר חָמֵץ): elimination of leavened products from one's possession

bris milah (בְּרִית מִילָה): the convenant of circumcision

carpas (כַּרְפַּס): parsley or celery dipped in salt-water and eaten at beginning of *Pesach *Seder

Chabad (חַבַּ"ד; acronym): branch of *Chassidism founded by Rav Shneur Zalman of Liadi

Chachamim (חֲכָמִים; lit., "sages"): a) the Rabbis of the Talmudic era; b) those holding the majority view in a debate recorded in the Talmud

chadash (חָדָשׁ; lit., "new"): the prohibition against using the new crop of grain until after the second day of *Pesach

chag (חַג): festival

Chagigah, see *Korban Chagigah*

chalifin (חֲלִיפִין): momentary exchange of a handkerchief or similar object in order to confirm a transaction

challah (חַלָּה): a mandatory contribution of dough for the *kohen; (also: the braided loaf baked in honor of *Shabbos and *Yom-Tov)

chamei Tveryah (חַמֵּי טְבֶרְיָה): the hot-springs of Tiberias

chametz (חָמֵץ): leavened products forbidden for use on *Pesach

chametz nukshe (חָמֵץ נוּקְשֶׁה): inedible *chametz

Chanukah (חֲנוּכָה; lit., "consecration"): eight-day festival of lights in commemoration of the Maccabees' rededication of the Temple in the second century B.C.E.

charoses (חֲרוֹסֶת): mixture of chopped fruits, chopped nuts, spices, and wine, into which the *maror is dipped at the *Pesach *Seder

chassid (חָסִיד; pl., *chassidim*): adherent of *Chassidism

Chassidism (Heb.: חֲסִידוּת): pietist movement founded by Reb Yisrael Baal Shem Tov in the eighteenth century

Chatas-offering, see *Korban Chatas*

chatzos (חֲצוֹת): midnight; noon

chavurah (חֲבוּרָה): group of people sharing one *korban Pesach.

chazakah (חֲזָקָה): a) a legal presumption (especially of valid property rights resulting from occupation or use; b) a method of legally acquiring real property through an overt act demonstrating ownership *chazeres* (חֲזֶרֶת); herb used for the *mitzvah of *maror

chazzan (חַזָּן): cantor; person (sometimes professional) who leads a prayer service

cheresh, shoteh, ve-katan (חֵרֵשׁ, שׁוֹטֶה, וְקָטָן; lit., "deaf-mute, mentally incompetent, or minor"): types of person with limited rights and responsibilities

chiddush (חִדּוּשׁ; pl., *chiddushim*): innovative commentary or hitherto unrecorded legal conclusion

chimutz (חִמּוּץ): fermentation leading to *chametz

chol (חוֹל): an ordinary weekday, neither *Shabbos nor *Yom-Tov

Chol HaMo'ed (חוֹל הַמּוֹעֵד): the days (of lesser sanctity than *Yom-Tov*) between the opening and the closing festive days of *Pesach and *Sukkos

chovas gavra (חוֹבַת גַּבְרָא): an obligation inherent in the person (rather than in objects)

chrein (חֲרֵיין; *Yid.*): horseradish used by some for the *mitzvah of *maror at the *Pesach *Seder

chullin (חוּלִין): ordinary, non-sanctified food for lay use

Chumash (חוּמָשׁ; pl., *Chumashim*): the Five Books of Moses; Pentateuch

chuppah (חוּפָּה): a) the wedding canopy; b) the ceremony constituting the legal completion of the marriage *(nisuin)*

Churban (חוּרְבָּן): the Destruction of the First or the Second Temple

commandment, negative, see *mitzvas lo saaseh*

commandment, positive, see *mitzvas aseh*

commandment, Rabbinic, see *mitzvah derabbanan*

cusemes (כּוּסֶמֶת; in Mishnaic Hebrew *cusmin*, (כּוּסְמִין): spelt, one of the five kinds of grain that can become *chametz; not to be confused with the modern Hebrew word for buckwheat (kasha), which is not one of the five species

dagan (דָּגָן): grain

Daily Sacrifice, see *Korban Tamid*

davar she-yesh lo matirin (דְּבָר שֶׁיֵּשׁ לוֹ מַתִּירִין): something that is presently prohibited but which has some way of becoming permissible

dayeinu (דַּיֵּינוּ; "it would have been sufficient"): song sung during the *Pesach *Seder

demai (דְּמַאי): produce from which one is uncertain whether tithes have been taken

derabbanan, see *mitzvah derabbanan*

derashah (דְּרָשָׁה): interpretation of Biblical words, in order to derive a *halachah, in accordance with one of a number of exegetical principles (e.g., *kal vachomer) handed down by the Sages; (also: a sermon or an aggadic exposition)

derush (דְּרוּשׁ; pl., *derushim*): a) discourse, spoken or written, usually aggadic in content and form, to inspire and instruct; b) an instance of *derashah

din (דִּין): a law; a *halachah

dinar (דִּינָר): a coin of Talmudic times

divrei Torah (דִּבְרֵי תּוֹרָה): a) *mitzvah deoraysa; b) a law given orally to Moshe Rabbeinu at Sinai; (also: discourse or conversation on Torah subjects)

Elul (אֱלוּל): the sixth month; the month of stocktaking before *Rosh HaShanah

emurim (אֵמוּרִים): parts of a sacrifice which were burned on the Altar

Eretz Yisrael (אֶרֶץ יִשְׂרָאֵל): the Land of Israel

erev (עֶרֶב): the day before [a given day]; (also: the evening which begins a [Jewish] day)

esrog (אֶתְרֹג; pl., *esrogim*): citron, one of the Four Species in the *Sukkos ceremony

Evening Service, see *Maariv*

exegesis, see *derashah*

Four Cups (אַרְבָּעָה כּוֹסוֹת): the cups of wine which one is commanded to drink at the *Pesach *Seder

Gaon (גָּאוֹן; pl., *Geonim*; lit., "magnificent"): a Torah genius; especially, the head of one of the Babylonian academies from the seventh to the eleventh centuries, C. E.

Gemara (גְּמָרָא; Aram.): that part of the Talmud which expounds the *Mishnah (see also vol. II, p. 333.)

get (גֵּט): a bill of divorce

geulah (גְּאוּלָה): redemption

gezerah (גְּזֵרָה): enactment of the Sages to avert halachically undesirable situations (see also vol. II, p. 335)

gezerah shavah (גְּזֵרָה שָׁוָה): exegetical means of drawing halachic conclusions from the occurrence of certain pairs of identical words or phrases in different Scriptural contexts

gid hanasheh (גִּיד הַנָּשֶׁה): the sciatic nerve, forbidden for eating

gluska (גְּלוּסְקָה; pl., *gluskaos*): a fine white roll

Golah (גּוֹלָה): the Diaspora; formerly, Babylonia

Grace after Meals, see *Birkas HaMazon*

haaramah (הַעֲרָמָה): a device for circumventing a prohibition

haavarah (הַעֲבָרָה): the prohibition of carrying an object four cubits in *reshus harabim* on *Shabbos

hadlakos (הַדְלָקוֹת): the practice of burning valuable items at the tomb of a *tzaddik*

Haftarah (הַפְטָרָה; pl., *Haftaros*): a passage from the Prophets which is read on *Shabbos* and *Yom-Tov* after the Torah reading and related to that reading

hagalah (הַגְעָלָה): see *hagalas kelim*

hagalas kelim (הַגְעָלַת כֵּלִים): placing a metal vessel or utensil in boiling water to remove the taste of any prohibited substance absorbed into its walls; before *Pesach this is done to remove absorbed *chametz*

Haggadah, the (הַגָּדָה): text recited at the *Pesach *Seder*, recounting the Story of Redemption from Egypt

halachah (הֲלָכָה; pl., *halachos*): a) [upper case] the whole body of Jewish law; b) an individual law; c) the accepted ruling in cases of disagreement

Hallel (הַלֵּל): Psalms of praise and thanksgiv-ing recited on certain festive days (Psalms 113-118 with added blessings)

Hallel HaGadol (הַלֵּל הַגָּדוֹל): Psalms 136, recited during the *Pesach *Seder*

hanaah (הֲנָאָה): a) benefit; b) enjoyment

harshaah (הַרְשָׁאָה): document empowering one to perform a transaction on another's behalf

hashbasah (הַשְׁבָּתָה; lit. "causing to cease"): spec. with reference to destruction of *chametz* before Pesach

HaShem (הַשֵּׁם; lit., "The Name"): God; (in this book the word is spelled HASHEM when used for the Ineffable Name as it appears in a verse of Scripture)

Havdalah (הַבְדָּלָה): ceremony marking the transition from *Shabbos* or *Yom-Tov* to a day of lesser sanctity

hefker (הֶפְקֵר): ownerless property

hekesh (הֶקֵּשׁ): an exegetical means of drawing halachic conclusions from the juxtaposition of Scriptural texts or from a comparison stated explicitly in the text

heseibah (הֲסָבָה): leaning or reclining on the left side at the *Pesach *Seder*, to symbolize the state of freedom

heteira bala (הֶתֵּירָא בָּלַע): the absorption into the walls of a vessel of a substance that is presently permitted but that will become prohibited at a later time (e.g., *chametz before *Pesach)

hiddur [mitzvah] (הִדּוּר מִצְוָה): enhancement or meticulous observance of a *mitzvah beyond the basic requirements

hilchos (... הִלְכוֹת): "the laws of ... " (see *halachah)

hilula (הִלּוּלָא): a wedding celebration; the yearly celebration at the tomb of Rabbi Shimon bar Yochai

Hoshana Rabbah (הוֹשַׁעְנָא רַבָּה): the seventh day of the festival of *Sukkos, when seven circuits are made around the Altar in the *Beis HaMikdash or the *bimah in the synagogue

hotzaah (הוֹצָאָה): (a) the prohibition of removing objects from a private to a public domain (or vice versa) on *Shabbos; (b) removing the Pesach sacrifice from its *chavurah*

Isru Chag (אִסְרוּ חַג): the day following any one of the three *Pilgrim Festivals

issur (אִסּוּר): prohibition

issur cheftzah (אִסּוּר חֶפְצָא): a prohibition inherent in an object (rather than in a person)

issur gavra (אִסּוּר גַּבְרָא): a prohibition inherent in a person (rather than in an object)

issur hanaah (אִסּוּר הֲנָאָה): prohibition against deriving any benefit from an object

Iyyar (אִיָּר): the second month; the month in which Lag BaOmer is celebrated

Kabbalah (קַבָּלָה; lit., "received tradition"): the body of Jewish mystical teachings

kadashim (קָדָשִׁים): items sanctified for Temple use

kadashim kalim (קָדָשִׁים קַלִּים): *kadashim of a relatively lower level of Sanctity

Kaddish (קַדִּישׁ; Aram.; lit., "holy"): passage with congregational responses recited by *sheliach tzibur* or a mourner

kal vekalush (קַל וְקָלוּשׁ): (in reference to tastes absorbed into vessels:) "light and weakened"

kam lei biderabbah minei (קָם לֵיהּ בְּדְרַבָּה מִינֵיהּ): the rule that, in some instances, one who commits an act incurring both a severe and a less severe penalty receives only the severe one

kares (כָּרֵת): divine punishment by spiritual excision

katan, see *cheresh, shoteh, ve-katan*

kavanah (כַּוָּנָה): intent (in performing a mitzvah)

kazayis (כְּזַיִת): the volume equivalent of an olive

ke'arah (קְעָרָה): the plate of symbolic foods used at the *Pesach *Seder

kedei achilas pras (כְּדֵי אֲכִילַת פְּרָס; lit., "enough [time] to eat half a loaf of bread"): a unit of time (— a few minutes), variously defined

kedushah (קְדוּשָׁה): sanctity

Kedushah (קְדוּשָׁה): passage of congregational responses in repetition of the *Amidah

kemach shmurah (קֶמַח שְׁמוּרָה): flour made from grain guarded since harvesting from contact with moisture

kesubos (כְּתוּבוֹת); sing., *kesubah):* document attesting to the legal obligations of a man to his wife

kezeisim (כְּזֵיתִים): pl. of *kazayis

Kiddush (קִדּוּשׁ; lit., "sanctification'): blessing, usually over wine, expressing the sanctity of *Shabbos or a *Yom-Tov

kilayim (כִּלְאַיִם): the prohibition of growing certain differing species of plants in proximity to each other

kimelo lugmav (כִּמְלֹא לוּגְמָיו): a minimum measure of drinking: "one cheekful"

kinyan (קִנְיָן): a halachic means of acquisition

kinyan agav (קִנְיָן אַגַב): acquisition of movable goods as an adjunct to the acquisition of real estate

Kislev (כִּסְלֵו): the ninth month; the month in which Chanukah begins

kitnios (קִטְנִיּוֹת): edible seeds, other than those five kinds which can become *chametz*

kli rishon (כְּלִי רִאשׁוֹן): a vessel which has stood directly on the fire

kli sheni (כְּלִי שֵׁנִי): a vessel into which the contents of a *kli rishon* have been put

kodesh (קוֹדֶשׁ): sanctity

kodshei kodashim (קָדְשֵׁי קָדָשִׁים): sacrifices of the highest degree of sanctity

kohen (כֹּהֵן; pl., *kohanim):* descendant of the priestly family of Aharon

kohen gadol (כֹּהֵן גָּדוֹל): High Priest

kolshehu (כָּלְשֶׁהוּ): term indicating the lack of any fixed minimum for a given substance

korban (קָרְבָּן; pl., *korbanos):* sacrifice or offering

Korban Chagigah (קָרְבָּן חֲגִיגָה): a sacrifice offered up at each of the *Pilgrim Festivals

Korban Chatas (קָרְבָּן חַטָּאת): sacrifice in expiation of certain specified transgressions

Korban Minchah (קָרְבָּן מִנְחָה): a meal offering

Korban Musaf (קָרְבַּן מוּסָף): additional sacrifice offered on behalf of the community in honor of *Shabbos*, festivals, and *Rosh Chodesh

Korban Pesach (קָרְבַּן פֶּסַח): the Passover sacrifice offered on the eve of the festival

Korban Shlamim (קָרְבַּן שְׁלָמִים): peace offering, part of the sacrifice being eaten by the offerer and his guests

Korban Tamid (קָרְבַּן תָּמִיד): the sacrifice offered in the Temple twice daily on behalf of the community

Korban Tzibur (קָרְבַּן צִבּוּר): any sacrifice offered on behalf of the entire House of Israel

korech (כּוֹרֵךְ): the sandwich of *matzah* and bitter herbs eaten at the *Pesach *Seder

kosher (כָּשֵׁר): halachically fit for its purpose

krichah (כְּרִיכָה): synonym for *korech*

Ksuvim (כְּתוּבִים; lit., "Writings"): the third part of the *Tanach, comprising *Psalms*, the Five Scrolls, and other Books; the Hagiographa

kukureizen kemach (yid.): the flour of Indian corn or maize

Lag BaOmer (לַ"ג בָּעוֹמֶר): the thirty-third day of the *Omer; a minor festival falling between *Pesach and *Shavuos

lav hanitak le-aseh (לָאו הַנִּיתָּק לַעֲשֵׂה): a negative commandment for which there is a counteractive positive commandment

lav she-ein bo maaseh (לָאו שֶׁאֵין בּוֹ מַעֲשֶׂה): a prohibition involving no definite action

lechayim (לְחַיִּים; lit., "To life"!): greeting exchanged over strong drink

Lechem HaPanim (לֶחֶם הַפָּנִים): the twelve loaves placed on the Table in the *Beis HaMikdash

lechem oni (לֶחֶם עוֹנִי): "the bread of poverty," i.e., *matzah

leshon bnei adam (לְשׁוֹן בְּנֵי אָדָם): ordinary speech

levi'im (לְוִיִּם): Levites; descendants of the Tribe of Levi, with special duties in the Temple

libun (לִבּוּן): heating a metal vessel or utensil to red heat to remove the taste of any prohibited substance absorbed into its walls; before *Pesach this is done to remove absorbed *chametz

linah (לִינָה): staying overnight (in Jerusalem on Pilgrim Festivals and on the night after one has offered a sacrifice in the *Beis HaMikdash*)

lishmah (לִשְׁמָה): intended for the sake of a (particular) mitzvah

lulav (לוּלָב): palm branch; one of the Four Species in the *Sukkos ceremony

Maariv (מַעֲרִיב): the nightly Evening Service, corresponding in time to the burning of the remnants of the day's sacrifices on the Altar

maasar ani (מַעֲשַׂר עָנִי): a tithe given to the needy

maasar behemah (מַעֲשַׂר בְּהֵמָה): a tithe of certain animals, part of which was offered on the Altar, and part eaten by the owners

maaseh (מַעֲשֶׂה): an act

maaser (מַעֲשֵׂר; pl., *maasros*): tithe

maaser sheni (מַעֲשֵׂר שֵׁנִי; lit., "the second tithe"): sanctified farm produce (or the coins with which it has been redeemed) to be consumed in Jerusalem

machshirin (מַכְשִׁירִין): preparatory activities

maftir (מַפְטִיר): a) congregant given the honor of reading a passage from the Prophets (*Haftarah) after the public Torah reading; b) the brief concluding passage in the Torah over which he recites two blessings

malkus (מַלְקוּת): lashing as a court imposed punishment

mamon (מָמוֹן): money; property

mamzer (מַמְזֵר): offspring of adulterous or incestuous union

mamzeress (מַמְזֶרֶת): fem. of *mamzer*

maror (מָרוֹר): the "bitter herb" eaten during the *Pesach *Seder

Mashiach (מָשִׁיחַ): the Messiah

mashkon (מַשְׁכּוֹן): item given as security on a loan

maskilim (מַשְׂכִּילִים): Jews, esp. of 19th-cent. Europe who preferred modern "enlightened" ideas and life-styles over those of the Torah

matzah (מַצָּה; pl., matzos): unleavened bread eaten on *Pesach

matzah ashirah (מַצָּה עֲשִׁירָה; lit., "rich matzah"): *matzah containing other ingredients besides flour and water

matzah shmurah (מַצָּה שְׁמוּרָה): *matzah made from grain guarded against any contact with moisture from the time it is harvested until it is ready to be kneaded into dough

matzas mitzvah (מַצַּת מִצְוָה): *matzah used to perform the mitzvah of eating matzah on the first night of *Pesach

mayim she-lanu (מַיִם שֶׁלָּנוּ): water which has stood overnight

mechirah clallis (מְכִירָה כְּלָלִית): the sale of *chametz to a non-Jew by one man on behalf of a whole community

me-ein sheva (מֵעֵין שֶׁבַע): a short recapitulation of the Amidah prayer, recited after the Maariv service on the eve of *Shabbos by the *sheliach tzibur and (in part) by the congregation

mehadrin (מְהַדְּרִין): those who are meticulous in the observance of the *mitzvos

mehadrin min hamehadrin (מְהַדְּרִין מִן הַמְּהַדְּרִין): those who are exceedingly meticulous in the observance of the mitzvos

mei peros (מֵי פֵּרוֹת; lit. "fruit water"): liquids other than water

megillah (מְגִילָה): scroll

mesirus nefesh (מְסִירוּת נֶפֶשׁ): self-sacrifice

mezuzah (מְזוּזָה): small parchment scroll affixed to doorpost, and containing the first two paragraphs of *Shema Yisrael

Mikdash (מִקְדָּשׁ; lit., "Sanctuary"): scriptural and mishnaic term for the *Beis HaMikdash

mikveh (מִקְוֶה): bath especially constructed for ritual immersion

mil (מִיל): a measure of distance equalling 2,000 cubits (approx. 1 km.)

Minchah (מִנְחָה): a) the daily Afternoon Service, corresponding in time to one of the two daily sacrifices in the Temple; b) *korban Minchah

minhag (מִנְהָג; pl., minhagim): custom (see also vol. II, p. 335)

minim (מִינִים): apostates

minyan (מִנְיָן): a) quorum of ten, needed for public prayer; b) a congregation

Mishkan (מִשְׁכָּן): the movable Sanctuary erected by Moshe Rabbeinu in the wilderness; the Tabernacle

mishmeres (מִשְׁמֶרֶת; construct form of mishmorah; lit., "watch"; pl., mishmaros): shift of duty in the priestly rota in the Beis HaMikdash

Mishnah (מִשְׁנָה; lit., "learned by repetition"): a) that part of the Talmud which states the kernel of the law, and which is debated by the Gemara; b) [lower case] any particular paragraph from one of the Six Orders of the Mishnah (see also vol. II, p. 333)

mishnayos (מִשְׁנָיוֹת): pl. of *mishnah

misnaged (מִתְנַגֵּד): one who opposes *Chassidim

mitzvah (מִצְוָה; pl., mitzvos): a commandment (see also vol. II, p. 334)

mitzvah derabbanan (מִצְוָה דְּרַבָּנָן; lit., "commandment from the Rabbis"; Heb. / Aram.): term describing laws enacted by the Sages, as distinguished from those appearing in the Torah (see also vol. II, p. 334)

mitzvah habaah be-aveirah (מִצְוָה הַבָּאָה בַּעֲבֵרָה): a *mitzvah performed by means of a transgression

mitzvah she-hazman grama (מִצְוָה שֶׁהַזְמַן גְּרָמָא): a *mitzvah which must be performed at a certain time

mo'ed (מוֹעֵד; pl., moadim): festival; holy day

mohel (מוֹהֵל): a specialist in ritual circumcision

Morning Service, see Shacharis

Motzaei (מוֹצָאֵי): the evening and night following [a given day]; specifically, Motzaei *Shabbos and Motzaei *Yom-Tov

mumar (מוּמָר): one who rejects part or all of the Torah

Musaf (מוּסָף): either a) the sacrifice (in the *Beis HaMikdash; see *Korban Musaf) or b) the *Amidah (in the prayers) added in honor of *Shabbos, *Yom-Tov, and *Rosh Chodesh

musar (מוּסָר): a body of Torah teaching aimed at fostering spiritual and ethical self-refinement

nasi (נָשִׂיא): the national leader during Talmudic times

nazir (נָזִיר): one who sets himself apart for divine service by the acceptance of certain ascetic restrictions

nechar (נֵכָר; usually ben nechar): a gentile

neder (נֶדֶר): a vow

Nefilas Apayim (נְפִילַת אַפַּיִם): a) the act of "prostration" during prayer, i.e., burying one's face in one's arm; b) the supplications recited during this act

neharos (נְהָרוֹת): bodies of flowing water — i.e., rivers and lakes, as opposed to Okeanus, the ocean

netilah (נְטִילָה): see netilas yadayim

netilas yadayim (נְטִילַת יָדַיִם): ritual washing of hands

nevelah (נְבֵלָה): an animal which died from a cause other than kosher slaughtering

Nevi'im (נְבִיאִים): a) prophets; b) the Prophetic Writings

New Moon, see Rosh Chodesh

niddah (נִדָּה): a woman who is ritually impure due to menstruation; in general, the laws of family purity

Nissan (נִיסָן): the first month; the month in which *Pesach is celebrated

ochel nefesh (אוֹכֶל נֶפֶשׁ): food for a person

Omer (עֹמֶר): a) a dry measure; b) an offering of barley flour, offered up each year on the 16th of Nissan when the Temple is standing

olah (עוֹלָה): a sacrifice which is burned in its entirety on the Altar

oneg Shabbos (עֹנֶג שַׁבָּת): the pleasure of Shabbos; (also: a special gathering in honor of Shabbos)

Oral Law, see vol. II, p. 333

orlah (עָרְלָה): a) the prohibition against deriving benefit from fruit produced by a tree in its first three years; b) the fruit so prohibited

parashah (פָּרָשָׁה): a Torah passage

pasul (פָּסוּל): halachically disqualified for its purpose

perusah (פְּרוּסָה): a broken piece; specifically, a broken piece of matzah

Pesach (פֶּסַח): Passover, one of the three *Pilgrim Festivals, beginning on 15 *Nissan

Pesach Sheni (פֶּסַח שֵׁנִי; lit., "the second Pesach"): opportunity given to certain persons who were unable to offer the Pesach sacrifice (*Korban Pesach) to do so one month later on 14 *Iyar

pidyon haben (פִּדְיוֹן הַבֵּן): ceremony of Redemption of the Firstborn

Pilgrim Festivals (שָׁלוֹשׁ רְגָלִים): *Pesach, *Shavuos, and *Sukkos, when all Israel are commanded to bring offerings to the Temple

piyyut (פִּיּוּט): a liturgical poem

posek (פּוֹסֵק; pl., poskim): scholarly authority who rules on disputed halachic issues

Prushim (פְּרוּשִׁים; lit., "separated"): a) in the Talmudic era groups who were punctilious in the observance of the laws of purity or who undertook certain ascetic restrictions in response to the Destruction; b) the halachic descendants of the Gaon of Vilna (Gra) in Eretz Yisrael

prutah (פְּרוּטָה): minimal Talmudic coin

pulim (פּוֹלִים): beans

Rabban (רַבָּן; Aram.): "our teacher"

Rabbanan (רַבָּנָן; "our teachers"; Aram.), see *Chachamim

rabbanim (רַבָּנִים): plural of *rav

Rabbeinu (רַבֵּנוּ): "our Teacher"

rav (רַב): rabbi

regel (רֶגֶל; pl., *regalim*): one of the three *Pilgrim Festivals

reshus harabim (רְשׁוּת הָרַבִּים): the public domain

revi'is (רְבִיעִית): lit., "a quarter" [of a *log*]): liquid measure variously defined (about 4 oz.)

Rishon (רִאשׁוֹן; pl., *Rishonim*): a Torah authority of the period between the era of the *Geonim and the publication of *Shulchan Aruch* in the sixteenth century

Rosh Chodesh (רֹאשׁ חֹדֶשׁ; pl., *Rashei Chadashim*): New Moon, i.e., one or two semi-festive days at the beginning of the month

Rosh HaShanah (רֹאשׁ הַשָּׁנָה): the New Year festival, celebrated on 1 and 2 *Tishrei

Sadducees (צְדוֹקִים): a sect in Mishnaic times who interpreted the Torah literally, rejecting the Rabbinic interpretations contained in the Talmud

safek (סָפֵק): doubt about a law, or about the specific circumstances to which the law must be applied

Sages, see *Chachamim*

Sanctuary, see *Mishkan*

Sanhedrin (סַנְהֶדְרִין): supreme legislative and judicial body

Se'ah (סְאָה): a measure of volume

Seder (סֵדֶר): the festive *Pesach meal, with all its prescribed symbolic acts and foods, including the recitation of the *Haggadah*

sefeik-sefeika (סְפֵק־סְפֵקָא): a compound doubt (see *safek)

sefekos (סְפֵקוֹת): plural of *safek

Sefirah (סְפִירָה): see *Sefiras HaOmer*

Sefiras HaOmer (סְפִירַת הָעוֹמֶר): the count of forty-nine days beginning on 16 *Nissan (when the *Omer was offered in the *Beis HaMikdash) and ending the day before *Shavuos

sela (סֶלַע): a coin of Talmudic times

Sephardi (סְפָרַדִי): pertaining to the Jewry of southern Europe, North Africa, and Asia

seudah (סְעוּדָה): meal, especially a festive one

Seudah Shlishis (סְעוּדָה שְׁלִישִׁית): the third Shabbos meal, normally held after *Minchah

seudas mitzvah (סְעוּדַת מִצְוָה): festive meal celebrating the performance of a commandment

Seventh of Adar (ז' אֲדָר): anniversary of the passing of Moshe Rabbeinu

shaas hadechak (שְׁעַת הַדְּחָק): a time of extraordinary difficulty

Shabbos (שַׁבָּת; pl. *Shabbosos*): the Sabbath

Shacharis (שַׁחֲרִית): the daily Morning Service, corresponding in time to the morning daily sacrifice

shalmei chagigah (שַׁלְמֵי חֲגִיגָה): peace offerings sacrificed at each of the three *Pilgrim Festivals

Shavuos (שָׁבוּעוֹת: lit., "weeks"): one of the three *Pilgrim Festivals, celebrated seven weeks after the second day of *Pesach

Shechinah (שְׁכִינָה): the Presence of God in the world

shechitah (שְׁחִיטָה): kosher slaughtering

Shehecheyanu (שֶׁהֶחֱיָנוּ): blessing of thanksgiving for joyous occasions

shekel (שֶׁקֶל; pl., *shekalim*): Biblical and Talmudic coin

sheliach tzibur (שְׁלִיחַ צִבּוּר): congregant called upon to lead the prayer service

Shema Yisrael (שְׁמַע יִשְׂרָאֵל; lit., "Hear, O Israel"): the opening words of the Jew's twice-daily declaration of faith

Sheva Berachos (שֶׁבַע בְּרָכוֹת): the seven blessings recited under the wedding canopy; (also, a meal of celebration held during the week following the wedding, at which these blessings are repeated)

shevi'is (שְׁבִיעִית; lit., "the seventh"), see *Shmitah

shevus (שְׁבוּת): Rabbinic prohibition of work

shfoch chamascha (שְׁפוֹךְ חֲמָתְךָ): a passage in the *Haggadah calling for divine retribution against the enemies of Israel *shir* (שִׁיר): song; psalm

shiur (שִׁעוּר); a) required measure or dimension for the fulfillment of a mitzvah; b) a lesson

Shlamim (שְׁלָמִים): see *Korban Shlamim*

Shmini Atzeres (שְׁמִינִי עֲצֶרֶת): in *Eretz Yisrael* a one-day festival, the day after Sukkos, coinciding with Simchas Torah; outside *Eretz Yisrael* a two-day festival, the second day of which is Simchas Torah

Shmitah (שְׁמִיטָה): the sabbatical year; the year of rest given to the land (*Eretz Yisrael*) once every seven years

Shmoneh Esreh (שְׁמוֹנֶה עֶשְׂרֵה): see *Amidah*

shmurah (שְׁמוּרָה): guarded (i.e., *matzah* guarded from contact with moisture)

shochet (שׁוֹחֵט): ritual slaughterer

shofar (שׁוֹפָר; pl., *shofaros*): (ram's) horn blown on Rosh HaShanah and at conclusion of Yom Kippur

shoteh, see *cheresh, shoteh, ve-katan*

Showbread, see *Lechem HaPanim*

shtar (שְׁטָר; pl., *shtaros*): legal document

shtei halechem (שְׁתֵּי הַלֶּחֶם; "the two loaves"): the offering baked from the new season's wheat harvest, and brought to the *Beis HaMikdash* on *Shavuos*

Shvat (שְׁבָט): the eleventh month; the month in which the New Year of the Trees (*Tu BiShvat*) falls

Siddur (סִדּוּר; pl., *siddurim*): prayer book

simchah (שִׂמְחָה): joy

sin-offering, see *Korban Chatas*

sirchon (סִרְחוֹן): "rotting" (as opposed to *chimutz*)

situmta (סְטוּמְתָּא; Aram.): a method of legally transferring property deriving its validity from the fact that it is an established custom

Sivan (סִיוָן): the third month, the month in which the festival of *Shavuos* is celebrated

sugya (סוּגְיָא; Aram.): a passage or debate on a given topic in the Talmud

sukkah (סוּכָּה): booth with covering of branches, etc., lived in during the festival of *Sukkos*

Sukkos (סוּכּוֹת; lit., "booths"): one of the three *Pilgrim Festivals, beginning on 15 *Tishrei

suma (סוּמָא): a blind person

taam ha-elyon (טַעַם הָעֶלְיוֹן) and *taam hatachton* (טַעַם הַתַּחְתּוֹן): two different prescribed melodies for the chanting of the Ten Commandments

taaroves chametz (תַּעֲרוֹבֶת חָמֵץ): a mixture of *chametz with some other substance

Tachanun (תַּחֲנוּן): the penitential prayers recited following the *amidah on all non-festive days

taharah (טָהֳרָה): ritual purity (also: the ritual preparation of the dead for burial)

tahor (טָהוֹר): ritually pure

takkanah (תַּקָּנָה; pl., *takkanos*): Rabbinic enactment (see also vol. II, p. 334)

tallis (טַלִּית): fringed shawl worn in prayer (*tallis gadol*), or the smaller garment (*tallis katan*) worn constantly, usually under the outer garments

talmid chacham (תַּלְמִיד חָכָם; pl., *talmidei chachamim*): Torah scholar of standing

Talmud (תַּלְמוּד), see vol. II, p. 333

Talmud Yerushalmi (תַּלְמוּד יְרוּשַׁלְמִי; lit., "the Jerusalem Talmud"): the *Talmud which was completed in the Land of Israel at the end of the fourth century, C.E.

tameh (טָמֵא): ritually impure

Tamid, see *Korban Tamid*

Tammuz (תַּמּוּז): the fourth month; the month during which the Three Weeks of mourning for the Destruction of the *Beis HaMikdash* begin

Tanach (תַּנַ"ךְ): acronym for Torah (the Five Books of Moses), Nevi'im (the Prophetic Books), and Ksuvim (the Writings)

Tanna (תַּנָּא; pl. *Tannaim*; Aram.): an authority cited in the *Mishnah*, or one who lived in the Mishnaic era (see also vol. II, p. 333)

Tanna kama (תַּנָּא קַמָּא; Aram.): the anonymous *Tanna* whose opinion is cited first in a Talmudic debate

taryag (תַּרְיַ"ג): the letters whose numerical equivalent is 613 — the number of Biblical commandments

tashlumin (תַּשְׁלוּמִין): compensatory sacrifices, prayers, or other *mitzvah acts, to make up for those not performed at the preferred time

tavshil (תַּבְשִׁיל): a cooked item

techum (תְּחוּם): bounds, such as those delimiting the permissible walking distance on *Shabbos*

tefach (טֶפַח; pl. *tefachim*): a unit of length corresponding to the width of a fist

tefillah (תְּפִלָּה; pl. *tefillos*): prayer; esp. (in the Talmud) the *Amidah

tefillin (תְּפִלִּין): small black leather cubes containing parchment scrolls inscribed with *Shema Yisrael* and other Biblical passages, bound to the arm and forehead at weekday morning prayers

Temple, see *Beis HaMikdash*

Tenth of Teves (עֲשָׂרָה בְּטֵבֵת): fast commemorating the beginning of Nevuchadnetzar's siege of Jerusalem

teshuvah (תְּשׁוּבָה; lit., "return"): repentance; (also: a halachic responsum)

tevel (טֶבֶל): produce forbidden for consumption because it is untithed

Teves (טֵבֵת): the tenth month

tevillah (טְבִילָה): ritual immersion in a *mikveh

Tishah BeAv (תִּשְׁעָה בְּאָב; lit., "the Ninth of Av"): fast commemorating the Destruction of both the First and the Second Temples

Tishrei (תִּשְׁרֵי): the seventh month; the month in which the festivals of *Rosh HaShanah, *Yom Kippur, and *Sukkos occur

tosefes (תּוֹסֶפֶת): addition, supplement (esp., time added at either end of a holy day)

trefah (טְרֵפָה): meat forbidden for consumption (not kosher) because of certain defects in the animal; also, colloquially, meat not slaughtered according to the law or any food stuff of animal derivation (e.g., blood, certain fats, etc.) prohibited for consumption

trumah (תְּרוּמָה; pl., *trumos*): the portion of one's produce which is set aside for the *kohen

Tu BiShvat (ט"ו בִּשְׁבָט; lit., "the fifteenth of *Shvat"): the New Year of the Trees; the determining date for several commandments concerning the fruit of trees

tumah (טוּמְאָה): ritual impurity

tzaddik (צַדִּיק): righteous or saintly person

tzedakah (צְדָקָה): a) justness or righteousness; b) charity

Tzedokim (צְדוֹקִים): see Sadducees

tzitzis (צִיצִית): the fringes worn at the corners of the *tallis

yash (יַיִן שָׂרָף; יַ"שׁ): spirituous liquor

yerek (יֶרֶק; pl., *yerakos*): green vegetables

yeshivah (יְשִׁיבָה; pl. *yeshivos*): Talmudic academy

Yom HaKippurim, see Yom Kippur

Yom Kippur (יוֹם כִּפּוּר): the Day of Atonement; Biblical fast observed on 10 *Tishrei

Yom Lag BaOmer (יוֹם לַ"ג בָּעוֹמֶר); see Lag BaOmer

Yom-Tov (יוֹם טוֹב; pl., *Yamim-Tovim*): a festival day sanctified by almost complete prohibition of work

Yovel (יוֹבֵל): the fiftieth or Jubilee Year, when during most of the first Temple era all land previously sold reverted to its original owner, and bondmen were freed

zal (ז"ל; abbreviation of זִכְרוֹנוֹ לִבְרָכָה; lit., "May his memory be a blessing"): epithet appended to name of a deceased person (see also *zatzal*)

zatzal (זַצַ"ל; abbreviation of זֵכֶר צַדִּיק לִבְרָכָה; lit., "The memory of a tzaddik is a blessing"): epithet appended to name of a particularly righteous, deceased person

zav (זָב): one who has a specific type of discharge which renders him ritually impure zavah (זָבָה); fem. of *zav

zerizin (זְרִיזִין): those who are swift and meticulous in performing *mitzvos

zevach (זֶבַח; pl., zevachim): a sacrifice

zimun (זִמּוּן): a) in Talmudic times, the practice by which one person recited the Grace after Meals on behalf of himself and two or more others; b) an introductory passage of invitation to the Grace after Meals when three or more men have eaten together

zman (זְמָן): a) time; b) Talmudic term for *Shehecheyanu

zroa (זְרוֹעַ): a) the arm or upper limb of a person or animal; b) the bone of meat placed on the *ke'arah

zuz (זוּז): Talmudic coin equivalent to a *dinar.